INVENTION OF THE FIRST-CENTURY

SYNAGOGUE

ANCIENT NEAR EAST MONOGRAPHS

General Editors
Alan Lenzi
Jeffrey Stackert
Juan Manuel Tebes

Editorial Board
Reinhard Achenbach
Jeffrey L. Cooley
C. L. Crouch
Roxana Flammini
Christopher B. Hays
René Krüger
Graciela Gestoso Singer
Bruce Wells

Number 22

INVENTION OF THE FIRST-CENTURY

SYNAGOGUE

by
Lidia D. Matassa

Edited by
Jason M. Silverman and J. Murray Watson

Atlanta

Copyright © 2018 by SBL Press

All rights reserved. No part of this work may be reproduced or transmitted in any form or by any means, electronic or mechanical, including photocopying and recording, or by means of any information storage or retrieval system, except as may be expressly permitted by the 1976 Copyright Act or in writing from the publisher. Requests for permission should be addressed in writing to the Rights and Permissions Office, SBL Press, 825 Houston Mill Road, Atlanta, GA 30329 USA.

Library of Congress Control Number: 2018951474

Printed on acid-free paper.

This book is dedicated to my mother and father, Maria Nardone and Antonio Matassa, whose support has been constant.

Table of Contents

Editors' Foreword	ix
Preface	xi
Acknowledgements	xiii
Abbreviations	xv
List of Illustrations and Tables	xviii

1. INTRODUCTION — 1
Terminology — 7
Literature Review — 20
Conclusions — 34

2. DELOS — 37
Introduction — 37
History of Delos — 38
History of the Excavations — 40
The Ancient Sources — 42
The Archaeological Evidence — 57
Literature Review — 67
Conclusions — 76

3. JERICHO — 79
Introduction — 79
History of Hasmonaean-Herodian Jericho — 81
The Ancient Sources — 83
The Excavation Reports — 86
Literature Review — 103
Conclusions — 106

4. MASADA — 109
Introduction — 109
Josephus's Masada Narrative — 110
The Masada Acropolis — 112
History of the Excavations at Masada — 113
The Ancient Sources — 121
The Excavation Reports — 127
My Analysis of the Excavation Reports and Building Phases — 132
Literature Review — 142
Conclusions — 155

5. HERODIUM — 159
Introduction — 159
Josephus's Herodium Narrative — 160
The Ancient Sources — 161
Construction of the Fortress of Herodium — 163
History of the Excavations — 165
The Excavation Reports — 166
Literature Review — 177
Conclusions — 183

6. GAMLA — 187
Introduction — 187
Josephus's Gamla Narrative — 189
Identification of the Synagogue — 191
The Excavation Reports — 194
Food for Thought (A Prototype Aedicula?) — 206
Conclusions — 210

7. CONCLUSIONS — 211

BIBLIOGRAPHY — 217
ANCIENT SOURCES INDEX — 255
MODERN AUTHORS INDEX — 261

Editors' Foreword

This monograph is published posthumously. The author, Dr. Lidia Matassa, passed away suddenly in January 2016. She had been working on revising this manuscript for publication, with the goal of adding additional case-studies, after a few years' delay due to a serious injury. She had been looking forward to taking up a fellowship period for this purpose in Jerusalem, originally for the Fall 2015, that she had had to postpone.

Knowing that Lidia had been working on this manuscript (as well as several others) at the time of her untimely death, the editors sought to see what we could do to preserve her work and legacy. We were able to receive copies of the entire manuscript in its original form as well as some other materials from her brother, Rocco. We are grateful to him and Lidia's father, Antonio, for facilitating this posthumous publication. Unfortunately, however, we could not find any of the more updated versions of these chapters in her rescued electronic files beyond a few oral presentations and preparations for several conference volumes. Her more recent files were presumably saved in the cloud, where they are inaccessible to us. Therefore, the version of the work edited here was the version that she had completed in 2010. It is worth noting that the chapter on Gamla was written *prior* to the final publication of that site, though with reference to pre-published materials that had been shared by Danny Syon. The editors are very grateful to Danny Syon for his assistance in updating the references towards the published Gamla excavation reports.

We have taken a conservative approach and restricted our editorial work to formatting and typesetting. On occasion, we have added a clarifying note for the readers in the footnotes. These are in square brackets and marked "–eds." On occasion, Lidia had cited some web links that are no longer viable; these we deleted and indicated in the notes. Contrary to typical SBL style, we have retained Lidia's original, British orthography. Any remaining errors may be attributed to our neglect.

We are grateful to the editors of the ANEM series for all their cooperation in facilitating the publication of this work, and pleased that their anonymous reviewers concurred with our belief that the material herein remains of relevance to the field, despite the delay in its publication.

Previous versions of several chapters in this book have already appeared in print. An early version of chapter 2 was published as "Unravelling the Myth of the Synagogue on Delos," *Strata: Bulletin of the Anglo-Israeli Archaeology Society* 25 (2007): 81–115 and reprinted in the *Encyclopedia Britannica*. Chapter 3 was first published as "Problems with the Identification of a Synagogue in the Hasmonean Estate at Jericho," 95–132 in *Text, Theology, and Trowel: Recent Research into the Hebrew Bible,* edited by Lidia D. Matassa and

Jason M. Silverman (Eugene, OR: Pickwick, 2011). Chapter 5 was first published as "The Synagogue at Herodium: Problematic Fact or Problematic Fiction?," 13–40 in *A Land Like Your Own*, edited by Jason M. Silverman with Amy Daughton (Eugene, OR: Pickwick, 2010).

May this work be a service to the guild and an enduring testament to Lidia.

Jason M. Silverman	Helsinki, Finland
J. Murray Watson	Barrie, Ontario
	March 2018

Preface

Each of the case study sites has been approached in the same way: by gathering every possible excavation detail, as well as literary, epigraphic, and other sources and material evidence. Each site has been painstakingly and closely examined so as to illustrate the specifics of the excavations, the known history of those sites, and any literary, epigraphic, or other information that might cast light on their function in their ancient context, as well as on specific problems with excavations and subsequent analyses over the years.

I have visited and photographed each site, drawn plans showing the relevant contexts and the relationship between elements of the sites, as well as the locations of artefacts, inscriptions, and architectural and other physical elements, and have analysed the individual elements that led to each identification. This methodology has had a completely unexpected benefit in that it has enabled illustration of the points at which scholarly opinion and interpretation of the archaeology has departed from fact (and sometimes reason!), and where this has been built on, over time, to produce the identification mythologies that we now see in relation to these five sites. As a consequence of this, it also became necessary to separate out some of the more specific claims made in relation to each of the individual sites and to locate them within the case studies. Therefore, in each chapter, there is a recitation of the main scholarly interpretations of the particular site, showing where these have relied on previous scholarship, or on misinterpretation rather than on the reality of the archaeological, epigraphic, or textual evidence.

ANCIENT SOURCES

The sources used in researching this monograph were the New Testament, the Hebrew Bible, the Pseudepigrapha, Josephus, Philo, and other Graeco-Roman writers who make any relevant reference (even if only in passing), including Strabo, Pliny the Elder, Suetonius, Tacitus, Juvenal, and others. I have also consulted, where available, epigraphical material, ancient texts, ostraca and graffiti from sites.

TRANSLATIONS

Throughout this book, quotations from and references to Josephus, Philo, and any other Graeco-Roman writers are taken from the Loeb Classical Library translations (see bibliography for specific details). Where I have quoted Greek inscriptions, I have produced the texts as they are inscribed on stelae, without diacritical marks and accents.

The Bible used throughout this monograph is *The Jewish Study Bible* (Oxford: Jewish Publication Society, 2004). I have also used the *BibleWorks 7* programme to search for terms in Hebrew, Greek, and English, which I have then cross-checked against the *Jewish Study Bible*. For New Testament material, I have used *The Harper Collins Study Bible*, New Revised Standard Version, but have then cross-checked via *BibleWorks 7* to search for terms in Hebrew, Greek, and English.

IMAGES AND PLANS

Other than five photographs and one map (figures 4a, 4b, 11, 17, 49 and 50), all illustrations used in this book are my own. For ease of reference I have integrated all illustrations into the body of the text.

Acknowledgements

I owe a monumental debt of gratitude to my supervisor, Dr. Catherine Hezser, Professor of Jewish Studies at SOAS in London, without whose support, intellectual openness and great patience this book could never have been written. Her guidance has been an asset to me throughout the research and writing of this work and I am astonished and thankful that she continued to be my supervisor and did not give up on me during the unproductive years in the middle.

I am grateful to the School of Religions and Theology at Trinity for its support over the years. I will be eternally grateful to Dr. Maria Diemling (now at Canterbury University) for her mentorship whilst she was at Trinity.

I am grateful to Prof. John Dillon of the School of Classics and The Dublin Centre for the Study of the Platonic Tradition at Trinity for his support, advice and help with Greek translations of the Delos and other inscriptions.

I thank the École française d'Athènes, which maintains a number of houses on the island of Delos, and am most grateful to their Director of Studies, Michèle Brunet, for arranging to open one of their dig houses for me out of season, so that I might stay on the island alone. I am also grateful to Panayotis Chatzidakis of the 21st Ephoreia of Prehistoric and Classic Antiquities, for giving me permission to stay on the island in October of 2003. This was an unforgettable experience, and one I shall treasure. To have slept on the island of Delos is to have been favoured by the gods.

I thank the Kenyon Research Institute in Jerusalem and its past Directors, Dr. Robert Allen and Dr. Yuri Stoyanov and past Assistant-Director, Tim Moore, for always making me feel welcome and comfortable when I visited, and for enabling me to travel into areas to which I would otherwise not have had access. And I am particularly grateful to the present Director of the Institute, Dr. Jaimie Lovell for driving me to Herodium on 14 February 2009 when all other avenues of travel had failed.

I thank my dear friend, Dr. Orit Peleg-Barkat, of the Institute of Archaeology at the Hebrew University of Jerusalem, for her friendship and support over the years. I will always be grateful for her good humour and kindness, and for the many discussions we've had about the Herodian period, its architecture and history, as well as for her help in interpreting the decorative material at Gamla, for the many translations she did for me and, of course, for showing me her magnificent collection of Temple Mount marbles and stones from the Western Wall Excavations. I am also very grateful to her for re-photographing the *triclinium* on Herodium for me after conservation work was carried out by the Hebrew University of Jerusalem in June/July of 2009, so I could see some of the structures that had not been visible when I visited in 1999,

2004, 2005, 2006, and February 2009, and for allowing me to use her photograph of the basilica lintel from Gamla in this monograph.

I thank my dear friend Tal Vogel for the pleasure of her company, her support and interest in my research and for showing me her work on the Masada textiles at the Hebrew University of Jerusalem and explaining the processes involved in their manufacture.

I thank my dear friend Amiram Barkat for his good humour, friendship and kindness and for giving me, a complete stranger at the time, a place to lay my head the first time I visited Jerusalem back in 1999.

I thank the staff of the Institute of Archaeology at the Hebrew University in Jerusalem for allowing me to use the library and for always being helpful and informative. In particular, I thank Prof. Ehud Netzer, who was generous with his time and advice despite the fact that I disagreed with practically everything he said, and I congratulate him on his discovery of the tomb of Herod the Great in 2009, a magnificent achievement by any measure!

I am grateful to Motti Aviam of the Institute for Galilean Archaeology at the University of Rochester for meeting me in Tiberias and driving me up to Gamla in 2005 and for our long discussion about the archaeology of the site.

I owe a particular debt of gratitude to Danny Syon of the Israel Antiquities Authority for giving me access to all the maps and plans from the Gamla excavation reports, as well as copies of the as-yet unpublished chapters of the excavation reports, and for his cogent and generous answers to the many vague questions I posed.

I am immensely and eternally grateful to Dr. Shimon Gibson for the opportunity to work with him at the Cave of John the Baptist at Tzuba, and to see for myself his legendary fastidious and methodical approach to archaeology. His knowledge of all things archaeological in Israel and Palestine is staggering, and it is a good thing for the world of archaeology that he publishes as much as he does.

I am very grateful to my landlord, John Dowling, who died on 21 May 2010. I miss our doorstep conversations about the ancient world.

And last, but by no means least, I thank my fellow PhD candidates in the School of Religions at Trinity: Jason Silverman, Amy Daughton, Audrey Barnett, and Murray Watson, Jason McCann, and Claire Carroll for their friendship, for the general environment of supportive fellowship, and for the intellectual and "other" discussions we have shared. Without our regular postgraduate seminars in "Paris," the last few years at Trinity would have been a lot less fun.

Abbreviations

ABD	*Anchor Bible Dictionary*
AJA	*American Journal of Archaeology*
AJP	*American Journal of Philology*
AJSL	*American Journal of Semitic Languages and Literatures*
AJSR	*Association for Jewish Studies Review*
ANRW	*Aufstieg und Niedergang der römische Welt*
ASAE	*Annales du service des antiquités de l'Égypte*
ASHAD	Urman, Dan, and Paul V. M. Flesher, eds. *Ancient Synagogues, Historical Analysis and Archaeological Discovery*. Vol. 1. Leiden: Brill, 1995.
BA	*Biblical Archaeologist*
BAR	*Biblical Archaeology Review*
BASOR	*Bulletin of the American Schools of Oriental Research*
BAIAS	*Bulletin of the Anglo-Israel Archaeological Society*
BCH	*Bulletin de Correspondance Hellénique*
BEHJ	*Bulletin des Études Historiques Juives*
BIOSCS	*Bulletin of the International Organisation for Septuagint and Cognate Studies*
BJPES	*Bulletin of the Jewish Palestine Exploration Society*
BJRL	*Bulletin of the John Rylands Library*
BMC	British Museum Catalogue
BSKG	*Bulletin de la sociéte khédiviale de géographie*
BSP	Black Sea Project
BT	*Bible Today*
CBQ	*Catholic Biblical Quarterly*
CIJ	*Corpus inscriptionum judaicarum*
CIL	*Corpus inscriptionum latinarum*
CIRB	*Corpus inscriptionum regni bosporani.* Moscow: Institute of History of the Soviet Academy of Sciences, 1965.
CIS	*Corpus inscriptionum semiticarum*
ConBNT	Coniectanea Biblica, New Testament Series
CPJ	*Corpus papyrorum judaicarum*
DACL	*Dictionnaire d'archéologie chrétienne et de liturgie*
DJD	Discoveries in the Judean Desert
EI	*Eretz Israel*
EJ	*Encyclopaedia Judaica*
FRLANT	Forschungen zur Religion und Literatur des alten und neuen Testaments

HSCP	*Harvard Studies in Classical Philology*
HTR	*Harvard Theological Review*
HUCA	*Hebrew Union College Annual*
IEJ	*Israel Exploration Journal*
IMJ	*Israel Museum Journal*
INJ	*Israel Numismatic Journal*
ISBE	*International Standard Bible Encyclopedia*
JAAR	*Journal of the American Academy of Religion*
JAS	*Journal of Archaeological Science*
JBL	*Journal of Biblical Literature*
JHS	*Journal of Hellenic Studies*
JJA	*Journal of Jewish Art*
JJS	*Journal of Jewish Studies*
JPOS	*Journal of the Palestine Oriental Society*
JQR	*Jewish Quarterly Review*
JRH	*Journal of Religious History*
JRS	*Journal of Roman Studies*
JSJ	*Journal for the Study of Judaism*
JSNT	*Journal for the Study of the New Testament*
JSOT	*Journal for the Study of the Old Testament*
JSP	*Journal for the Study of Pseudepigrapha*
JSQ	*Jewish Studies Quarterly*
JTS	*Journal of Theological Studies*
LA	*Liber Annuus.* Franciscan Biblical Centre, Jerusalem.
LPGN	*Lexicon of Personal Greek Names.* 6 vols. Ed. P. M. Fraser and Elaine Matthews. Oxford: Clarendon, 1987–2018.
MGWJ	*Monatsschrift für Geschichte und Wissenschaft des Judentums*
NEAEHL	Stern, Ephraim, Ayelet Lewinson-Gilboa, and Joseph Aviram, eds. *New Encyclopedia of Archaeological Excavations in the Holy Land.* Jerusalem: Israel Exploration Society; New York: Simon & Schuster, 1993–2008.
NTS	*New Testament Studies*
PAAJR	*Proceedings of the American Academy for Jewish Research*
PBSR	*Papers of the British School at Rome*
PEQ	*Palestine Exploration Quarterly*
PG	*Patrologia Graeca*
PL	*Patrologia Latina*
PO	*Patrologia Orientalis*
POC	*Proche-Orient Chrétien*
POXY	*Oxyrhynchus Papyri*
RA	*Revue archéologique*
RB	*Revue Biblique*
REG	*Revue des Études Grecques*

REJ	*Revue des Études Juives*
RPh	*Revue Philologique*
RQ	*Revue de Qumrân*
SCI	*Scripta Classical Israelitica*
SEG	Supplementum Epigraphicum Graecum
ZDMG	*Zeitschrift der Deutschen Morgenländischen Gesellschaft*
ZDPV	*Zeitschrift für den Deutschen Palästina Vereins*
ZNW	*Zeitschrift für die neutestamentliche Wissenschaft und die Kunde der älteren Kirche*
ZPE	*Zeitschrift für Papyrologie und Epigraphik*

List of Illustrations and Tables

All images are the author's own, unless otherwise indicated.

DELOS

Fig 1	The Cycladic Islands. Author's own, using Google Earth. © 2010 DigitalGlobe and CNES	37
Fig 2	Delos in context	38
Fig 3	GD 80 ("the synagogue") in context	41
Fig 4	GD 80 (its environs and where the inscriptions were found)	46
Fig 4a	ID 2329 (front and top view of inscription stele). Image reproduced from Waldemar Déonna, *Le Mobilier délien, Délos* (Paris: De Boccard, 1938). Used by permission.	47
Fig 4b	ID 2331 (front view of inscription stele). Image reproduced from Waldemar Déonna, *Le Mobilier délien, Délos* (Paris: De Boccard, 1938). Used by permission.	50
Fig 5	Plan of GD 80	57
Fig 6	The benches and marble throne in GD 80	58
Fig 7	GD 91 (Sarapeion A)	59
Fig 8	GD 80 (from the stylobate down to the sea)	60
Fig 9	GD 89 (House of the Hermes)	62
Fig 10	Floor plans of GDs 80, 89, 111, and 57	62
Fig 11	The lamp from the cistern. Image reprinted from Waldemar D Déonna, *Le Mobilier délien, Délos* (Paris: De Boccard, 1938). Used by permission.	64
Fig 12	The cistern from room B (looking south to Mount Cynthus)	65
Fig 13	The lime kiln in Room A (looking west)	66
Fig 14	Satellite image of GD 80 and its environs. Courtesy of Google Earth (Matassa accessed this image before 2010. Attribution of the map via Google Earth at the time of editing is © 2018 CNES / Airbus)	72
Fig 15	The niche in GD 80 (and other niches on Delos)	75

JERICHO

Fig 16	View over Hasmonaean-Herodian Jericho (looking north)	79
Fig 17	Hasmonaean-Herodian Jericho (context and locations)	80
Fig 18	The courtyard house (phase 1)	86
Fig 19	Comparison of courtyard houses	90
Fig 20	The courtyard house (phase 2)	93
Fig 21	The peristyle courtyard (looking east)	96
Fig 22	The niche (looking south)	100

| Fig 23 | The stepped cistern | 102 |
| Fig 24 | The courtyard house (phase 3) | 103 |

MASADA

Fig 25	Masada (looking west)	109
Fig 26	Masada (context and locations)	110
Fig 27	Locus 1042 (excavators' phase 1)	128
Fig 28	Locus 1042 (excavators' phases 2/3)	130
Fig 29	Locus 1042 (my phase 2a)	133
Fig 30	Locus 1042 (my phase 2b)	134
Fig 31	Locus 1042 (my phase 3)	135
Fig 32	Locus 1042 (floor level and benches)	137
Fig 33	Locus 1042 (my phase 4)	138
Fig 34	View of Loci 1038, 1039 and 1042 (looking west)	140
Fig 35	Locus 1042 (seating capacity)	141

HERODIUM

Fig 36	Herodium (looking south from Bethlehem)	159
Fig 37	Plan of the upper palace-fortress	164
Fig 38	Plan of the *triclinium*	167
Fig 39	Location of *mikveh,* kiln, *triclinium* and water installation	172
Table 1	Coins from the period of the first rebellion	173
Table 2	Coins from the period of the second rebellion	174
Table 3	Coins from miscellaneous periods	174
Fig 40	Comparison of Locus 1042 on Masada and Herodium *triclinium*	179

GAMLA

Fig 41	Gamla (looking west across to Galilee)	187
Fig 42	The breach in the fortifications	191
Fig 43	Replica catapult (looking west to the breached wall)	192
Fig 44	The public building (looking southwest)	192
Fig 45	The public building (floor plan)	194
Fig 46	The northern wall (cupboard)	197
Fig 47	The ancillary room	199
Fig 48	The *mikveh*/cistern	200
Fig 49	The rosette lintel from the second western doorway. Photograph © Danny Syon/Gamla Excavations. Used by permission.	201
Fig 50	The rosette lintel from the basilica. Photograph by O. Peleg-Barkat. Used by permission.	202
Fig 51	The badly carved capitals	203

List of Illustrations

Fig 52	The swastika/double meander pattern at Bet She'an	204
Fig 53	The unidentified structure behind the central stylobate	207
Fig 54	Another view of the unidentified structure (looking northeast)	208
Fig 55	A prototype aedicula?	209

1
INTRODUCTION

This monograph deals with the processes by which the five sites at Delos, Jericho, Herodium, Masada, and Gamla were identified as first-century synagogues. *The five sites discussed in this monograph were chosen for the simple reason that they are consistently used in modern scholarship as comparators for all other early synagogues and are the archaeological foundation upon which the chronological development of the early synagogue stands.* Understanding the assumed links between these five sites, as well as the interpretations of the material that led to their identifications, is vital to the subject of early synagogue studies as a whole, and it is the aim of this study to take a fresh look at the material that has been used in this way.

The identification of pre-70 CE synagogues in the land of Israel and the Graeco-Roman diaspora is fraught with difficulties, but this has not prevented new identifications being made every year.[1] The material evidence contributing to

---

[1] For example, in September of 2009, a synagogue identification was made in a Jewish village at Magdala in the Galilee. Having seen some photographs and media coverage of the site, as well as receiving some photographs from the site from colleagues, it seems clear that what has been found is indeed an early synagogue. However, I am certain it will be dated to the second or third century on the basis that the style and execution of the carved decorative elements is not the norm for the first century and that the excavators themselves are not yet sure that it can be safely dated to the first century. The excavations are being conducted along the northern fringes of Magdala, along the shores of Lake Kinneret. Pottery fragments were found which the excavators think are dated to the early Roman period, but they are somewhat equivocal about this and say that these pottery fragments are no later than the second century CE. The site is being excavated by Dina Avshalom-Gorni and Arfan Najar of the Israel Antiquities Authority. See http://www.ynet.co.il/articles/0,7340,L-3775237,00.html (accessed 21.10.2009) [another, now broken link also originally appeared here –Eds.]; see also Boaz Zissu and Amir Ganor, "Horvat 'Ethri—A Jewish Village from the Second Temple Period and the Bar Kokhba Revolt in the Judaean Foothills," *JJS* 60.1 (2009): 90–136, in which there is a discussion about whether the public building 'M' is a prototype synagogue dating to before 70 CE. The excavators argue that it is a pre-70 CE synagogue, despite the fact that they say remodelling work in the third century CE removed features such as stone

those identifications has frequently been meagre, and interpretations of that material evidence has tended to be speculative, because often there have been no archaeological reports to support the identifications, either because those reports have not been published or because they have never been written.

In this monograph, we will see that there have been substantial errors in both the analysis and transmission of archaeological and historiographical information in relation to the five case study sites, as well as how this has resulted in the generation of a flawed process that has allowed identifications of first-century synagogues based on broad and simplistic assumptions that have not been established. Of course, none of this is to say that the five sites discussed in this study could not have been synagogues; only that we shall see that there is little or no evidence that they were.

The five case studies of this study are ordered so as to show the progression of specific identification errors, rather than on the basis of any internal or external chronology, because, as it turns out, a chronology of the sites from earliest to latest date is not particularly helpful. Moreover, while it might seem obvious that Masada could have been used as the first case study, because it is the most famous of the sites to have been identified as a first-century synagogue, this would have presented its own set of problems, since the site is often, in effect, used as a comparator for itself as well as for the other four sites discussed in this monograph. As will be illustrated in the case studies, each of these five first-century synagogue identifications has become caught up in a web of scholarly, epigraphical, and archaeological tautology.

Because of the paucity of literary information on synagogues in the land of Israel in the first century BCE/CE (the only contemporary works that mention the synagogue in a Jewish context are Josephus, Philo, and the New Testament, plus occasional references in the Latin and Greek literature of the era, such as in Juvenal's *Satire 3*)[2], it is impossible now to recover precisely how the early

---

benches *for which there is now no evidence*; and see also Yitzhak Magen et al., *The Land of Benjamin* (JSP 3; Jerusalem: Civil Administration of Judea and Samaria, Israel Antiquities Authority) about the village and "synagogue" at Kiryat Sefer). The publication of the Kiryat Sefer material is not a full excavation report, consisting instead of a descriptive and assumed historical context for the site as well as some archaeological details. It is not clear when the site will be fully published, but there is certainly no evidence that the building identified is a synagogue at all, much less that it is a first-century one.

[2] Juvenal, *Satires* (Morton-Braund, LCL), "He stands facing me and tells me to stop. I've no choice but to obey. After all, what can you do when a lunatic forces you, and he's stronger as well? 'Where have you been?' he yells. 'Whose sour wine and beans have blown you out? Which shoemaker has been eating spring onions and boiled sheep's head with you? Nothing to say? Tell me or you'll get a kicking! Say, where's your pitch? Which *proseuchē* shall I look for you in?' ["in qua te quaero proseucha?"] Whether you try to say something or silently

synagogue functioned or, indeed, how it developed.³ This has resulted in a substantial disconnect between the terminology and definitions used in modern discussions about early synagogue identification and the archaeological and material record. In recent years, academic understanding has purposefully deconstructed the physical institution of the early synagogue into a multipurpose communal assembly space which was used for everything from commercial trading to threshing floor, from school to law court and, of course, to a locus of religious activity in some form or another.

Broadening the criteria by which the theoretical—but potentially physical—first-century synagogue is defined has been necessary to mainstream scholarship, because otherwise identification is all but impossible (or has been so far). However, broadening the definition has also had the effect of making it harder to make a physical identification of a first-century synagogue—on the basis that any building in a demonstrably Jewish setting with a reasonably large internal space with benches around its walls could be a synagogue and, simultaneously, easier to make an identification—on precisely the same basis. As a result, evidence for first-century synagogue identifications is non-specific and is riddled with inaccuracies and presumptions which have been built on over time and have been accepted almost without question into scholarship on the subject. This process will be illustrated in the case studies contained in this book.

We can define and identify later purpose-built synagogues easily enough as spaces in which liturgy and prayer are used in the pursuit of worship, and where the space may also be used for other communal activities including teaching. These (late Roman/Byzantine period) synagogues contain a physical focal point, such as a raised platform (a *bema*) on which a reader stands so as to be both visible and audible, and are designed to facilitate reading to a gathered congregation and participation in prayer by that congregation. Moreover, there can be decorative, architectural, and storage elements used in these later structures that have a specifically Jewish character (such as Torah shrines, *menorahs*, *ethrogs*, *lulavs*, and other motifs we now associate with the synagogue). We also see dedicatory

---

retreat, it's all the same. They beat you up just the same and then, still angry, they sue for assault."

³ All excerpts from Philo, Josephus, and other Graeco-Roman authors, in Greek or English, are taken from the LCL editions (see bibliography).

4 INVENTION OF THE FIRST-CENTURY SYNAGOGUE

inscriptions[4] and certain decorative features on columns and door lintels.[5] We can see instances and combinations of all these elements in later synagogues in Israel, such as those at Nabratein, Kfar Baram, Hammat Tiberias, Capernaum, Khirbet Shema, Gush Halav, Sepphoris, Bet Alpha, Meiron (all in the Galilee and the Golan), En Gedi, Eshtemoa, Na'aran, Ma'on, Ma'on Nirim, (all in Judaea), and, in the Diaspora, at Priene and Sardis (Turkey), Dura Europos and Apamea (Syria), Ostia (Italy), Stobi (Macedonia), Aegina and Miletus (Greece), Gerasa (Jordan), as well as many others, all dating to the late Roman/Byzantine period.[6] Certainly, by the Byzantine period, Torah shrines in purpose-built apses have become a common fixture of the architecture of the synagogue, as have raised speakers' platforms (*bema*) and orientation towards Jerusalem.[7]

Our problem only becomes fully apparent when we try to identify the first-century architectural precursors to these later well-established and identified synagogues. None of the foregoing architectural or decorative elements are present in any of the five case study sites, with the *possible* exception of the purpose-built public building at Gamla, which is discussed in detail in chapter 6 herein.

---

[4] Martin Hengel, "Proseuche und Synagoge: Jüdische Gemeinde, Gotteshaus und Gottesdienst in der Diaspora und in Palästina," in *The Synagogue: Studies in Origins, Archaeology and Architecture*, The Library of Biblical Studies (New York: KTAV, 1975): 27–54; Aryeh Kasher, "Synagogues as 'Houses of Prayer' and 'Holy Places' in the Jewish Communities of Hellenistic and Roman Egypt," in *Ancient Synagogues: Historical Analysis and Archaeological Discovery* (ed. Dan Urman and Paul V. M. Flesher; New York: Brill, 1995): 1:205–20; Catherine Hezser, *Jewish Literacy in Roman Palestine* (Tübingen: Mohr Siebeck, 2001), 397–413; Lea Roth-Gerson, *Greek Inscriptions from the Synagogues in Eretz-Israel* (Jerusalem: Ben Zvi Institute, 1987); Jürgen Zangenberg, Harold W. Attridge and Dale B. Martin, eds., *Religion, Ethnicity and Identity in Ancient Galilee* (Tübingen: Mohr Siebeck, 2007); Frowald Gil Hüttenmeister and Gottfried Reeg, *Die Antiken Synagogen in Israel* (2 vols.; Wiesbaden: Reichert, 1977).

[5] Danny Syon and Zvi Yavor, "Gamla 1997–2000," in *Atikot* 50 (2005): 16–23; Orit Peleg, "The Decorated Architectural Elements," in *Gamla II: The Shmaryah Gutman Excavations, 1976–1989—The Architecture* (IAA Reports 44; ed. Danny Syon; forthcoming) [Matassa cited the unpublished version; it has subsequently been published (2010) –Eds.]; Lee I. Levine, ed., *Ancient Synagogues Revealed* (Jerusalem: Israel Exploration Society, 1982): 95–97, 106, 108.

[6] Steven Fine, ed., *Sacred Realm: The Emergence of the Synagogue in the Ancient World* (New York: Oxford University Press, 1996).

[7] Rachel Hachlili, "The Niche and the Ark in Ancient Synagogues," *BASOR* 223 (1976): 43–54; Rachel Hachlili, "Torah Shrine and Ark in Ancient Synagogues: A Re-evaluation," *ZDPV* 116.2 (2000): 147; Rachel Hachlili, "Aspects of Similarity and Diversity in the Architecture and Art of Ancient Synagogues and Churches in the Land of Israel," *ZDPV* 113 (1997): 92–115; Lee I. Levine, *The Ancient Synagogue: The First Thousand Years* (New Haven: Yale University Press, 2000), 213–22.

INTRODUCTION 5

Delos, the first study in this monograph (and the earliest of the sites to be identified as a first-century synagogue), is sometimes dated to the mid-third century BCE. As we shall see, beginning with the case of Delos, but in common with three of the other four case study sites, there is a trail of epigraphical and archaeological evidence that has been misunderstood and misinterpreted, and these errors are still being transmitted and built on by modern scholars as though they represent established fact.

There is no safe way to identify a first-century synagogue. There is no canonical architectural style other than a central open space, a feature common to many buildings, both public and private. There are otherwise few commonalities, and there appears to be an unbridgeable gap between the five case study sites of this study and the sites that can be unequivocally identified as synagogues, all of which date to at least the late Roman-Byzantine period. Moreover, there is no useful comparison to be made between other contemporary structures, in Jewish contexts or otherwise, and the five case study sites. Where there are even superficially comparable structures, they are discussed in the context to which they directly relate in this study but, even then, they are largely unhelpful, as the case studies will show.

Additionally, there is something of a curiosity here, and it is this: why are encircling benches (around the walls) of an assembly space taken as indicators of synagogue usage? I have been unable to find where the suggestion originates. In an assembly space such as a council chamber, encircling benches are useful. They become less useful in terms of cultic function, that is, where movement of objects in and out of the space is required. It seems that the presence of benches in assembly spaces has entered the scholarship as a *factoid*: without support. It makes far more sense, in a public building designed and/or intended for religious use, to have a long central space with moveable seating or no seating at all, whereas encircling benches make perfect sense within the context of a public building designed to accommodate discussion and debate.

A good example of how the argument about benches tends to lead us nowhere is the cautionary tale of the little structure at Magdala identified in 1974 by Corbo and Loffreda as a first-century synagogue on the basis that its layout, with encircling benches around the walls and a central open space, is the same as that of the public building at Gamla (publicly identified as a first-century synagogue by Shmaryahu Gutman in 1976[8]). Closer and later examination of the Magdala site revealed its dedicated and extensive water systems and shortly thereafter that

---

[8] Ehud Netzer, "Did the Spring-House at Magdala Serve as a Synagogue?," in *Synagogues in Antiquity* (ed. Aryeh Kasher, Aharon Oppenheimer, and Uriel Rappaport; Jerusalem: Ben Zvi, 1987), 165–72.

it was a fountain house built in the style of a public building.[9] Clearly, we cannot simply use a rectangular structure with open internal space and benches around its walls as the basis for identifying early synagogues.

It is this gap between the theoretical scholarship on the identification of early synagogues and the physical evidence and its interpretation that informs the body of this monograph, focused through the lens of the five case studies. As will become clear through them, the physical similarity between each of the sites in this book is tenuous and superficial. In addition, these five synagogue identifications were made—at best—on little more than the fact that the spaces identified as synagogues had benches around their walls, as uncomfortably unlikely and fanciful as this may seem.

There are no certainties here and any potential descriptors must remain—of necessity—tentative. In these circumstances, what can possibly help to identify what a first-century synagogue might have been, in the absence of specific identifiers and markers? Let us assume that, if we are looking for a physical structure, then it must be of sufficient size to hold a number of people from its community, let us say a minimum of ten people.[10] We may also need space for seating or standing or kneeling. This seating need not be fixed in place—such as stone benches—as, if our potential structure is a multi-purpose building, the space may need to be utilised in other ways at other times.

If, on the other hand, the building is designed to function solely as a synagogue as we now understand it, then perhaps, in addition to the open space sufficient to accommodate at least ten people, we may look for traces of architectural features that appear in later synagogues, such as a reading platform[11] (although, of course, this could easily be portable in the same way as seating might be). We will see in the case study of the purpose-built public building at Gamla that there is a structure that could—just possibly—be the foundation for a platform which might fit this bill. We might also expect to find some sort of external indication of what the building was, such as an identifying inscription, donor inscriptions, or perhaps a door lintel with rosettes carved into it (such as the one found at one of the entrances to the public building in Gamla).

---

[9] The little fountain house at Magdala is a different building to the synagogue identified in 2009 (for which see n. 1 above). See also Richard Bauckham, *Gospel Women: Studies of the Named Women in the Gospels* (Grand Rapids: Eerdmans, 2002), 143; LaMoine F. De Vries, *Cities of the Biblical World* (Peabody, MA: Hendrickson, 1997), 327–28; Levine, *Ancient Synagogues*: 67; Carol Meyers, Toni Craven, and Ross S. Kraemer, eds., *Women in Scripture: A Dictionary of Named and Unnamed Women in the Hebrew Bible, the Apocryphal/Deuterocanonical Books and New Testament* (New York: Houghton Mifflin, 2000); Lidia D. Matassa, "Magdala," in *Encyclopaedia Judaica* (2nd ed.; Detroit: Thomson, 2007), 13:335.
[10] A Mishnaic *minyan*.
[11] A *bema*.

INTRODUCTION

It is possible, though by no means assured, that our putative synagogue may have water systems that feed an installation such as a *mikveh*,[12] or even a handwashing basin (such as the one at Gamla). We might also look for a building which is part of a larger complex that might perhaps offer accommodation for visitors, such as that described in the Theodotos Inscription (discussed below).

In the absence of these architectural identifiers, we are left with only a single possible criterion with which to identify a synagogue—either as a single or multi-purpose building—and that is that its internal configuration consisting of an open space need only be sufficient to accommodate a group of people gathered together for some purpose. This is clearly not an adequate or satisfactory basis on which to make an identification of a first-century synagogue. Unfortunately, for the moment, and looking at the case studies in this monograph, this may be an insurmountable difficulty (except, perhaps, in relation to Gamla).

TERMINOLOGY

Arguments surrounding the origins of the synagogue, where they refer to structures that predate the destruction of the temple in Jerusalem, are wholly based on literary and epigraphical evidence, in which the Greek terms προσευχή and συναγωγή are used to describe what we have come to know as houses of prayer or synagogues.[13] Other words that are used in the Hebrew Bible (and sometimes interpreted as relating to the synagogue) are עדה (congregation)[14] and קהל (assembly),[15] but these describe an assembly of people not a place in which to assemble.[16] In any event, none of the Hebrew Bible references to congregation or assemblies relate to any synagogue-like institution or activity, but instead to the

---

[12] Water installation for ritual purification.
[13] Rachel Hachlili, "The Origin of the Synagogue: A Reassessment," *JSJ* 28.1 (1997): 39; Hengel, "Proseuche und Synagoge," 27–29; Anders Runesson, *The Origins of the Synagogue* (Uppsala: Almqvist & Wiksell, 2001), 171–73; Samuel Krauss, *Synagogale Altertümer* (Berlin: Hildesheim, 1922), 15–17.
[14] עדה at: Exod 16:22; 38:25; Prov 9:14; Jer 6:18; Num 1:16, 18; 3:7; 4:34; 6:19; 8:9; 10:2–3; 13:26; 14:1–2, 10, 35–6; 15:24, 33, 35–6; 16:3, 5, 9, 19, 21–22, 24, 26, 45; 17:7, 10–11; 20:1, 8, 11, 22, 27, 29; 25:7; 26:9–10; 27:2–3, 14, 16, 19, 21–22; 31:13, 26–27, 43; 32:2; 35:12, 24–5; Lev 4:15; 8:3–5; 9:2, 5; 10:6, 17; 24:14, 16; Judg 20:1; 21:10, 13, 16; Josh 9:15, 18–19, 21; 20:6, 9; 22:12, 30; 1 Kgs 12:20; Job 15:34.
[15] קהל at Exod 16:3; Lev 4:13–4, 21; 8:3; 16:33; Num 1:18; 8:9; 10:7; 15:15; 16:33; 17:12; 19:20; 20:2, 6, 10; 22:4; Deut 4:10; 9:10; 10:4; 18:6; 31:12; Josh 18:1; 22:12; Judg 21:8; 2 Sam 20:14; 1 Kgs 8:2; 1 Chr 13:4; 29:1, 10, 20; 2 Chr 1:3; 5:3; 20:14; 23:3; 28:14; 29:28, 31–32; 30:2, 4, 23, 25; Esth 9:15; Ezra 2:64; 10:1, 12, 14; Neh 5:13; 7:66; 8:2, 17.
[16] Joseph Gutmann, "Synagogue Origins: Theories and Facts," in *Ancient Synagogues: The State of the Research* (ed. Joseph Guttmann; Chico, CA: Scholars Press, 1981), 1.

assembly of people for particular events or announcements.¹⁷ The Hebrew term בית כנסת (house of assembly) is also sometimes used in modern scholarship to refer to synagogues of this period, but is a term that comes to us from the late Roman-Byzantine period. According to rabbinic literature, after the return from the Babylonian exile, Jews gathered in secular assembly houses all over the country (*t. Sukkah* 4, 5). Unfortunately, the rabbinic material is not helpful in discussion of particular identifications because, although a significant volume of work, it takes the form of biblical commentaries (*midrash*), translations (*targums*), collections of rabbinic rules (*Mishnah*), and discussions of those rules (*Talmud*), all of which were only written down from around 200 CE onwards and worked and reworked over the following centuries to create a purposeful uniformity.¹⁸ It should not be surprising, given this framework, that the earliest rabbinic texts project some of the most significant aspects of rabbinic Judaism, including details about the fully realised synagogue of the later periods, back into the past.¹⁹ The rabbinic collections incorporate many traditions, some of which surely predate their integration into the redacted texts, but the extent of their redaction is such that recovery of specific historiographic detail is fraught with difficulties that fall far outside the scope of this book.

Schürer, in 1879, sought to classify the origins of the synagogue as relating to Graeco-Roman voluntary institutions, such as *collegia*.²⁰ Voluntary associations are a Hellenistic phenomenon which developed in urban centres.²¹ In a sense, all such voluntary and guild associations were religious, inasmuch as piety was embedded in ancient culture. The benefits of professional *collegia* came in the form of patronage in support of communal assembly and common meals, and a wealthy patron might be persuaded to buy buildings to be used by the assembly for such meetings.²²

Recently, Levine has asked whether Roman use of such terminology was meant to precisely define something specifically Jewish, or was simply the use of

---

[17] See nn. 12 and 13 above.
[18] Steven D. Fraade, "The Early Rabbinic Sage," in *The Sage in Israel and the Ancient Near East* (ed. John G. Gammie and Leo G. Perdue; Winona Lake, IN: Eisenbrauns, 1990), 417; Jacob Neusner, *The Mishnah: An Introduction* (Northvale, NJ: Jason Aronson, 1989), 1; Jacob Neusner, *The Talmud: What It Is and What It Says* (Lanham, MD: Rowman & Littlefield, 2006), 19.
[19] Fraade, "The Early Rabbinic Sage," 424.
[20] Emil Schürer, *Die Gemeindeverfassung der Juden in Rom in der Kaiserzeit* (Leipzig: Hinrichs, 1879), 15–17; Lee I. Levine, "The First-Century Synagogue: Critical Reassessments and Assessments of the Critical," in *Religion and Society in Roman Palestine: Old Questions, New Approaches* (ed. Douglas R. Edwards; New York: Routledge, 2004), 73.
[21] John S. Kloppenborg and Stephen G. Wilson, eds., *Voluntary Associations in the Graeco-Roman World* (London: Routledge, 1996), 17.
[22] Kloppenborg and Wilson, *Voluntary Associations*, 18.

a term which was familiar to the Roman authorities and which could be applied to a Jewish community without attempting to be exact. If the use of the term *collegium* (a voluntary association or guild association) was deliberate, did it in fact describe a synagogue?[23] The term is never used in any Jewish document or inscription.[24]

There are a number of other terms that are sometimes claimed to refer to early synagogues, such as ἱερόν (temple), ἱερόν περίβολον (a wall enclosing a sacred precinct), ναός (the inner sanctum of a temple), and τόπος (a district), which may be a form of shorthand for τὸ ἅγιος τόπος (holy place), although this is by no means certain. Moreover, the terms ἱερόν περίβολον, τὸ ἅγιος τόπος, and ἱερός τόπος suggest that the space referred to is enclosed in some way, and that access was not universal, nor was it arranged for communal prayer or assembly.[25] The term Σαββατεῖον indicates a gathering, but not the activity undertaken at that gathering. Nonetheless, the use of Σαββατεῖον must indicate that the social or religious act or institution to which it refers, in whatever form it took, was built around Sabbath observance. The term οἴκημα is sometimes thought to refer to converted house synagogues.[26]

However, in the broad spectrum of *possible* references to Jewish religious structures and institutions outside Jerusalem, the only terms that are used relatively consistently, in Egypt, in the Graeco-Roman Diaspora, and in the land of Israel, as we shall see, are προσευχή and συναγωγή. And, of course, while all of the terminological possibilities are interesting, there is no way to link them with the subject matter of this book, the identification of five specific structures as synagogues. Thus, we will concentrate on the Greek terms προσευχή and συναγωγή insofar as we can track their usage geographically and chronologically to some degree, using contemporary sources.

Hengel, in his discussion of the development of the early synagogue, argued for origins in the Graeco-Roman diaspora, which developed as a response to the centralisation of the cult, and not as a direct replacement for the temple. According to him, the development of the synagogue in the land of Israel came only later, with Hasmonaean policies of territorial expansion.[27] In his seminal work on the

---

[23] Levine, "The First Century Synagogue," 73; Levine, *The Ancient Synagogue*, 90.
[24] Levine, "The First Century Synagogue," 74.
[25] Schürer, *Die Gemeindeverfassung*, 15–17.
[26] James F. Strange, "Ancient Texts, Archaeology as Text, and the Problem of the First-Century Synagogue," in *Evolution of the Synagogue: Problems and Progress* (ed. Howard Clark Kee and Lynn H. Cohick; Harrisburg, PA: Trinity Press International, 1999), 32–33.
[27] Martin Hengel "Proseuche und Synagoge: Jüdische Gemeinde, Gotteshaus und Gottesdienst in der Diaspora und in Palästina," in *Tradition und Glaube: Das frühe Christentum in seiner Umwelt* (ed. Gert Jeremias, Heinz-Wolfgang Kuhn, and Hartmut Stegemann; Göttingen: Vandenhoeck & Ruprecht, 1971), 181–82; Hengel, *Judaism and Hellenism*:

influence of Hellenisation on Judaism, he argued that, about the middle of the third century BCE, all Judaism was effectively Hellenistic, and differentiation was only discernible between the Greek-speaking Judaism of the western diaspora and the Aramaic/Hebrew-speaking Judaism of Palestine and Babylonia. From the time of the Ptolemies to the destruction of the temple, "a sizeable minority" in Jerusalem would have had Greek as their mother tongue, as evidenced by the epigraphy.[28] Thus, in the third century BCE, even those who observed Mosaic law were subject to Greek influence.[29]

According to Hengel, the earliest evidence for the existence of the institution of the synagogue came from Ptolemaic Egypt, where two inscriptions from the reign of Ptolemy III (247–221 BCE) refer to the προσευχή as a *house of prayer*.[30] Philo used the word προσευχή eighteen times. However, according to Hengel, it is unclear whether all of these instances refer to the synagogue as a building or as an assembly of people.[31] Nevertheless, the term προσευχή came to be used to describe the place of Jewish religious assembly in the Graeco-Roman diaspora.[32]

The use of the Greek word προσευχή in the context of a *house of prayer* originated in Ptolemaic Egypt, but its influence spread to the rest of the Mediterranean and to the land of Israel.[33] Thus it was that the synagogue—as a religious institution—developed in the diaspora earlier than in Palestine,[34] and it is likely that its development in Palestine was facilitated by local communities.[35]

Moreover, προσευχή, according to Hengel, as well as referring to the building in which assembly took place, refers to prayers (like תפלה),[36] and that prayer was part of Jewish ritual assembly.[37] Hengel says that the term בית כנסת came to be used in the late Roman/Byzantine period to refer to a *house of assembly*,[38] and that the term בית תפלה was sometimes claimed to be an interpretation of the Greek προσευχῆς (contained in the LXX of Isa 56:7, 60:7, and 1 Macc 7:37).[39]

Hengel's influence on early synagogue studies remains particularly strong, especially in relation to the terms which survived and were commonly used into

---

Studies in their Encounter in Palestine during the Early Hellenistic Period (London: SCM, 1974).
[28] Hengel, *Judaism and Hellenism*, 104.
[29] Hengel, *Judaism and Hellenism*, 248.
[30] Hengel, "Proseuche und Synagoge," 158–59.
[31] Hengel, "Proseuche und Synagoge," 169.
[32] Hengel, "Proseuche und Synagoge," 179.
[33] Hengel, "Proseuche und Synagoge," 179.
[34] Hengel, "Proseuche und Synagoge," 180.
[35] Hengel, "Proseuche und Synagoge," 180
[36] Hengel, "Proseuche und Synagoge," 161.
[37] Hengel, "Proseuche und Synagoge," 157–84.
[38] J. Gwyn Griffiths, "Egypt and the Rise of the Synagogue," in *ASHAD* 1:7.
[39] Hengel, "Proseuche und Synagoge," 166.

the Roman period, that is, προσευχή and συναγωγή. It is fair to say that there is little evidence that the other terminology relates to specific buildings or to a particular type of religious institution in the Jewish world of the late Hellenistic and early Roman periods.

DEFINITIONS OF προσευχή

The Greek noun προσευχή means "a prayer," or "an offering," although in our context it has also come to mean, or it has come to be understood to mean, a *place of prayer*.[40] We find the earliest usage of the word προσευχή in a Jewish context in Hellenistic-Roman Egypt in inscriptions that refer to donations and benefactions to προσευχαί made by, or on behalf of, Egyptian Jews. It seems certain, based on the Egyptian inscriptions, that the Jews of Egypt had some form of building dedicated to their particular ethnic and/or communal and/or religious needs.

REFERENCES TO προσευχαί IN THE EGYPTIAN GRAECO-ROMAN INSCRIPTIONS. No. 13 of Horbury and Noy's *Jewish Inscriptions of Egypt* is a plaque with an inscription dated to around 37 BCE, from Gabbary near Alexandria, which refers to Alypus who *made the proseuchē*. No. 21 (dating to the second or first century BCE) is an inscription in which the Jews of Arthribis *dedicate the proseuchē* to the Most High God. No. 22 is the earliest epigraphical reference to the προσευχή of the diaspora Jewish community, and dates to around 246–221 BCE. No. 24 is an inscription dating to 140–116 BCE dedicating the *gateway of the proseuchē*. No. 25, also dating to 140–116 BCE is an inscription dedicating the *proseuchē and its appurtenances*. No. 28 is an inscription from Arthribis, dedicating the *exedra of a proseuchē*. No. 105 is an inscription from Leontopolis, dating to the mid- to early second century BCE, possibly dedicating a προσευχή to God the Highest. No. 117 is an inscription from Arsinoe-Crocodilopolis dated to 246–221 BCE dedicating the προσευχή. No. 125 is an inscription of uncertain origin, dating to around 145–116 BCE, proclaiming the προσευχή *to be inviolate*. No. 126 is an inscription, also of unknown origin, dating to around the first or second century CE, referring to Papous who *built the proseuchē*.[41]

It is difficult to understand precisely how these inscriptions relate to the existence of synagogues as we have come to understand them, as none of them is associated with any physical structure and some of the references may not be Jewish at all (since the term was also used in non-Jewish contexts). However, the inscriptions do indicate the existence of some form of physical structure in which

---

[40] Henry George Liddell and Robert Scott, *A Greek-English Lexicon* (9th ed. with revised Supplement; Oxford: Oxford University Press, 1996).
[41] William Horbury and David Noy, *Jewish Inscriptions of Greco-Roman Egypt* (Cambridge: Cambridge University Press, 1992).

Jews assembled regularly, whether that structure was used for religious purposes or not. We must infer from the specific use of the word προσευχή ("a prayer") in the Egyptian inscriptions that the place itself was dedicated as part of an offering, although none of the inscriptions gives us details of how the structures functioned, and whether religious worship of any sort was undertaken there.[42]

REFERENCES TO προσευχαί IN PHILO. In addition to the Egyptian inscriptions, the Alexandrian Jewish philosopher, Philo, writing in the first half of the first century CE, describes how communities of Jews in Alexandria met on Sabbaths to read the law (for example, *Hypothetica* 7:13; *Special Laws* 2:62). This gives us a clear link between a physical structure and a regularised and communal behaviour. However, Philo never once refers to praying as being part of the tradition of assembly, even though his accounts of these assemblies are otherwise quite specific (at least about the reading of the law on the Sabbath).[43] Of course, we might assume this to be the case, given the use of the word προσευχή to describe the assembly.

While an argument from silence may be risky, the προσευχή inscriptions and Philo's accounts do suggest, at least as regards Graeco-Roman Egypt and specifically in relation to Alexandrian Jews, that communal prayer may not have been part of a regularised Sabbath assembly and, thus, that the προσευχή of Graeco-Roman Egypt in the first century (and earlier) did not function as religious

---

[42] Horbury and Noy, *Jewish Inscriptions*; Giuseppe Botti, "Le inscrizioni cristiane di Alessandria d'Egitto," *Bessarione* 7 (1900): 270–81; Giuseppe Botti, "Les inscriptions de Schédia," *BSKG* 10 (1901): 611–17; Aryeh Kasher, "Three Jewish Communities of Lower Egypt in the Ptolemaic Period," *SCI* 2 (1975): 113–23; Aryeh Kasher, "First Jewish Military Units in Ptolemaic Egypt," *JSJ* 9 (1978): 57–67; Ross Shepherd Kraemer, "Hellenistic Jewish Women: The Epigraphical Evidence," in *SBL 1986 Seminar Papers* (Atlanta: Scholars Press, 1986): 183–200; Ross Shepherd Kraemer, "Non-Literary Evidence for Jewish women in Rome and Egypt," in *Rescuing Creusa: New Methodological Approaches to Women in Antiquity* (ed. Marilyn Skinner; Lubbock: Texas Tech University Press, 1986), 75–101; Ross Shepherd Kraemer, "On the Meaning of the Term 'Jew' in Greco-Roman Inscriptions," *HTR* 82 (1989): 35–54; H. Leclerq, "Judaïsme," in *DACL* 8.1: cols. 1–254; Gustave Lefèbvre, "Inscriptions grecques d'Égypte," *BCH* 26 (1902): 440–66; Gustave Lefèbvre, "Inscriptions gréco-juives," in *ASAE* 24 (1924): 1–5; David M. Lewis, "The Jewish Inscriptions of Egypt," in *CPJ* (1964): 138–66; L. A. Mayer and A. Reifenberg, "A Jewish Titulus from Egypt," *ASAE* 33 (1933): 81–82; David Noy, "A Jewish Place of Prayer in Roman Egypt," *JTS* 43.1 (1992): 118–22; and M. Schwabe, "On the Interpretation of a Jewish Inscription from Alexandria," *BEHJ* 1 (1946): 101–3.

[43] C. Mosser, "Torah Instruction, Discussion, and Prophecy in First-Century Synagogues," in *Christian Origins and Hellenistic Judaism: Literary and Social Contexts for the New Testament* (ed. Stanley E. Porter and Andrew Pitts; Leiden: Brill, forthcoming) [Matassa cited a prepublished version; it was subsequently published in 2012, 523–51, doi: 10.1163/9789004236394_020 –Eds.].

institutions in the way later synagogues did, or, perhaps instead that it was such a ubiquitous part of the Sabbath assembly that it was simply not mentioned. However, even given these parameters, it is also very likely that the term προσευχή must refer to a physical space in at least some of the Egyptian inscriptions, and from the accounts in Philo (*Embassy to Gaius* and *Flaccus*) that attacks on Alexandrian Jews were launched when resentments built up among the Roman, Greek, and native Egyptian populations as a result of the perceived separateness of the Jewish community in general.

REFERENCES TO προσευχαί IN JOSEPHUS. When we move away from Egypt and into the second half of the first century CE, we see that the use and meaning of the word προσευχή shifts somewhat.[44] Josephus, writing about events during the rebellion against the Romans (when his opponents seek to discredit him), for example, refers to a προσευχή in Tiberias as a place of assembly: "On the next day, they all came into the *proseuchē*; it was a large edifice, and capable of receiving a great number of people; Jonathan went in there, and though he dared not openly speak of a revolt, yet did he say that their city stood in need of a better governor than it then had."[45] Josephus refers to that same meeting in the προσευχή as a council ("so Jonathan and his colleagues put off their council till the next day, and went off without success").[46] Later, Josephus says he was making a prayer (καὶ πρὸς εὐχὰς), when Jesus began to question him "about the furniture and uncoined silver which had been confiscated after the conflagration of the royal palace."[47] It seems clear from this passage at least that the προσευχή in Tiberias to which Josephus refers is an assembly space and/or council chamber. Unfortunately, other

---

[44] Josephus uses the term προσευχή only three times: *A.J.* 14.258 (to decree relating to Halicarnassus and the right of Jews there to pray at the seaside according to their traditional customs; *C. Ap.* 2.10 (refuting claims that Moses prayed in the open at Heliopolis facing the city walls); and *Vita* 277–295 (where Josephus refers to a large προσευχή at Tiberias).

[45] Josephus, *Vita* 277: "κατὰ τὴν ἐπιοῦσαν οὖν ἡμέραν συνάγονται πάντες εἰς τὴν προσευχὴν μέγιστον οἴκημα καὶ πολὺν ὄχλον ἐπιδέξασθαι δυνάμενον. εἰσελθὼν δὲ ὁ Ἰωνάθης φανερῶς μὲν περὶ τῆς ἀποστάσεως οὐκ ἐτόλμα λέγειν, ἔφη δὲ στρατηγοῦ κρείττονος χρείαν τὴν πόλιν αὐτῶν ἔχειν." See also Josephus, *Vita* 280, 293–294. See also Josephus, *Vita*, 279, 280, 293–294, and, specifically, 295: "ἤδη δ' ἡμῶν τὰ νόμιμα ποιούντων καὶ πρὸς εὐχὰς τραπομένων ἀναστὰς Ἰησοῦς περὶ τῶν ληφθέντων ἐκ τοῦ ἐμπρησμοῦ τῆς βασιλικῆς αὐλῆς σκευῶν τοῦ ἀσήμου ἀργυρίου ἐπυνθάνετό μου, παρὰ τίνι τυγχάνει κείμενα. ταῦτα δ' ἔλεγεν διατρίβειν τὸν χρόνον βουλόμενος, ἕως ἂν ὁ Ἰωάννης παραγένηται [...]."

[46] Josephus, *Vita* 279: "καὶ οἱ περὶ τὸν Ἰωνάθην εἰς τὴν ἐπιοῦσαν ὑπερθέμενοι τὴν βουλὴν ἀπῄεσαν ἄπρακτοι."

[47] Josephus, *Vita 295:* "ἤδη δ' ἡμῶν τὰ νόμιμα ποιούντων καὶ πρὸς εὐχὰς τραπομένων ἀναστὰς Ἰησοῦς περὶ τῶν ληφθέντων ἐκ τοῦ ἐμπρησμοῦ τῆς βασιλικῆς αὐλῆς σκευῶν τοῦ ἀσήμου ἀργυρίου ἐπυνθάνετό μου, παρὰ τίνι τυγχάνει κείμενα. ταῦτα δ' ἔλεγεν διατρίβειν τὸν χρόνον βουλόμενος, ἕως ἂν ὁ Ἰωάννης παραγένηται."

than being describing it as "large," Josephus gives no details concerning the structure or its layout.

In another passage, referring to a decree from Halicarnassus, Josephus mentions a προσευχή in a context in which he could be referring to the act of praying or, possibly, to going to a place to pray, or even having a fixed or regular place to pray, though this passage is open to interpretation: "[…] we have decreed, that as many men and women of the Jews as are willing so to do, may celebrate their Sabbaths, and perform their holy offices, according to Jewish laws; and may make their *proseuchai* at the seaside, according to the customs of their forefathers […]."[48]

Even though, as with the Egyptian inscriptions, none of the references in Josephus have a physical analogue, they do strongly suggest that whatever the προσευχή was, it was sometimes a physical structure in which groups of Jews met, whether it was for the purposes of holding town councils, or even as a place in which an individual could pray. There is nothing in Josephus, however, to help us identify what shape that structure took, although, in relation to the προσευχή at Tiberias, we know that it was a large building, and we might suppose, if it was intended for general or council assemblies, that we would see a building with an open space surrounded by encircling benches. While Josephus mentions praying in the προσευχή, it is noteworthy that there is no mention of organised communal prayer, nor of liturgy. As it was normal for blessings for rulers and benefactors to be given at the start of formal proceedings in public meetings, we may assume that this was the case for proceedings in the προσευχή at Tiberias.[49] Although,

---

[48] *AJ* 14.258: "δεδόχθαι καὶ ἡμῖν Ἰουδαίων τοὺς βουλομένους ἄνδρας τε καὶ γυναῖκας τά τε σάββατα ἄγειν καὶ τὰ ἱερὰ συντελεῖν κατὰ τοὺς Ἰουδαίων νόμους καὶ τὰς προσευχὰς ποιεῖσθαι πρὸς τῇ θαλς, ἄττῃ κατὰ τὸ πάτριον ἔθος. ἂν δέ τις κωλύσῃ ἢ ἄρχων ἢ ἰδιώτης, τῷδε τῷ ζημιώματι ὑπεύθυνος ἔστω καὶ ὀφειλέτω τῇ πόλει."

[49] Some of the general literature discussing Judaism and synagogues in the Galilee can be found at Mark A. Chancey, *The Myth of a Gentile Galilee: The Population of Galilee and New Testament Studies* (Cambridge: Cambridge University Press, 2002); Mark A. Chancey, *Greco-Roman Culture and the Galilee of Jesus* (Cambridge: Cambridge University Press, 2005); Jörg Frey, Daniel R. Schwartz, and Stephanie Gripentrog, eds., *Jewish identity in the Greco-Roman World* (Leiden: Brill, 2007); Seán Freyne, *Galilee, Jesus and the Gospels: Literary Approaches and Historical Investigations* (Dublin: Gill & Macmillan; Fortress, 1988); Seán Freyne, *The Geography, Politics and Economics of Galilee and the Quest for the Historical Jesus* (Leiden: Brill, 1994); Seán Freyne, *Galilee: From Alexander the Great to Hadrian, 323 BCE to 135 CE: A Study of Second Temple Judaism* (London: T&T Clark, 1998); Seán Freyne, "Behind the Names: Galilaeans, Samaritans, *Ioudaioi*," in *Galilee through the Centuries* (ed. Eric M. Meyers; Winona Lake, IN: Eisenbrauns, 1999): 39–56; Seán Freyne, *Galilee and Gospel: Collected Essays* (Tübingen: Mohr Siebeck, 2000); Martin Hengel, *The Four Gospels and the One Gospel of Jesus Christ* (London: SCM, 2000); Sylvie Honigman, *The Septuagint and Homeric Scholarship in Alexandria. A Study in the Narrative of the Letter of Aristeas* (London: Routledge, 2003); W. G. Jeanrond and A. D. H. Mayes,

whether offering prayers and benedictions is sufficient reason to ascribe a "religious" dimension to use of the space is debatable.

REFERENCES TO προσευχαί IN THE NEW TESTAMENT. In the New Testament,[50] the term προσευχή is used to refer to prayer and praying. Only in five of the forty-three references in the New Testament does the term relate to anything more than a simple prayer or an act of praying, and three of these refer to the same incident in which Jesus refers to the Jerusalem temple as a προσευχή (Matt 21:13,[51] Mark 11:17,[52] and Luke 19:46).[53] The other references are in Acts 12:5,[54] where prayer was made by the assembly for Peter who was in jail, and, finally, in Acts 16:13, there is an incident recounting how the Apostles went to a riverside where they supposed there to be a place of prayer.[55] There are no occurrences of προσευχή in the New Testament that imply an assembly space, as with the Egyptian inscriptions, Philo, and Josephus.

Based on Egyptian προσευχή inscriptions, Philo, Josephus, and the New Testament, we cannot take for granted that the various instances of the term προσευχή in those texts necessarily denote the same thing. A house of assembly, a place of assembly, and participation in an assembly are very different things, though they may share some commonalities. We cannot now know precisely how

---

eds., *Recognising the Margins: Developments in Biblical and Theological Studies: Essays in Honour of Seán Freyne* (Dublin: Columba Press, 2006); John S. Kloppenborg, *The Shape of Q: Signal Essays on the Sayings Gospel* (Minneapolis, MN: Augsburg Fortress, 1994); John S. Kloppenborg, *Excavating Q: The History and Setting of the Sayings Gospel*, (Minneapolis, MN: Augsburg Fortress, 2000), 222; Frederick J. Murphy, *An Introduction to Jesus and the Gospels* (Nashville, TN: Abingdon, 2005); Stan Purdum, *He Walked in Galilee: The Days of Jesus' Ministry* (Nashville, TN: Abingdon, 2005); Anthony J. Tomasino, *Judaism Before Jesus* (Downers Grove, IL: InterVarsity Press, 2003); and Georg Walser, *The Greek of the Ancient Synagogue: An Investigation on the Greek of the Septuagint, Pseudepigrapha and the New Testament* (Lund: Almquist & Wiksell, 2001).

[50] The Tanakh used throughout this monograph is *The Jewish Study Bible* (Jewish Publication Society; Oxford: Oxford University Press, 2004). For the New Testament I have referred to Harold W. Attridge, ed., *The Harper Collins Study Bible* (New York: Harper One, 2006). [The Greek derives from *BibleWorks 7* –Eds.]

[51] "καὶ λέγει αὐτοῖς· γέγραπται ὁ οἶκός μου οἶκος προσευχῆς κληθήσεται, ὑμεῖς δὲ αὐτὸν ποιεῖτε σπήλαιον λῃστῶν."

[52] "καὶ ἐδίδασκεν καὶ ἔλεγεν· οὐ γέγραπται ὅτι ὁ οἶκός μου οἶκος προσευχῆς κληθήσεται πᾶσιν τοῖς ἔθνεσιν; ὑμεῖς δὲ πεποιήκατε αὐτὸν σπήλαιον λῃστῶν."

[53] "λέγων αὐτοῖς· γέγραπται καὶ ἔσται ὁ οἶκός μου οἶκος προσευχῆς, ὑμεῖς δὲ αὐτὸν ἐποιήσατε σπήλαιον λῃστῶν."

[54] "ὁ μὲν οὖν Πέτρος ἐτηρεῖτο ἐν τῇ φυλακῇ προσευχὴ δὲ ἦν ἐκτενῶς γινομένη ὑπὸ τῆς ἐκκλησίας πρὸς τὸν θεὸν περὶ αὐτοῦ."

[55] "τῇ τε ἡμέρᾳ τῶν σαββάτων ἐξήλθομεν ἔξω τῆς πύλης παρὰ ποταμὸν οὗ ἐνομίζομεν προσευχὴν εἶναι καὶ καθίσαντες ἐλαλοῦμεν ταῖς συνελθούσαις γυναιξίν."

the προσευχή functioned in each of the different references; whether it was a prayer, or an offering, a location, or a particular building, the congregants themselves, or even different combinations of those elements. And, as we see in the collection of socially, politically, geographically, and chronologically diverse documents that make up the New Testament, the word προσευχή is only used to denote prayer not a specific, built place.

Definitions of συναγωγή

The Greek noun συναγωγή means a bringing-together, or a uniting, or an assembly, or a place of assembly. In its verb form it can also mean a bringing in [of a harvest], a drawing together, a contracting of, a forming of [an army in a column], a pursing of the lips or wrinkling of the face, or even the closing up of a wound.[56] In our context, the noun has come to mean an assembly of people and/or a place of assembly, though it is not universally used this way in Greek texts.[57]

References to συναγωγή in the New Testament. Moving to the New Testament, we find numerous occurrences of the word συναγωγή where it clearly denotes a physical structure or a physical space. From the missions of Jesus to those of the apostles we see clear indicators that by the time the gospels were redacted into their canonical form, the term συναγωγή had become common (at least in those texts). Unfortunately, not a single one of these references describes a single physical feature of the synagogues mentioned. They do, however, mention reading of scripture, discussions of scripture, preaching, teaching, scourging (of miscreants), law courts, and the collection of monies. It is notable that there is no mention of prayer in the synagogue—communal or otherwise, nor of liturgy, although, of course, this may simply be because this was a ubiquitous part of communal and/or ritual activity in a synagogue.[58] And, while it is fascinating to note that the places where the synagogue is seen to be developing in the first century are some distance from Judaea—either in the Graeco-Roman

---

[56] Liddell and Scott, *A Greek-English Lexicon*.
[57] See Horbury and Noy, *Jewish Inscriptions*, in general; see also n. 20 above.
[58] Συναγωγή, "synagogue": Matt 12:9; 13:54; Mark 1:21–3, 29; 3:1; 5:22, 35, 36, 38; 6:2; Luke 4:16, 20, 28, 33, 38; 6:6; 7:5; 8:41, 49; 13:14; John 6:59; 9:22; 12:42; 18:20; Acts 5:15–21; 6:9; 13:14, 15, 42; 14:1; 17:10, 17; 18:4, 7, 8, 17, 19, 26; 19:8; 22:19; 26:11; Rev 2:9; 3:9.
Κηρύσσω, "preach": Matt 4:17; 10:7, 27; 11:1; Mark 1:4, 38; 3:14; 16:15; Luke 4:18, 19, 43; 9:2, 60; Acts 5:42; 10:42; 14:15; 15:2; 16:6, 10; 17:3; Rom 1:15; 10:8, 15; 15:20; 1 Cor 1:17, 23; 9:14, 16, 18; 15:11; 2 Cor 2:12; 4:5; 10:16; Gal 1:8, 9; 2:2; 5:11; Eph 3:18; Phil 1:15, 16; Col 1:28; 2 Tim 4:2; Rev 14:6.
Διδάσκω, "teach": Matt 11:1; 28:19; Mark 4:1; 6:2, 34; 8:31; Luke 11:1; 12:12; John 7:35; 9:34; 14:26; Acts 1:1; 4:18; 5:28, 42; 16:21; 1 Cor 4:17; 11:14; 14:19; 1 Tim 1:3; 3:2, 6:3; 2 Tim 2:2, 4; Heb 5:12; 8:11; 1 John 2:27; Rev 2:20.

diaspora or in the north of Israel in the Galilee or Golan[59]—this does not help us to identify any of our case study sites. There is no uniformity in the way the two terms, προσευχή and συναγωγή, are used in the New Testament, and that ambiguity may represent the way in which the institution we have come to know as the synagogue was developing and evolving.

REFERENCES TO SYNAGOGUES IN JOSEPHUS. In Josephus, we find the word συναγωγή used five times. In *A.J.* 1.10, Josephus refers to the translation of the Septuagint into Greek for Ptolemy II;[60] in *A.J.* 19.300–305, Josephus refers to a συναγωγή at Dor (just 8 km north of Caesarea) where a statue of the emperor is erected;[61] in *B.J.* 2.285, Josephus mentions a συναγωγή to which access is being deliberately blocked by its Greek owner;[62] at *B.J.* 2.289 Josephus refers to a συναγωγή outside of which a local youth sacrificed a number of fowl so as to offend Jews;[63] and a reference at *B.J.* 7.74 where Josephus refers to the successors of Antiochus Epiphanes allowing the Jews of Antioch to restore their συναγωγή to its former state and granting them equal privileges with Greek citizens.[64]

These five passages clearly indicate that the synagogues referred to by Josephus were buildings in which there was some element of religious activity

---

[59] Peter Richardson, "Early Synagogues as Collegia in the Diaspora and Palestine," in *Voluntary Associations in the Graeco-Roman World* (ed. John S. Kloppenborg and Stephen G. Wilson; London: Routledge, 1996), 100.

[60] *A.J.* 1.10: "Εὗρον τοίνυν, ὅτι Πτολεμαίων μὲν ὁ δεύτερος μάλιστα δὴ βασιλεὺς περὶ παιδείαν καὶ βιβλίων συναγωγὴν σπουδάσας ἐξαιρέτως ἐφιλοτιμήθη τὸν ἡμέτερον νόμον καὶ τὴν κατ' αὐτὸν διάταξιν τῆς πολιτείας εἰς τὴν Ἑλλάδα φωνὴν μεταβαλεῖν."

[61] *A.J.* 19.300 & 305: "παντάπασιν δὲ ὀλίγου χρόνου διελθόντος Δωρῖται νεανίσκοι τῆς ὁσιότητος προτιθέμενοι τόλμαν καὶ πεφυκότες εἶναι παραβόλως θρασεῖς Καίσαρος ἀνδριάντα κομίσαντες εἰς τὴν τῶν Ἰουδαίων συναγωγὴν ἀνέστησαν" [...] "τἀναντία δὲ πάντα πρᾶξαι, συναγωγὴν Ἰουδαίων κωλύοντας εἶναι διὰ τὸ μεταθεῖναι ἐν αὐτῇ τὸν Καίσαρος ἀνδριάντα, παρανομοῦντας οὐκ εἰς μόνους Ἰουδαίους, ἀλλὰ καὶ εἰς τὸν αὐτοκράτορα, οὗ ὁ ἀνδριὰς βέλτιον ἐν τῷ ἰδίῳ ναῷ ἢ ἐν ἀλλοτρίῳ ἐτίθετο καὶ ταῦτα ἐν τῷ τῆς συναγωγῆς τόπῳ, τοῦ φύσει δικαιοῦντος ἕνα ἕκαστον τῶν ἰδίων τόπων κυριεύειν κατὰ τὸ Καίσαρος ἐπίκριμα."

[62] *B.J.* 2.285: "πρὸς δὲ τὸ μέγεθος τῶν ἐξ αὐτοῦ συμφορῶν οὐκ ἀξίαν ἔσχεν πρόφασιν: οἱ γὰρ ἐν Καισαρείᾳ Ἰουδαῖοι, συναγωγὴν ἔχοντες παρὰ χωρίον, οὗ δεσπότης ἦν τις Ἕλλην Καισαρεύς, πολλάκις μὲν κτήσασθαι τὸν τόπον ἐσπούδασαν τιμὴν πολλαπλασίονα τῆς ἀξίας διδόντες."

[63] *B.J.* 2.289: "Τῆς δ' ἐπιούσης ἡμέρας ἑβδομάδος οὔσης τῶν Ἰουδαίων εἰς τὴν συναγωγὴν συναθροισθέντων στασιαστής τις Καισαρεὺς γάστραν καταστρέψας καὶ παρὰ τὴν εἴσοδον αὐτῶν θέμενος ἐπέθυεν ὄρνεις. τοῦτο τοὺς Ἰουδαίους ἀνηκέστως παρώξυνεν ὡς ὑβρισμένων μὲν αὐτοῖς τῶν νόμων, μεμιασμένου δὲ τοῦ χωρίου."

[64] *B.J.* 7.44: "Ἀντίοχος μὲν γὰρ ὁ κληθεὶς Ἐπιφανὴς Ἱεροσόλυμα πορθήσας τὸν νεὼν ἐσύλησεν, οἱ δὲ μετ' αὐτὸν τὴν βασιλείαν παραλαβόντες τῶν ἀναθημάτων ὅσα χαλκᾶ πεποίητο πάντα τοῖς ἐπ' Ἀντιοχείας Ἰουδαίοις ἀπέδοσαν εἰς τὴν συναγωγὴν αὐτῶν ἀναθέντες, καὶ συνεχώρησαν αὐτοῖς ἐξ ἴσου τῆς πόλεως τοῖς Ἕλλησι μετέχειν."

being observed and where regular practise could be disrupted by local gentiles. Unfortunately, none of the references to synagogues include any detail as to precisely what the synagogue was, or how it was used by the local Jewish community. Still, it seems certain that during the period about which Josephus was writing, there were synagogues in some shape or form in northern Israel.

THE THEODOTOS INSCRIPTION. Perhaps most the most tantalising use of the word συναγωγή appears on the Theodotos inscription found in a cistern filled with rubble from both the pre-70 CE and post-70 CE periods in the City of David in Jerusalem. This inscription is thought by many scholars to attest to the existence of a synagogue in Jerusalem in the first century CE:

> Theodotos, son of Vettenos the priest and *archisynagogos*, son of an *archisynagogos* and grandson of a *archisynagogos*, who built the synagogue for purposes of reciting the Law and studying the commandments, and the hostel, chambers and water installations to provide for the needs of itinerants from abroad, and whose father, with the elders and Simonides, founded the synagogue.[65]

Kloppenborg, writing in 2000, says that there is near consensus on the dating of the inscription. This is on the basis of both a close palaeographic analysis of the lettering inscribed on it and the location and archaeological context in which the inscription was found.[66] On a close analysis of the palaeography, using comparisons with Greek and other Near Eastern inscriptions (but not inscriptions from Jerusalem), Kloppenborg acknowledges that the "dating of undated inscriptions is far from an exact science"[67] and that "it is important to note again that shifts in lettering styles are not sufficiently sharply defined to enable one to exclude a second century date or one even later."[68] He notes that there are very few Greek inscriptions from the Herodian and early Roman period from Jerusalem from which to draw a direct palaeographic parallel.[69] Kloppenborg concludes that, "while it is still possible that the lettering is from later than the first century CE— the result of traditionalism or deliberate archaizing—nothing requires such a dating, and all of the indications are consistent with the Herodian period."[70]

In relation to the archaeological context, Kloppenborg strongly argues for an early date on the basis that the area in which the inscription was found in the City

---

[65] Paul V. M. Flesher, "Palestinian Synagogues Before 70 C.E.: A Review of the Evidence," in *ASHAD* 1:33.
[66] John S. Kloppenborg, "Dating Theodotos (CIJ II 1404)," *JJS* 51.2 (2000): 243–44.
[67] Kloppenborg, "Dating Theodotos," 265.
[68] Kloppenborg, "Dating Theodotos," 276.
[69] Kloppenborg, "Dating Theodotos," 269.
[70] Kloppenborg, "Dating Theodotos," 276.

of David has clear signs of destruction from the period around the razing of Jerusalem. In general, the late Roman period is generally ill-represented throughout the entire City of David in the areas east, northeast, and north of Weill's excavations. The City of David seems to have been unoccupied after 135 CE until around 460 CE. There was nothing found that could be dated to the period immediately after 70 CE, and dateable finds from the area only begin to emerge again in the Byzantine period so that, on this basis too, it is likely that the inscription dates from the pre-70 CE period.[71]

Although Kloppenborg's intention is to support the dating of the Theodotos inscription to the pre-70 CE period, the evidence on which he makes his argument is, unfortunately, inherently ambiguous and, while it is possible, and even likely, that the Theodotos inscription can be dated to the first century CE, it is also possible that it belongs to a much later period. Thus, the Theodotos inscription remains perhaps the single most frustrating pieces of evidence relating to first-century synagogues in the land of Israel because information about its discovery—including whether it was found below, in, or above the destruction layer of 70 CE—was not recorded, and it is now impossible to reconstruct the information which might have helped support a definitive first-century date.[72]

In spite of the ambiguity of the evidence both for and against an early dating of the Theodotos inscription, it may be appropriate to take a more positive position and leave the matter open. If Kloppenborg is correct about the pre-70 CE dating of the Theodotos inscription, it would prove to be enormously helpful in any ongoing search for physical manifestations of the first-century synagogue, and it would, in fact, provide some of the criteria of possible identifiers outlined above, such as the presence of water installations and hostel accommodation for visitors and, of course, a specific reference to reading the law in the synagogue itself. The inscription would also be useful in relation to the identification of the public building at Gamla, which is not yet completely excavated, but which is thought to have been part of a far more extensive complex of integrated buildings.

As we shall see in the case studies in this monograph, even though we may use somewhat nebulous terms to discuss what we have come to know as the *synagogue*, and whichever terms we use to describe that institution, be it προσευχή, συναγωγή, עדה or קהל, and however we choose to interpret the textual and epigraphic evidence, there is a separation between modern scholarship's theoretical constructs of what a first-century synagogue might have been,

---

[71] Kloppenborg, "Dating Theodotos," 260–61. There is good supporting evidence for this argument to be found in the current excavations of the Givati Parking Lot in the City of David, where a team led by Doron Ben-Ami of the Hebrew University of Jerusalem has found that after the destruction layer of 70 CE only Roman and then later Byzantine material has been excavated. [Matassa orignally cited a press release from the IAA website that she had accessed 17 May 2011 but is no longer extant –Eds.].
[72] Flesher, "Palestinian Synagogues," 33.

LITERATURE REVIEW

Modern scholarship on the identification of early synagogues cannot fill in the missing link between the Hellenistic/early Roman period and the late Roman/Byzantine period, when synagogues become fully realised and dedicated physical structures. This is because the contemporary sources which they interpret are neither specific nor detailed, and there is no link between any of the *synagogē* and *proseuchē* references in the literature, the epigraphy, and a physical structure anywhere. On the face of it this seems an extraordinary statement given the amount that has been written on the subject (only a tiny portion of which is included in this overview). Scholars in this field have constructed a veritable creed of synagogue development that is endlessly regurgitated and expanded without ever having properly been tested against the five buildings which it has identified as first-century synagogues. Very few scholars writing about the continuing search for the origins of the synagogue deal with the archaeological record and, of the ones that do, there are only a few who deal with the material as relating to particular sites. These few are discussed in context in the case studies herein. The overwhelming majority of the rest of the scholarship on the subject deal with the archaeological origins of the synagogue by surveying past scholarship, and by adding new speculations to those accounts.

We can identify the beginnings of modern synagogue scholarship with Kohl and Watzinger's 1905–1907 survey of eleven Galilaean and Golan synagogues, which was published in 1916 under the title *Antike Synagogen in Galilaea*. Kohl and Watzinger argued that the earliest synagogues (at that time) dated to the late second and early third centuries CE and were modelled along Romano-Syrian temple structures.[73] In 1934, Sukenik identified a series of basilica-like structures, also in the Galilee, which he said originated in the sixth and seventh centuries CE and belonged to a completely different and later synagogue type.[74] In the 1950s, a third type of synagogue, the broadhouse, was proposed by Goodenough and Avi-Yonah.[75] The common thread in these identifications was that synagogue architecture was thought to have developed along a chronological and physical

---

[73] Heinrich Kohl and Carl Watzinger, *Antike Synagogen in Galilaea* (Leipzig: Hinrichs, 1916).
[74] Eleazar Sukenik, *Ancient Synagogues in Palestine and Greece* (Schweich Lectures of the British Academy; London: Oxford University Press, 1934).
[75] Erwin Goodenough, *Jewish Symbols in the Greco-Roman Period* (Princeton, NJ: Princeton University Press, 1988 [1953]).

continuum and that at any time there was a dominant architectural model with some overlapping styles.[76]

To date, and beginning with Kohl and Watzinger's work, there has not been one single identification related to any physical structure which can be definitively identified as a synagogue **and** dated to earlier than the late Roman/Byzantine period. The earliest phase of Nabratein in the Galilee *may* be late second century CE, but is probably later,[77] and the synagogue excavated at Magdala in 2009 may be second century, but since the site has not been published, there is not much evidence on which to base any judgement. Even so, various scholars have argued for the establishment of synagogues from as early as the ninth century BCE.[78] Some prominent streams of scholarship thought that the development of the synagogue was a direct product of the reforms of Ezra-Nehemiah,[79] while others suggested establishment dates from the fourth to the first centuries BCE, distributed over a post-exilic diaspora setting.[80]

Writing in the 1920s and 1930s, E. L. Sukenik's approach fed into the *Zeitgeist* of the time, using what became known as *biblical archaeology* to connect the emerging modern state of Israel to its ancient past.[81] Sukenik's excavations at Bet Alpha took synagogue studies into the media spotlight in Israel.[82] He argued that the origins of the synagogue lay in the Babylonian diaspora, and that the early synagogue was a place of assembly, study, and worship, through his discussion of the synagogues at Na'aran, Bet Alpha, Jerash, Delos, Miletus, Aegina, and Priene. However, while Sukenik argued for Babylonian origins, his excavations and studies of synagogue sites were unable to provide physical evidence of anything that dated before the late Roman/Byzantine period, and he was making an assumption that what could be seen in that later period was also the case for the earlier period.[83] This, as we shall see in the context of the specific case studies in this book, has been the standard approach to the subject as a whole.

---

[76] Levine, *Ancient Synagogue*, 10.
[77] Fine, *Sacred Realm*, 13.
[78] Gutmann, *Ancient Synagogues*, 1.
[79] Gutmann, *Ancient Synagogues*, 1.
[80] Levine, Ancient Synagogue, 20.
[81] Sukenik's excavation of the synagogue at Bet Alpha inspired his son Yigael Yadin to develop his own interest in early synagogues and eventually led to his identification of Locus 1042 on Masada as a first-century synagogue.
[82] Eleazar L. Sukenik, "The Present State of Ancient Synagogue Studies," in *Bulletin of the Lewis M. Rabinowitz Fund* 1 (1949): 8–23.
[83] Sukenik, "Present State," 8–23. Sukenik famously changed his mind about the Delos case after reading B. Mazur's 1935 discussion of the site and, in 1949, wrote that "the case of the so-called 'Synagogue' at Delos shows how misleading incomplete research can be." His revised position is explained in the Delos case study in this monograph.

M. Hengel, writing in the 1970s, argued for synagogue origins in the Hellenistic period diaspora, which developed as a response to the centralisation of the cult, and not as a direct replacement for the temple. According to Hengel, the development of the synagogue in the land of Israel came only later, with Hasmonaean policies of territorial expansion and the rise of the Pharisees. Hengel tied his argument together by saying that the diaspora synagogue was then influenced by Palestinian customs, beginning under the Hasmonaeans.[84] This argument took the debate even further from the physical reality of identifiable structures into the realm of the wholly *notional* synagogue, almost removing any requirement for corroboration in the material record and laying open the way for subsequent definitions of the early synagogue as a multi-purpose public building.

S. Zeitlin (1975) argued for an institution whose focus was the reading of the law, and for communal prayer and, like Hengel, said that this institution arose out of Pharisaic attempts to "democratise" temple worship into a communal act.[85] This argument about Pharisaic influence and involvement is based in its entirety on supposition and, along with Hengel's position, serves to broaden the definition of the early synagogue to something that could have served virtually any communal or public function. But, because the definition has become so vague, it does not get any closer to what the early institution of the synagogue might actually have been or how it might have worked.

J. Gutmann (1981) noted that "Edward Carr wisely cautioned that 'the facts of history cannot be purely objective, since they become facts only in virtue of the significance attached to them by the historian [...].'"[86] He also said that nothing testifies to this more than the problem of synagogue origins where the same facts lead to radically different theories of origins, from the rabbinic tradition of Mosaic origins to more modern hypotheses ascribing origins to the Babylonian exile or to Hellenistic Egypt.[87] According to him, there is no archaeological evidence for the synagogue, nor is there textual evidence in the Hebrew Bible. Even the Septuagint, which uses the term συναγωγή to translate the Hebrew words קהל and עדה, does not refer to a building, despite claims to the contrary.[88] Increasingly frustrated by myriad claims about synagogue origins, he said that all hypotheses in support of an early origin for the synagogues are arguments from silence, and the proofs offered up for the early existence of the synagogue are merely semantics, ripping words from their biblical context in the belief that the meaning of the word remains static and that one may infer the same meaning for a word

---

[84] Hengel, "Proseuche und Synagoge," 181–82.
[85] Solomon Zeitlin, "The Origin of the Synagogue: A Study in the Development of Jewish Institutions," in *The Synagogue: Studies in Origins, Archaeology and* Architecture (ed. Joseph Gutmann; New York: Ktav, 1975), 56–58.
[86] Gutmann, *Ancient Synagogues*, 1.
[87] Gutmann, *Ancient Synagogues*, 1.
[88] Gutmann, *Ancient Synagogues*, 1.

found both in a biblical and a rabbinical context.[89] Even taking for granted that such institutions existed in Babylonia, it does not follow that these were synagogues.[90]

Moreover, the references to the so-called *houses of prayer* or the *proseuchē* of Hellenistic Egypt do not necessarily imply the existence of the synagogue and, according to Gutmann, whatever the *proseuchē* was, it was not a synagogue, but was some localised form of Judaism that had responded to the specific environmental challenges.[91] Gutmann may be making too sceptical a claim here as regards the Egyptian inscriptions because, while we cannot account for the precise meaning of the use of the term *proseuchē* in the inscriptions, the word does mean *a prayer* or *for a prayer*, and the dedication of a *proseuchē*, or its appurtenances, implies that it had a physical element or purpose which could be offered in some way [to a god]. And, according to Gutmann, if we cannot rely on finding the origins of the synagogue in semantic arguments, then we can at least see that it is attested in the first century by Josephus and the New Testament, even though archaeological corroboration is lacking.[92]

J. D. Newsome (1982) argues that the synagogue may initially have been an institution dedicated to the reading of and instruction in the Torah. This would have been especially true in the diaspora where Jews comprised a minority in the local population. After the destruction of the temple at Jerusalem, the synagogue took on greater significance within the community, and became the place where Jews met for worship, instruction, and fellowship.[93] This is a sufficiently vague claim as to be probably correct, but does not add weight or credibility to any of the identifications of first-century synagogues so far made. Newsome further argues that as regards the origins of the synagogue, all that can be stated with any certainty is that it flourished in the Hellenistic and Roman periods, first in the diaspora, and later in Palestine.[94] But this, as we have seen in the section on the terminology and sources, above, is not the case. Since, with the best will in the world, we do not know exactly what the *proseuchē* was, or how its physical manifestation worked, we cannot claim that whatever it was it was flourishing in a given time period, or that it was a synagogue at all. Consequently, Newsome's

---

[89] Gutmann, *Ancient Synagogues*, 1–2.
[90] Gutmann, *Ancient Synagogues*, 3.
[91] Gutmann, *Ancient Synagogues*, 3.
[92] Gutmann, *Ancient Synagogues*, 3. Indeed, it is attested in the New Testament in a myriad of references, some to physical structures, some to congregations or assemblies (see n. 38 above).
[93] James D. Newsome, *Greeks, Romans, Jews* (Currents of Culture and Belief in the New Testament World; Philadelphia: Trinity Press Intl, 1992), 27–28.
[94] Newsome, *Greeks, Romans, Jews*, 27–28.

claim that communities in Palestine, where the population was almost entirely Jewish, would mirror the membership of the local synagogue is untenable.[95]

J. T. Burtchaell (1992) notes that while the books of Maccabees describe in detail Seleucid efforts in the second century BCE to wipe out every institution and observance precious to Jews, no mention is made of synagogues, which therefore did not exist at that time, at least not in the sense of being a religious institution.[96] Using their own nomenclature, the Jews themselves were the assembly and this covenantal belief was so typical that it provided the term by which one referred to the Jews.[97] It is difficult to argue with this viewpoint, as it is undoubtedly correct, but it does not add anything to the means by which we can identify the institutions and physical structures that developed out of this self-designation.

I. Elbogen, writing in 1993, argues that the developing Jewish liturgy was completely unique in the history of religions, because it was completely independent of a sacrificial cult. Because liturgy was central to post-70 CE Judaism, and because it was community based, it was able to spread easily throughout the Graeco-Roman world.[98] Again, this has to be correct, but still does not address the use of liturgy in the period before the destruction of the temple or in its immediate aftermath, or how it was adapted for synagogue use or even how much adaptation was required to move it from place to place.

L. L. Grabbe (1995) tries to locate a finite point in time after which synagogues existed.[99] While he accepts there were "synagogues" in Egypt in the third century BCE, he argues that they did not develop in the land of Israel until the third century CE.[100] Using the Theodotos inscription and the New Testament to support his argument, he says that the institution that existed before the destruction of the Jerusalem temple was well placed to transform Judaism into a non-sacrificial cult.[101] His position is interesting in a number of ways, not least of which is because he is using the term "synagogue" in a way that it is not used even in the Egyptian inscriptions to which he refers. The Egyptian inscriptions uniformly use the term *proseuchē*. This is a minor point, however, as Grabbe is scathing on the use of assumptions in history writing, and says that these can be so strong that evidence often makes little impact against the tide of tradition and is confounded by "that most persistent and hardy of species—the impregnable defence of 'what everybody knows,' the incontrovertible argument of 'what must

---

[95] Newsome, *Greeks, Romans, Jews*, 27–28.
[96] James Tunstead Burtchaell, *From Synagogue to Church: Public Services and Offices in the Earliest Christian Communities* (Cambridge: Cambridge University Press, 1992), 203–4.
[97] Burtchaell, *From Synagogue to Church*, 209.
[98] Ismar Elbogen, *Jewish Liturgy: A Comprehensive History* (Philadelphia: The Jewish Publication Society, 993), 304.
[99] Lester L. Grabbe, "Synagogues in Pre-70 Palestine: A Re-Assessment," in *ASHAD*, 1:17.
[100] The Egyptian inscriptions refer to *proseuchai* and not *synagogues*, however.
[101] Runesson, *Origins of the Synagogue*, 153.

have been.'" According to Grabbe, this results in flimsy evidence being used to support major conclusions, often without reference to any primary data, and where data is referenced, data from different periods and geographical areas is mixed.[102]

Z. Safrai (1995) argues that the main function of the בית הכנסת (*house of assembly*[103]) was not for public prayer but as a place for the reading and study of Torah, and that this was the main function of the synagogue.[104] Here, the terminology is being obfuscated because the phrase used in the passage at Ezek 11:16 to which Safrai is referring is מקדש מעט (a small sanctuary), which *t.Sukkah* 4, 5 interprets as *house of assembly* (בית הכנסת).[105] There is no historical basis on which to imply that the early synagogue was the equivalent of a religious sanctuary or whether the one developed from the other.

A. Kasher (1995) argues that the two most important non-sacrificial functions of the Jerusalem temple, praying and Torah reading, were adopted in Egypt after the Torah was translated into Greek during and after the reign of Ptolemy II (285–246 BCE). According to Kasher, the description of daily prayer in the *Letter of Aristeas* provided a model for imitation, and there is a line of development from *The Letter of Aristeas* through to the writings of Philo and his descriptions of synagogue activity in Alexandria.[106] The central place of the synagogues means that one can assume wherever there is such an institution, there is also an organised Jewish community. Such an institution can only be built where a sizable Jewish community required its services, which means that the synagogue was situated at the very heart of the area of settlement.[107]

Kasher, like Grabbe, is using the word *synagogue* to discuss Philo's accounts of Jewish religious activity in Egypt. In fact, Philo refers to the *proseuchē* as a place to assemble seventeen times (*Flaccus* 41, 45, 47, 48, 49, 53, 122; *Embassy* 132, 134, 137, 138–9, 148, 152, 156–8, 165, 191, 371), and to the *synagogē* as a place to assemble only three times (*Embassy* 311, 346; *Good Person* 81–83), and to the *synagogē* as a congregation twice (both in *Posterity* 67). Moreover, while Philo describes assemblies where the law is read and where instruction is given, nowhere does he refer to any acts of communal prayer, which is what Kasher is implying here. This thesis would work well if it were combined with that of H. A. McKay, who wrote in 1995 that, if the use of sacred texts should be regarded as a

---

[102] Grabbe, "Synagogues in Pre-70 Palestine," 17.
[103] The phrase is an interpretation of the passage at Ezek 11:16 which refers to מקדש מעט, not בית הכנסת.
[104] Z. Safrai, "The Communal Functions of the Synagogue in the Land of Israel in the Rabbinic Period," in *ASHAD*, 181.
[105] Safrai, "The Communal Functions," 182.
[106] Aryeh Kasher, "Synagogues as 'Houses of Prayer' and 'Holy Places' in the Jewish Communities of Hellenistic and Roman Egypt," in *ASHAD*, 211.
[107] Kasher, "Synagogues as 'Houses of Prayer,'" 213–14.

sacred act, it has to be accompanied by other rituals that define the event as "a planned session of worship."[108]

A. T. Kraabel (1995) argues that in the diaspora, the sanctity of the synagogue increased, particularly after the destruction of the Jerusalem temple. The synagogue gradually became more than a "prayer house," and secular functions became restricted to side rooms. Kraabel says that this must have happened in the diaspora even before the temple was destroyed.[109] Unfortunately, again, there is no evidence that this was the case. And, while Kraabel refers to an institution that gradually became "more than" a prayer house, we still do not know exactly what a prayer house was (if that is what a *proseuchē* was), and when or where this might have happened. The only reference we have to prayer in the *proseuchē* comes to us from the passage in Josephus where he refers to praying in the large *proseuchē* at Tiberias.[110]

P. V. M. Flesher (1995) notes that in the period prior to 70 CE, in the numerous Jewish documents, there is little information about synagogues, and only three texts even mention synagogues in Palestine—the New Testament, Josephus, and Philo. All other documents are silent.[111] Flesher tries to discover the origins from a specific context in Palestine, and argues that it was that an institution that arose where there was no easy access to the Jerusalem temple. He looks for a central and mainstream institution in Jewish towns and villages in which religious functions (and other things took place). He finds this mainstream institution in northern Palestine only, and says the only evidence for synagogues in Judaea (Acts 6:9[112] and the Theodotos Inscription) are references to institutions for diaspora Jews.[113] This is quite interesting in that it raises the question of why—if he is right—the institution existed for foreign nationals only and whether, therefore, it functioned in any religious capacity. Of course, if it is correct that the Theodotos inscription relates to a later period, then the *only* evidence for synagogues in Judaea comes to us from Acts.

R. Reich (1995) argues that both the literary and archaeological evidence make it clear that the synagogue emerged in the Second Temple period, although

---

[108] Heather A. McKay, *Sabbath and Synagogue: The Question of Sabbath Worship in Ancient Judaism* (Leiden: Brill, 1995), 3.

[109] Alf Thomas Kraabel, "The Diaspora Synagogue: Archaeological and Epigraphic Evidence Since Sukenik," in *ASHAD*, 120–21.

[110] *Vitae* 295 (καὶ πρὸς εὐχάς).

[111] Paul V. M. Flesher, "Palestinian Synagogues Before 70 CE, a Review of the Evidence," in *ASHAD*, 30–31. Actually, we do see a reference to a *proseuchē* in Juvenal's third satire, but as the reference is part of a vituperative [albeit satirical] attack on a poor person in Rome, it is difficult to understand precisely what is being referred to (see n. 2 above).

[112] A reference to the "synagogue of the freedmen."

[113] Runesson, *Origins of the Synagogue*, 157, referring to Flesher, "Palestinian Synagogues," 29–30.

its precise origins remain unclear.[114] This claim does not stand up to scrutiny, as will be made clear in the case studies, and while there is some evidence in the textual sources, it is by no means overwhelming. There is certainly literary evidence for the existence of synagogues in the New Testament, and *proseuchai* as places of assembly in the Egyptian inscriptions and in Philo, but there is no archaeological evidence to support a claim that they emerged in the Second Temple period. Linking the literary material to non-existent or later archaeological evidence has created a very artificial space in which to look for the synagogue of the first century CE.

P. Richardson (1996) argues that the earliest evidence for synagogues is from the diaspora, where they took the form of voluntary associations and guilds, and that as they spread and came to be adopted in Palestine, they retained this structure, even though the terminology changed.[115] Again, we have an interesting theory here, but no supporting evidence, either in the material record or in the texts. Because of the nature of Philo's writings, and his presumed audience, it is not clear whether he is describing religious institutions or voluntary associations and guilds when he discusses assemblies of Jews.

According to Eric Meyers (1996), the identification of early synagogues in the land of Israel was initially heavily influenced by nationalistic concerns.[116] Meyers, like Levine (and the vast majority of other scholars writing on the subject of early synagogues) identifies synagogues at Masada, Herodium, and Gamla, and dates them to the first century CE.[117] He lists general support for this in the writings of Philo, Josephus, and the New Testament, but also uses rabbinic literature to support his thesis that synagogues were common in first-century Palestine, citing *y. Meg.* 3:1, 738, which says there were 480 synagogues in Jerusalem during the reign of the emperor Vespasian (although he acknowledges that this number derives from a later homiletic and not a historical perspective).[118] According to Meyers's position, which is broadly similar to Levine's, there are distinct elements in synagogue buildings and their settlements; these are a focus on the importance of reading the law, an attachment to Jerusalem, and a commitment to make houses of assembly the locus of all sorts of activities.[119] Meyers says that the synagogue enabled Judaism to survive the destruction of the temple and that liturgy and communal functions increased, to the point where they

---

[114] Ronny Reich, "The Synagogue and the Miqweh in Eretz-Israel in the Second-Temple, Mishnaic, and Talmudic Periods," in *ASHAD*, 289.
[115] Richardson, "Early Synagogues as Collegia," 90–93.
[116] Eric M. Meyers and Steven Fine, "Ancient Synagogues: An Archaeological Introduction," in *Sacred Realm: The Emergence of the Synagogue in the Ancient World* (ed. Steven Fine; Oxford: Oxford University Press, 1996), 3–6.
[117] Meyers and Fine, "Ancient Synagogues," 8.
[118] Meyers and Fine, "Ancient Synagogues," 9.
[119] Meyers and Fine, "Ancient Synagogues," 18.

28   INVENTION OF THE FIRST-CENTURY SYNAGOGUE

then influenced the physical form the early synagogue took.[120] While he may use general sources as support for his thesis, there are no references to synagogues in any of these places, and the material record, as will be seen in the case studies, does not support his contention. This problem, while reproduced in a somewhat repetitive manner in this overview, is representative of the scholarship on the subject as a whole.

L. Feldman (1996) is sceptical about the use of epigraphical evidence relating to the identification of early synagogues. He notes correctly that these texts are not informative about the religious beliefs and practises of Jews and often do not specify dates. He also argues that there are problems with identifying which inscriptions are Jewish and which are Christian, and names, where they are not specifically Jewish, add to the ambiguity of the epigraphic evidence as a whole. According to Feldman, even where an inscription or papyrus refers to people who held honorary positions in synagogues, it does not necessarily follow that this relates to a Jewish community with a building called a synagogue. Feldman also notes that the overall picture taken from the epigraphy and papyri is skewed because more than a third of all inscriptions come from Rome, which had only a small percentage of the total Jewish population of the diaspora.[121]

S. Fine (1996) sees the development of synagogues as part of a trend in the Graeco-Jewish world, evidenced in the proliferation of voluntary associations and guilds. For Fine, the period after the destruction of the temple saw an explosion in the sorts of religious activities carried out in synagogues, and the most important of these was liturgical when, for the first time, prayer became an important part of synagogue life.[122] According to Fine, prayer modelled on temple liturgy played a major part in the sanctification of the synagogue from the late first to the early third century CE, and the focus of community assembly in a religious context enabled Judaism to survive the destruction of the central cult at Jerusalem.[123] Fine argues that the synagogue is one of the most influential religious institutions in Western civilisation, and that it allowed a much more democratised religious experience than had existed before, one which became a model for the early Christian church.[124] According to Fine, the "overwhelming impression" to be taken from the extant sources is that early synagogues were

---

[120] Meyers and Fine, "Ancient Synagogues," 18.

[121] Louis H. Feldman, "Diaspora Synagogues: New Light from Inscriptions and Papyri," in *Sacred Realm: The Emergence of the Synagogue in the Ancient World* (ed. Steven Fine; Oxford: Oxford University Press, 1996), 49–50.

[122] Steven Fine, "From Meeting House to Sacred Realm," in *Sacred Realm: The Emergence of the Synagogue in the Ancient World* (ed. Steven Fine; Oxford: Oxford University Press, 1996), 26–28.

[123] Fine, "From Meeting House," 47.

[124] Fine, "From Meeting House," 21.

places of communal scripture reading and instruction.[125] All of which is perfectly logical, except we do not know anything about synagogue liturgy in the first century, or its development, and we can only surmise that the extant liturgies possibly relate to synagogues. The paucity of information has resulted in Fine, like so many other scholars, constructing an argument about the development of the early synagogue on little more than supposition and the projection backwards of information from later periods, and from the heavily redacted body of work that is the rabbinic material.

R. A. Horsley (1996) does not try to pinpoint the origins of synagogues and argues only that early synagogues were not religious buildings, but rather intended for communal and public assemblies. While he does not rule out a religious aspect, he says that this did not define the function of the space.[126] He makes a good point here, because the internal configuration of space intended for public assembly for discussions and the configuration of space intended for religious functions may be quite different.

Rachel Hachlili (1997) emphasises the destruction of the Jerusalem temple as the key to the development of the synagogue as a religious institution in which liturgical activities developed.[127] The sacrificial cult of the Jerusalem temple, conducted by an elite group of priests, was replaced by an egalitarian assembly, organised communally, which put the study of the Torah and prayer at its centre.[128] According to Hachlili, the synagogue, as a purpose-built structure, with Torah shrines, only began to appear in the land of Israel at a much later date, and construction of new synagogues and renovations of old ones continued into the seventh and eighth centuries CE.[129] It certainly seems clear from the literature that the study of Judaism was central to the developing institution and although we might suppose prayer played a role in this, we do not have any sources or material to confirm this.

D. Binder (1999), argues for the beginnings of the synagogue in the city gate, and traces the development via the Jerusalem temple to a form which was heavily influenced by Hellenistic architecture. He has concluded that early synagogues were extensions of the Jerusalem temple cult, and functioned as satellite temples,

---

[125] Fine, "From Meeting House," 22–23.

[126] Runesson, *Origins of the Synagogue*, 153, citing Richard A. Horsley, *Archaeology, History, and Society in Galilee: The Social Context of Jesus and the Rabbis* (Valley Forge, PA: Trinity Press Intl, 1996), 155–56.

[127] Runesson, *Origins of the Synagogue*, 153, citing Rachel Hachlili, "The Origin of the Synagogue: A Reassessment," *JSJ* 28.1 (1997): 46.

[128] Rachel Hachlili, "Aspects of Similarity and Diversity in the Architecture and Art of Ancient Synagogues and Churches in the Land of Israel," *ZDPV* 113 (1997): 92.

[129] Hachlili, "Aspects of Similarity and Diversity," 93.

of sorts.[130] Binder's work can be troublesome as it leans heavily on presumptions and suppositions about the nature of the early synagogue, and he ties some of these presumptions to the physical structures identified as first-century synagogues at Delos, Herodian Jericho, Masada, Herodium, and Gamla. His specific claims in relation to these sites are discussed in the case studies in this book to illustrate how unproven claims have become part of the accepted scholarship on the subject.

E. P. Sanders (1999) takes the view that the origin of the synagogue lies in the diaspora, and that it was natural for immigrant groups to join together in clubs or associations and societies, which were popular throughout the Graeco-Roman world.[131]

H. C. Kee, writing in 1999, advocates a late date for the development of synagogues. He argues for the development of the synagogue from voluntary gatherings through to institutionalised structures and concludes that this took place from the second century CE onwards. Before this time, he argues, the term *synagogue* referred only to informal gatherings in private houses and public buildings, and not to purpose-built structures.[132]

L. I. Levine's seminal work, *The Ancient Synagogue* (2000), which spans a thousand years of synagogue history, has effectively become *the* textbook for synagogue studies because of the breadth of information it covers. Levine defines the early synagogue as a location for regular prayer, study of Mosaic law, sacred meals, a communal treasury, law courts, general assembly, a hostel, and a residence for synagogue officials. According to Levine, both the first-century CE synagogue and the *proseuchē* were communal institutions where a variety of activities took place; thus, it may have been used as a courtroom, school, or hostel, or for political meetings, social gatherings, keeping treasury funds, slave manumissions, meals (sacred or otherwise), and religious-liturgical functions.[133] There is evidence for all of this, except for the last claim which we must, for the purposes of his monograph, assume to be a ubiquitous part of the institution of synagogue (or *proseuchē*). Levine argues that the synagogue (as a formal institution) was well-established by the early Roman period, and the basis on which he enunciates this position (and constructs his list of synagogal functions)

---

[130] Donald D. Binder, *Into the Temple Courts: The Place of the Synagogues in the Second Temple Period* (SBLDS 169; Atlanta: Society of Biblical Literature, 1999), 218–20.

[131] E. P. Sanders, "Common Judaism and the Synagogue in the First Century," in *Jews, Christians, and Polytheists in the Ancient Synagogue: Cultural Interaction during the Greco-Roman Period* (ed. Steven Fine; London: Routledge, 1999), 1.

[132] Runesson, *Origins of the Synagogue*, 149–50; Howard Clark Kee, "Defining the First-Century CE Synagogue: Problems and Progress," in *Evolution of the Synagogue: Problems and Progress* (ed. Howard Clark Kee and Lynn H. Cohick; Harrisburg, PA: Trinity Press Intl, 1999), 7–26.

[133] Levine, *Ancient Synagogue*, 27.

is primarily the Theodotos inscription, although he also refers to Acts, Philo, and Josephus.[134] The thrust of Levine's argument is that the origins of the synagogue lay in its role as a community centre, and that it did not develop as a religious institution until the destruction of the Jerusalem temple, although it had had religious elements present from its beginnings.[135] Levine says that even if the synagogue was a post-70 CE institution, its origins lay earlier and its role only changed in the period after the destruction of the Jerusalem temple.[136] Like Hengel, Kasher, Kraabel, and Grabbe, Levine uses terms to discuss the identification of first-century synagogue that are so broad as to be virtually useless in relation to the search for specific, early (first-century CE) sites. Levine says that, of the hundred or so synagogue sites excavated in the land of Israel, only four can be dated to the pre-70 CE period. These four are Masada, Gamla, Herodium, and the synagogue referred to in the Theodotos inscription,[137] and he asks why, if the synagogue was already a central communal institution by that period, there should be so few remains. He concludes that the topography of Israel contributes greatly to this, and we see this phenomenon even in the cities that flourished during the period with which we are concerned (such as Caesarea, Tiberias, Sepphoris, and Jericho).[138] It is true that topography contributes to the scarcity of remains, but it is notable that none of the literature relates to any of these supposed synagogues and, as we have already seen, the archaeological context of the Theodotos inscription has been lost, rendering it impossible to date accurately. Even Josephus, discussing events on Masada at the end of the rebellion against Rome, and at pains to give details of all aspects of life there, does not once mention the existence of a synagogue. In the case study on Masada in this book, it will be clear why this is so, and the extent to which a mythology has developed around the existence of a synagogue there.

A. Runesson, writing in 2001, says there is no consensus as to the earliest history of the synagogue, and that if, for instance, Jesus or the Apostles taught or spoke in any place they thought fit, this place need not have been in a synagogue building.[139] Runesson says that even though there are no specific sources to

---

[134] Lee I. Levine, "Ancient Synagogues: A Historical Introduction," in *Ancient Synagogues Revealed* (ed. Lee I. Levine; Jerusalem: Israel Exploration Society, 1982), 33–34.
[135] Levine, *Ancient Synagogue*, 3.
[136] Lee I. Levine, "The Nature and Origin of the Palestinian Synagogue Reconsidered," *JBL* 115.3 (1996): 443–48.
[137] Lee I. Levine, "The Revolutionary Effects of Archaeology on the Study of Jewish History: The Case of the Ancient Synagogue," in *The Archaeology of Israel: Constructing the Past, Interpreting the Present* (JSOTSup 237; ed. Neil Asher Silberman and David B. Small; Sheffield: Sheffield Academic Press, 1997), 171. Masada, Herodium, and Gamla are discussed in the detailed case studies in this monograph.
[138] Levine, "Revolutionary Effects," 171.
[139] Runesson, *Origins of the Synagogue*, 478.

support this claim, it is likely that "charismatics, prophets, and scholars" used public spaces in Jerusalem to teach at times other than those dedicated to communal Torah reading on the Sabbath.[140] Runesson sees the vector of synagogue development as deriving from Torah-reading rituals in public assemblies as early as the reign of Artaxerxes I in the fifth century BCE. Thus, the institutional aspects of the early synagogue were established before the liturgy, and they functioned in an official capacity from the start. He says that, through the Hellenistic period, changing national authorities did not impose any direct control over the teaching of the law, and so the emphasis changed from national to local, while still retaining an official nature.[141] At some stage in the late Hellenistic period, the first signs of non-official institutions dedicated to communal reading and study began to emerge, and these were most likely influenced by voluntary associations and guilds as seen in the broader Graeco-Roman world.[142] In the diaspora, evidence of Jewish institutions was limited to temple cults around which the Jewish community organised, and that by around the second century BCE the evolution from sacrificial cult to one of public Torah-reading had been incorporated into the institution. He argues that the *proseuchai* of the Egyptian inscriptions were probably temples, as is supported by Philo's account that offerings were part of the ritual activities of the first century CE.[143] This meant that by the first century CE, various Jewish groups had developed their own agendas, separate from the cult dictated from Jerusalem, and this led to public assemblies where anyone could put forward their views, and no one group controlled synagogues in general.[144] Runesson says that, although the destruction of the Jerusalem temple in 70 CE is often seen as a pivotal point in the development of the synagogue, it actually mattered little because the institution had begun to evolve from as early as the Hellenistic period, so that by the time the temple was destroyed, the synagogue already had an established organisational pattern.[145] According to Runesson, the aspect that points to a continuity between the origins and the developing synagogue was the reading and teaching of the Torah.

Runesson's thesis is reasonable, and he is generally careful not to link too much of his theoretical construct to the material record, which is helpful. Moreover, he makes what is a very important claim, that while the early rabbinic material on Torah reading provides a link between the multifaceted origins of the synagogue and the later mainstream institution, *the origin of the rabbinic*

---

[140] Runesson, *Origins of the Synagogue*, 218.
[141] Runesson, *Origins of the Synagogue*, 479.
[142] Runesson, *Origins of the Synagogue*, 480.
[143] Runesson, *Origins of the Synagogue*, 481.
[144] Runesson, *Origins of the Synagogue*, 482–84.
[145] Runesson, *Origins of the Synagogue*, 485–86.

synagogue is not the same as the origins of the early synagogue.[146] This is a particularly useful point, and it may go some way towards explaining the gap between the somewhat nebulous *proseuchē* or *synagogē* of the earlier period and the proliferation of rabbinic synagogues in the late Roman/Byzantine period.

C. Claussen (2003) says that despite the fact that it is now twenty years after Kraabel wrote his essay on "The Diaspora Synagogue: Archaeological and Epigraphic Evidence since Sukenik," we are still dealing with the same archaeological evidence, and the findings from Sardis, Priene, Dura Europos, Delos,[147] and that Ostia and Stobi are still the only reliable architectural remains of synagogues in the diaspora.[148] P. Richardson (2003) also points to the diaspora for the origins of the synagogue, but suggests that this is merely a hypothesis, and other theories are possible, but these rely on arguments from silence or complex processes for which there is no evidence.[149]

I. Nielsen (2005) notes that the period before the destruction of the temple in Jerusalem is the least known in the synagogue's history, but that there are some preserved synagogues and written sources, such as the Theodotos inscription, although the dating of that inscription is disputed.[150] Nielsen points out that the absence of any reference to prayer is a glaring omission from the Theodotos inscription.[151] In Acts 6:9, there is a reference to a "synagogue of the freedmen" in Jerusalem,[152] but the term *synagogē* is more frequently applied to Galilee and northern Palestine, where Jesus frequently preached.[153] Nielsen notes that seven buildings have been identified as synagogues in Palestine in the pre-70 period. These are at Gamla, Magdala, Capernaum, and Chorazin (in Galilee) and Jericho, Masada, and Herodium (in Judaea). The view of some scholars, mostly non-archaeologists, according to Nielsen, is that none of these sites should be regarded as *proper* [my emphasis] synagogues, but only as public buildings for assembly,

---

[146] Runesson, *Origins of the Synagogue*, 192–93.
[147] In the Delos case study herein this identification is vigorously disputed.
[148] Carsten Claussen, "Meeting, Community, Synagogue—Different Frameworks of Ancient Jewish Congregations in the Diaspora," in *The Ancient Synagogue from its Origins until 200 CE* (ConBNT 39; ed. Birger Olsson and Magnus Zetterholm; Stockholm: Almqvist & Wiskell Intl, 2003), 157.
[149] Peter Richardson, "An Architectural Case for Synagogues as Associations," in *The Ancient Synagogue from Its Origins until 200 CE* (ConBNT 39; ed. Birger Olsson and Magnus Zetterholm; Stockholm: Almqvist & Wiskell Intl, 2003), 113.
[150] Inge Nielsen, "Issues of Current Interest: Synagogue (*synagoge*) and Prayerhouse (*proseuche*): The Relationship between Jewish Religious Architecture in Palestine and the Diaspora," *Hephaistos* 13 (2005): 74.
[151] Nielsen, "Issues of Current Interest," 74.
[152] τῆς συναγωγῆς τῆς λεγομένης Λιβερτίνων.
[153] See n. 38 above.

whereas she claims that most scholars accept all or most of these identifications.[154] Nielsen opines that, if a building for assembly is found in Jewish surroundings, whether in a city-quarter, a palace area, or a fortress, it is likely to be a synagogue, since this was the form the Jewish communal building took. When the Jerusalem temple was destroyed, holiness was gradually transferred to the synagogue, a process traceable both in the written and the archaeological sources.[155] This is not supported in any way, either in the literary evidence or material record. Nielsen does not address the problems with the dating of the buildings at Capernaum and Chorazin, neither of which provides evidence for a pre-70 public building, let alone for a synagogue.

CONCLUSIONS

The above are the main positions of scholarship on the subject of early synagogues to date, and the nagging problem that is the problem of the gap between theoretical modern constructions, the ancient literature, and the archaeological evidence cannot be resolved. This is not the only problem: while purporting to write about the identification of early synagogues, many scholars survey what has already been written in general terms and apply it to specific sites, a practice that is potentially (and in some cases actually) damaging to the process of identification, as will be clear in the five case studies.

The field of synagogue studies continues to grow apace, with material from archaeological excavations, secondary studies, and from increasingly refined methodological approaches. The earlier and simplistic model of chronologically linked and overlapping types promoted by Goodenough, Avi-Yonah, and others in the early years has been overtaken by the intricate and multifaceted approaches of modern scholarship, which take a more technical and scientific approach to the archaeology, as well as an increasingly critical approach to the ancient sources, including the Hebrew Bible, the New Testament, the works of Josephus and Philo, and the Rabbinic literature.[156]

Unfortunately, while these new methods are being used to make new identifications, they are not being used to analyse those identifications already made (such as Delos, Jericho, Herodium, Masada, and Gamla, the five case studies herein). Thus we have a situation where the early identifications are still being used to shore up subsequent identifications, thereby weaving old errors and presumptions into the new work being done. As against the increasingly numerous claims of early foundations, only three sources (Josephus, Philo, and the New Testament) refer to pre-70 CE synagogues and/or *proseuchai*, and the terminology

---

[154] Nielsen, "Issues of Current Interest," 74.
[155] Nielsen, "Issues of Current Interest," 74.
[156] Levine, *Ancient Synagogue*, 13.

is not used in the same way throughout the sources, as we have seen. Moreover, in the Hebrew Bible and deuterocanonical literature (including First and Second Maccabees, Tobit, and Ben Sira), throughout all known extra-biblical pseudepigrapha, in texts such as the Hellenistic *Letter of Aristeas*, in all of the apocalyptic literature and in the Qumran texts, there remains a deafening and lengthy silence on the subject of the synagogue.[157]

No physical site has yet been matched to any of the epigraphical or literary or other evidential material for pre-70 CE synagogues in the land of Israel. And, almost without exception, assumptions about early synagogues are made based on the identifications of Delos, Jericho, Herodium, Masada, and Gamla, and commonalities between their architecture and synagogues from later periods. Moreover, the model of the synagogue as a multi-purpose public building, whether in the Graeco-Roman diaspora or the land of Israel, is unhelpful and allows for a plethora of public buildings to be identified as synagogues without any requirement for supporting evidence.

While theory and speculation is useful in the discussion of what a first-century synagogue might have been and how it might have functioned, too much has been made too often of too little archaeological and other evidence, resulting in the development of complex accounts and descriptions of the function and layout of specific first-century and earlier synagogues without unambiguous evidential support. The problem with the definition of what the early synagogue might have been is bound up in the fact that many of the arguments are circular. Thus, because the structures at Masada, Herodium, Gamla, and Delos are assumed to be synagogues—that is what we should be looking for in an early synagogue. This naturally creates problems and inconsistencies. This argument will be clearly borne out by the evidence presented in the case studies that follow.

---

[157] Flesher, "Palestinian Synagogues," 30–31; Grabbe, "Synagogues," 20.

2
DELOS

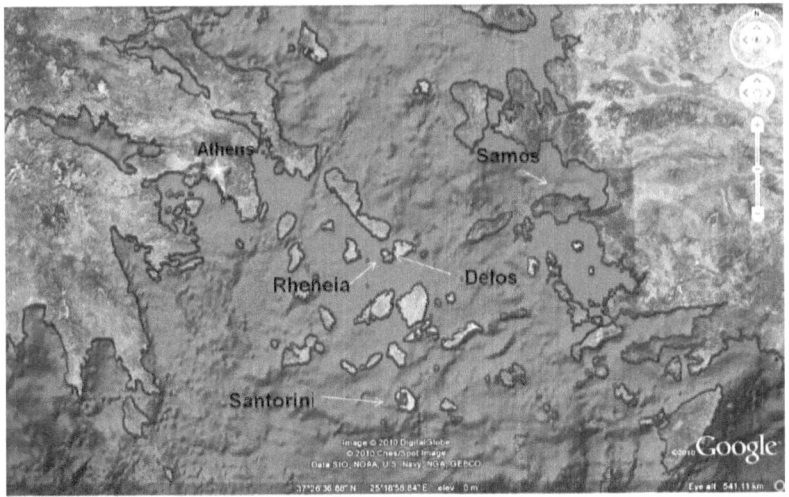

Figure 1 – The Cycladic Islands
Author's own, using Google Earth. © 2010 DigitalGlobe and CNES

INTRODUCTION

The identification of a synagogue on Delos has been problematic ever since it was first made in 1913, because, while there is some evidence relating to Jews and/or Samaritans on Delos, not one single piece of it refers to a synagogue or association house. When we come to look at the material relating to how a building on this tiny Greek island came to be identified as a synagogue, we find a surprisingly large gap between what was originally proposed—and widely accepted—and what has been found. To this day, scholarship continues to build upon the original and quite erroneous identification. The building with which we are here concerned, GD 80, lies on the north-eastern shoreline of the Greek island of Delos, in the Bay of Gournia, outside the town walls. It stands in the area just east of the stadium and northeast of the gymnasium (fig. 2 below).

38 INVENTION OF THE FIRST-CENTURY SYNAGOGUE

Figure 2 – Delos in context

It is important to note that there is nothing in the structure of GD 80 that is specifically Jewish in nature, although I am always mindful of Levine's comment that Jews and Jewish architecture have always been influenced by local material culture.[158]

HISTORY OF DELOS

Delos is a small island in the Cyclades, measuring just 5 km north to south and 1.3 km east to west (see figs. 1 and 2 above). The mythological birthplace of the gods Apollo and Artemis, it was a major cultic centre, and it is mentioned in Homer's *Odyssey* (6.160–169) and in Homeric Hymn 3 to Apollo.[159]

Delos arrived at its prominent political and economic status almost by default. According to Thucydides (*Peloponnesian Wars* 1.96.2; 6.76.3), the Persian Emperor Xerxes had razed the Athenian sanctuaries during raids into mainland Greece. In 478 BCE, the Greek city-states responded by forming a defensive alliance funded by its member states. To avoid the danger of any one of the city-states becoming too powerful, the Athenian-controlled island of Delos was chosen

---

[158] Levine, "Ancient Synagogues," 6; Lee I. Levine, *Judaism and Hellenism in Antiquity: Conflict or Confluence?* (Seattle: University of Washington Press, 1998), 23; Levine, *The Ancient Synagogue*, 581.

[159] Michael Crudden, *The Homeric Hymns* (Oxford: Oxford University Press, 2001), 23–42.

to hold the treasury of what came to be known as the Delian League. Delos became a hub of commercial, military, maritime trading, and slaving activity (the main slave markets were at Rhodes, Delos, and Crete) whilst continuing to be a major cultic centre.[160] Delos became independent from Athens in 314 BCE, and, when the Delian League was finally dissolved in the mid-third century BCE, its independence continued, along with its economic boom.[161]

Later, after Delos came under Roman rule, Athens lobbied the Roman Senate for the return of some of its erstwhile territories. In 166 BCE, the Roman Senate returned Delos to Athenian control, and it was made a cleruchy of Athens.[162] To accommodate this, Delian citizens were exiled and their land turned over to the colonists. Even so, people still flocked to Delos from all over the Aegean, many establishing businesses, cults, and associations on the island.[163]

The downside of being a thriving and strategically placed cultic, trade, and slaving centre was that Delos was often caught between warring factions vying for control of the Aegean. During the first Mithridatic war (88–84 BCE), Delos was raided by Menophaneses, one of Mithridates Eupator's generals. According to Pausanias (*Descr.* 3.23.2) and Appian (*Mithridateios* 28), some 20,000 of the island's inhabitants were slaughtered during that incursion. There was a further major destruction during the second Mithridatic war (83–81 BCE), and another (led by the pirate Athenodoros) during the third Mithridatic war (74–63 BCE).[164] The problem of piracy in the Aegean was so widespread that Cicero complained to the Roman Senate in 66 BCE, saying that the friends, allies, and subjects of Rome had been at the mercy of pirates until Pompey finally drove them away. In 69 BCE, Gaius Triarius, Legate to the Roman Consul Lucullus, repaired some of the damage and built a defensive wall round the town centre of Delos.[165]

By the mid-first century BCE, the rise of other trading centres (such as Puteoli and Ostia in Italy), as well as the constant raids and destructions, had taken their toll, and trade routes altered to accommodate these changes, pushing Delos further outside the commercial loop. Eventually it was in such decline that Athens did not even bother sending its official representatives to the island, and the priest of Apollo on Delos left to live in Athens, only returning for the traditional annual ceremonial sacrifice of twelve animals.[166]

---

[160] Philip de Souza, *Piracy in the Graeco-Roman World* (Cambridge: Cambridge University Press, 1999), 61.
[161] de Souza, *Piracy*, 61.
[162] A colony of military veterans, given land as a settlement.
[163] B. Hudson McLean, "The Place of Cult in Voluntary Associations and Christian Churches on Delos," in *Voluntary Associations in the Graeco-Roman World* (ed. John S. Kloppenborg and Stephen G. Wilson; London: Routledge, 1996), 189.
[164] de Souza, *Piracy*, 162–63; McLean, "Place of Cult," 188.
[165] de Souza, *Piracy*, 162–63.
[166] McLean, "Place of Cult," 189.

40   INVENTION OF THE FIRST-CENTURY SYNAGOGUE

The decline continued apace and, in the second century CE, the philhellenic Emperor Hadrian's attempt to revive the old Delian festivals was unsuccessful. By then, according to Pausanias (*Descr.* 8.33.2), the island was already very sparsely inhabited.[167] The agricultural land in the southern part of Delos continued to be cultivated until the last person left, probably during the fifth century CE.[168]

HISTORY OF THE EXCAVATIONS

The École française d'Athènes commenced excavations on Delos in 1873. Between 1904 and 1914, much of the island was excavated. There were further extensive excavations between 1958 and 1975. The École française d'Athènes continues to run excavations on the island in conjunction with the Cycladic Ephoreia (the governing body for archaeological excavations, museums, and conservation in the Cycladic Islands), and it maintains a permanent presence there.[169] All structures on the island will be referred to according to their designations in Bruneau and Ducat's seminal guide to the excavations on Delos, the *Guide de Délos*, and I will refer to all inscriptions found on the island according to their designations in the collections of inscriptions from Delos, the *Inscriptions de Délos* (ID). Using this format, the building known as the synagogue is GD 80 (see fig. 3 below).

IDENTIFICATION OF THE SYNAGOGUE (GD 80)

It was André Plassart of the École française d'Athènes who, during the excavations of 1912 and 1913, identified GD 80 as a synagogue. His identification relied on six inscriptions. Rather astonishingly, the principal inscription, around which the entire identification was made, was found not in GD 80, but rather some 90 m north of it, in a complex of residential buildings on the east side of the stadium district, and was not associated with GD 80 until sometime later. This inscription, ID 2329, contained the donor names *Agathoklēs* and *Lysimachos* and

---

[167] McLean, "Place of Cult," 189.

[168] In conversation with Michelè Brunet in October 2003, discussing the extent of agriculture on Delos until its abandonment. See Michelè Brunet, "Contribution à l'histoire rurale de Délos aux époques classique et hellénistique," *BCH* 114.2 (1990): 669–82, which looks at aspects of the countryside of Delos and its historic cultivation.

[169] The École française d'Athènes maintain a number of houses on the island for the purpose of accommodating their archaeologists during the digging seasons, and I am most grateful to their Director of Studies, Michèle Brunet for arranging to open one of their dig houses for me, and to Panayotis Chatzidakis of the 21st Ephoreia of Prehistoric and Classic Antiquities, for giving me permission to stay overnight on the island in October of 2003.

the word *proseuchē* which, Plassart said, referred to a Jewish "house of prayer" or "synagogue."[170]

Plassart's other five inscriptions were found scattered around GD 80, and among those was one which contained one of the donor names found in ID 2329 above. Three of the inscriptions contained the epithet *Theo Hypsisto* ("god most high"), and one contained the epithet *Hypsisto* ("most high"). Plassart's final inscription retained only two legible words, *genomenos eleutheros* ("became free").[171]

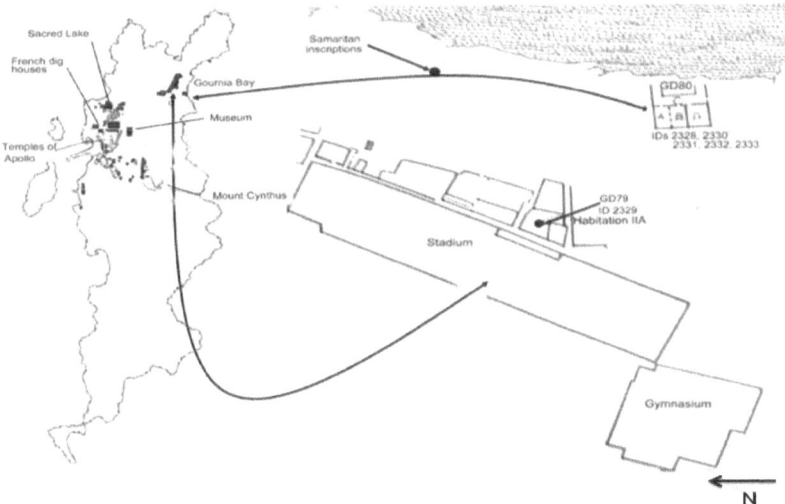

Figure 3 – GD 80 ("the synagogue") in context

In an article written in 1913, André Plassart laid out his argument that the use of the epithets *Hypsisto* ("most high") or *Theo Hypsisto* ("god most high") indicated a religious tendency towards monotheism, and therefore referred to the Jewish deity. However, in the same article, he noted that an inscription had recently been found in Lydia, bearing the epithet *Thea Hypsista*, probably referring to the great mother goddess of Asia Minor, and that other similar inscriptions had been found in relation to the Thracian-Phrygian deity Dionysos-Sabazios and to the Syrian Zeus of Heliopolis.[172]

---

[170] André Plassart, "La Synagogue juive de Délos," in *Mélanges Holleaux, recueil de mémoires concernant l'antiquité grecque* (Paris: Picard, 1913): 201–15; André Plassart, "La synagogue juive de Délos," *RB* 23 (1914): 523–34.
[171] Plassart, "La synagogue juive," *RB*, 528.
[172] Plassart, "La synagogue juive," *RB*, 529.

Thus, despite being aware of the non-Jewish uses of the term *Theos Hypsistos* and its application to different divinities, male and female, and, despite the fact that the inscription on which he was basing his argument was not found in GD 80 (see fig. 4 below), he proceeded to use it as proof that GD 80 was a synagogue. According to his argument, since the word *proseuchē* signified a later Jewish use and context, he associated the *proseuchē* and *Lysimachos* inscriptions with one another. Combining the use of *Theos Hypsistos* and *Hypsistos* in the other inscriptions, and looking at the configuration of the furnishings of the building (arguing that it was similar to later synagogues), Plassart declared GD 80 to be a synagogue.[173]

However, as we shall see, the word *proseuchē* in the context in which André Plassart found it refers to the fulfilment of a prayer or votive offering, not to a building and, indeed, possibly not to a Jewish context at all. Moreover, the occurrences of the names *Lysimachos* and *Agathoklēs* are entirely coincidental, and the arguments relating to the form, style, furnishings, and artefacts found in GD 80 are irrelevant to its identification as a synagogue. In short, there are no compelling reasons to consider GD 80 a synagogue.

The Ancient Sources

There is very little literary evidence relating to Jews on Delos, and, while what does exist is useful in establishing the presence of Jews in the region, it does not allude to the existence of a synagogue, nor indeed to any specifically Jewish physical structure on Delos. The earliest reference to Jews on Delos is found in the first book of Maccabees and incorporates a letter from Lucius, a Roman consul:

> Then Numenius and his companions arrived from Rome, with letters to the kings and countries, in which the following was written: "Lucius, consul of the Romans, to King Ptolemy, greetings. The envoys of the Jews have come to us as our friends and allies to renew our ancient friendship and alliance. They had been sent by the high priest Simon and by the Jewish people and have brought a gold shield weighing one thousand minas. We therefore have decided to write to the kings and countries that they should not seek their harm or make war against them and their cities and their country, or make alliance with those who war against them. And it has seemed good to us to accept the shield from them. Therefore if any scoundrels have fled to you from their country, hand them over to the high priest Simon, so that he may punish them according to their law." The consul wrote the same thing to King Demetrius and to Attalus and Ariarathes and Arsaces, and to all the countries, and to Sampsames, and to the Spartans, and to Delos, and to Myndos, and to Sicyon, and to Caria, and to Samos, and to

---

[173] Plassart, "La synagogue juive," *RB*, 528–29.

Pamphylia, and to Lycia, and to Halicarnassus, and to Rhodes, and to Phaselis, and to Cos, and to Side, and to Aradus and Gortyna and Cnidus and Cyprus and Cyrene. They also sent a copy of these things to the high priest Simon. (1 Macc 15:15–23)

In this passage, the Jews, through the High Priest Simon, have made an offering to the Romans of a valuable shield in return for which the Romans have renewed an old alliance and offered their protection. There is an ongoing debate concerning the chronology of this text, but it is not relevant here.[174] While this text is useful in that it suggests that the Delians may have had some interaction with Jews, it may be that because we have already assumed that there are Jews on the island, we see the text as confirming their presence there. This has the potential of becoming an entirely circular argument. What the text *actually* says is that the Romans have renewed their friendship with the Jews, via a delegation sent to Rome by the high priest Simon, as a consequence of which Rome asked its allies to hand over to the Jewish authorities those who harassed the Jews and "scoundrels" who, having made war against the Jews, fled to the locations listed in the letter. Notably, there is no mention of *Jews on Delos* nor of any Jewish buildings, houses, or associations.

The second text is Josephus's account of the same event. There are variables in this version in that Josephus identifies the Lucius mentioned in the 1 Macc passage as the praetor Lucius Valerius, and the island of Delos is not mentioned at all. The chronological context of this passage is also disputed.[175]

Lucius Valerius, son of Lucius the praetor, consulted with the senate on the Ides of December in the Temple of Concord. And at the writing of the decree there were present Lucius Coponius, son of Lucius, of the Colline tribe, and Papirius of the Quirine tribe. Whereas Alexander, son of Jason, Numenius, son of Antiochus, and Alexander, son of Dorotheus, envoys of the Jews and worthy men and allies, have discussed the matter of renewing the relation of goodwill and friendship which they formerly maintained with the Romans, and have brought as a token of the alliance a golden shield worth fifty thousand gold pieces, and have asked that letters be given them to the autonomous cities and kings in order that their country and ports may be secure and suffer no harm, it has been decreed to form a relation of goodwill and friendship with them and to provide them with all the things which they have requested, and to accept the shield which they have brought. (Josephus, *A.J.* 14.145–148)[176]

---

[174] For the essentials of the debate on the chronology, see Jonathan A. Goldstein, *1 Maccabees* (AB; New York: Doubleday, 1976) and John R. Bartlett, *1 Maccabees* (Sheffield: Sheffield Academic Press, 1998).
[175] Bartlett, *1 Maccabees*, 93–94.
[176] Trans. Ralph Marcus (LCL 1943).

While the text is very similar to the text of the Maccabees passage, there is no reference whatsoever to Delos or, again, to the presence of Jews on Delos. Again, past and modern scholarship has assumed that this text refers to Jews on Delos because we presuppose that, because of its similarity to the passage at 1 Macc 15, it must be so. Again, the text actually only notes the renewal of Roman-Jewish friendship and the request made by a Jewish delegation that Jews not be harassed in the autonomous ports and cities of the Mediterranean.

The third text is the most interesting and most substantial. Again, it comes to us via Josephus, in the form of a letter dealing specifically with the Jews of Delos. This text is thought to date to about the middle of the first century BCE.

> Julius Gaius, Praetor, Consul of the Romans, to the magistrates, council and people of Parium, greeting. The Jews in Delos and some of the neighbouring Jews, some of your envoys also being present, have appealed to me and declared that you are preventing them by statute from observing their national customs and sacred rites. Now it displeases me that such statutes should be made against our friends and allies and that they should be forbidden to live in accordance with their customs and to contribute money to common meals and sacred rites, for this they are not forbidden to do even in Rome. For example, Gaius Caesar, our consular praetor, by edict forbade religious societies to assemble in the city, but these people alone he did not forbid to do so or to collect contributions or to hold common meals. Similarly do I forbid other religious societies but permit these people alone to assemble and feast in accordance with their native customs and ordinances. And if you have made any statutes against our friends and allies, you will do well to revoke them because of their worthy deeds on our behalf and their goodwill towards us. (Josephus, *A.J.* 14.213–216)[177]

According to this text, at some point in the middle of the first century BCE, the Jews of Delos (and other Jews) were being prevented by the magistrates, council, and people of Parium *from observing their national customs and sacred rites*. They were not being allowed to meet for religious purposes, to collect religious tithes, to pay for common meals, or to assemble, even though assembly by religious societies in Rome had been forbidden *except for the Jews* who were not forbidden ... *to do so or to collect contributions or to hold common meals*. The letter asked that the religious prohibitions against the Jews of Delos (and other neighbouring Jews) be revoked.

We can hypothesise, based on this letter, that the Jews on Delos (and some of the neighbouring Jews) were for some time not permitted the same privileges as Jews in Rome. Thus, at the time of this letter, the Jews at Rome could assemble, collect contributions, and hold common meals, but the Jews on Delos (and some of the neighbouring Jews) could not. Apart from any other interpretation of the

---

[177] Trans. Ralph Marcus (LCL 1943).

text, it does not suggest that the Jews on Delos were in a position to have had a physically identifiable synagogue or other communal building to use for their traditional practices, given that those practices were forbidden by the magistrates, council, and people of Parium. It is evident that for at least some unknown time there was a statute of some sort in place forbidding Jews to live in accordance with their native customs, to assemble, and to contribute money to communal meals and sacred rites, and it is apposite to note that the prohibition against Jewish practices mentioned in it relates to precisely the period when GD 80 is said to have functioned as a synagogue, that is from the middle of the first century BCE.

Despite these problems and despite the lack of corroborating evidence, Plassart used the foregoing passage as support for his identification of GD 80 as a synagogue. He said that the text "undertook to repeal the decree" by which the Jews had been forbidden from observing their ancient customs and, in particular, from organising communal meals that would have taken place "in the vast premises of the synagogue."[178] While it is possible that the appeal by Josephus presupposed that the Jews on Delos had had the facilities to practise common worship, which practise had been prohibited by decree, there is no evidence to suggest that GD 80 functioned as such a facility.

There is not one shred of evidence connecting GD 80 with a reading of the letter about the Delian Jews in Josephus other than Plassart's original assumption (based on his association of the inscriptions mentioned above and discussed in more detail below) that it was a synagogue.

The foregoing passage in Josephus does not allude to a synagogue or house being used as a synagogue, and then being prevented from being used as a synagogue. Indeed, it only says that Jews on Delos (and other neighbouring Jews) were being prevented from following their traditional practices and that the Romans thought it desirable that this should change, in line with Roman administrative leniency relative to Jews.

At best, therefore, we have one direct reference to Jews on Delos (and other neighbouring Jews; either on the island or elsewhere in the region either in the Cyclades or the Dodecanese, or even Aegina, Crete, Rhodes or Cyprus; and not necessarily on Delos at all), in the first century BCE, suggesting that they were, for some unknown period of time, prevented from following their traditional practices.

As this text provides the only clear reference we have to the presence of Jews on the island of Delos, it must be examined in that context. So, what we do have is what appears to be a reliable and plausible reference to the presence of Jews on the island of Delos, albeit one that is wholly dependent on Josephus. What we do not have is a reference to a synagogue or association house or community building of the Jews on Delos.

---

[178] Plassart, "La synagogue juive," *RB*, 529.

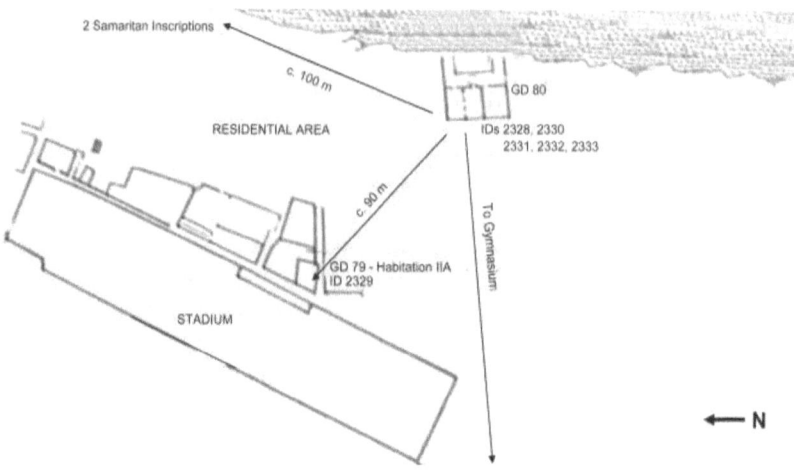

Figure 4 – GD 80 (its environs and where the inscriptions were found)

THE PLASSART INSCRIPTIONS

As stated above, Plassart's evidence for the identification of GD 80 as a synagogue consisted of six inscriptions. The principal inscription was found in house IIA of GD 79 in the densely packed residential area, some 90 m northwest of GD 80 (see figure 4 above).

Inscription 1 (ID 2329)

Αγαθοκλης και Λυσιμαχος επι προσευχη[179]

("Agathoklēs and Lysimachos for an offering/prayer")[180]

This inscription is the one on which Plassart based his identification of GD 80 as a synagogue. It is notable that ID 2329 was, however, found in the cistern of house IIA of GD 79 beside the stadium, about 90 m northwest of GD 80 (see figure 4 below). This inscription has been dated to around the first century BCE and is carved on a plain rectangular marble stele with a cut on the top side

---

[179] Pierre Roussel and Marcel Launey, *Inscriptions de Délos: Décrets Postérieurs à 166 av. J.–C. (Nos. 1497–1524). Dédicaces Postérieures à 166 av. J.-C. (Nos. 1525–2219)* (Librairie Ancienne; Paris: Honoré Champion, 1937a): 295; Plassart, "La Synagogue juive de Délos," in *Mélanges*, 205.

[180] My translation.

containing the remnants of a lead fixing, indicating it held a statue or some other votive offering.

Figure 4a – ID 2329 (front and top views)[181]
Image reproduced from Waldemar Déonna, *Le Mobilier délien, Délos* (Paris: De Boccard, 1938). Used by permission.

The presence of the lead fixing for a votive offering is some support for the argument that this inscription may not be a Jewish one. It is also support for the argument that if ID 2329 was indeed a Jewish inscription, then whatever was affixed to the top of the stele was what was being offered.[182] Moreover, as there is no definite article used in the wording of the inscription, it is plausible that the words επι προσευχη (in this context) may not refer to a building at all and should be translated as reading "for an offering" or simply as a "prayer" (in the sense that a prayer to a deity is always an offering) and not "for the synagogue" (as Plassart translated it in his 1913 article) and as others have continued to do.[183] It is, of course, possible that the inscription does indeed refer to a physical structure and

---

[181] Waldemar Déonna, *Le Mobilier délien, Délos* (Paris: De Boccard, 1938), (pages unnumbered).
[182] Possibly a model of a decorative vase or urn of a standard type.
[183] Plassart, "La Synagogue juive de Délos," in *Mélanges*, 205.

that the standards of Greek used in literary writing simply cannot or should not be applied to the inscribing of dedicatory inscriptions.

ID 2329 contained the names *Agathoklēs* and *Lysimachos*, and the word *proseuchē*, which, Plassart said, referred to a Jewish "house of prayer" or "synagogue" (and following Plassart most scholars have agreed with this interpretation).[184] On the basis of his presumption that ID 2329 indicated the existence of a synagogue, Plassart identified the two names listed on it as Jewish.[185] However, in addition to the presence of those two names on ID 2329, there are other contemporary instances of the name *Agathoklēs* from Delos, including one from the Agora of the Competalists (ID 1760);[186] one from the Portico of Antigone (ID 1965);[187] one from a list of donors and subscribers found in and belonging to Sarapeion C (ID 2618);[188] one from an *Ephebium* list (ID 2598);[189] one on a decree of the Athenian cleruchy in honour of the musician *Amphikles* (ID 1497);[190] and one on a white marble stele found in the Sanctuary of the Syrians (ID 2263).[191]

Inscription 2 (ID 2328)

Λυσιμαχος υπερ εαυτου Θεω Υψιστω χαριστηριον[192]

("Lysimachos for himself [to] God Most High [for a] votive/thank-offering")[193]

ID 2328 is carved on a small piece of white marble. It was found lying at the foot of a wall in GD 80. This inscription is also dated to the first century BCE. It was the use of the name *Lysimachos* in this inscription that caused Plassart to associate IDs 2329 and 2328 together, resulting in the identification of GD 80 as a synagogue.

---

[184] Roussel and Launey, *Inscriptions de Délos (Nos. 1497–1524)*, 295; Plassart, "La Synagogue juive de Délos," in *Mélanges*, 205.
[185] P. M. Fraser and Elaine Matthews, eds., *Lexicon of Greek Personal Names: Volume I: The Aegean Islands* (Oxford: Clarendon, 1987). [On the basis of Plassart –Eds.]
[186] Roussel and Launey, *Inscriptions de Délos (Nos. 1497–1524)*, 119.
[187] Roussel and Launey, *Inscriptions de Délos (Nos. 1497–1524)*, 188.
[188] Pierre Roussel and Marcel Launey, *Inscriptions de Délos: Dédicaces Postérieures à 166 av. J.-C. (Nos. 2220–2528); Textes Divers, Listes et Catalogues, Fragments Divers Postérieurs à 166 av. J.-C. (Nos. 2529–2879)* (Librairie Ancienne; Paris: Honoré Champion, 1937b), 395.
[189] Roussel and Launey, *Inscriptions de Délos (Nos. 2220–2528)*, 374.
[190] Roussel and Launey, *Inscriptions de Délos (Nos. 1497–1524)*, 1.
[191] Roussel and Launey, *Inscriptions de Délos (Nos. 2220–2528)*, 78.
[192] Roussel and Launey, *Inscriptions de Délos (Nos. 2220–2528)*, 295; Plassart, "La Synagogue juive de Délos," in *Mélanges*, 205, n. 2; Plassart, "La synagogue juive," *RB*, 527, n. 2.
[193] My translation.

Again, there are other contemporary inscriptions from Delos containing the name *Lysimachos*. The name appears on ID 1764,[194] relating to the Association of Competalists, and on ID 2616,[195] a list of donors and subscribers to Sarapeion C.

The fact that the names *Lysimachos* and *Agathoklēs* both appear in lists of donors and subscribers to Sarapeion C is interesting, and it is well worth mentioning here that the internal configuration of GD 80 (our supposed synagogue), GD 91 (Sarapeion A), and GD 100 (Sarapeion C) is very similar—with benches placed around the internal walls (we will return to this point in the discussion of the archaeological evidence below).

Inscription 3 (ID 2330)

Λαωδικη Θεωι Υψιστωι σωθεισα ταις υφ αυτου θαραπηαις ευχην[196]

("Laodikē [to] God Most High for healing him of his infirmities, an offering")[197]

ID 2330 is carved on a rectangular base of white marble. It was found in GD 80, and has been dated to around 108/107 BCE. It is an inscription in the style of a Greek votive rather than a Jewish dedication.

The name *Laodikē* is identified in the *LPGN* as possibly being Jewish, but this is again on the basis of Plassart's identification. There is one other instance of the name *Laodikē* from Delos, ID 2628,[198] among a list of donor and subscriber names on a marble plaque, which was discovered in the Theatre of the Syrian Sanctuary.

Inscription 4 (ID 2331)

Ζωσας Παριος Θεω Υψιστω ευχην[199]

("Zozas of Paros [to] God Most High, an offering")[200]

---

[194] Roussel and Launey, *Inscriptions de Délos (Nos. 1497–1524)*, 122.
[195] Roussel and Launey, *Inscriptions de Délos (Nos. 2220–2528)*, 389.
[196] Roussel and Launey, *Inscriptions de Délos (Nos. 2220–2528)*, 296; Plassart, "La Synagogue juive de Délos," in *Mélanges*, 205, n. 3; Plassart, "La synagogue juive," *RB*, 527.
[197] My translation.
[198] Roussel and Launey, *Inscriptions de Délos (Nos. 2220–2528)*, 401–2.
[199] Roussel and Launey, *Inscriptions de Délos. (Nos. 2220–2528)*, 296; Plassart, "La Synagogue juive de Délos," in *Mélanges*, 205, n. 4; Plassart, "La synagogue juive," *RB*, 527.
[200] My translation.

ID 2331 was found on a bench in the western side of room A in GD 80. It is carved on a small base of white marble (fig. 4b). Plassart described it as "slightly pyramid-shaped," but it is actually in the shape of a horned altar.

Figure 4b – ID 2331[201]
Image reprinted from Waldemar Déonna, *Le Mobilier délien, Délos* (Paris: De Boccard, 1938). Used by permission.

This inscription has been dated to the first century BCE, and the name *Zozas* is identified in the *LGPN* as possibly belonging to a manumitted slave, but not specifically identified as a Jewish name. The style of this base and that of ID 2328 is very similar, and there are many examples of this type of inscribed base all over Delos itself (and indeed all over the ancient Near East).

There was no other instance of the name *Zozas* in the ID. However, there are other instances of the name *Zozas* in the context of the first rebellion against Rome in Josephus (*B.J.* 4.235; 5.249; 6.92; 6.148; and 6.380), and all the references are to the same person: one James, *son of Sosas*, an Idumaean general who mustered forces to march on Jerusalem in support of the Zealot faction. This could be support for a Jewish identification of ID 2331, although it is not an association Plassart or any other following scholar made, and, of course, it could be entirely coincidental and/or unrelated.

---

[201] Déonna, *Le Mobilier délien, Délos*, (pages unnumbered).

Inscription 5 (ID 2332)

Ὑψίστω ευχὴν Μαρκια[202]

("Most High [from] Markia")[203]

ID 2332 was found on a bench in the west of room A in GD 80. It is carved on a small, white marble base and dates to the first century BCE. The name *Markia* is again identified as Jewish in the *LGPN* on the basis of Plassart's identification. It is the only instance of this name on an inscription from Delos.

Inscription 6 (ID 2333)

γενομενος ελευθερος[204]

("... became free")[205]

ID 2333 is carved on a small rectangular base of white marble and was found in GD 80. The marble is very badly damaged and only those two words can be made out. Given the position of Delos as one of the main Aegean centres of the slave trade, it is hardly surprising to find that there are inscriptions relating to the freeing of slaves found there. Furthermore, there were other inscription bases found in GD 80 which neither Plassart nor subsequent scholars have chosen to mention, and whose texts are illegible.[206] It is evident, thus, that other than its proximity to the other four inscription bases found in GD 80 (and the one found some 90 m away in the stadium district) and discussed by Plassart, there is nothing Jewish about ID 2333, and it is merely Plassart's association of the inscriptions that has linked it with the others.

It becomes clear, when looked at in the light of all of the foregoing, that the inscriptions used by Plassart to identify GD 80 as a synagogue are unrelated. They, like many of the other pieces of marble on the island, have ended up together in building GD 80 where there is a lime kiln (for melting down marble to make lime),

---

[202] Roussel and Launey, *Inscriptions de Délos (Nos. 2220–2528)*, 296; Plassart, "La Synagogue juive de Délos," in *Mélanges*, 205, n. 5; Plassart, "La synagogue juive," *RB*, 528.
[203] My translation.
[204] Roussel and Launey, *Inscriptions de Délos (Nos. 2220–2528)*, 296; Plassart, "La Synagogue juive de Délos," in *Mélanges*, 206, n. 6; Plassart, "La synagogue juive," *RB*, 528, n. 6.
[205] My translation.
[206] Specifically, two small inscription bases whose texts are illegible. See Déonna, *Le Mobilier délien, Délos*, Pl. CXII, photographs 969 and 970 (the pages are unnumbered).

and we will return to this point below in the discussion of the archaeological remains.

However, there are two further inscriptions which are very interesting indeed.

THE SAMARITAN INSCRIPTIONS

In 1979, two inscriptions were found by Philippe Fraisse of the École française d'Athènes. These two inscriptions are the only specifically Jewish (Samaritan) pieces of material found on the island. They were both found in an unexcavated area just beneath current ground level, where they had fallen from the exterior wall onto which they had apparently been fixed, near the shoreline about 100 m north of GD 80. Both inscriptions are written in Greek, and both are dedicated by the "Israelites who offer to Holy Argarizein" (presumably Mount Gerizim in Samaria).

These two inscriptions do provide evidence of Samaritans on the island. It is possible that, if there were a Samaritan (or Jewish) community on Delos, that it came there in the same way as the other multinational migrants, to benefit from the free trade status of Delos and to deal in merchandise and slaves from around the Mediterranean region.

Unfortunately, other than these two inscriptions, there is no literary, archaeological, or epigraphic evidence to tell us anything about Samaritans on Delos. Of course, it is possible to theorise, based on the inscriptions and on the passage in Josephus (*A.J.* 14.213–216) above, that the references to the Jews on Delos could relate to Samaritans, and that the building from which the two inscriptions came could have been a Samaritan synagogue.

Samaritan Inscription 1

Οι εν Δηλω Ισραελειταο οι
απαρχομενοι εις ιερον
Αργαριζειν στεφανουσιν
χρυσω στεφαω Σαραπιωνα
Ιασονος Κνωσιον ευεργεσιας
ενεκεν της εις εαυτους[207]

"The Israelites on Delos who make first-fruit offerings to Holy Argarizim crown with a golden crown Sarapion son of Jason of Knossos for his benefactions on their behalf."[208]

---

[207] Philippe Bruneau, "Les Israélites de Délos et la juiverie délienne," *Bulletin de Correspondance Hellénique* 106 (1982): 469.
[208] Bruneau, "Les Israélites de Délos," 469.

DELOS

This inscription has been dated to somewhere between 150 and 50 BCE.²⁰⁹ There is substantial damage to the upper area of the stele, but it does not affect the text.²¹⁰ The inscription honours *Sarapion* (son of Jason of Knossos) for his benefactions on behalf of the "Israelites on Delos" but does not offer any details as to the presence of a permanent community of Samaritans on the island, and it is not clear whether the *Sarapion* honoured in the text is a Samaritan, Jew, or pagan. It does, however, identify the dedicators as "the Israelites on Delos," which certainly indicates a community of Israelites on the island, be it a temporary, seasonal or permanent one.

Samaritan Inscription 2

Ισραηλιται οι απαρχομενοι εις ιερον Αργαριζειν
ετιμησαν vac. Μενιππον Αρτεμιδωρου
Ηρακλειον αυτον και τους εγγονους αυτου
κατασκευασαντα και αναθεντα εκ των ιδιον επι
προσευχη του θε[ου] TON[- - - - - - - - - - - - -]
ΟΛΟΝ ΚΑΙ ΤΟ[- - - - - και εστεφανωσαν] χρυσω
στε[φα -]νω και [- - - - - - - - - - - - - - - -]
ΚΑ - - -
Τ - -²¹¹

"[The] Israelites who make first-fruit offerings to holy Argarizim honour Menippos, son of Artemidoros of Heraclea, himself as well as his descendants to have established and dedicated its expenses, for an offering/prayer [to God], [- - - - - - -] and [- - - - -] and crowned it with a golden crown and [- - -]"²¹²

The second Samaritan inscription is tentatively dated to between 250–175 BCE and is carved onto a white marble stele.²¹³ There is a great deal of damage to the bottom portion of the text, with the second half of the text entirely missing. This inscription refers to a donation of some unknown thing or act. It is unfortunate that this second inscription, whose damaged portion probably contained the details of the donation, has not survived intact and thus, unfortunately, the two Samaritan inscriptions do not clear up the mystery for us. It is to be hoped that the bottom fragment of the second inscription might at some point be found and the text fully reconstructed so that we might at least know what was offered.

---

²⁰⁹ Bruneau, "Les Israélites de Délos," 469–74.
²¹⁰ Bruneau, "Les Israélites de Délos," 474.
²¹¹ Bruneau, "Les Israélites de Délos," 471–74.
²¹² Bruneau, "Les Israélites de Délos," 471–74.
²¹³ Bruneau, "Les Israélites de Délos," 469–74.

The second inscription is very similar to the first and honours Menippos (son of Artemidoros of Heraclea) for his benefactions in establishing something somewhere on Delos (perhaps the place where the stele fell to the ground and was ultimately found), and again offers no clues as to the presence of a permanent community of Samaritans on the island. Again, it is not clear whether the Menippos of the text is a Samaritan or pagan himself. It is the "Israelites" who honour Menippos, but unlike the first Samaritan inscription, *the text of the second inscription does not include the phrase "the Israelites of Delos."*

The text of the second inscription has been interpreted on the basis that it must be worded like the first. However, it is inscribed on a reused marble stele with an earlier text blocked out and, as noted above, whoever inscribed the new text over the old did not include the words *on Delos*, although there is space to do so. Nevertheless, Philippe Bruneau of the École française d'Athènes reconstructed it as though it did contain that phrase and subsequent scholarship has followed suit.[214] It is possible that this dedication, like the first, might relate to a permanent, seasonal or even a non-resident donor or group of Samaritans, or to a group who did not have the same legal status on Delos as those who dedicated the first stele.

To add some further confusion to the translation and interpretation of the two Samaritan inscriptions, Plassart's initial translation of the phrase επι προσευχη (from ID 2329) as "for the synagogue," has led to a number of scholars translating the same phrase in the second Samaritan inscription in that way, leading them to think that the building from which the Samaritan inscription came was a synagogue. Moreover, Bruneau translated the phrase επι προσευχη in the second Samaritan inscription as "in ex-voto" (for a vow/offering), whereas in relation to ID 2329 he accepted Plassart's reading of it as "for the synagogue."[215]

In any event, the two Samaritan inscriptions provide at least some indication that the texts referring to the Jews on Delos in Josephus and Maccabees might relate to a permanent or seasonal community of Samaritans and possibly to the existence of a building related to their presence there. The dating of the inscriptions is broad (c. 250–50 BCE), and it could be that offerings were sent to Mount Gerizim while the temple still stood there, or that offerings continued to be made and sent to Samaria after the destruction of the temple. Or, indeed, it could be that the offerings, in whatever form they took, were made on Delos only, perhaps in the form of votives.

In the light of the discovery of two Samaritan inscriptions, it has been suggested that there were communities of both Jews and Samaritans on Delos, and that the letter recorded in Josephus refers to both,[216] and it must be at least

---

[214] Bruneau, "Les Israélites de Délos," 474.

[215] L. Michael White, "The Delos Synagogue Revisited: Recent Fieldwork in the Graeco-Roman Diaspora," *HTR* 80.2 (1987): 142.

[216] White, "The Delos Synagogue Revisited," 153.

possible that this is so. However, while the reference in Josephus (*A.J.* 14.213–216) to the "Jews in Delos and some of the neighbouring Jews" does indicate that there was more than one Jewish community in the area, it is possible that these "neighbouring Jews" may have been on other islands, either in the Cyclades or the Dodecanese, or indeed other larger islands in the region, such as Crete, Rhodes, or Cyprus. Since we know of the Jewish population on Delos only from Josephus, and of the Samaritans only from the two Samaritan inscriptions, it is difficult to see how this conundrum can be resolved without substantial excavations of the area immediately east of the stadium.

Θεος Ὕψιστος / Ὕψιστος

Writing in 1914, Plassart outlined his belief that the use of the epithets Ὕψιστος or Θεος Ὕψιστος (in the inscriptions found in GD 80) indicated "a tendency towards monotheism," and Jewish monotheism in particular.[217] However, the inscriptions that refer to *Hypsistos* may also refer to the Greek deity *Zeus Hypsistos*, whose cult (a healing cult, and a more likely association given the physical form of the inscription bases) also used these epithets to describe their chief deity. The sanctuary of the cult of *Zeus Hypsistos* is located on Mt. Cynthus, less than 500 m southwest of GD 80 (see fig. 3 above).

Plassart only identified the names from the group of inscriptions he considered to be related (see above) as being Jewish without looking at other occurrences of those names on Delos. Additionally, as already stated, he noted an occurrence of the term *Thea Hypsista*, which he acknowledged as referring to a Near Eastern female deity, possibly the Great Goddess of Asia Minor.[218] Taking this together with the recurrences of the names contained in the inscriptions, Plassart's argument is considerably and correctly diminished. Furthermore, the names on the two Samaritan inscriptions may or may not be Jewish and could be the names of non-Jewish Cretan donors. If, at some future point, it were possible to relate the two names (Menippos and Jason) from Crete to a Jewish family there, it would be a significant advance in the scholarship on the subject.

Writing in 1935, Belle Mazur noted that the style of the inscribed bases was inconsistent with Jewish practice, in particular the *proseuchē* and the *Lysimachos* inscriptions which had lead fixings in place for votive offerings or statues.[219] She made the first connection with the Greek cult of *Zeus Hypsistos,* in whose sanctuary on the Athenian Pnyx were found similar inscribed bases, and to the cult of *Theos Hypsistos* from Asia Minor. Mazur was also the first scholar to note

---

[217] Plassart, "La synagogue juive," *RB*, 529.
[218] Plassart, "La synagogue juive," *RB*, 529.
[219] Belle D. Mazur, *Studies on Jewry in Greece* (Athens: Printing Office "Hestia," 1935): 21–22.

that Plassart's translation of the phrase επι προσευχη as meaning "for the synagogue" was incorrect because the definite article is absent from the inscription. She translated it as "for a prayer/votive."[220]

AN ILLUSTRATIVE DIGRESSION – THE CULT OF THE HYPSISTARIANS

There is another cult that used the epithets *Hypsistos* and *Theos Hypsistos*: the *Hypsistarians*, who, while they recognised other gods, considered theirs as being above all. Part of their ritual is described in an inscription carved on one of the blocks of the Hellenistic inner face of the city wall of Oenoanda in northern Lycia.[221]

> Born of itself, untaught, without a mother, unshakeable, not contained in a name, known by many names, dwelling in fire, this is god. We, his angels, are a small part of god. To you who ask this question about god, what his essential nature is, he has pronounced that Aether is god who sees all, on whom you should gaze and pray at dawn, looking towards the sunrise.[222]

According to descriptions of their practices, the Hypsistarians stood in the open air facing east, looking up to heaven and offering their prayers. Lamps and fire were an essential part of their cult, which was associated with heaven and the sun, and, by the dedication of light, it was thought possible to establish a link with the deity.[223]

GD 80, our putative synagogue, is oriented eastwards, is unroofed, and 40 lamps were found in it by Plassart's excavation team. While it is impossible (and, indeed, would be absurd) to attribute the use of the final phase of GD 80 to the Hypsistarians, there is nothing to suggest that the lamps could not have been used in a ritual such as that described in the Oenoanda Oracle. There is certainly no known Jewish ritual with which to compare this, and, to add further to this idea, even as late as the fourth century CE, Hypsistarians were sometimes mistaken for Jews.[224] In any event, the cult of the Hypsistarians has been offered for consideration *only* to illustrate how tenuous and tendentious the identification of GD 80 as a Jewish and/or Samaritan synagogue is.

---

[220] Mazur, *Studies on Jewry*, 21–22.
[221] Stephen Mitchell, "The Cult of Theos Hypsistos between Pagans, Jews and Christians," in *Pagan Monotheism in Late Antiquity* (ed. Polymnia Athanassiadi and Michael Frede; Oxford: Clarendon, 1999), 193–94. I am most grateful to John Dillon, Emeritus Professor of Greek in the School of Classics at Trinity College in Dublin, for pointing out this interesting parallel, during a conversation in Athens.
[222] Mitchell, "The Cult of Theos Hypsistos," 93–94.
[223] Mitchell, "The Cult of Theos Hypsistos," 91–92.
[224] Mitchell, "The Cult of Theos Hypsistos," 93–94.

THE ARCHAEOLOGICAL EVIDENCE

GD 80 lies on the northeastern shoreline of Delos in the Bay of Gournia, outside the defensive town walls. It stands in the area just east of the stadium and northeast of the gymnasium (figs. 2, 3, and 4 above). When Plassart excavated GD 80 in 1912, he found a large rectangular room measuring 16.90 m (north to south) by 14.40 m (west to east). The floor of this room had a coarse flaked marble/gravel-like covering, and there was some plaster left on the base of some of the walls, as well as some roof tiles scattered around the floor. The building directly abuts the shoreline which has advanced over time and has consumed its eastern side (see fig. 5 below).

Dividing the main rectangular space (Rooms A and B) into two almost equal parts is an east-west wall with three doorways, with room A in the north and room B in the south. This wall was erected some unknown time after the north, west and south walls (it is not bonded into them, and is therefore a later addition), and is made up of gneiss, rubble, and reworked marble from abandoned or destroyed buildings, including pieces of capitals, marble inscription bases, triglyphs and thresholds.[225] There is also a further space, room D, along the south of the building, parallel with rooms A and B, which was divided into smaller chambers and which may have contained a stairwell. Running beneath part of rooms B and D is the cistern around which the building was constructed.[226]

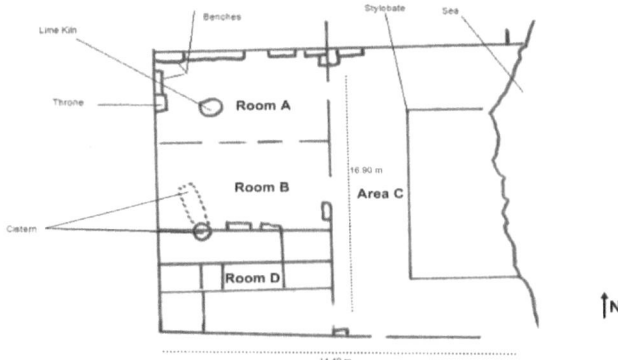

Figure 5 – Plan of GD 80

According to Plassart—based on his assumptions about inscriptions ID 2329 and ID 2328 and on the letter preserved in Josephus—rooms A and B served as the assembly halls of a synagogue. There are some white marble benches in place in this area dating to the period he argued GD 80 was in use as a synagogue (from

---

[225] Plassart, "La synagogue juive," *RB*, 523–34.
[226] Plassart, "La synagogue juive," *RB*, 523–34.

around the middle of the first century BCE). There are also benches running along the south and west inner walls of room B, and some more benches running along the south, west and north walls of area C (the corridor between the main rectangular space and the peristyle courtyard to the east).[227]

In the centre of the west wall of room A is a white marble throne (see fig. 6 below). This was found *in situ* with the marble benches on either side, along the inside west wall of the area A.[228]

Figure 6 – The benches and marble throne in GD 80

The marble throne in GD 80 is very similar to the first century BCE throne for the priest of Dionysos in the theatre in Athens, the stone thrones in the Ampherion at Oropos, and to others all over the Graeco-Roman world. In a world of limited resources, the reuse of objects was a common way to reduce the cost of furnishing any given space, and the throne is likely to have come from the theatre on Delos, on the west side of the island.

Likewise, the benches in GD 80 are made up of various reused architectural pieces which are similar to those still left in the nearby gymnasium, from whence they may have been removed after its destruction and abandonment around 74–63 BCE.[229] Of course, this does not prove that GD 80 was not used as a synagogue, but it is also striking that the internal furnishing of other buildings on the island have a similar layout, including the use of similarly reused benches in Sarapeion A near the theatre district on Delos (see fig. 7 below). Thus, the internal configuration of GD 80 cannot in itself be evidence that it was used as a synagogue.

---

[227] Plassart, "La synagogue juive," *RB*, 523–34.
[228] Plassart, "La synagogue juive," *RB*, 526.
[229] Around 200 m distant from *GD* 80. The *Ephebium* is where the education of *ephebes* took place under the supervision of the *Gymnasiarch*. The construction of the benches there is very similar to the construction of the benches in GD 80, and the throne would probably have been used by the *Gymnasiarch* who instructed the *ephebes*. The throne could, alternatively, have come from the theatre as it is identical to other theatre "VIP" chairs.

Figure 7 – GD 91 (Sarapeion A)

In terms of the Sarapeia, there is also the connection between the names from the inscriptions found in and near GD 80 and the donor names on the Sarapeion C list of subscribers (and the associations of Hermaists and the Poseidonists). The list was found in, and specifically refers to, that structure. In fact, more than one hundred and seventy dedicatory and votive offerings and inscriptions relating to Isis, Sarapis, and Anubis were found in Sarapeion C alone.[230]

Furthermore, there are other buildings on the island with this sort of benching still apparent, such as in the Heraion, the Italian Agora, in the semi-circular exedra of the Sanctuary of Apollo, the Ephebium, and in the orchestra of the theatre, as well as others dotted around the island.[231]

It is possible to date—approximately—the second phase GD 80 by reference to the material used in the rebuilt areas of the internal walls, and especially to the marble taken from the nearby gymnasium. A second century BCE inscribed base (ID 1928) of the Gymnasiarch *Poses* was used in rebuilding one of the walls of GD 80, after the destruction or removal of the statue which it carried. Another gymnasium inscription base (ID 1923b) relating to *ephebes* under the rule of the *Gymnasiarch Diotimos Theodosion* (126–125 BCE) was also found in another rebuilt wall.

Other inscriptions from the gymnasium ended up being reused in the Palaestra of the Lake on the western side of the island. As the gymnasium was plundered during the pirate raids of the Mithridatic wars, it is only from this time

---

[230] Philippe Bruneau and Jean Ducat, *Guide de Délos* (3rd ed.; Paris: De Boccard, 1983), 227.
[231] Déonna, *Le Mobilier délien, Délos*, Pl. CXII, photographs 64, 67, 68, 69 (pages unnumbered).

(74–63 BCE) that GD 80 could have been adapted for the sort of use that required the seating arrangement found there.[232]

On the eastern side of the building is area C, the remains of the corridor and step or stylobate leading out into what was originally a peristyle courtyard. The peristyle would have measured approximately 18 x 18 m, but has now been destroyed by the sea almost up to the line of the stylobate (fig. 8 below). In October 2003, the northern and southern walls of the existing structure extended to almost the same point of collapse into the sea, some 1.5 m beyond the stylobate, and rooftiles were found along the inside of these perimeter walls indicating that they were at least partially covered.

Figure 8 – GD 80 (from the stylobate down to the sea)[233]

The seaward side of area C retains a section of a stylobate running parallel just over 6 m from the easternmost wall. The visible section is made of blocks of white marble resting on a gneiss foundation. This line stops approximately 5 m from the north and south walls of area C. Just one metre in front of the stylobate is a sharp drop-off to the beach (marked in the photograph by the clumps of sea grass), and the rest of the courtyard and whatever was on the other side of it has been consumed by the encroaching sea.

Plassart and other scholars (most notably, Mazur 1935; Bruneau 1970; White 1987, 1990; Binder 1999; and Trümper 2004) interpreted the physical layout of the Hellenistic house in several ways, none of which has much bearing on its identification as a synagogue, other than the fact that, in the final phase of the structure, it had benches arranged around the walls of the two main areas and that the final phase is oriented towards the east. However, as I mentioned above, this seating arrangement is something of an archaeological red herring given the configuration of Sarapeion A (fig. 7 above) and other buildings on the island.

In the final ruined phase of GD 80, Rooms A and B are bisected by an east-west wall with three doorways (see fig. 5 above). This wall was erected some

---

[232] Plassart, "La synagogue juive," *RB*, 532.
[233] The stylobate can also be clearly seen in the satellite image at fig. 14 below.

unknown time after the north, west and south walls, as it is not bonded to them. When it was excavated in 1912–1913 its three doorways were found walled up. This east-west wall is made up of local gneiss, rubble, and reused material from other buildings, including pieces of capitals, marble inscription bases, and thresholds. There are also three doorways on the east side of the structure, providing access to areas A and B from the peristyle courtyard along the shoreline.

On Delos, it was normal for some of the larger Hellenistic houses to have two courtyards; one courtyard was often deeper and sometimes taller than the other, in order to enhance the entrance to a reception room.[234] GD 80 is similar in size and layout to a number of other houses on Delos, such as the House of the Hermes (GD 89) near the theatre, which had at least three storeys, accessed from various external and internal stairways (see figs. 9 and 10 below).

The floor plan of GD 89 (House of the Hermes) is very similar to the floor plan of GD 80 (the "synagogue"), as well as to the floor plans of GD 111 (House of the Dauphins) and GD 57 (House of the Poseidonists), as can be seen in the comparison of floor plans below (figure 10). In the photograph of GD 89 (figure 9 below), the preserved and restored section of the house is built around the central peristyle courtyard and other areas of the house were ranged around the courtyard with access through that central area as well as from the exterior of the building.

As can be seen in the floor plans, each of these houses had a peristyle courtyard around which was arranged the habitation areas of the house. Moreover, each building comprised two to three storeys, and each had a second, smaller domestic courtyard. However, there is nothing in the layout of GD 80 which can in any way be ascribed to its having been used a synagogue. Its final usage, in a ruined state, included benches around the space which originally had been the domestic courtyard.

Other than lamps, antefixes, roof-tiles, and inscription blocks, there was nothing found in GD 80 that would enable it to be absolutely identified as belonging to a particular group, religious or otherwise, although the number of lamps found in the structure is quite curious in itself, as was referred to above in the section on the Hypsistarians. Specifically, there was no artefact, structure, or inscription found within GD 80 which was Jewish in nature.

---

[234] Simon Price, "The History of the Hellenistic Period," in *Greece and the Hellenistic World* (Oxford History of the Classical World; eds. John Boardman, Jasper Griffin, and Oswyn Murray; Oxford: Oxford University Press, 1988), 388.

Figure 9 – GD 89 (House of the Hermes, looking northwest)

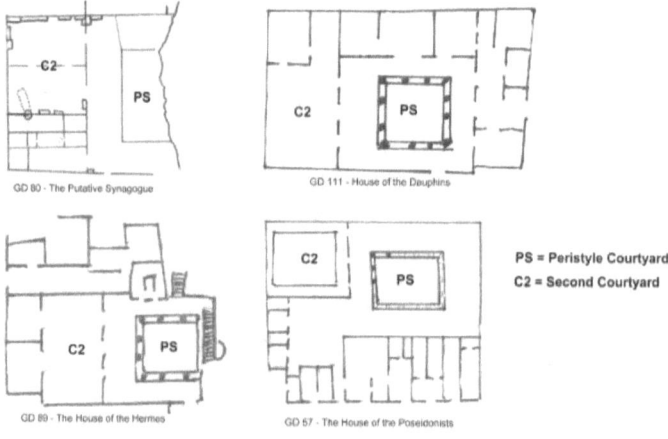

Figure 10 – Floor plans of GDs 80, 89, 111, 57

As already discussed above, and as described by Mazur in 1935, a number of the inscription or statue bases found in GD 80 are in the form of Greek and Near Eastern "horned" altars, including two of the bases cited as Jewish (Inscription 2 [ID 2328] and Inscription 4 [ID 2331]) by Plassart in 1913/1914.

The Cistern

Uniquely on the island, GD 80 appears to have been constructed over a rock-fault which was extended into a cistern by means of vaulting. This cistern lies beneath the main east-west wall between rooms B and D (see fig. 5 above). For those who built the house, this rock fault must have represented a convenient location, since it meant the degree of excavation necessary to provide the house with its water supply was considerably reduced. Philippe Bruneau, of the École française d'Athènes, is the only person, following Plassart, who has excavated on the site of GD 80. In 1962 he excavated part of the floor around the arch (on both sides of the wall) so that he could access and clean out the well/cistern which Plassart had left untouched. Unfortunately, the list of finds from the cistern is not complete, but it included a piece of bluish marble, a fragment of a bluish marble bowl, three antefixes of beige/pink clay decorated with palmettes, some fragments of a vase with a ringed wall, and three fragments of blown glass (Plassart had also found numerous fragments of small glass vases in GD 80, but not in the cistern). In the cistern, Bruneau recovered the only lamp not found during the original excavations of GD 80 (see fig. 11 below).

Only the area immediately underneath the arch of the cistern was accessible when it was in use, and although the floor is now quite opened out, this is only because of Bruneau's 1962 excavations. The floor in this area originally came right up to the wall, leaving only the space immediately beneath the arch open into this room.[235] Even *with* the excavated opening, access from room B is both difficult and precarious as the opening lies under, and extends only a metre from, the arch. There is a sharp and sheer drop from the floor level to the bottom of the cistern. There are no steps built into the cistern, and there is insufficient space in the opening in rooms B or D (on the other side of the wall) for access via a ladder for the purposes of bathing.

---

[235] Philippe Bruneau, *Recherches Sur Les Cultes de Délos à L'Époque Hellénistique et à L'Époque Impériale* (Paris: De Boccard, 1970), 481.

Figure 11 – The lamp from the cistern[236]
Image reprinted from Waldemar Déonna, *Le Mobilier délien* (Paris: De Boccard, 1938). Used by permission.

The cistern is deep—the bottom of the fault lies at 4 m in places—and is by no means a level surface, running some 6.08 m in length, under a vaulted roof, and was probably constructed before the rest of the building was finished.[237] The arch over the opening to the cistern serves not only as access for the drawing of water, but also bears weight for the wall that divides rooms B and D, so that the floor does not collapse into the cistern.

It has been suggested that the cistern in GD 80 could have been used as a *mikveh*.[238] This claim can be completely dismissed. The arch above the cistern provides limited access to the cistern from both B and D, and at its *highest* point the arch is just 32cm off the original floor level (see fig. 12 below). The top of the cistern arch does not rise above the top of the benches.

---

[236] Déonna, *Le Mobilier délien*, (pages unnumbered).
[237] Bruneau, *Recherches*, 481.
[238] Binder, *Into the Temple Courts*, 306.

Figure 12 – The cistern from room B (looking south to Mount Cynthus)

Binder also says that Bruneau suggests that a wooden ladder or stairs may have been used to enter the cistern for ritual ablutions,[239] but what Bruneau actually said was that if it is possible to take water from room B via an opening in the wall framed by the arch, this is only because part of the original floor is now missing (removed during the excavation process).[240]

Furthermore, while there may be water in the well/cistern from the water table, there is no direct means for rainwater to flow into the cistern, and it would undoubtedly have presented a most unsatisfactory manner in which to bathe, ritually or otherwise. As Bruneau noted, emptying this cistern would have been impossible, especially as it is partly fed from the aquifer.[241] Most importantly, on an island devoid of a surface supply of water, bathing would have rendered the cistern useless for the collection of water for domestic purposes. This, in turn, would suggest that the building ought to have had a separate domestic water supply if it had had a *mikveh*. It does not.

Binder cites Bruneau as having said that the cistern in GD 80 was unusual in that it allowed for human access.[242] He is incorrect on *three* counts. The first is that there is no room for human access into the cistern in GD 80, as is clear from the photograph and description above. The second is that many of the cisterns on

---

[239] Binder, *Into the Temple Courts*, 306.
[240] Bruneau, *Recherches*, 482.
[241] Bruneau, *Recherches*, 481.
[242] Binder, *Into the Temple Courts*, 306.

Delos are constructed to incorporate stone stairways specifically designed for human access.[243] The third is that Binder did not understand what Bruneau said, which was that *according to Plassart* (who had not excavated the cistern), it is possible to take water from room B via an opening in the wall framed by a marble arch, but that he had been unable to do so.[244] In any case, access is somewhat better from room D, and it is likely that it was properly accessed from there when the cistern was in use. Even from room D, however, the height of the access to the cistern is just 30 cm and the floor before it was excavated went right to the wall.

THE LIME KILN

In room A of GD 80 there is a substantial lime kiln measuring some 2 m in diameter (figure 13 below). Produced by melting down marble and limestone, lime was a valuable commodity in the ancient world. In agriculture, it was used as a fertiliser and to improve drainage. Lime was also used in construction. Mortar for laying masonry was made by mixing lime with sand. Concrete was made by mixing the lime with crushed or natural stone. Plaster was covered with a similar mix to mortar. Lime white is a mixture of lime and water and was used for whitening walls, the traditional "whitewash," and lime plaster was used to waterproof cisterns.

Figure 13 – The lime kiln in Room A (looking west)

---

[243] The cistern of GD 79 (the building where ID 2329 was found), for example, has a stone staircase leading down into that cistern.
[244] Bruneau, *Recherches*, 482.

The town centre of Delos, as it became further and further removed from the commercial and strategic centres of the Mediterranean, lay abandoned and in ruins. The marble lying around the island remained one of its final commercial assets. The lime kiln in GD 80 was likely put in place in the post-abandonment phase of the site as the burning or melting down of marble for lime generally only occurred when the Mediterranean marble trade was tapering off, that is, from about the third century CE, and possibly as late as the fourth century CE. There was agriculture and viticulture on the southern part of the island up until the beginning of the fifth century CE, when the island was finally abandoned, so some of that obsolete marble would have been burned down to make lime to use for this purpose.[245]

When Plassart found the marble inscription bases in rooms A and B of GD 80, he stated (without explaining his reasoning) that they were not associated with the kiln.[246] Given that a number of large marble column barrels (see figure 13 above) and inscription bases were also found in GD 80, probably waiting to be sawn into smaller pieces before being burned down, and given also the variety of the inscription bases found in GD 80—including two small marble inscription bases with no visible text or with wholly eroded text, which were found by Plassart in the same area as IDs 2330, 2331, and 2332, discussed earlier—it is logical to expect that the marble found in this building was destined for the kiln.[247]

LITERATURE REVIEW

ANDRÉ PLASSART (1913, 1914)

André Plassart of the École française d'Athènes identified GD 80 as a synagogue during excavations of 1912 and 1913. He identified the structure as a Hellenistic house with a formal portico entranceway on its eastern extremity. He found six inscriptions, the principal one of which was found some 90 m away from GD 80; the other five inscriptions were found within GD 80, which combined with the internal configuration of GD 80 caused him to interpret it as a synagogue.[248] Plassart's identification of the inscriptions as Jewish is incorrect (see section on inscriptions above). Not only was his translation of ID 2331 incorrect, but he ignored occurrences of the same names (as those from his "Jewish" inscriptions) found elsewhere on the island. In relation to the archaeological evidence, he ignored other buildings on the island with the same internal configuration, such as the Sarapeia (see fig. 7 above).

---

[245] Brunet, "Contribution à l'histoire," 669–82.
[246] Plassart, "La synagogue juive," *RB*, 526.
[247] Déonna, *Le Mobilier délien, Délos*, photos 969–970 (loose, unnumbered pages).
[248] Plassart, "La synagogue juive," *RB*, 523–34.

BELLE D. MAZUR (1935)

Mazur interpreted the main structure as a Hellenistic house with a peristyle courtyard, rather than a portico (as Plassart had suggested). Both options are equally possible. Mazur's reconstruction of it was based on parallels of size and layout with other houses on the island.[249] Mazur's was the first and only dissenting voice on the subject of the so-called synagogue on Delos, and, while her interpretation of the physical structure of the building was very similar to that of Plassart and others, her interpretation of the inscriptions and statue bases found in the building was not. She argued that their form (votive bases with lead fixings for decorative attachments) was not consistent with a Jewish context, that Plassart's inscriptions were therefore not Jewish and that GD 80 was not a synagogue, but some sort of establishment belonging to the Greek cult of *Theos Hypsistos*, whose sanctuary was on the summit of Mount Cynthus just 500 m south of GD 80.[250] Mazur also retranslated the text of the principal inscription (ID 2329), and pointed out that there is no definite article used in the wording of the inscription, and that the words επι προσευχη in this context cannot refer to a building and must be translated as reading "for an offering" or simply as a "prayer."[251] Mazur's arguments in terms of the form of the inscription bases and the inscriptions themselves are convincing. Her translations are accurate and careful. In terms of her discussion of GD 80 itself, as to whether it had a portico or peristyle courtyard, etc., this is entirely irrelevant. How GD 80 was adapted for use in its final phase is unrelated to its original purpose.

ELEAZAR LIPA SUKENIK (1934, 1949)

Sukenik initially accepted André Plassart's interpretation of GD 80. However, once he had read Mazur's 1935 analysis of the evidence, he changed his mind. Writing in 1949, he said "the case of the so-called 'Synagogue' at Delos shows how misleading incomplete research can be," and went on to conclude, based on Mazur's argument, that the word προσευχή could only mean "prayer" and not "synagogue" because of the absence of the definite article in the inscription; that the deity referred to as "*hypsistos*" was the Greek god Zeus; and that the form of the inscribed bases was pagan and not Jewish.[252]

---

[249] Mazur, *Studies on Jewry*, 17–18.
[250] Mazur, *Studies on Jewry*, 21.
[251] Mazur, *Studies on Jewry*, 21.
[252] Sukenik, "Present State," 8–23.

PHILIPPE BRUNEAU (1970, 1982)

Bruneau was the only other archaeologist to have excavated at GD 80 other than Plassart. Bruneau accepted Plassart's synagogue identification and dismissed Mazur's rebuttal of Plassart's work, along with Sukenik's later acknowledgement of the correctness of her rebuttal.[253] He insisted that the inscriptions showed that GD 80 was a sanctuary of the Jewish God Most High, *Theos Hypsistos*, since the name *Zeus Hypsistos* does not appear on the inscriptions and since the cult of *Zeus Hypsistos* had its own sanctuary on Mount Cynthus.[254] Bruneau also rejected Mazur's argument concerning the format and style of the inscribed bases, saying that the Hellenised Jews of the Diaspora assimilated certain pagan customs which over time became established in their religion. Peculiarly, even though he agreed with Mazur's translation of the phrase επι προσευχή as "for a prayer/offering," he accepted Plassart's reading of it as "for the synagogue" and insisted that προσευχή remains "an essentially Jewish term," concluding that GD 80 was a synagogue of an exceptional type, and that the endurance of the Jewish cult on Delos even after the destructions of 88 BCE and 69 BCE confirms the references in the literary sources.[255] The ancient sources, however, do not refer to any structure at all, let alone to a synagogue. At the very best, they confirm the presence of Jews on Delos (and other *neighbouring* Jews), and indicate that the Jews on Delos were for some time unable to follow their customary religious practices. Moreover, the fact that there is a large lime kiln in GD 80, together with many pieces of marble, suggests that much of the material in this locus was being melted down to make lime. Moveable objects, such as the inscription bases, could easily have been taken from other areas to GD 80 for this purpose. The presence of the *theos hypsistos* inscriptions in GD 80 does not mean that they belonged in this building.

L. MICHAEL WHITE (1987, 1990)

White concluded that because there is some external evidence of a Jewish community on Delos, GD 80 would have fitted their needs and that in all likelihood it was a Samaritan synagogue that was founded.[256] Like many other buildings on the island, GD 80 *could* have been a synagogue. It is only that there is no evidence that it *was* a synagogue, be it Jewish or Samaritan.

---

[253] Bruneau, *Recherches*, 465–504.
[254] Bruneau, *Recherches*, 486–87. However, one of the inscriptions (ID 2332) contains has the epithet *hypsistos* and not *theos hypsistos*.
[255] Bruneau, *Recherches*, 485–88.
[256] White, "The Delos Synagogue Revisited," 133–60; L. Michael White, *Building God's House in the Roman World: Architectural Adaptation among Pagans, Jews, and Christians* (Baltimore, MD: Johns Hopkins University Press, 1990), 138.

A. Thomas Kraabel (1992)

Kraabel came to the conclusion that GD 80 was a synagogue on the basis of the earlier debate (rejecting Mazur's critique and Sukenik's support of it), and relying on Bruneau's presentation of the material. His main argument for the identification of GD 80 as a synagogue rests on the epigraphical references to *theos hypsistos* in the inscriptions found by André Plassart which, he says, "do not offer an obviously pagan use of the term at a time when references to one or other pagan deity as *hypsistos* are not uncommon."[257] As outlined above, the inscriptions are out of context and unrelated. Whilst Kraabel acknowledged the ambiguity of the *proseuchē* inscription, he concluded it was nonetheless Jewish. He did not remark on the form or style of the inscribed bases, nor did he note or refer to the cuttings for lead fixings.[258]

B. Hudson McLean (1996)

McLean took the two Samaritan inscriptions as proof that GD 80 was a synagogue, albeit a Samaritan one. In McLean's interpretation of the physical structure (adopted from White's), he noted that there was no provision in GD 80 for cultic rites, that there was no altar or shrine, and that therefore the congregation "related to a remote external cult, namely the Samaritan cult practiced at Mount Gerizim."[259]

Peter Richardson (1996)

Richardson interpreted GD 80 as a "remodelled house adapted to the needs of the worshipping community." He accepted that Plassart and all those who followed on from his work were correct, and that GD 80 was a synagogue.[260]

Donald Binder (1999)

Binder made what is probably one of the most ambitious of all the interpretations of the building. Based only on the letter preserved in Josephus (*A.J.* 14.213–216) and on Plassart's and Bruneau's interpretation of the material he found, he described GD 80 as "a synagogue with an ancillary banquet hall used to hold feasts on sacred days" and argued that the dividing wall between Rooms A and B

---

[257] Reprinted in *Diaspora Jews and Judaism: Essays in Honor of, and in dialogue with, A. Thomas Kraabel* (ed. J. Andrew Overman and Robert S. MacLennan; Atlanta: Scholars Press, 1992), 491, 493.
[258] In Overman and Robert, *Diaspora Jews*, 493.
[259] McLean, "Place of Cult," 195.
[260] Richardson, "Early Synagogues as Collegia," 97.

presented "the first serious architectural evidence suggesting the division of the sexes within the synagogue."[261] He deemed that access to the cistern from rooms B and D was part of the proof for this claim, on the basis that it was possible that the cistern might have functioned as a *mikveh*.[262] In general, Binder's argument is that there were two possible patterns of occupation of GD 80. In the first scenario, GD 80 was originally a cultic hall of a pagan association in the second century BCE. During the Mithridatic war of 88 BCE and/or the pirate raids of 69 BCE, the building was severely damaged and eventually abandoned by the association to whom it belonged. Then the building was "transformed into a synagogue," and remained as such until the second century CE.[263] In his second scenario, the building was originally constructed as a synagogue, damaged in the first century BCE and afterwards modified with a dividing wall constructed perhaps as a result of the earlier damage.[264]

Both of Binder's occupation scenarios are irrelevant to the identification, since the identification was made on the basis of the inscriptions (the principal one of which was not found in GD 80 at all), and the benches around the Rooms A and B. His suggestion regarding the use of the cistern as a *mikveh* is both physically and domestically unlikely.[265] Moreover, he has misunderstood—in quite a basic way—Philippe Bruneau's descriptions of the structure he excavated. Since he relies wholly on Bruneau's description as the basis for his understanding of the cistern, this proves an insurmountable problem for his interpretation.

LEE I. LEVINE (2000)

Levine accepted Bruneau's conclusion that GD 80 was a synagogue, and referred to the 1970s as the point at which a scholarly consensus was arrived at (apparently on the basis of Philippe Bruneau's publication of the site).[266] Levine described IDs 2328, 2330, 2331, 2332 as having been inscribed on "column bases," which is incorrect. These inscriptions are actually on carved stelae, some in the shape of horned altars, some rectangles with lead fixings. Levine further mentioned ID 2329 (the *proseuchē* inscription), noting that it could have been used in a pagan context but that, combined with the other ancillary evidence and the discovery in 1979 of the two Samaritan stelae by Philippe Fraisse of the École française d'Athènes, added up to sufficient evidence to identify GD 80 as the earliest synagogue thus far found.[267] As we have seen, the Samaritan inscriptions found

---

[261] Binder, *Into the Temple Courts*, 299.
[262] Binder, *Into the Temple Courts*, 306, n. 153.
[263] Binder, *Into the Temple Courts*, 314.
[264] Binder, *Into the Temple Courts*, 314.
[265] Binder, *Into the Temple Courts*, 316–17.
[266] Levine, *The Ancient Synagogue*, 100.
[267] Levine, *The Ancient Synagogue*, 100–101.

by Fraisse and the inscriptions found by Plassart are unrelated, and, while the Samaritan inscriptions are unquestionably evidence of some sort of Samaritan community on Delos, Plassart's inscriptions are unlikely to be Jewish. Levine asked whether there were two separate synagogues (one Jewish, one Samaritan) or one synagogue serving both communities.[268] He went on to conclude that the location of the Delian Jewish community was in a "relatively isolated part of the island." In fact, GD 80, the *proseuchē* inscription, and the two Samaritan inscriptions were found in densely populated areas, each not more than 100 m or so from the others, abutting a heavily occupied residential area on the east side of the stadium. This area has not been fully excavated yet, but it is evident from Bruneau's plans, my own observations in October 2003, and by cursory examination of satellite views of the site from the *Google Earth* website (see fig. 14 below), that there are sub-surface and above-surface walls all over the area, so that there is practically no unused ground in that quarter. There was simply no room in the town and town-adjacent areas of this small island for isolation of any sort.

Figure 14 – Satellite image of GD 80 and its environs[269]

MONIKA TRÜMPER (2004)

According to Trümper, the "synagogue on Delos is the earliest known to date, either in the Diaspora or in Palestine," and that in the last thirty years a consensus has emerged that the building was an assembly hall for Jews or Samaritans.

---

[268] Levine, *The Ancient Synagogue*, 103.
[269] From Google Earth. Visible are GD 80, the gymnasium, the stadium district, and the residential area. [Matassa accessed this image before 2010. Attribution of the map via Google Earth at the time of editing is © 2018 CNES / Airbus. –Eds.]

Trümper argues that the building was a purpose-built synagogue from the time of its initial construction in the period before 88 BCE.[270]

Trümper discusses the inscribed stelae as found within the building. Four of them, she says, include vows to Θεω Υψιστω, a "God Most High." Although the identity of *theos hypsistos* and the nature of the cult are debatable, she says that it is generally agreed that this epithet was certainly, though not exclusively, used by Diaspora Jews (and also Samaritans) to refer to their god. These inscriptions are regarded as primary evidence for the identification of GD 80 as a synagogue.[271] Even though the two earliest votives are dated to the first century BCE, they do not testify with certainty to such an early Jewish or Samaritan use of the building because they, like the other three, are small and movable and might easily have been transported from one building to another. Therefore, the possibility that the two oldest votives were set up in another building and were transferred to GD 80 only in the last (fifth) phase of its use cannot be ruled out.[272] She goes on to discuss "three other Jewish and Samaritan inscriptions." One, she says, was discovered in a private house nearby, in the Quartier du stade, and the other two, on two stelae, were found in an unexcavated area some 90 m north of GD 80. She asks whether these inscriptions originally belonged to GD 80, but were displaced in a later period, or were they discovered in their original contexts, thus bearing witness to Jewish or Samaritan ownership of the respective buildings.[273]

Trümper also says, quite correctly, that the use of the benches and the throne are only datable to the last phase of GD 80 and hypothetical for all previous phases, and that this holds true for all other movable furniture found in the building.[274] She also discusses the carved palmette decoration on the back of the throne (which cannot be seen, because it was designed for use in a theatre or other public building where it would not have stood against a wall) and says that suggesting it is of a Jewish or Samaritan provenance is to be regarded with extreme caution. These palmettes, which appear on the marble throne, on antefixes, and on a marble lintel (of the third century CE), and rosettes, which decorate an inscribed votive offering, might be among the prominent motifs of later Jewish and Samaritan art, but they were certainly no less prominent in non-Jewish and non-Samaritan pagan art. According to Trümper, it is difficult to know whether the decorated objects were made for Jewish or Samaritan use, whether they were deliberately chosen out of a large stock of spoil material for Jewish or Samaritan reuse, or whether no special meaning could be assigned to their presence in this building because of the extensive diffusion of these motifs

---

[270] Monika Trümper, "The Oldest Original Synagogue Building in the Diaspora: The Delos Synagogue Reconsidered," *Hesperia* 73.4 (2004): 513–14.
[271] Trümper, "Oldest Original Synagogue," 569–70.
[272] Trümper, "Oldest Original Synagogue," 570.
[273] Trümper, "Oldest Original Synagogue," 571.
[274] Trümper, "Oldest Original Synagogue," 572.

throughout the ancient world.²⁷⁵ Trümper acknowledged that the identification of GD 80 as a synagogue was made primarily on the basis of the inscriptions and furnishings. She cited just three scholars, Bruneau, White, and Binder, as being sufficient to explain the history and use of GD 80 "because no substantially differing views have been presented in the literature."²⁷⁶ In a footnote she goes on to qualify this with the statement that the earlier opponents to the "synagogue" argument (Mazur and Sukenik) "can be ignored here."²⁷⁷

Trümper's article is largely a discussion of the architectural arrangement of GD 80, as taken from Bruneau's (not Plassart's) excavation reports, and there is much in it with which I agree. Her discussion of the architecture of the structure, and the limitations of the possibility of making identifications based on decorative embellishments are of particular use.

However, ultimately, because of her dismissal of any opposing opinions as irrelevant, Trümper is drawn into a circular argument of her own making, whereby she cannot acknowledge the full force of the Mazur's argument against the identification of GD 80 as a synagogue, and is hindered in her view by not having read Mazur's 1935 article.²⁷⁸

Moreover, there are a number of errors in Trümper's analysis. She cites, for example, the *four* inscriptions found in GD 80 that bear the name *theos hypsistos*. She is incorrect in this detail: only three of the inscriptions bear the epithet *theos hypsistos* (IDs 2328, 2330, and 2331). One of the inscriptions bears only the epithet *hypsistos* (ID 2332). She goes on to say that the use of this epithet is still debated, although it is now generally agreed that it was used (although not exclusively) "by Diaspora Jews (and also Samaritans) to refer to their god."²⁷⁹ This may well be the case from about the middle of the first century CE for the use of the epithet *theos hypsistos*, but it is by no means certain in the first century BCE or earlier—the period to which Trümper refers. By using later evidence to support earlier data without any corroboration she creates yet another circular and potentially misleading argument.

Trümper goes on to make another error, saying that there is an ongoing discussion about the *three other* Jewish and Samaritan inscriptions: "One was discovered in a private house nearby, in the *Quartier du stade*, and the other two, on stelae, were found in an unexcavated area some 90 m north of GD 80."²⁸⁰ Here

---

²⁷⁵ Trümper, "Oldest Original Synagogue," 573–74.
²⁷⁶ Trümper, "Oldest Original Synagogue," 569.
²⁷⁷ Trümper, "Oldest Original Synagogue," 569, n. 121.
²⁷⁸ Trümper, "Oldest Original Synagogue," 519, n. 17, says that she had no access to Mazur's "book." I had no difficulty in obtaining a photocopy (of what is actually a short article) from the École française d'Athènes while I was staying in Athens in 2003 before travelling south to Delos, as they hold it in their library.
²⁷⁹ Trümper, "Oldest Original Synagogue," 569.
²⁸⁰ Trümper, "Oldest Original Synagogue," 571.

she has confused two things. The two Samaritan stelae to which she alludes were discovered in 1979 by Philippe Fraisse of the École française d'Athènes (see the section above on inscriptions). However, the *third* inscription to which she refers is the original *proseuchē* inscription that Plassart found back in 1912 (ID 2329), which was indeed found in the stadium district, in Habitation IIA of GD 79 (see section on inscriptions, above) and to which she refers separately and earlier in her article. Thus, she has accidentally duplicated a piece of evidence and treated it as though its existence supports her argument that it and the Samaritan inscriptions may have originated in GD 80.

There are a number of other claims made by Trümper to which I must also refer. One is that a niche in the wall of room A postdates the construction of the wall and is "rather crudely made" (see fig. 15 below).[281]

Figure 15 – The niche in GD 80 (and other niches on Delos)

The GD 80 niche (and the other niches) clearly do not postdate the construction of the wall, but are instead an integral part of its construction. Trümper suggests the niche could have been used to contain lamps.[282] These niches could indeed have been used, as Trümper suggests, for placing lamps to light building interiors. It is also possible that they were shrines of some sort, as

---

[281] Trümper, "Oldest Original Synagogue," 584–85.
[282] Trümper, "Oldest Original Synagogue," 585.

were those recorded by Colin Renfrew during his extensive excavations on Phylakopi.[283]

Trümper also says that the stelae on which the inscriptions were found resemble "altar incense burners," and were probably used in the "synagogue" on Delos, a claim, for which, again, there is no evidence whatsoever.[284] Trümper cites Anders Runesson here as support for this argument, but Runesson does not offer any support for this specific contention, and indeed his comments on meal and incense offerings relate only to the petition to restore the Jewish Temple at Elephantine some time before its ultimate abandonment, and not to any purported synagogue usage, then or later.[285]

CONCLUSIONS

Because we know so very little about early synagogues, it is important to proceed carefully with the available evidence and not to reach for inherently teleological solutions to explain that for which we do not yet have answers. The problem with the foregoing and other interpretations of the structure, identification, and internal furnishings of GD 80 is that they are predicated on the pre-existing belief, following Plassart, that GD 80 is a synagogue. They are not based on the physical, literary, or epigraphic evidence. The argument, for instance, that the Samaritan inscriptions provide *additional* proof that GD 80 was a synagogue is spurious since it is clear from all the evidence that the initial identification of GD 80 as a synagogue was made on the basis of the tenuous association of two inscriptions by Plassart, and that *that* initial association is clearly not supported by the evidence.

Plassart's identification of GD 80 as a synagogue seems to have given rise to an historical distortion in the chronology of the development of synagogues in the diaspora. Indeed, some scholars have dated the "Delian synagogue" not even to the last phase of the building (when the benches were added), but to its Hellenistic origins in the third century BCE, and all on the basis of the first inscription that Plassart discovered 90 m north of GD 80.

The question to ask must surely be, if Plassart had not originally associated the inscriptions from GD 79 and GD 80, whether such an identification could ever have been made. The answer to that question is clearly "no," such an identification of GD 80 as a synagogue on such tenuous material would be deemed implausible. It is safe to say that while there is nothing that would exclude GD 80 from being

---

[283] Colin Renfrew, *The Archaeology of Cult: The Sanctuary at Phylakopi* (Athens: the British School of Archaeology at Athens; London: Thames & Hudson, 1985), 11–12 and plate 12b.
[284] Trümper, "Oldest Original Synagogue," 585.
[285] Runesson, "Origins of the Synagogue," 437.

a synagogue, there is not one piece of evidence that would suggest that it actually *was* a synagogue.

All that can be said is that there were Jews or Samaritans (or both) on Delos from some time in the first (or possibly second) century BCE, and that they were prevented from following their traditional customs for an unknown period of time during the first century BCE. While it is possible that there was a synagogue (Samaritan or Jewish, or both) on Delos, there is as yet no evidence that it has been found. Because of the restrictions on the traditional practices of some cults and associations, including the Jews, in the first century BCE, it is also possible that if Jews assembled for religious purposes, they did so in private dwellings, not in cultic establishments, in which case they would have remained hidden and unidentifiable. Moreover, the letter preserved in Josephus (*A.J.* 14.213–216) relating to the Jews being forbidden to follow their religious traditions and customs is dated to precisely the time that it is argued GD 80 functioned as a synagogue, that is, to the middle of the first century BCE.

As already stated, the issue of physical evidence is complicated because in this period it is not certain that we should be looking for synagogues, since religious structures are bound to be of an ambiguous nature if that worship was forbidden by local law. An obvious example would be that when Christians were being persecuted under Roman rule there were no purpose-built Christian churches or basilicas. Private houses, bath houses, crypts, and even catacombs were used as meeting places, and overt architectural statements of identity only emerged when the political climate of religious tolerance made it safe for them to develop.

All in all, it is impossible to identify GD 80 as a synagogue on the available evidence. It is furthermore impossible to identify any other structure on the island as a synagogue. It is also clear that, other than the two Samaritan (Israelite) inscriptions, nothing specifically pertaining to Jews or Samaritans has been found on the island. It is also clear that the names *Lysimachus* and *Agathoklēs* are not indicators of Jewishness on the island and appear elsewhere in very specifically non-Jewish contexts on the island. The only names associated with a Jewish or Samaritan context on Delos are those of Jason of Knossos and Artemidoros of Heraclea, both apparently from Crete. And again, we do not know if these were Samaritan benefactors, or pagan donors or patrons.

We must conclude, therefore, that the vexed question of the existence of a synagogue on Delos remains open, and that we must hope for specifically Jewish and/or *more* Samaritan material to be found to help with any potential identification.

3
JERICHO

Figure 16 - View over Hasmonaean/Herodian Jericho (looking north)

INTRODUCTION

During the course of excavations at the Hasmonaean and Herodian palace estates near Jericho in 1998, Ehud Netzer of the Hebrew University at Jerusalem identified a courtyard building in the north-eastern section of the estate as a Hasmonaean period synagogue. The building was identified on the basis of its physical layout, which is a Hellenistic period villa built around an internal courtyard. The identification, in the main, relies on the shape and construction of the villa along with some specific architectural features, such as an assembly space, a triclinium, and a niche, all of which will be discussed below. Looking at the data relating to the site, it is clear that there is no evidence to support the identification, and, in this case, it is possible to show how the identification is specifically mistaken. It also must be noted here that the ancient sources relating to the Hasmonaean period are particularly scant and deal with the date and balsam plantations on the estate and not the occupants of the palaces, much less with the

80 INVENTION OF THE FIRST-CENTURY SYNAGOGUE

political, economic, social, and/or religious dimensions thereof. Moreover, the building which is the subject of this chapter, the courtyard house, was destroyed in an earthquake in 31 BCE, and Herod the Great built over the ruins, never reconstructing the destroyed building.

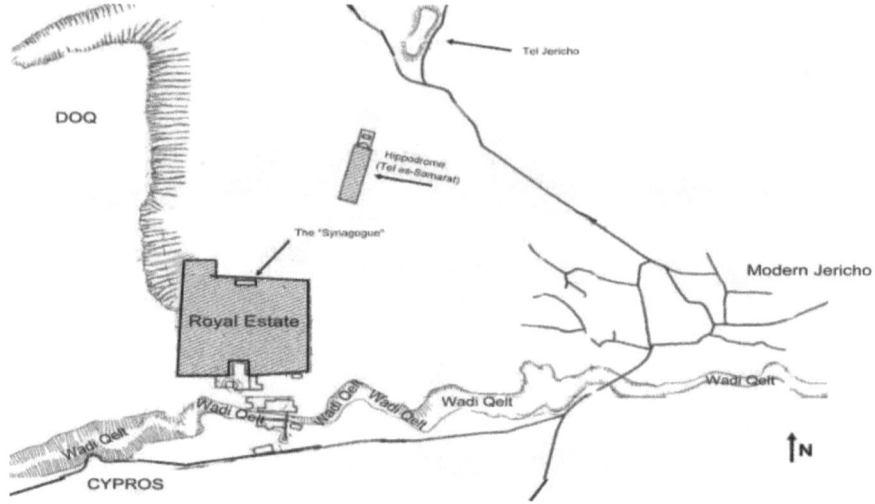

Figure 17 – Hasmonaean / Herodian Jericho (context and locations)

It is possible that the Hasmonaean royal estate began to be constructed as early as the mid-second century BCE, but this is uncertain.[286] Even accepting a later date for its construction, we do not know which of the Hasmonaeans built the estate, precisely when, or under what circumstances it was built, although construction is tentatively attributed by the excavators approximately to the reigns of Alexander Jannaeus (106–76 BCE) and his widow Alexandra (76–67 BCE).[287] Nor do we have any idea what, if anything, occupied the site before the Hasmonaeans built on it although, logically, it must have been occupied because the area of the estate is an oasis.

---

[286] [Inna Pommerantz, unattributed], *Excavations and Surveys in Israel 1982*, Volume 1 (Jerusalem: Israel Department of Antiquities and Museums, 1984), 45 (English Edition of *Hadashot Arkheologiyot*, Archaeological Newsletter of the Israel Department of Antiquities and Museums, Numbers 78–81, Jerusalem, 1982).

[287] [Pommerantz], *Excavations and Surveys in Israel 1*, 45.

History of Hasmonaean/Herodian Jericho

Even though little is directly known about the Hasmonaean/Herodian estates at Jericho, it may be possible to surmise a little of the history of occupation of the area by reference to the nearby site of Tel Jericho. Tel Jericho is one of the oldest continuously inhabited cities in the world, and the remains of some twenty successive settlements dating back to around 9000 BCE have been excavated on that site. Tel Jericho sits barely 2 km north-east of the Hasmonaean/Herodian palace site (see fig. 17 above).

The first archaeological explorations of Tel Jericho were made by Charles Warren of the British Royal Engineers in 1868. Following this, two German archaeologists, Carl Watzinger and Ernest Sellin, conducted excavations at Tel es-Sultan (Tel Jericho) and Tulul Abu el-Alayiq (Hasmonaean/Herodian Jericho) from 1907 to 1909 and in 1911.[288] From 1952–1958, Kathleen Kenyon's excavations provided a flood of information, and she was able to set out a chronology of Tel Jericho through its entire history.[289]

In terms of the local population, we know that, after the Babylonian exile, Tel Jericho was abandoned, but it is thought that there was a settlement somewhere nearby, because, of the people who returned with the biblical Ezra to Judaea after the Babylonian exile, three hundred and forty-five men (and their families, servants, slaves, etc.) returned to the Jericho area (Ezra 2.34).[290]

Despite these shadows of earlier Persian period occupation, there are few monumental remains dating to this period.[291] This scarcity is sometimes attributed to a widespread destruction at the end of the First Temple period (although this explanation is by no means universally accepted).[292] In any event, the scarcity of monumental remains probably relates as much to local construction methods and materials used (mud brick and wood), as to any specific destruction event or series of events.

There are quite significant gaps in what we know of Jericho from the Persian period through the Hellenistic and Roman periods. However, Tel Jericho appears

---

[288] Ernst Sellin and Carl Watzinger, *Jericho die Ergebnisse der Ausgrabungen* (1913; repr. Osnabrück: Zeller, 1973), 58; Carl Watzinger, "Zur Chronologie der Schichten von Jericho," *ZDMG* 80 (1926): 131–36.

[289] Kathleen Kenyon, *Digging Up Jericho* (London: Benn, 1957); Kathleen Kenyon, *The Bible and Recent Archaeology* (Atlanta: John Knox Press, 1987); Kathleen Kenyon, *Excavations at Jericho*, 5 vols. (London: British School of Archaeology in Jerusalem, 1960–1983). Kenyon was Director of the British School of Archaeology at Jerusalem at that time (now the Kenyon Research Institute in Sheikh Jarrah in East Jerusalem).

[290] Ephraim Stern, *Material Culture of the Land of the Bible in the Persian Period 538–332 BC* (Warminster: Aris & Phillips; Jerusalem: Israel Exploration Society, 1982), 38.

[291] Stern, *Material Culture*, 47.

[292] Stern, *Material Culture*, 47.

to have been fortified during the Hellenistic period (1 Macc 9:50). During the Roman conquest of Judaea and after he conquered Jerusalem, the Roman general Pompey the Great undertook to "cleanse Judaea of the haunts of robbers and the treasure-holds of the tyrants," two of which were along the route leading to Jericho (Strabo, *Geogr.* 16.2.40). Under Roman rule, Gabinius made Jericho one of the five administrative centres of Palestine (Josephus, *B.J.* 1.170).

The modern Arab name of the Hasmonaean/Herodian palace site is *Tulul Abu el-Alayiq*.[293] The site is located in the western area of the Jericho plain, spanning both sides of the Wadi Qelt not far from the Qelt source in the hills to the north. It lies some 7 km west of the River Jordan, 10 km north of the Dead Sea, 1.5 km west of the modern city of Jericho, 2 km south of Tel Jericho, and about 27 km east-north-east of Jerusalem. The site encompasses palatial, residential, administrative, and storage buildings, aqueducts, pools, water installations, balsam and date plantations, and gardens (see figs. 16 and 17 above).

The area around Jericho is balmy and generally dry all year round, with average summer temperatures of 32–39° C and average winter temperatures of 20–23°. The rainfall is between 50 mm and 200 mm, falling almost entirely between October and April in short heavy showers during which the desert soil can only absorb a limited amount of water, which results in sudden (and often dangerous) wadi floods.[294] As a result of the unpredictability of the rain, ancient Jericho relied on aqueducts, cisterns, wells, and springs for its water supply, and there was and still is a plentiful water supply from the nearby springs at Ain es-Sultan (Elisha's Spring: 2 Kgs 2:19–22), Ain Duq, Ain Nu'eima, the three springs of Wadi Qelt, and the springs of Auja el-Tahta and Na'aran in the hills just northwest of the Hasmonaean/Herodian site.[295]

Because of its location, we may surmise that the royal estate was built to take advantage of the local climate, the nearby water resources, and the agricultural conditions on the oasis. And whilst we do not know who originally built the estate, we do know a little about the agricultural produce of the estate, because Jericho was a centre for the production of balsam and dates. From the scale of the palatial estate, the variety of dates, and the valuable balsam produced there, along with the quality of the architectural decoration of the site as a whole, it is possible to say that it was a place of some commercial importance both to the Hasmonaeans and, later, to the Herodians.[296]

---

[293] The Arabic plural of *Tel*. The site is built over two hillocks.

[294] Günter Garbrecht and Yehuda Peleg, "The Water Supply of the Desert Fortresses in the Jordan Valley," *BA* 57.3 (1994): 161–62.

[295] Ehud Netzer, *The Architecture of Herod, the Great Builder* (Tübingen: Mohr Siebeck, 2006), 43; G.W. Bromiley et al., eds., *The International Standard Bible Encyclopedia* (Grand Rapids: Eerdmans, 1982), 2:995; Ephraim Stern, ed., "Jericho," *NEAEHL* (Jerusalem: Israel Exploration Society, 1993), 2:683.

[296] See Strabo 16.2.41 (trans. H. L. Jones, LCL).

Adding to the problem of the paucity of historiographic material, the site itself is difficult to access. It is located in the Palestinian territories 1.5 km west of the modern town of Jericho. Israelis have not been permitted to visit the site since the Intifada of 2000, and foreign schools do not excavate there. Getting through the border checks (both Israeli and Palestinian) can be tense. The site is not on the tourist trail and few locals know it exists. Tourists who do venture into the area are taken to see nearby Tel Jericho and the Arabic site of Hisham's Palace (Khirbet al-Mafjar), but not Hasmonaean/Herodian Jericho. Moreover, the site is not actively protected by the Palestinian Authority, and Bedouins camp on the site.[297] Bedouin families farm the arable land of the oasis and graze goats, which means visitors have to walk through their fields to get to the site. The site is directly overlooked by the Israeli military posts at Cypros and Doq high in the hills above (see figs. 16 and 17 above). All of this combines to make visiting the site something of an unsettling experience.[298]

THE ANCIENT SOURCES

The most informative of the ancient references available to us are from Strabo, Pliny the Elder, and Josephus, and these relate to the geography and agricultural produce of the area. As already stated, the ancient references to Jericho are few and far between, and those that do refer specifically to the Hasmonaean estate are even fewer. None refer to religious activity and none to the existence of a synagogue anywhere on the site.

In Strabo, we find a description of the area and the balsam and dates which were grown there.

> Hiericus is a plain surrounded by a kind of mountainous country, which, in a way, slopes towards it like a theatre. Here is the Phoenicon,[299] which is mixed also with other kinds of cultivated and fruitful trees, though it consists mostly of palm trees; it is one hundred stadia in length, and is everywhere watered with streams

---

[297] Among the Bedouin who live on the site is the same family—though a different generation—mentioned in Egon H. E. Lass's memoir *The Seasons of Tulul* ([No location]: Xlibris, 2005). *Seasons* is a memoir of the period between January 1974 and April 1976 during which Lass, one of the archaeologists working on the excavation of Hasmonaean/Herodian Jericho, lived alongside and befriended a Bedouin family camped at the Wadi Qelt.

[298] I visited and photographed the site four times: the first just before the Intifada of 2000, the second in 2004, the third in 2006, and most recently in February 2009. Each time I visited, less of the archaeology was visible. There is now a Bedouin family camped on top of the main Na'aran aqueduct that runs past the building complex with which this chapter is concerned, and the aqueduct has partially collapsed as a result.

[299] Palm grove.

and full of dwellings. Here are also the palace[300] and the balsam park. The balsam is of the shrub kind, resembling Cytisus[301] and terminthus,[302] and has a spicy flavour. The people make incisions in the bark and catch the juice in vessels. This juice is a glutinous, milk white substance; and when it is put up in small quantities it solidifies; and it is remarkable for its cure of headache and of incipient cataracts and of dimness of sight. Accordingly, it is costly; and also for the reason that it is produced nowhere else. Such is also the case with the Phoenicon, which alone has the caryotic palm,[303] excepting the Babylonian and that beyond Babylonia towards the east. Accordingly, the revenue derived from it is great. And they use the xylobalsam[304] as spice. (Strabo, *Geogr.* 16.2.41)

Strabo's text seems to refer to Hasmonaean/Herodian Jericho and to the plantations and palaces on the royal estate, and it gives us some insight into how the economy of the area must have functioned, given that the balsam produced there apparently grew nowhere else.

Pliny the Elder refers only to the administrative district of Jericho and to the palm groves and numerous water sources there:

Beyond Idumaea and Samaria stretches the wide expanse of Judaea. The part of Judaea adjoining Syria is called Galilee, and that next to Arabia and Egypt Peraea. Peraea is covered with rugged mountains, and is separated from the other parts of Judaea by the river Jordan. The rest of Judaea is divided into ten Local Government Areas in the following order: the district of Jericho, which has numerous palm-groves and springs of water, and those of Emmaus, Lydda, Joppa, Accrabim, Jufna, Timnath-Serah, Beth-lebaoth, the Hills, the district that formerly contained Jerusalem, by far the most famous city of the East and not of Judaea only, and Herodium with the celebrated town of the same name. (Pliny the Elder, *Nat.* 5.15.70)[305]

Pliny's text does not specifically mention Hasmonaean/Herodian Jericho, but it does mention the plantations and the numerous water sources. Our next source is Josephus, who wrote a great deal about the palace estates in the time of the Hasmonaeans and Herod and who we can assume visited the site (because his descriptions of the buildings and layout are so detailed), but he does not mention

---

[300] Herod's palace.

[301] *Medicago Arborea*. The Jericho balsam was a plant with a resinous secretion whose effects were healing and/or soothing. We cannot identify the exact plant from which ancient balsam was produced, but we do at least know that Jericho was a centre for its production.

[302] The terebinth tree, *pistacia terebinthus*, from which turpentine is extracted and which also produces edible nuts.

[303] *Palma caryota*, with a walnut-like fruit.

[304] The liquid that oozes from the cut branches of the plant.

[305] Trans. H. Rackham, LCL.

a synagogue (or the lack of one). He too makes particular reference to the palm trees and to the balsam produced in the area:

> Now when Pompey had pitched his camp at Jericho (where the palm tree grows), and that balsam which is an ointment of all the most precious, which, upon any incision made in the wood with a sharp stone, distils out thence like a juice) [...] (Josephus, *A.J.* 14.54)

While Josephus's text does not directly refer to the Hasmonaean/Herodian estates, it seems clear that he is discussing them when he discusses Cleopatra's desire to control their agricultural produce during the Herodian period:

> When Cleopatra had obtained thus much, and had accompanied Antony in his expedition to Armenia, as far as Euphrates, she returned back, and came to Apamea and Damascus, and passed on to Judaea; where Herod met her, and farmed of her parts of Arabia, and those revenues that came to her from the region about Jericho. This country bears that balsam, which is the most precious drug that is there, and grows there alone. The place bears also excellent palm trees, both many in number, and those excellent in their kind. (Josephus, *A.J.* 15.96)

The next Josephus text also refers to the royal estates, but only relates to the Herodian period, where it appears the economy remained reliant on the produce of the plantations:

> Indeed, this spring [at Jericho] irrigates a larger space of ground than all others, and passes within a plain of seventy furlongs long, and twenty broad; wherein it affords nourishment to those most excellent gardens that are thick set with trees. There are in it may sorts of date palms that are watered by it, different from each other in flavour and name; the better sort of them, when they are pressed under foot, yield an excellent kind of honey, not much inferior in sweetness to that of bees, which are also abundant in this region. Here, too grow the juicy balsam, which is the most precious of all fruits in that place, cypress trees also, and those that bear myrobalanus, so that he who would pronounce this place to be divine would not be mistaken, a spot in which the rarest and the most excellent plants are produced in abundance. (Josephus, *B.J.* 4.467–470)

Unfortunately, not one of the foregoing texts provide any assistance in terms of a discussion of the existence of a synagogue on the Hasmonaean palace estate. We are therefore left with nothing but archaeology through which to analyse the structure the excavators identified as a Hasmonaean period synagogue; that is, the courtyard house complex in the eastern sector of the estate. Because there is no corroborating textual or epigraphic material, the interpretation of the archaeological material is particularly important.

86   INVENTION OF THE FIRST-CENTURY SYNAGOGUE

THE EXCAVATION REPORTS

THE EXCAVATION REPORTS (PHASE 1)

The building identified as a synagogue is a courtyard house that forms part of a complex of buildings along the north-eastern section of the Hasmonaean estate. It belongs specifically to the Hasmonaean period, as it was destroyed by an earthquake in 31 BCE and never reconstructed or reused after that.

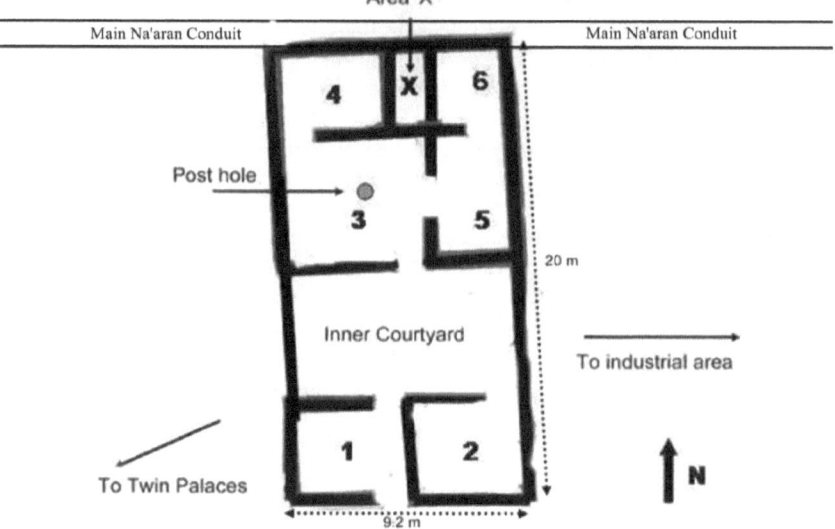

Figure 18 – The courtyard house (phase 1)

THE COURTYARD HOUSE (PHASE 1)

The courtyard house is located at the western end of a row of nine residential buildings. At the eastern end of this row of buildings, which stretches some 165 m, is an industrial area. To the southwest of the courtyard house is a large villa structure the excavators describe as twin palaces. To the west of the courtyard house complex is a large swimming pool complex and a garden. As the courtyard house complex is located between an industrial area and the twin palaces, it may have marked some sort of delineation between the industrial area to the east and the series of palace complexes to the west. The main water conduit from Na'aran runs east across the northern wall of the courtyard house.[306]

The courtyard house was the first phase of this building complex to be constructed. According to the excavators, it was built slightly off-axis to the plan of the neighbouring buildings abutting the industrial area to the east. It is more or less rectangular in shape and measures some 20 x 9.2 m. It comprises a central courtyard between rooms on the north and south and was built of local materials—that is, mud brick on top of rough stone foundations and rubble from the wadi.[307]

Throughout the entire Hasmonaean (and the Herodian) palace estates at Jericho, mud brick and fieldstones were used for construction and then plastered over so as to look more substantial and costly: a common economisation. This technique was used in many parts of the site, including the courtyard house referred to in this section.

While in use the courtyard house would have been indistinguishable from buildings constructed of solid masonry.[308] It is of a size that would suggest it was used by some official of the ruling household, be it an estate employee or a family member, and is of a type common throughout the Mediterranean area in the late Persian, Hellenistic, and early Roman periods.[309]

The floor plan of the first phase of the house reveals six rooms built around an internal courtyard (see fig. 18 above). The rooms are divided into two rooms to the south and four to the north. The entrance to the courtyard house is at the southern end of the building and leads into the courtyard from between the two

---

[306] Ehud Netzer, *Hasmonaean and Herodian Palaces at Jericho: Final Reports of the 1973–1987 Excavations* (Jerusalem: Israel Exploration Society; Institute of Archaeology, The Hebrew University of Jerusalem, 2004), 2:159.

[307] Netzer, *Hasmonaean and Herodian Palaces*, 2:160.

[308] As the excavator Ehud Netzer rightly and persuasively argues—in an unpublished article and in a conversation with me in Jerusalem in September of 2006—the building he identified as a synagogue would undoubtedly have provoked much more public attention had it been constructed of stone ashlars, even if it lacked mosaic floors, carved architectural features, and other decorative elements. The unpublished article, "A Synagogue in Jericho from the Hasmonaean Period," was emailed to me following my conversation with Prof. Netzer in September 2006, and very kindly translated from Hebrew to English by Dr. Orit Peleg of the Institute of Archaeology at the Hebrew University of Jerusalem.

[309] For general examples ses residential houses in Yizhar Hirschfeld, *The Palestinian Dwelling in the Roman-Byzantine Period* (Studium Biblicum Franciscanum, Collectio Minor 34; Jerusalem: Franciscan Printing Press; Israel Exploration Society, 1995); Nicholas Cahill, *Household and City Organization at Olynthus* (New Haven: Yale University Press, 2002), 125, 201, 231; the axonometric reconstruction of the Mason de la Colline on Delos and the Herdraum house at Ammotopos in Lisa C. Nevett, *House and Society in the Ancient Greek World* (Cambridge: Cambridge University Press, 1999), 24–25; the comparisons of courtyard houses in Thorikos in Bradley A. Ault and Lisa C. Nevett, eds., *Ancient Greek Houses and Households* (Philadelphia: University of Pennsylvania Press, 2005), 86.

southern rooms. Internally, the courtyard leads into the rooms of the northern part of the house.

As they are accessed only by one door, the rooms on the north side of the courtyard may have been part of the private quarters of whoever lived and worked in this building. The rooms on the south of the courtyard could have been reception rooms, office spaces, or for other use altogether. Indeed, their use need not have been fixed, as many elements used in the household would have been portable (desks, chairs, braziers, cooking equipment, etc.). Sleeping quarters would have been on upper floors and on the roof.

Water was easily accessible and the main aqueduct from the springs at Na'aran in the hills above the palace site runs beside and partly underneath the northernmost wall of the courtyard house for the entire width of the building.[310] The importance of this will become clear when we come to look at Phase 2 of the courtyard house, its water installations, and what Netzer has identified as a niche and possible *genizah*.[311]

THE ENTRANCE (ROOM 1). The entrance room is located at the southern end of the courtyard house and measures 4.4 m x 3.4 m. A doorway from the outside of the building leads through the entrance room into the central courtyard.[312] The floor of the entrance room was made up of beaten earth above wadi rubble. Underneath the floor of the entry room, in line with the doorway, there is a small water channel that comes from the Na'aran conduit.[313] This channel feeds part of a later water installation (see phase 2 below).

ROOM 2. Room 2 is located directly to the east of the entrance room. It measures some 3.65 m x 3.4 m. This room was accessed via the courtyard on the east side of the building. The floor consisted of the same material as that of the entrance room, that is, beaten earth above wadi fill.[314]

THE INTERNAL COURTYARD. The internal courtyard is located in the centre of the courtyard house, along its entire width, and situated between Rooms 1 and 2 on the south and Rooms 3 and 5 on the north. It measures 9.2 m x 5.1 m wide and was entered from the south via the entrance between Rooms 1 and 2. A doorway on the north of the courtyard provided access to Room 3, from which the other

---

[310] Netzer, *Hasmonaean and Herodian Palaces*, 2:184.
[311] Storage archive for sacred and important documents which have gone out of use but cannot be destroyed for religious reasons.
[312] Netzer, *Hasmonaean and Herodian Palaces*, 2:162.
[313] Netzer, *Hasmonaean and Herodian Palaces*, 2:162.
[314] Netzer, *Hasmonaean and Herodian Palaces*, 2:162.

rooms on the north could be reached.[315] The floor of the courtyard consisted of beaten earth.[316]

ROOM 3. Room 3 is the large southwestern room on the northern end of the building and measures 5.45 x 4.85 m. The room was accessible from the courtyard on the south via a doorway on its eastern side. There are two other doorways leading from Room 3 to other rooms in the northern part of the courtyard house; one on the east providing access to Rooms 5 and 6, and two on the north, both leading into Room 4 in the northwestern part of the house. The excavators thought this might have been a second courtyard.[317]

The floor was covered with a layer of mud brick debris which contained Hasmonaean pottery sherds, and it was made up of beaten earth over soil. Since the ground surface was not entirely horizontal here, wadi material was piled on top of it to form a level base for the floor. In the centre of the room there is evidence of what might have been a setting for a wooden column base. It consisted of red burnt clay and ash.[318]

It may be assumed that this was the location of a column or pillar to support a partially roofed section of the courtyard, as the placement of this post hole is directly analogous to a second/third-century CE insula in the lower part of the city of ancient Meiron, where we see a pillar base in the same place as the Jericho courtyard house posthole.[319]

However, posthole aside, the second/third-century CE insula at ancient Meiron is not the only analogue to the second/first-century BCE courtyard house at Hasmonaean/Herodian Jericho. There are other similar buildings, such as a third/fourth-century BCE house at Beth Yerah, a second century BCE house at Mount Gerizim, a third/second-century BCE house at Samaria-Sebaste, and countless others not listed here.[320]

This type of domestic building construction was used from as early as the beginning of the second millennium BCE and can be seen all over the Mediterranean and the ancient Near East.[321] These buildings are constructed around central courtyards because the Mediterranean climate enables extensive

---

[315] Netzer, *Hasmonaean and Herodian Palaces*, 2:162.
[316] Netzer, *Hasmonaean and Herodian Palaces*, 2:163.
[317] Netzer, *Hasmonaean and Herodian Palaces*, 2:164.
[318] Netzer, *Hasmonaean and Herodian Palaces*, 2:164.
[319] Eric M. Meyers, et al., *Excavations at Ancient Meiron, Upper Galilee, Israel 1971–2, 1974–5, 1977*, Meiron Excavation Project Volume III (Cambridge, MA: The American Schools of Oriental Research, 1981), 34–35 (the posthole is in the upper left of the plan).
[320] Meyers, et al., *Excavations*, 34–35. The posthole is in the upper left of the floor plan at fig. 18 above.
[321] Hirschfeld, *The Palestinian Dwelling*, 57.

use of outdoor space, and it means that various activities needed only be moved indoors during the rainy or cold season.³²²

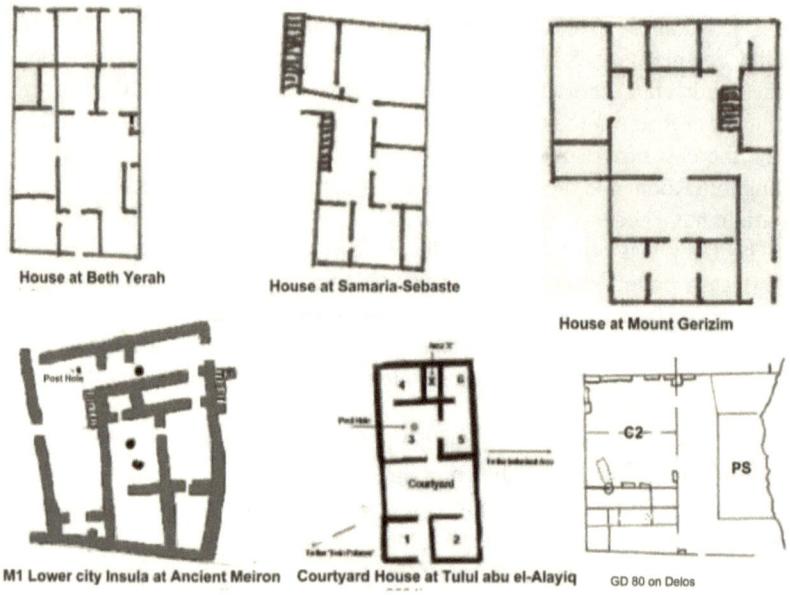

Figure 19 – Comparison of courtyard houses

ROOM 4. Room 4 of the Jericho courtyard house, located in the northwestern corner of the house, measured 4 x 3 m. Some mud brick was preserved on top of the fieldstone foundations of part of the eastern and western walls of this room. The room was originally entered from the south via two doorways but, at some point, the eastern door was eliminated.³²³ The floor consisted of beaten earth over soil. Some lime plaster remains on the south face of the northern wall of this room.³²⁴

ROOM 5. Room 5 is located to the east of Room 3 from which it is entered. It measures 4.8 x 2.75 m. In it, there is an internal doorway leading to another room (room 6) on the north. The floor consisted of beaten earth over virgin soil and

---

³²² Hirschfeld, *The Palestinian Dwelling*, 272.
³²³ Netzer, *Hasmonaean and Herodian Palaces*, 2:164.
³²⁴ Netzer, *Hasmonaean and Herodian Palaces*, 2:165.

covered with ash, above which was a layer of mud brick debris which contained Hasmonaean pottery sherds.[325]

ROOM 6. Room 6 is located in the north-eastern corner of the house, and measures 2.8 x 2.5 m. Some mud brick is preserved on part of its western wall. Entry to the room was via room 5. The floor of room 6 also consisted of beaten earth over virgin soil. A small installation consisting of a quarter-circle formed by a row of pebbles and containing ash was revealed in the north-eastern corner of the room. This may have served as a small fixed fireplace or oven.[326]

AREA X. Area X, a narrow space measuring 2.8 x 1.25 m in size, is located between rooms 4 and 6. No doorway was found here. The excavators argued that this space was entered via an opening located at a higher level in one of the walls.[327] However, it is more likely that this space represents the base of a stairway that accesses the upper storey of the house. This argument is supported by the fact that the floor in this area, when excavated, was some 32cm higher than that of the other rooms, suggesting it had been compacted to a degree sufficient to support the base of a stairway.[328] Indeed, a direct parallel to this can again be seen in the insula of the lower city of Meiron, where a stairway lays along the eastern wall of the internal courtyard and leads to the upper floor of the house (see fig. 19 above).[329]

In many ways, the insula at ancient Meiron corresponds to the layout of the courtyard house under discussion here. The centremost element of the insula has the same rectangular structure with an entryway, two rooms just inside, a central courtyard and then rooms leading off to the north, east, and west of the building. In the first phase of the Jericho courtyard house complex, the room marked "3" (in fig. 18 above) is similar to the internal courtyard in the insula in ancient Meiron, where there is a column post in the same place as in the corresponding room at Jericho.

Netzer suggests that the entire internal courtyard at Jericho was covered. As an analysis of the lower city insula at Meiron reveals, only a small portion of the courtyard was covered (see fig. 19 above).[330] This makes a great deal of sense in terms of utilisation of space and retention of views of the lower parts of the house and the courtyards (both the internal one and the porticoed one).[331] This applies to the Jericho courtyard house as much as it does to the insula at ancient Meiron.

---

[325] Netzer, *Hasmonaean and Herodian Palaces*, 2:164.
[326] Netzer, *Hasmonaean and Herodian Palaces*, 2:165.
[327] Netzer, *Hasmonaean and Herodian Palaces*, 2:165.
[328] Netzer, *Hasmonaean and Herodian Palaces*, 2:165.
[329] See also figs. 9 and 10 on Delos.
[330] Meyers et al., *Excavations*, 34–35.
[331] Meyers et al., *Excavations*, 34–35.

Moreover, from observation and from photographs of the site at Jericho, it appears that the entirety of the courtyard house complex has not been excavated, and that, in fact, there are at least two further ground floor rooms on the east side of the original building. Again, this is directly analogous to the lower city insula at ancient Meiron and elsewhere (see examples at fig. 19 above), and I would suggest that at least the ground floor structure of the Hasmonaean courtyard house and the insula in the lower city of ancient Meiron, and the other examples given, share many commonalities. The excavators say that the courtyard house is not built along the same axis as the residential row to the east.[332] However, if I am correct about the ground floor layout, and the unexcavated walls, then the easternmost wall abuts the residential area precisely, thus utilising the available space fully, as with the insula at Meiron.

THE EXCAVATION REPORTS (PHASE 2)

In the second phase of the building, according to the excavation reports, what the excavators describe as an assembly hall (measuring 16 x 11.5 m) was added along the western wall of the original courtyard house, with some reconstruction taking place to accommodate those changes. This included opening up two doorways in the western wall of the courtyard house: one leading to the new space, and one leading into the chambers on the south.

THE COURTYARD HOUSE (PHASE 2). What the excavators describe as an assembly hall is a simple peristyle courtyard and is part of an architectural tradition which reflects Graeco-Roman influences.[333] That this style is seen in the building programmes of the Hasmonaeans is interesting, but should not trouble us, as it is a common feature of Hellenistic and Roman houses throughout the Mediterranean region.

---

[332] Netzer, *Hasmonaean and Herodian Palaces*, 2:160.
[333] Hirschfeld, *Palestinian Dwelling*, 85–86.

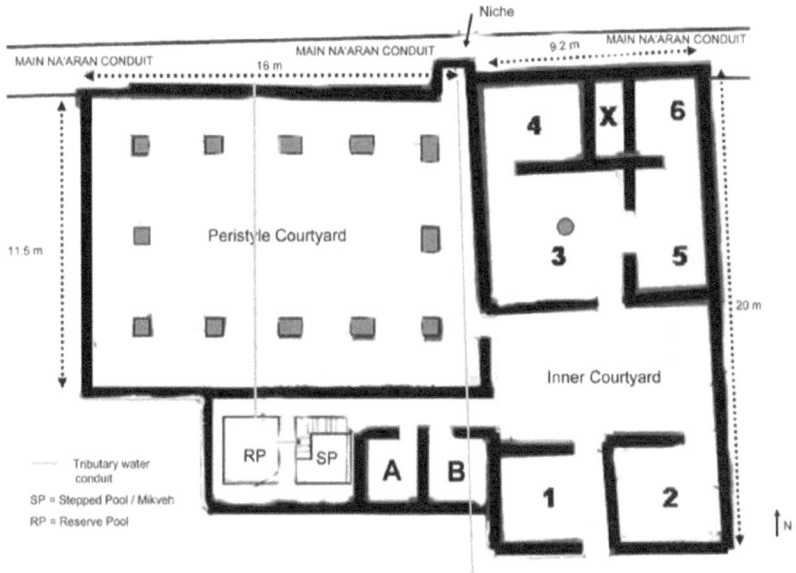

Figure 20 – The courtyard house (phase 2)

The excavator, Netzer, argues that what he describes as the assembly space could not be a second courtyard, because other courtyards in the estate had a visual connection with the buildings with which they are connected.[334] In fact, a second, usually larger and more formal, peristyle courtyard is a standard component of a courtyard house of this type in the Hellenistic period.[335] The visual connection the excavator refers to would have certainly existed in the view from the upper floor(s) of the original courtyard house to the peristyle courtyard below. Netzer contradicts his own argument on line-of-sight when he argues that, in a later phase of the building, one of the columns between the courtyard and the triclinium was moved to provide a line of sight from the triclinium to the courtyard. Thus, there were actually *three* lines of visual connection to this second courtyard: the first from the upper floors of the original courtyard house, the second from the triclinium, and the third from the entrance of the original courtyard house into the peristyle courtyard (see fig. 20 above).

The excavator argues that the so-called assembly hall was originally covered because the floor consisted of beaten earth, which is normally used in covered rooms.[336] However, there is a practical problem with his thesis, as covering the

---

[334] Netzer, *Hasmonaean and Herodian Palaces*, 2:184.
[335] Boardman, Griffin, and Murray, *Greece and the Hellenistic World*, 388.
[336] Netzer, *Hasmonaean and Herodian Palaces*, 2:185.

peristyle courtyard would have removed the light source for most of the rest of the ground floor of the original courtyard house.[337] The ground floor rooms looking onto both of the courtyards would have had windows, so that any light blockage (e.g., by roofing the space) would cut off that light source.[338] Moreover, the use of beaten earth (pulverised with hoes and rakes) had another purpose. It reduced moisture evaporation from parched soil and helped drainage so that pooling of rainwater would have been minimised.[339]

The excavators also argue that it was the custom to have a peristyle courtyard at a slightly lower level in order to drain rainwater, and that therefore the assembly hall could not be a courtyard.[340] However, while in the Hellenistic period double-courtyard houses sometimes had one of the courtyards built at a slightly lower level, this was designed to enhance the view and entrance into the house proper.[341] The fact that the peristyle courtyard of this building is at the same level as the rest of the complex is irrelevant to drainage, but it adds substance to the line-of-sight argument.

Another of the excavators' contentions about the assembly hall is that it was covered and had clerestory windows because, otherwise, there is no explanation for the use of the massive pillars in its construction.[342] The pillars themselves do not survive. However, the bases on which they stood survive, and these are rectangular in shape and vary in diameter, averaging some 85 x 70 cm.[343] The pillar bases sit on top of the remains of a stylobate and the best preserved base stands only 50 cm high. The fact that the bases are not of a uniform size lends further credence to the argument that they were not designed to support a full roof. Moreover, as with other structural elements on the estates, the bases are constructed of local field stones bonded with mud and were probably plastered over to make them look like stone (see fig. 21 below). The upper parts of the pillars that do not survive were most likely mud brick (made in the industrial area to the east). They were likely to have been of a narrower gauge than the bases and would have been plastered and painted to look like solid masonry.

Thus, the pillars referred to by the excavator were in no way massive and were there to support a colonnade which would have been no higher than the external walls of the courtyard. The colonnade was designed to be a decorative feature of such courtyards and to provide some shade in the glaring summer heat and some protection from the winter rain, whilst simultaneously leaving the

---

[337] This is illustrated in fig. 9, the photograph of the House of the Hermes on Delos in the previous chapter. There is building *around* the courtyard, but it is not covered.
[338] Nevett, *House and Society*, 24–25.
[339] Richard J. Forbes, *Studies in Ancient Technology* (2nd ed.; Leiden: Brill, 1965), 2:43–44.
[340] Netzer, "A Synagogue in Jericho," unpublished.
[341] Boardman, Griffin, and Murray, *Greece and the Hellenistic World*, 388.
[342] Netzer, "A Synagogue in Jericho," unpublished.
[343] Netzer, *Hasmonaean and Herodian Palaces*, 2:166–67.

central area open to the elements and to line of sight. Covering a walled courtyard and building clerestory windows (with the consequent bulking out of the courtyard house complex) is highly unlikely and would be a redundant design feature. Not only would a covered courtyard have been aesthetically unappealing and out of character for this type of building,[344] but it would also have been unnecessary and, more importantly, would have interfered with light penetration into the ground floor of the house. There would have been no external windows looking out onto the external street, whereas there would have been windows looking into the courtyard and these would have been thereby rendered obsolete.

The excavators say that the assembly hall is not in proportion to the size of the courtyard house, and that this adds support to the argument that the building is a synagogue, as there is otherwise no reason for the scale of the assembly/reception hall.[345] They also say that the assembly hall is missing a proper residential building which would justify a reception hall on this scale and that the courtyard house itself is not a residence for this hall.[346] However, as is clear from the parallel examples given, both in Israel and Greece, not only is the courtyard house entirely in proportion to the peristyle courtyard, but was also at least a two-storey building.[347] And, as already stated, there were probably at least two more rooms on the ground floor of the eastern side of the house, as in the parallels at Meiron and elsewhere. The original courtyard house was therefore wider and more capacious than the excavation reports would suggest. The walls of the easternmost end of the building would then abut, at a slight angle, the residential buildings to the east. There can be no question that the courtyard house is the residence attached to the peristyle court. This is a normal configuration, as is seen from the floor plan and the examples of other courtyard houses given above.

The excavation reports describe the peristyle courtyard as a nave surrounded by aisles with square pillars along all four sides. They further argue that the aisles are situated about 40 cm higher than the nave, and that this 40 cm difference enabled the supportive walls that were built between the pillars and separated the nave from the aisles to be used as benches, which then allowed about 150 people to sit in the hall.[348]

---

[344] Cahill, *Household and City Organization*; Nevett, *House and Society*; Ault and Nevett, *Ancient Greek Houses and Households*; Hirschfeld, *Palestinian Dwelling*; Meyers et al., *Excavations*.
[345] Netzer, *Hasmonaean and Herodian Palaces*, 2:186.
[346] Netzer, *Hasmonaean and Herodian Palaces*, 2:186, n. 67.
[347] Cahill, *Household and City Organization*; Nevett, *House and Society*; Ault and Nevett, *Ancient Greek Houses and Households*; Hirschfeld, *Palestinian Dwelling*; Meyers et al., *Excavations*.
[348] Netzer, *Hasmonaean and Herodian Palaces*, 2:165–66.

There is, however, no evidence of benches having been in place; there are certainly no visible remains of such. The only raised areas are the platforms on which the pillar bases stand, and these simply encircle the courtyard (see fig. 21 below). There is no regular differentiation in floor levels between what Netzer called the nave and the aisles. The few irregular differences in the ground level can be accounted for by soil erosion, earthquake damage, and the excavation process itself. This is a peristyle courtyard and is, like the design of the original courtyard house itself, a fairly standard feature of houses of this type.[349]

Figure 21 – The peristyle courtyard (looking east)[350]

Of course, even if the structure was a courtyard and not an assembly hall, this would not preclude its use as a synagogue. There is no question that the layout of the courtyard could easily have been used for the reading of the Torah to people gathered there. But, equally, any sufficient space—exterior or interior—could serve this purpose.

Finally, Netzer finally sets up a straw man argument, positing his position against a group of unrealistic alternatives. He asks what the space could possibly have been used for if not as a meeting place and a place for receptions and

---

[349] Boardman, Griffin, and Murray, *Greece and the Hellenistic World*, 388.
[350] Taken in February 2009, this photograph also shows a Bedouin habitat sitting on top of the main Na'aran conduit along the northern wall of the original courtyard house complex. The line cutting through the middle of the courtyard is one of the Na'aran conduit's tributaries and leads from the main conduit south and into the water installations, which are just visible on the right of the photograph. The courtyard house lies beyond the peristyle, just beneath the caravan. The wall at the bottom of the photograph is part of a later Herodian palace complex built over the earthquake-damaged Hasmonaean structure.

banquets. He says that it was unlikely to have been used for industrial activity, unlikely to have been a storage facility, and unlikely to have been a place for housing animals, and that therefore it must have been the assembly hall of a synagogue.[351]

Netzer is clearly correct that this space was not used for industrial activity, for storage, or for animals, but this argument ignores and avoids the conclusion that it was a straightforward peristyle courtyard for use by the occupants of and visitors to the courtyard house complex. Here, in this courtyard house complex, a peristyle courtyard is merely a peristyle courtyard.

THE AQUEDUCTS OF HASMONAEAN/HERODIAN JERICHO

Providing the supply of water to the palace estates were extensive Hasmonaean and Herodian aqueducts. Excavations conducted from 1973 through 1981 near where the Wadi Qelt flows into the western plains of Jericho found remains of extensive water systems linked with the Hasmonaean estate.[352] Sections of these aqueducts are still visible along the surface near the western edge of the Jericho plain and were first surveyed by the British Survey of Palestine in the 1880s.[353]

The excavations of the 1970s and 1980s revealed that there were two separate systems drawing water from the springs in the Wadi Qelt and from the springs at Na'aran and Ain el-Auja.[354] These systems brought the water directly from the source to the palace estates using a system of channels and sluice gates set along the conduits to control flow to different areas.[355] A sluice gate (on an ancient aqueduct) is normally just a wooden, stone, or metal plate which slides into grooves in the sides of the channel and is operated manually. Sluice gates were used to regulate the flow of water. Raising a sluice gate allows water to flow under it, and the level of the sluice gate can be adjusted to control the volume and speed of the water passing through the aqueduct. While the excavators found stones on either side of some conduit openings to facilitate sluice gates in the Hasmonaean estate, they did not find any built-in grooves for them, which suggests that the

---

[351] Netzer, *Hasmonaean and Herodian Palaces*, 2:187.
[352] Ehud Netzer and Günter Garbrecht, "Water Channels and a Royal Estate of the Late Hellenistic Period in Jericho's Western Plains," in *The Aqueducts of Israel* (Journal of Roman Archaeology Supplementary Series 46; ed. David Amit, Joseph Patrich, and Yizhar Hirshfeld; Portsmouth, RI: 2002), 367.
[353] Netzer and Garbrecht, "Water Channels," 367, n. 3; C. R. Conder and Horatio Herbert Kitchener, *The Survey of Western Palestine III: Judaea* (London: Committee of the Palestine Exploration Fund, 1883), 190, 222, 227-28.
[354] Netzer and Garbrecht, "Water Channels," 367.
[355] Netzer and Garbrecht, "Water Channels," 377.

sluice gates were a later or even an *ad-hoc* addition to the system as the water systems were extended and adapted.[356]

There are two main systems of aqueducts in the Wadi Qelt. One runs along the north bank of the wadi while the other runs along the south bank, and there are also three channels that are fed by seasonal rains.[357] The longest of the aqueducts is the one that travels from the Wadi Qelt to the hill fortress of Cypros and then back downhill into the plantations of the Hasmonaean/Herodian palace estate.[358]

Bearing in mind the tentative nature of the dating of the site, the excavators thought it may have been during the reigns of Alexander Jannaeus (106–76 BCE), or his widow Alexandra (76–67 BCE), that the Na'aran Conduit was built along the mountain ridges and down to the Hasmonaean site.[359] While this aqueduct served many parts of the Hasmonaean estate, its main conduit went directly to the plantations on the eastern end of the estate.[360] The addition of this aqueduct allowed tributary conduits for swimming pools, cisterns, ritual baths, and irrigation and drainage systems to be constructed.[361]

The Na'aran and other later aqueducts also enabled the production of rich harvests, particularly of balsam[362] and dates. Balsam plants take several years to reach maturity before they can be harvested and processed into perfume oils and various other unguents. Date palms likewise become productive only after a dozen or so years and, according to Josephus (*B.J.* 4.467–470) and as seen in the literary texts above, Jericho produced a number of distinct varieties which could be processed into various varieties of food and wine. Given the long-term planning and expense involved in producing balsam and dates, and the horticultural expertise required to maintain productive plantations, it would appear that the estate of the Hasmonaeans and Herodians at Jericho functioned as an administrative, trade, and agricultural centre, as well as a pleasant winter resort for the Hasmonaean and Herodian royal courts.

---

[356] Netzer and Garbrecht, "Water Channels," 377.

[357] Yosef Porath, "Hydraulic Plaster in Aqueducts as a Chronological Indicator," in *The Aqueducts of Israel* (Journal of Roman Archaeology Supplementary Series 46; ed. David Amit, Joseph Patrich, and Yizhar Hirshfeld; Portsmouth, RI: Journal of Roman Archaeology, 2002), 29.

[358] David Amit, Joseph Patrich, and Yizhar Hirshfeld, eds., *The Aqueducts of Israel* (Journal of Roman Archaeology Supplementary Series 46; Portsmouth, RI: Journal of Roman Archaeology, 2002), 19.

[359] Porath, "Hydraulic plaster," 31.

[360] Netzer, *Architecture of Herod*, 42.

[361] Stern, *NEAEHL*, 685.

[362] Balsam is a plant resin that is healing and/or soothing in its effect. It is not possible to identify the specific plant from which ancient balsam was produced, but Jericho was a centre for its production.

THE NICHE/*GENIZAH*

Another reason the excavators identified this building as a synagogue was that they found what is described in the excavation reports as a "niche" in the north-eastern corner of what they describe as the assembly hall (see fig. 20 above).[363] According to the excavators, the floor of this niche was half a metre lower than the floor of the main assembly space.[364] They said that the niche contained a wooden cupboard which was later replaced by a cupboard made of fieldstones and mud divided into two compartments, one above the other. The lower one, they argued, could have served as a *genizah*, or storage space for worn-out scrolls and documents. A wooden plate (a sort of a horizontal door) would have covered the lower space of the niche, and the upper space could have been accessed more often.[365] The reconstruction of this niche in the excavation report allows for a horizontal "door" to be raised or lowered to allow access to the internal compartments, one above the other. According to the excavators, the lower compartment may have been used to store sacred scrolls and other important documents. The excavators say that what was initially a wooden interior to the niche was eventually replaced with stone, transforming the space into a two-tiered compartment[366] and that the wooden structure was replaced because of fire destruction.[367] They claim that because the niche (both the upper and lower tier) was entirely coated with lime plaster, it was used for the storage of sacred scrolls and was, in fact, a *genizah*.[368]

There are obvious problems with the excavators' understanding of this space. One is that the "niche" is an integral part of and lies directly *beneath* the main Na'aran conduit. In figure 22 below, looking south,[369] you can clearly see the Na'aran channel running east and west and the tributary channel running south (through the peristyle courtyard and down towards other areas of the estate including the palaces and swimming pools).[370] This structure is quite obviously part of the aqueduct system and is in fact a sluice gate designed to regulate water flow in the main channel (see figs. 20, 21 above, and 22 below).[371] The branching

---

[363] Netzer, *Hasmonaean and Herodian Palaces*, 2:168.
[364] Netzer, *Hasmonaean and Herodian Palaces*, 2:171.
[365] Netzer, *Hasmonaean and Herodian Palaces*, 2:171.
[366] Netzer, *Hasmonaean and Herodian Palaces*, 2:168.
[367] Netzer, *Hasmonaean and Herodian Palaces*, 2:171.
[368] Netzer, *Hasmonaean and Herodian Palaces*, 2:171.
[369] A photograph I took in February 2009.
[370] This channel can also be seen towards the background of fig. 6, another photograph I took in February 2009.
[371] Although I formulated this theory about the function of the so-called "niche" back in 2004, it wasn't until I visited the site in February 2009, when quite a lot of erosion had taken place on the site, that it was possible to get a photograph showing the sluice gate as a clear

off into the south-flowing channel that runs under the centre of the peristyle courtyard disrupted the flow of water from the main aqueduct, and a sluice gate system to the tributary channel leading south was needed to control the still fast moving water of the aqueduct. Without this mechanism to control the disruption of flow, the water would have transmitted a shockwave backwards and forwards along the main aqueduct, damaging it and flooding the surrounding area.[372] This shockwave is known as *water hammer*, and it can destroy the conduit or pipe through which it passes.[373]

Figure 22 – The niche (looking south)

There are a number of points leading to and within the courtyard house building where the flow of water along the main conduit and its tributaries is controlled by sluice gates. The sluice gate (referred to by the excavators as a niche or *genizah*), makes certain that any water hammer could be safely contained. The tank could then be accessed for maintenance (and water collection) from the upper compartment.[374]

The excavators' reconstruction of the niche in the excavation reports is correct in almost all other respects. The placing and removal of a horizontal door between the two compartments is precisely how the overflow mechanism would

---

component of the aqueduct. Before this, all other photographs just showed a hole in the ground.
[372] A. Trevor Hodge, *Roman Aqueducts and Water Supply* (2nd ed.; London: Duckworth, 2002), 233.
[373] Hodge, *Roman Aqueducts*, 154.
[374] An overflow for a water conduit, in much the same position as at Jericho, can be seen at the fountain house of Theagenes; see Hodge, *Roman Aqueducts*, 26.

have functioned. The horizontal door would have been able to stay in place as long as the flow along the main Na'aran conduit was slow and regular. If the water was moving faster or deeper than usual, the upper compartment could have been opened to extend its containment.

At the very least, it would be an eccentric act to use such a mechanism in such a location for the safekeeping of sacred or valuable objects. All things taken into consideration, what the excavation reports describe as an assembly hall is a peristyle courtyard, and the niche is a simple overflow tank, an integral part of the water system in this building and in the palace estates as a whole.

THE CISTERN/*MIKVEH*

Also belonging to the second phase of the building are the three rooms south of the peristyle courtyard, the largest of which contains a substantial water installation. This installation consists of two pools, one with steps for access and the other a reserve tank of equal size, but without the stepped access. The excavation reports identify the water installation as a *mikveh* and a reserve tank, and they argue that the other two small rooms in this row of three rooms were probably dressing rooms or changing facilities.[375]

A small channel connects the reserve to the immersion pool, and that reserve pool is connected to the small tributary channel of the Na'aran conduit which runs under the floor of the peristyle courtyard some 8 metres west of the sluice gate discussed above. Two channels emerge from the corridor above Rooms A and B and then follow a line towards to the entranceway to the original courtyard house, leaving the building to the south. There is what appears to be another small sluice mechanism just along the wall of Room 1 on the courtyard side, controlling the flow of water out of the building and further down the north-south incline.[376]

In the event that this building is not a synagogue and that the water installations represent the totality of the water supply to the household, it would appear that this is not a *mikveh* complex, although, of course, it could also be a *mikveh* without being part of a synagogue complex. However, it appears that the water installations are rather too deep and too steep to be used for ritual purposes. The stepped pool is 2.25 x 2.25 m in size, is 3.65 m deep, and has ten steps, of unequal height. The reserve pool is 2.65 x 2.4 m in size and is 3.78 m deep.[377]

---

[375] Netzer, *Hasmonaean and Herodian Palaces*, 2:180.
[376] Netzer, *Hasmonaean and Herodian Palaces*, 2:163.
[377] Netzer, *Hasmonaean and Herodian Palaces*, 2:178–79.

Figure 23 – The stepped cistern[378]

With a water supply and sufficient space so readily available, it would have been more than possible to build a shallower and wider-stepped *mikveh* here specifically for ritual purposes. The pools are fed by a tributary channel of the Na'aran Conduit and were contained within a walled building, which was certainly covered. It seems that this is not a *mikveh*, but rather a cistern and reserve for the provision of water to this large household.

THE EXCAVATION REPORTS (PHASE 3)

In the third phase of the building, a *triclinium* was added to the assembly hall and this is another of the excavators' reasons for believing that this building was a synagogue, again based on similarity with other sites, such as the synagogue with *triclinium* at Herodium (see chapter on Herodium herein).[379] The reconstruction involved in this latter phase involved a wall being dismantled, and one corner of the building being completely eliminated. In order to add the *triclinium,* changes were made in the courtyard.

---

[378] Taken in 2004, the author is standing at the bottom of the stepped pool.
[379] Ehud Netzer (with Ya'akov Kalman and Rachel Laureys), "A Synagogue from the Hasmonean Period Recently Exposed in the Western Plain of Jericho," *IEJ* 49.3–4 (1999): 203–21; Ehud Netzer, "The Hasmonaean and Herodian Winter Palaces at Jericho," *IEJ* 25 (1975): 95.

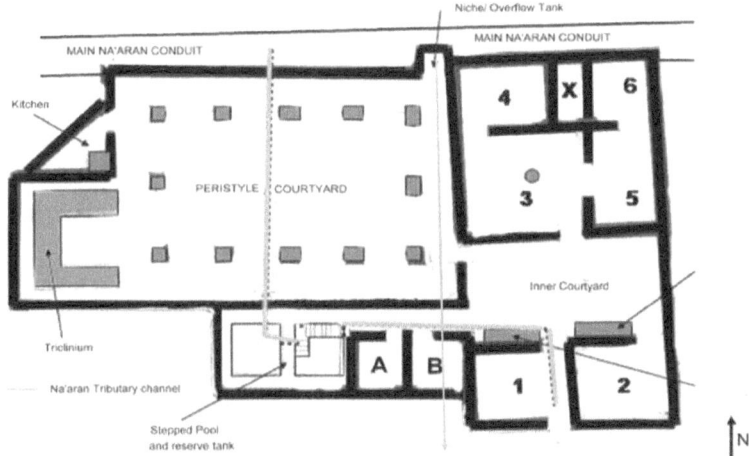

Figure 24 – The courtyard house (phase 3)

THE COURTYARD HOUSE (PHASE 3). To build the *triclinium*, part of the western wall was dismantled and one of the pillars (directly outside the *triclinium*) was moved about two metres to the north, so that there was a direct line of sight between the *triclinium* and the peristyle courtyard. The excavators argued that this was so that people dining in the *triclinium* could see the rest of the synagogue assembly during meals. It is more likely that the line of sight was altered so that diners could enjoy the decorative space, pleasant evening temperatures, and the probably fragrant garden outside. Adjacent to the *triclinium* is a triangular room that Netzer says was probably a kitchen. A podium in the right-angled corner bears evidence of fire and suggests that it may once have supported a stove. I have no argument with this interpretation.

LITERATURE REVIEW

SHANKS (2001)

Hershel Shanks, responding to Netzer's identification of the "synagogue" in Hasmonaean Jericho, takes the view that the building complex is important because of its architecture, but questions whether it is a synagogue on the basis that there is no clear archaeological evidence—that is, no architectural indicators, no epigraphy, and no donor plaques.[380] He lists the clues that led Netzer to

---

[380] Hershel Shanks, "Is It or Isn't It—A Synagogue? Archaeologists disagree over buildings at Jericho and Migdal," *BAR* 27.6 (2001): 51–57.

consider the building complex a synagogue, and he says that the first clue is the immersion pool and its reserve. Shanks also accepts this pool as a *mikveh* because it is a stepped pool with a supply coming from the Na'aran conduit and because it complies with the Rabbinic prescriptions for a *mikveh*. He concurs with Netzer that the other rooms along this section of the complex were probably dressing rooms.[381] Shanks repeats Netzer's assertion about the *triclinium* being the second clue to the building complex's identification as a synagogue, and goes on to say that *triclinia* are well known in the Roman world, but rare in Palestine.

He comes to the third clue, the niche, and has apparently accepted Netzer's contention as to its construction and use. Shanks asks if all these clues are sufficient to identify the Jericho building as a synagogue, and cites Netzer's claim that the most important basis for his conclusion is its similarity to the Gamla synagogue. He leaves acceptance or rejection of Netzer's thesis to the reader, but applies no scrutiny to Netzer's claims.

However, in his acceptance of Netzer's interpretation of the construction of the building, he necessarily leans towards agreement rather than otherwise. There is nothing in Shanks's brief discussion that adds anything to the debate; it is basically a recitation of Netzer's findings and conclusions.

YEHUDAH RAPUANO (2001)

Rapuano approaches Netzer's identification from a different angle. He looks at what the purpose of a synagogue might have been in the Hasmonaean period, when the earliest part of the courtyard house complex was built. He does not question Netzer's interpretation of the architecture of the building, nor of the uses to which it could have been put.[382] He asks whether the eastern part of the Jericho complex could have been used for the convening of a small core of original members or leaders, while the pillared hall, added at a later stage, was designated for larger assemblies.[383] This, however, does not seem particularly realistic, as the original phase of the courtyard house points towards its having been a residence, as already shown.

---

[381] Shanks, "Is It or Isn't It."
[382] Yehudah Rapuano, "The Hasmonaean Period 'Synagogue' at Jericho and the 'Council Chamber' at Qumran," *IEJ* 51.1 (2001): 54, n. 16; Netzer, Kalman, and Laureys, "A Synagogue from the Hasmonean Period," 216.
[383] Rapuano, "Hasmonean Period 'Synagogue,'" 55.

HOLGER SCHWARZER AND SARAH JAPP (2002)

Of the scholars who have looked at Netzer's identification, Schwarzer and Japp have looked the most closely and have offered various explanations for how the courtyard house complex might have developed throughout its three-phased existence until its destruction in 31 BCE. Because of the general lack of evidence to prove the identification, they do not accept Netzer's argument that the structure was a synagogue or that any part of it was designed as a synagogue.[384]

But whilst they do not reject Netzer's interpretation and reconstruction of the niche out of hand, they do say that its function is unknown and, further, that whilst it is clear that the niche at the synagogue at Gamla was used to store something valuable, this is not the case for the Jericho niche.[385] Schwarzer and Japp were unable to correctly identify the niche as what it actually is (an overflow tank or sluice gate, one of the components of the courtyard house complex's water supply directly linked into the main Na'aran Conduit), but they were able to say that it may not have functioned as a *genizah,* as had been suggested by Netzer.[386]

INGE NIELSEN (2005)

Nielsen rejects arguments that compare the courtyard house complex to other synagogue buildings.[387] She says that one must take the surroundings and the cultural context into consideration. She accepts Netzer's interpretation of the remains, including a *mikveh* and a *genizah* and, having accepted his explanation, accepts the identification of a synagogue.[388]

LEE I. LEVINE (2005)

Levine acknowledges that, *if* Netzer's identification were found to be correct, then this site would be the earliest known synagogue in the land of Israel but that, "when all is said and done, there is very little hard evidence on which to base such a conclusion."[389] Levine says that there is no known synagogue parallel to the

---

[384] Holger Schwarzer and Sarah Japp, "Synagoge, Banketthaus oder Wohngebäude: Überlegungen zu einem neu entdeckten Baukomplex in Jericho/Israel," *Antike Welt* 33.3 (2002): 280.
[385] Schwarzer and Japp, "Synagoge, Banketthaus oder Wohngebäude," 279.
[386] Schwarzer and Japp, "Synagoge, Banketthaus oder Wohngebäude," 279.
[387] Inge Nielsen, "Synagogue (synagogé) and Prayerhouse (proseuché): The Relationship Between Jewish Religious Architecture in Palestine and the Diaspora," *Hephaistos* 23 (2005): 75.
[388] Nielsen, "Synagogue (synagogé)," 75.
[389] Lee I. Levine, *The Ancient Synagogue: The First Thousand Years* (2nd ed.; New Haven: Yale University Press, 2005), 73.

Jericho building, no evidence to suggest that the niche was ever used to store scrolls, and more differences between Jericho and the comparator Netzer used, Gamla, than commonalities. Moreover, he says that the location of this building is curious, as whom could it possibly serve, and that it is indeed similar to many Hellenistic and Roman villas.[390] Levine says that future excavations on the site may clarify the situation further.[391]

Conclusions

Of the courtyard house complex at Hasmonaean/Herodian Jericho identified as a synagogue, Ehud Netzer said that it was "an important contribution to a clearer picture of the appearance and functioning of synagogues from the Hasmonaean period (if not earlier), at least until the destruction of the Second Temple."[392] In a conversation in 2006 in Jerusalem, Prof. Netzer told me that his identification would be taken more seriously if the structure were monumental and built of stone.

It is clear that the contemporary historical record provides little in terms of our understanding of the Hasmonaean estate at Jericho. What we do have comes to us almost wholesale from the excavation reports. Given that there are so few historical references to this estate, there is no meaningful way in which we can assign ownership of particular areas of the site to any one group or person and so, even the excavators have only tentatively dated the site.

Curiously, the excavators do not consider what they have identified as Hasmonaean-period synagogue to have been part of the Hasmonaean palace complex and think it is not necessary that the palace had a synagogue. The excavators believe that this was a synagogue designed for and built by workers. They argue that there can be no reasonable alternative explanation for the function of the building, other than its being used as a place of assembly.[393] However, as it has been shown, there are very obvious alternative explanations, and there is no evidence whatsoever in any shape or form for the existence of a workers' synagogue at Hasmonaean-Herodian Jericho.

The excavators' identification and argument is also flawed in saying that this is a *prototype* of a synagogue, and that it fulfilled the requirement for assembly. This building did not survive far into Herod's use of the site, but was destroyed in the earthquake of 31 BCE and was left in ruins until part of Herod's second palace was built over it some five years later.

---

[390] Levine, *Ancient Synagogue*², 73.
[391] Levine, *Ancient Synagogue*², 74.
[392] Netzer, Kalman, and Laureys, "A Synagogue from the Hasmonean Period," 203–21.
[393] Netzer, Kalman, and Laureys, "A Synagogue from the Hasmonean Period," 203–21.

The excavators' arguments are highly speculative, arguing that the Hasmonaean stimulus to build in Jericho was the pursuit of pleasure; that the main purpose of the lavish and splendid pools complex was for entertainment and leisure, and that the gardens were areas of tranquillity.[394] As has been already stated, the excavators are extrapolating backwards from Herod (and his particularly lavish building programme), to the Hasmonaeans.[395]

All things considered, it would appear that this building complex, from its first phase as a courtyard house, through its second and third enlarging phases, was the dwelling of an official of the estate or even a member of the Hasmonaean household. It is wedged between the industrial estate to the east and the more luxurious elements of the estate to the west, and its use should therefore be related to its location.

Finally, adding to the delicate framework of the chronological development of the synagogue requires a great deal of care and attention, and more evidence is required before a building should be identified as being of religious significance. In the particular case of the courtyard house complex at Hasmonaean/Herodian Jericho, there is no reason to do so.

---

[394] Ehud Netzer, *Hasmonaean and Herodian Palaces at Jericho. Final Reports of the 1973–1987 Excavations*, Volume 1 (Jerusalem: Israel Exploration Society; Institute of Archaeology, The Hebrew University of Jerusalem, 2001), 335.

[395] David Stacey, "Was There a synagogue in Hasmonaean Jericho?," *The Bible and Interpretation* (2000), http://www.bibleinterp.com/articles/Hasmonean_Jericho.shtml.

4
MASADA

Figure 25 –Masada (looking west)

INTRODUCTION

Masada is a huge and complicated archaeological site, and, while many of its elements are interrelated—particularly those related to the period of the first rebellion and the Roman siege of Masada—an examination of its many elements and phases is not possible here, and we shall focus on the building identified as a synagogue by Yigael Yadin in 1963/64. Nevertheless, it is necessary to summarise Josephus's Masada narrative dealing with the period of the first Jewish rebellion against Rome, along with some details of geography and chronology, and the history of the excavations, to set the subject of this chapter, Locus 1042 (the synagogue), into context.

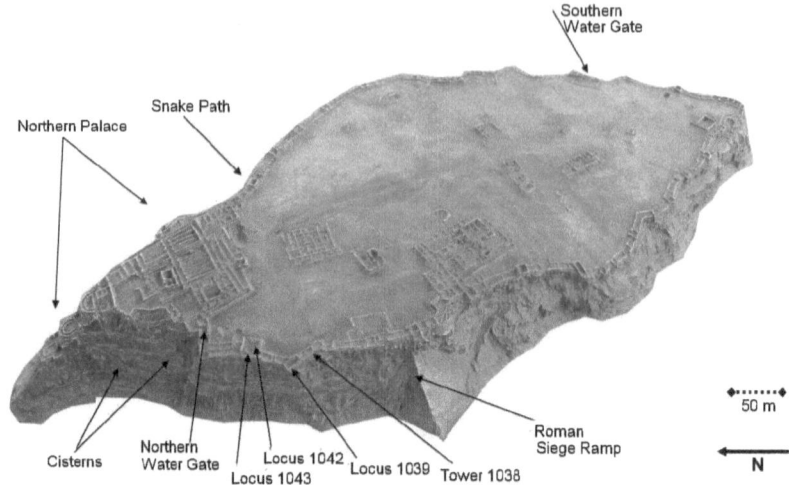

Figure 26 – Masada (context and locations)[396]

All buildings and structures on Masada with which we are here concerned will be referred to by the locus numbers they were assigned during the Yigael Yadin excavations. The relevant buildings here are Locus 1042 ("the Synagogue"); Locus 1043 (the "Genizah"), and Locus 1039 (the "Casemate of the Scrolls"), and all of these locations are identified in Figure 26 above. Locus 1042 is located on the northwestern side of the acropolis of Masada, near the Herodian northern palace complex, and was identified as a synagogue in the 1963/64 excavations run by Yigael Yadin.

JOSEPHUS'S MASADA NARRATIVE

Other than Josephus, the primary sources on the subject of Masada are limited to passing references to its geography in Strabo and Pliny the Elder. The only material we have relating to events on Masada at the end of the first Jewish war against Rome is found in Josephus, in *Antiquities*, *Bellum,* and *Vitae*. Josephus gives no account of the period between the death of Herod and the occupation of the site by the rebels.[397]

---

[396] Author's photograph of the scale model of Masada (on Masada).
[397] Hannah M. Cotton and Joseph Geiger, *Masada II: The Latin and Greek Documents, The Yigael Yadin Excavations 1963–1965; Final Reports* (Jerusalem: Israel Exploration Society, 1989), 3.

During the military and political turmoil that accompanied Herod the Great's struggle to become King of Judæa in 40 BCE and immediately prior to his journey to Rome to appeal to the Roman Senate for help, Herod sent members of his family and court to Masada (*B.J.* 1.267–285) to keep them safe from Malichus (an enemy of the Herodian family and the person who supposedly had had Herod's father, Antipater, poisoned only four years earlier).[398] This Malichus, at some earlier point, had maintained his own garrison on Masada (*A.J.* 14.296; *B.J.* 1.237–238).

Once Herod was established as king of Judæa with the assistance of the Romans, he began an enormous and ambitious construction programme on Masada, involving building palaces, barracks, baths, storehouses, workshops, and water systems (*B.J.* 7.285–300), including the subject of this chapter, Locus 1042, which is situated in the northwestern section of the acropolis (see figure 26 above).[399] Josephus says that Herod began building the fortress on Masada as a refuge in case there should be an attempt to oust him, either by his own people or by Cleopatra VII's machinations. Thus, he probably began building on Masada somewhere between 37 and 31 BCE (during which time Cleopatra's relationship with Mark Antony, according to Josephus [*B.J.* 7.300], threatened Herod's relationship with Rome). It is generally thought that Josephus must have visited Masada, as his descriptions of the Herodian building programme including the palatial structures, barracks, cisterns, swimming pools, and storage facilities are often accurate. Unfortunately, he makes no references to any of the casemate chambers that are the focus of this case study, nor to the existence of a synagogue at any stage before, during, or after the occupation of Masada by the rebels.

Nothing is known about Masada between the years following Herod's death in about 6 BCE and the Jewish war against Rome from 66–73 CE. When Josephus picks up the story of Masada again, it is 66 CE, at the start of the war against the Romans. A Roman garrison at Masada had been taken over by Jewish rebels using some sort of "treachery" (*B.J.* 2.408). Josephus refers to the rebels involved as *Sicarii*, and says they were led by a man named Eleazar (*B.J.* 7.297).[400]

Josephus reports that these *Sicarii*, and other rebel factions who joined them later, held the fortress of Masada until May of 73 CE, when it fell to the Roman Tenth Legion *Fretensis*, commanded by Flavius Silva. Josephus said that in the hours before the fortress fell, Eleazar, the rebel leader, had ordered his men to destroy everything except their food supplies to show that they had chosen to die rather than be captured by the Romans. According to Josephus's account, the

---

[398] *A.J.* 14.282. This was in 44 BCE, the same year that Julius Caesar, patron and friend of the Herodian dynasty, was assassinated.
[399] Avraham Negev and Shimon Gibson, eds., *Archaeological Encyclopedia of the Holy Land* (Rev. ed.; New York: Continuum, 2001), 320.
[400] Josephus, *B.J.* 2.425.

rebels drew lots and killed one another in turn, each man killing his family, on down to the last man, who would be the only one to have to take his own life (Josephus, *B.J.* 7.389–401).

The siege of Masada ended in 73 CE with the Romans breaking through the defensive walls only to find that all but two women and five children had died (*B.J.* 7.405–6). According to Josephus, these two women and five children had survived the suicide on Masada by hiding inside one of Masada's many cisterns, and it was from the women that the Romans learnt of events. After the siege and the re-establishment of a Roman garrison at Masada, the site was lost to the historical record until the nineteenth century.[401]

This, then, is broadly what Josephus tells us about Masada through to the end of the first Jewish war. It is important to note that there are some problems and inconsistencies with Josephus's accounts—which will not be explored here because they do not relate to the identification of Locus 1042 as a synagogue.[402] In any event, while Josephus's descriptions of the palatial and military buildings on Masada have proved to be quite accurate in their details, he never refers to a synagogue—or a requirement for one—in his narrative.

THE MASADA ACROPOLIS

The acropolis of Masada is encircled by a fortified double casemate wall (part of the Herodian construction phase), except for the area of the three-tiered Northern Palace of Herod the Great (see fig. 26 above). All of the rooms adjoining this wall were occupied during the period of the rebellion, and many were modified by their occupants for their use.[403] Objects, such as clothes, leather articles, papyri, sandals, nails, baskets, glass, stone, bronze vessels, food, gemstones, jewellery, seal rings, arrowheads, ballistas, and so on, were found scattered in the casemate rooms.[404] During the rebellion, towers along the casemate served as workshops, and some 350 bronze coins of the period of the rebellion lay scattered next to an oven in one of them.[405] Also discovered in the casemate rooms were hundreds of

---

[401] Although there was occupation of the site after the Jewish rebellion; there are late Roman/Byzantine church ruins on the acropolis, and it is likely that some of the occupation of the casemate chambers dates from this period.

[402] See Shaye J. D. Cohen, "Masada: Literary Tradition, Archaeological Remains and the Credibility of Josephus," *JJS* 33.1–2 (1982): 385–405, and David J. Ladouceur, "Josephus and Masada," in *Josephus, Judaism and Christianity* (ed. Louis H. Feldman and Gōhei Hata; Detroit: Wayne State University Press, 1989), 95–113. There are many other discourses on the subject of Josephus's reliability, none of which is relevant to the identification of a synagogue at Masada.

[403] Ronny Reich, "Baking and Cooking at Masada," *ZDPV* 119.2 (2003): 144.

[404] Netzer, "Masada," in *NEAEHL*, 980.

[405] Netzer, "Masada," 980.

MASADA   113

coins from the period of the rebellion, including a hoard of seventeen silver shekels, three of which were rare Year 5 shekels of the war (the year Jerusalem fell to the Romans) as well as a number of fragments of biblical and extra-biblical scrolls in Aramaic and Hebrew, letters in Latin and Greek, lists, and many *ostraca* and *tituli picti*.[406]

While many of the large buildings in the interior and at the northern end of the acropolis were razed during or at the end of the siege, few of the casemate chambers had been burned; however, their miscellaneous contents were strewn around on floors, ovens, and in niches in the walls. Piles of burnt material containing the remains of many different articles were found in the corners of some of the rooms, indicating that they had been collected and deliberately set alight.[407]

HISTORY OF THE EXCAVATIONS AT MASADA

The site of Masada was first identified in 1838 from a distance, but not explored until 1867, when Charles Warren of the British Royal Engineers climbed Masada's eastern side, tracing what Josephus referred to as the Snake Path.[408] All of the natural approaches to the summit of Masada are quite difficult: these are the White Rock on the west (*B.J.* 7.305), the southern and northern sides, and the Snake Path on the east (*B.J.* 7.282). There is also another route to the summit of Masada from the west, on a high sloping rock escarpment, along which the Roman siege ramp was built (*B.J.* 7.305–309; see fig. 26 above).[409]

Masada was excavated from October 1963 to April 1964 and again from December 1964 to March 1965 under the direction of the retired military general and archaeologist, Yigael Yadin (son of Eleazar Lipa Sukenik), and excavations and conservation continue, on a smaller scale, to this day.[410]

THE ZEALOTS AND *SICARII* ON MASADA

It is worth mentioning here that both Yigael Yadin (under whose leadership the excavations of Masada began) and Ehud Netzer (who wrote the text for the third volume of the Masada Final Reports, including the analysis of Locii 1042 and 1043, the subjects of this chapter) refer throughout to the rebels on Masada as the "Zealots." That this came about because of pre-existing expectations is clear when we look at what Yadin said in relation to the excavations on Masada:

---

[406] Netzer, "Masada," 980. *Tituli picti* are commercial stamps, usually on amphora handles, jugs, etc, which give details of manufacture, origin, destination, etc.
[407] Netzer, "Masada," 980.
[408] Netzer, "Masada," 974.
[409] Netzer, "Masada," 973–74.
[410] Netzer, "Masada," 974.

Before starting the excavations at Masada, we dreamed of the possibility of finding scrolls there. I say "dreamed" because the hope that we would could not be very bright. Hitherto, all the scrolls which had been found in the vicinity of the Dead Sea had been discovered only in caves, where they had been hidden intentionally, and where the damage they had suffered—comparatively slight—had been damage by nature, such as mild dampness, or by the nibbling of small animals. Now, as we approached Masada, we asked ourselves: "Had the Zealots hidden their writings before committing suicide? And if they had, would any of them still be preserved? And would we find them?"[411]

Yadin had a clear idea of what he was looking for, the form of the historical narrative he accepted, and where he intended looking for evidence to support his view before even starting to dig. There are a multitude of possible socio-political and personal reasons for Yadin to have taken this approach to digging on Masada, but they all fall outside the scope of this monograph, and they are not relevant to the analysis of the archaeological material relating to the subject of this chapter (Loci 1042 and 1043).

Because his work has reached such a wide audience, Yadin's use of the term "Zealot" has had a major impact on the interpretation of the archaeology and on the accepted history of Masada. It has fuelled much of the mythology around the Masada story, so that almost every reference to Masada includes a description of the Zealots who occupied it and who died defending it.[412] Certainly, there were

---

[411] Yigael Yadin, *Masada: Herod's Fortress and the Zealots' Last Stand* (trans. Moshe Pearlman; 1966; repr., London: Weidenfeld & Nicholson, 1977), 168.

[412] There are a multitude of discussions about who the *Sicarii* and the Zealots were, as well as how and where their roles overlapped, see (for example): Kenneth Atkinson and Jodi Magness, "Josephus's Essenes and the Qumran Community," *JBL* 129.2 (2010): 317–42; Cohen, "Masada: Literary Tradition," 385–405; Louis H. Feldman, *Josephus and Modern Scholarship (1937–1980)* (Berlin: de Gruyter, 1984); Martin Hengel, *The Zealots* (Edinburgh: T&T Clark, 1989); Ladouceur, "Josephus and Masada," 95–113; Netzer, "Masada," 973–85; E. Netzer, "The Rebels' Archives at Masada," *IEJ* 54.2 (2004): 218–29; Moshe Pearlman, *The Zealots of Masada* (London: Hamish Hamilton, 1967); Uriel Rappaport, "Where was Josephus' Lying—in His Life or in the War?," in *Josephus and the History of the Graeco-Roman Period: Essays in Memory of Morton Smith* (eds. Fausto Parente and Joseph Slievers; Leiden: Brill, 1994), 279–89; Seth Schwartz, *Josephus and Judaean Politics* (Leiden: Brill, 1990); Morton Smith, "Zealots and Sicarii, Their Origins and Relation," *HTR* 64 (1971): 1–19; Menahem Stern, "Zealots," in *Encyclopaedia Judaica Year Book* (Jerusalem: Encyclopaedia Judaica; New York: Macmillan, 1973), 135–53; Lisa Ullmann and Jonathan J. Price, "Drama and History in Josephus' *Bellum Judaicum*," *SCI* 21 (2002): 91–111; Yadin, *Masada: Herod's Fortress*; Y. Yadin, "Masada," *EJ* 11 (1971): 1078–1091; Yigael Yadin and Joseph Naveh, "The Aramaic and Hebrew Ostraca and Jar Inscriptions," in *Masada I, Final Reports* (Jerusalem: Israel Exploration Society; Hebrew University of Jerusalem, 1989); Solomon Zeitlin, "Masada and the Sicarii," *JQR*, New Series

Zealots on Masada during the rebellion, but there were also *Sicarii*, members of the priesthood, and general refugee groups, including women and children. The population of Masada during the seven years of the rebellion was not static, and there was a constant shifting of individuals and groups in and out as people fled from the Romans (and from each other, there being so much factional strife amongst the rebel groupings).[413]

As against this, since we only have one person's account of events on Masada, and since that source is Josephus, we must take some notice of his identifications of the involved parties, even though he can be confusing and contradictory.[414] It is also important, in the context of our discussion of the archaeological material pertaining to our site, not to place too much weight on who the *Sicarii* and Zealots on Masada were, how they interacted, and the reasons Josephus described them in particular ways, because, as will become clear in this chapter, there is no way to associate any particular group with the buildings with which this chapter is concerned. However, it is apposite to say a little about both groups since the issue remains so vexed.

Stern, writing his seminal article about the possible connections between the *Sicarii* and the Zealots, sees the *Sicarii* as having been run out of Jerusalem and active on Masada only after the death of their leader, Menahem, at the hands of the Zealots then in control of the Jerusalem Temple. He says that the *Sicarii* "continued to exist and it was they who were destined to be the last to hold aloft the standard of rebellion."[415] Thus, the rebels under the leadership of Eleazar ben Jair (who took over leadership of the *Sicarii* after Menahem's death) entrenched themselves on Masada, but their sphere of operations was confined to the adjacent area around En Gedi (*B.J.* 4.398–405).[416]

According to Stern, very few of the rebels fighting against Rome accepted the specific eschatological ideology of the *Sicarii* (as contained in Eleazar ben

---

55.4 (1965): 299–317; Solomon Zeitlin, "The Sicarii and Masada," *JQR*, New Series, 57.4 (1967): 251–70.

[413] As the Roman historian Tacitus remarked in terms of the factions vying for control of Jerusalem during the rebellion (*Hist.* 5.12.3–4), "There were three generals, three armies: the outermost and largest circuit of the walls was held by Simon, the middle of the city by John, and the temple was guarded by Eleazar. John and Simon were strong in numbers and equipment, Eleazar had the advantage of position: between these three there was constant fighting, treachery, and arson, and a great store of grain was consumed. Then John got possession of the temple by sending a party, under pretence of offering sacrifice, to slay Eleazar and his troops. So the citizens were divided into two factions until, at the approach of the Romans, foreign war produced concord." (Moore, LCL).

[414] Nachman Ben-Yehuda, *Sacrificing Truth: Archaeology and the Myth of Masada* (New York: Humanity Books, 2002), 35.

[415] Stern, "Zealots," 139.

[416] Stern, "Zealots," 140.

Jair's speech to his rebel cohorts before they committed suicide rather than be taken captive by the Romans after the fall of Masada).[417] Meanwhile, the Zealots retained overall control of Jerusalem, and Stern says there is little reason to doubt that the priests of Jerusalem were the "fomenting element among the Zealots."[418] Josephus, in fact, describes the Zealots as "lawless" and says that there was no "villainy recorded in history that they failed to emulate zealously… And yet they took their name from their professed zeal for virtue, either in mockery of those they wronged, so brutal was their nature, or reckoning the greatest of evils good" (*B.J.* 7.268–270).[419]

While some scholars see the Zealots as part of the same movement to which the *Sicarii* belonged, others reject the possibility of any connection. Stern concedes that there is "no clear evidence in the sources of any connection [...] during the Revolt" despite a [single] reference to the followers of the *Sicarii* under Menahem's leadership as "zealots" (*B.J.* 2.444).[420] Even so, Stern argues that there does seem to be a link and suggests, cautiously, that there was some cooperation "between the founders of the Zealots and of the Sicarii during the census of Quirinius, and that from the outset the difference between these two movements was a tangible one. This difference found its expression in the decisive schism which took place during the Revolt after a brief period of cooperation at its beginning."[421] Stern concludes that,

> although it cannot be denied that the picture given here of the various currents in the Jewish freedom movement is to a considerable extent hypothetical, one thing is nevertheless indisputably clear, namely, that the unifying factors among them outnumbered the divisive ones. From this point of view there is perhaps some justification for the view of those historians who are accustomed to speak generally of a Zealot movement which fearlessly raised the standard of revolt against the Roman Empire when it was at the height of its power.[422]

On the other hand, Hengel ultimately sees the two groups as interconnected and with common origins.[423] "If today we give these groups, including the *Sicarii*,

---

[417] Stern, "Zealots," 142. Of course, Stern ignores the view that ben Jair's speech and, all that follows it, is merely a literary construct designed by Josephus to induce some sympathy among his Roman audience for the Jewish rebels.

[418] Stern, "Zealots," 145.

[419] Stern, "Zealots," 142.

[420] Hengel, *Zealots*, 400. Hengel sees this reference as supporting evidence of the links between the *Sicarii* and the Zealots.

[421] Stern, "Zealots," 146.

[422] Stern, "Zealots," 153.

[423] Hengel, *Zealots*, 88–89. Hengel also refers to Locus 1042 on Masada as a "synagogue" without any analysis of the archaeology of the site, nor to its physical location on the

the name of 'Zealots,' it is certainly a correct name since they were all orientated towards Phinehas' paradigmatic act."[424] Hengel concedes, however, that "it cannot be denied that the problem of the 'party names' raises certain questions on the basis of the language used by our main source, Josephus."[425]

Hengel describes the Zealots as having taken control of Masada after their flight from Jerusalem:

> It was only when Jerusalem had decided to support the cause of revolt that the Zealots openly attacked the strongholds of the Roman occupation. They made a surprise attack against Masada on the Dead Sea. This fortress had been built by Herod and was almost impregnable, but the Zealots overcame the Roman occupying forces, seized control of it and occupied it themselves with their own people. The weapons and equipment that they found there were divided by their leader, Menahem, the son of Judas the Galilaean, among his followers and the population of the country.[426]

However, Josephus is quite specific on this point, and describes the group who took control of Masada as the *Sicarii* (*B.J.* 7.252ff). It is not clear why Hengel has chosen to refer to the rebel group who took control of Masada as the Zealots when Josephus does not use that term.

At the same time, Hengel talks of the group of Zealots who

> had demonstrated their military strength by their successful surprise attack against Masada. Either simultaneously or immediately afterwards, by virtue of his influential position and with the support of the Zealot majority of the lower clergy, Eleazar, the *sagan* who had come over to their side, managed to win the struggle for the Temple.[...] The Zealots had worked for two generations towards and had now achieved their aim. Almost the entire population had joined in the Holy War against Rome.[427]

This then implies that the only group in control of Masada was religiously founded, which, again, does not appear to be supported in the archaeology and is most assuredly not supported in Josephus's accounts of the rebels' thuggish raids into the countryside around to obtain supplies (*B.J.* 4.402–405), which seems to undermine Hengel's description of the *Sicarii* as a "closed and disciplined group

---

acropolis, and so has accepted Yadin's and Netzer's interpretation of the archaeological evidence.
[424] This Phinehas was described as a "zealot" in Num 25:10ff; 4 Macc 18:12; and *b. Sanh.* 82b.
[425] Hengel, *Zealots*, 403.
[426] Hengel, *Zealots*, 358–59.
[427] Hengel, *Zealots*, 363.

whose steadfastness was based on a determination to keep to the rule of God."[428] His central thesis, that the "Jewish freedom fighters" had been consolidating themselves as the "party of the Zealots" since the reign of Gaius Caligula (who wanted to erect a statue of himself in the Jerusalem temple) which was evidenced by the "ordinary people" being prepared to die as had done their "Zealot models, the *Sicarii*, in Masada,"[429] seems to be a circular argument, especially since the siege on Masada took place *after* the destruction of the Temple in Jerusalem. The rebels on Masada may indeed have represented the last pocket of Jewish resistance to the Romans but, by the time they fell, the war against Rome was over, the Zealot leadership vanquished, the Temple treasures already looted, taken to Rome, and paraded as part of Titus's triumph.

Josephus's tangled account of the parties involved in the fight for Jerusalem and the rebels on Masada makes it possible to claim, as Yadin did, that the rebels on Masada were Zealots, even though Josephus does not name them as such. Hengel has also, following Yadin, tied the Zealots and the *Sicarii* together, as forming different parts of one group, allowing him to refer to the rebels on Masada, uniformly, as Zealots. Neither Josephus's Masada narrative, nor Stern's and later Hengel's analyses of Josephus's account, unfortunately, leave us much wiser or able to make definitive statements as to the identity of either group. Thankfully, none of this impacts on the discussion of the archaeology of the site that follows.

THE IDENTIFICATION OF LOCUS 1042 AS A SYNAGOGUE

Yigael Yadin's excavations on Masada in the 1960s revealed occupation layers from the Herodian through to the Byzantine period, including the period of the Jewish rebellion (66–73 CE).[430] Almost all of the built-up areas of Masada were uncovered during this period, including Locus 1042; the subject of this chapter (see fig. 26 above).

In 1994, the World Heritage Committee launched the *Global Strategy for a Balanced, Representative and Credible World Heritage List*, aiming to ensure that the list reflected the world's cultural diversity of outstanding universal value, and Masada became a World Heritage Site in 2001.[431]

---

[428] Hengel, *Zealots*, 261.
[429] Hengel, *Zealots*, 265–66.
[430] Although Josephus refers to earlier occupation.
[431] See UNESCO: http://whc.unesco.org/en/list/1040. "Under criteria (iii), (iv) and (vi) of its charter: that Masada is a symbol of the ancient Jewish kingdom of Israel, of its violent destruction in the later first century CE, and of the subsequent Diaspora; that the palace of Herod the Great at Masada is an outstanding example of a luxurious villa of the Early Roman Empire, whilst the camps and other fortifications that encircle the monument constitute the finest and most complete Roman siege works to have survived to the present day; and that

The identification of Locus 1042 (see fig. 26 above) as a synagogue was made by Yigael Yadin during excavations on Masada in 1963/64. The first season of digging revealed a rectangular structure with benches around the walls.[432] In the northwestern corner of this building, the excavators found a separate small room attached (Locus 1043, the *"genizah"*).[433] When Locus 1042 was identified as a synagogue, it was immediately received into the historical record as the first pre-70 CE synagogue to be identified in the land of Israel.[434] Locus 1042 is pivotal to this entire study because all other synagogues attributed to the first century CE are compared to it.

It is important to note that the original phase of Locus 1042, built by Herod as part of his palace complex, was in use for possibly up to eighty years before being adapted to the form that is preserved today, which was in use at the time of the first rebellion. Unlike the buildings identified as synagogues at Delos, Hasmonaean/Herodian Jericho, Herodium, and Gamla, there are no architectural comparisons to be offered here. This is not an adapted villa or house, as is the case with the structures identified at Delos and Jericho, nor was Locus 1042 designed as a public building in the same way as the building identified as a synagogue at Gamla. Nor is it a converted *triclinium,* such as the building identified as a synagogue at Herodium (see chapters on Delos, Jericho, Herodium, and Gamla herein).

The excavators found some coins of the period of the first Jewish war in Locus 1042, and they saw that the benches, where the plaster was damaged, had been made out of quarried stone and broken pieces of dressed stone which had been taken from other buildings on Masada. It was therefore clear to the excavators that the benches had been built after the various parts of the palace had been destroyed, and that this structure had the character of an assembly space. This led Yadin to wonder what its purpose might have been.[435] Yet, even in that first season of digging, Yadin thought that Locus 1042 was a synagogue, on the basis that the building was [unintentionally but fortuitously] orientated towards Jerusalem, that an ostracon with the inscription *priestly tithe* had been found on the floor, and that coins of the period of the first Jewish war were also found there.[436] Yadin argued that if it was a synagogue, then it was a very important

---

the events during the last days of the Jewish rebels who occupied the fortress and palace of Masada make it a symbol both of Jewish cultural identity and, more universally, of the continuing human struggle between oppression and liberty."

[432] Yadin, *Masada: Herod's Fortress*, 181.
[433] Yadin, *Masada: Herod's Fortress*, 181.
[434] Louis H Feldman, "Masada: A Critique of Recent Scholarship," in *Christianity, Judaism and Other Greco-Roman Cults* (Studies for Morton Smith at Sixty, vol. 3; ed. J. Neusner; Leiden: Brill, 1975), 224.
[435] Yadin, *Masada: Herod's Fortress*, 184.
[436] Yadin, *Masada: Herod's Fortress*, 184.

discovery, because, up until this point, the earliest synagogues discovered in the land of Israel belonged to the end of the second or beginning of the third century CE.[437] As we shall see in the archaeological discussion below, there is no evidence of any sort that gives us any information in relation to how the earliest (Herodian) phase of Locus 1042 was used.

Excited by the prospect of identifying a first-century synagogue, Yadin's team of archaeologists continued to excavate Locus 1042, and during the second season of digging they discovered that there had been two clear stages of construction. In the first phase, the building was divided into two main sections comprising an antechamber and a main chamber with columns along its southern, western, and northern sides. The benches belonged to the second phase, as did Locus 1043, the smaller room. According to Yadin, at the point when the "Zealots"[438] came to add the small room and the benches, they removed two of the pillars from the western row, tore down the wall dividing the antechamber from the main room to its west and set up two pillars in its place.[439]

While Yadin could not determine the function of the building in the original Herodian phase, he suggested that even then it might have been a synagogue. He made this argument on three bases. First, he argued that it was unlikely that Herod would have denied a place of worship for the Jewish members of his family and other Jews who were members of his court. Second, he noted that the architectural plan is very reminiscent of the plan of several early synagogues discovered in Galilee.[440] The third argument, he said, was the existence of a strong conservative tradition in the location of houses of worship, and that it would be in keeping with this tradition that the Zealots, when deciding on their synagogue, specifically chose this place knowing that it had previously served as a synagogue. This, he said, would explain, too, why even the original building had been oriented towards Jerusalem.[441]

While making exploratory cuts in the small room (Locus 1043), the excavators uncovered a piece of rolled scroll, which later turned out to be sections from the book of Deuteronomy.[442] When the area of the cut was examined more closely, the excavators found that a pit had once been dug in this spot. The scroll fragment had been found at the bottom of this pit which had later been filled with

---

[437] Yadin, *Masada: Herod's Fortress*, 184.
[438] This is Yadin's appellation; there is no reference in Josephus or anything in the archaeological record to suggest that a particular group was responsible for Locus 1042 and its conversion.
[439] Yadin, *Masada: Herod's Fortress*, 185.
[440] By which he means the second and third century CE synagogues he has referred to already as being the earliest discovered in Israel.
[441] Yadin, *Masada: Herod's Fortress*, 185–87. Again, it is Yadin's presumption that Locus 1042 was a synagogue used by the Zealots.
[442] The team architects Munia-Immanuel (Izaak) Dunayevsky and Ehud Menzel.

earth and stones. Yadin said that Locus 1043 had therefore been a *genizah*, and the scroll may have been buried while the Zealots lived there. This discovery spurred the excavators into removing the whole of the second-phase floor to see if there were any other such pits.[443]

During this process, Moshe Cohen, a chief petty officer in the Israeli navy and enthusiastic amateur archaeologist, discovered a portion of floor was missing in the southern section of Locus 1043. Beneath the missing section of floor was a pit full of stamped-down earth in which, when he rifled through it with his bare hands, he found the remains of another scroll. This second scroll fragment was identified as containing sections of Ezek 37, the vision of the dry bones.[444] Thus, according to Yadin, the synagogue identification was made on the basis that the structural adaptations were the work of the Zealots, coupled with the nature of the finds. He reiterated also that the back wall of Locus 1042 was orientated exactly in the direction of Jerusalem.[445] While Yadin acknowledged the lack of material to help identify the "usual plan" of a Second Temple period synagogue, he said that we may assume that at this stage it served as a place of assembly and preaching, and that there could be no doubt that in its second stage it served as a place of public assembly, and as such it resembles the *ecclesiasteria* known to us from the Hellenistic period onwards.[446] Yadin said that we may therefore assume that at this stage Locus 1042 served first and foremost as a place of assembly and preaching. From this Yadin concluded that first-century synagogues were built on this model. He went on to suggest that if his hypothesis was correct, then this was not only the earliest synagogue ever discovered, but also the only one dating from the second temple period.[447] Since then, Locus 1042 has been treated as the standard paradigm of "ancient synagogue" in the scholarship.

THE ANCIENT SOURCES

Other than Josephus's accounts of Masada during the first Jewish war against Rome in *Antiquities* and *Bellum*, there are few descriptions of the area (let alone of its inhabitants) in any of the ancient literature. In Pliny we find a passing reference to Masada:

---

[443] Yadin, *Masada: Herod's Fortress*, 187. The removal of the floor will be important to an understanding of the phases of the building, which will be explored below.
[444] Yadin, *Masada: Herod's Fortress*, 187.
[445] Y. Yadin, "The Excavation of Masada—1963/64: Preliminary Report," *IEJ* 15.1–2 (1965): 78.
[446] Yadin, "Excavation of Masada," 78.
[447] Yadin, "Excavation of Masada," 79.

Next to it we come to Masada, a fortress on a rock, not far from Lake Asphaltites. This much concerning Judæa. (Pliny, *Nat.* 5.17.29–31)[448]

In Strabo there is a description of the area around the Dead Sea, including a reference to Masada:

> Many other evidences are produced to show that the country is fiery; for near Moasada are to be seen rugged rocks that have been scorched, as also, in many places, fissures and ashy soil, and drops of pitch that emit foul odours to a great distance [...] (Strabo, *Geogr.* 16.2.44)[449]

Finally, two documents were found at Wadi Murabba'at, located in the upper part of Nahal Dragot, which empties into the Dead Sea near Kibbutz Mitzpe Shalem, not far from Qumran. The first document is a deed of divorce (on papyrus) between Yehoseph son of Naqsan and his wife Miriam dated the "First of Marheshvan in the Year Six at Masada" (around 111 CE).[450] The second is the text of an ostracon which reads, in part, "and I ascended from there to Masada," which is dated to around 200 CE.[451]

---

[448] "And to the Essenes who lived in the area, as well as to the town of En Gedi: 'Lying on the west of Asphaltites, and sufficiently distant to escape its noxious exhalations, are the Esseni, a people that live apart from the world, and marvellous beyond all others throughout the whole earth, for they have no women among them; to sexual desire they are strangers; money they have none; the palm-trees are their only companions. Day after day, however, their numbers are fully recruited by multitudes of strangers that resort to them, driven thither to adopt their usages by the tempests of fortune, and wearied with the miseries of life. Thus it is, that through thousands of ages, incredible to relate, this people eternally prolongs its existence, without a single birth taking place there; so fruitful a source of population to it is that weariness of life which is felt by others. Below this people was formerly the town of Engadda, second only to Hierosolyma in the fertility of its soil and its groves of palm-trees; now, like it, it is another heap of ashes. Next to it we come to Masada, a fortress on a rock, not far from Lake Asphaltites. This much concerning Judæa'" (Rackham, LCL).

[449] "[...] and ruined settlements here and there; and therefore people believe the oft-repeated assertions of the local inhabitants, that there were once thirteen inhabited cities in that region of which Sodom was the metropolis, but that a circuit of about sixty stadia of that city escaped unharmed; and that by reason of earthquakes and of eruptions of fire and of hot waters containing asphalt and sulphur, the lake burst its bounds, and rocks were enveloped with fire; and, as for the cities, some were swallowed up and others were abandoned by such as were able to escape. But Eratosthenes [the work of Eratosthenes has been lost to history and is only known through reference to him by other historians and philosophers] says, on the contrary, that the country was a lake, and that most of it was uncovered by outbreaks, as was the case with the sea" (Jones, LCL).

[450] Pierre Benoit, J.T. Milik, and Roland de Vaux, eds., *Les Grottes de Murabba'at* (DJD 2; Oxford: Clarendon, 1961), 106ff.

[451] Benoit, Milik, and de Vaux, *Les Grottes*, 173.

Outside Josephus's accounts of the first Jewish war and the part Masada played in it, there is little information to be gleaned from the ancient sources. There are no corroborating sources for Josephus's accounts of the siege of Masada, and consequently there are numerous arguments about the accuracy and/or veracity of his reports, but this does not impact on the identification of Locus 1042 as a synagogue, since nowhere does Josephus discuss the religious practices of the rebels on Masada, let alone the existence of a synagogue there. On the other hand, since our only literary source for the occupation of Masada during the course of the Jewish war against the Romans *is* Josephus, we must turn to the archaeology for corroboration. A close analysis of the details of the excavation reports will be discussed below.

OSTRACA, COINS, AND DOCUMENTS

Over 700 ostraca in total were found on Masada.[452] More are continuing to be found as excavations and conservation work continue, many are still unpublished. Of those found, about half are inscribed with single letters or combinations of letters and most were found in or near the storerooms in the northern section of the acropolis, scattered about the place and/or in groups of the same type.[453]

The majority of the Hebrew and Aramaic (around 60 percent) ostraca were found in the area of the northern Water Gate (see fig. 26 above) and in an adjoining room. It is convincingly argued by the excavators that the Water Gate area was used to register the people who lived on Masada during the rebellion, and that it was therefore likely that personal or public documents were deposited here for safekeeping.[454] The ostraca found fall into the category of public documents, as they appear to have been used to define work patterns, to distribute food, and to draw up lists of people. It is clear that without some system to record the growing number of people present at any given time (given the logistical difficulties of feeding and housing them), life on Masada during the rebellion would have been chaotic.[455]

---

[452] In the excavation reports, *tituli picti* and *ostraca* are lumped together as though they are the same thing.
[453] Netzer, "Masada," 982.
[454] Ehud Netzer, "The Rebels' Archives at Masada," *IEJ* 54.2 (2004): 221–22.
[455] Netzer, "The Rebels' Archives," 225.

THE OSTRACON FOUND IN LOCUS 1042

Only one ostracon was found in Locus 1042; this was inscribed מעשר כהן (*priestly tithe*).[456] This was found just outside the threshold of Locus 1043 (see fig. 26 above and fig. 28 below). It is hard to know what to make of it, but certainly at the last stages of the siege on Masada, the population on Masada had been swollen by refugees from Jerusalem and elsewhere. The מעשר כהן ostracon certainly seems to imply the presence of some form of religious representation on Masada during the period of the revolt, but it does not follow that there was a synagogue to which this person was attached. And although this inscription is described as being on an ostracon, it was actually on the shoulder of a storage jar.[457] This is relevant because some people did not (or could not) deliver their tithes to the temple in Jerusalem, but instead gave them to priests living in their villages and towns. It is possible that at least some of the rebels and/or refugees on Masada followed this custom and kept their tithe offerings, hoping that the temple in Jerusalem would be restored after the war was over.[458]

TEXTS FOUND IN LOCUS 1042/1043

Other than the small fragments of Ezekiel and Deuteronomy, no texts were found in Locus 1042/1043.

TEXTS FOUND IN LOCUS 1039 / "THE CASEMATE OF THE SCROLLS"

A large number of documents were found in Locus 1039 (the so-called Casemate of the Scrolls). Locus 1039 (see fig. 26 above) was the location of a large hoard of documents and other materials, comprising biblical and extra-biblical texts, letters, and lists, in Greek, Latin, Aramaic, and Hebrew. This collection included a papyrus, written in Latin, and containing parts of lines from Virgil's *Aeneid* 4.9 (the section in which Dido writes to her sister describing her nightmares).[459] But there were also many other items found here, which had apparently been collected together. For example, the excavators found a red-orange cornelian seal of Victory/Nike along with a hoard of nineteen rebel period shekels, eighteen Latin

---

[456] Yadin refers to a second one with the name *Hezekiah* written on it, but in the excavation reports it is listed as having been found in Locus 1044, in the storeroom to the north of Locus 1042, and not associated with Locus 1042 at all.
[457] Yadin and Naveh, *Masada I*, 33.
[458] Yadin and Naveh, *Masada I*, 39.
[459] Hanan Eshel, "Josephus' View on Judaism without the Temple in Light of the Discoveries at Masada and Murabba'at," in *Gemeinde ohne Tempel*, WUNT 118 (ed. Beate Ego, Armin Lange, and Peter Pilhofer; Tübingen: Mohr Siebeck, 1999), 235.

papyri, and four Greek papyri.[460] Also found were a broken and burnt bone sword pommel,[461] a scabbard mount and a dagger suspension loop,[462] shield fragments,[463] and a belt-buckle tongue,[464] amongst other things. Many hundreds of siege items were found in Locus 1039, including ballista balls, arrows, arrowheads, and rolling stones. The defensive and offensive militaria need not concern us, as they relate to the last stages of the siege rather than to the general occupation of Masada and use of the structure by the rebels.

The excavators had particular difficulties putting together the report on Locus 1039 because the audio recordings of the discussions held during the period 13–22 November 1963 (when the more important finds in the locus were made) were lost.[465] Whilst there are photographs, basket lists, some locus cards, and a preliminary report, there is now nothing specifying the exact locations where items were found or the precise contexts in which they were found.[466]

Locus 1039 is more or less rectangular in shape. Like all the other casemate rooms, it was adapted during the period of the first rebellion, and all of the installations referred to herein relate to that period of occupation. In the southern part of the room, there is a small underground silo (perhaps for grain or oil) in the southeastern corner; there is a stove built against the eastern wall and a small lime-plaster lined basin (70 x 50 cm) built into the floor by the western wall. Finally, there is a pit dug into the southwestern corner of the room.[467]

A large concentration of material was found when clearing the upper layer of stone siege and roof debris from the southern extremity of Locus 1039. These objects were very closely packed together. First uncovered were fragments of reed baskets and fabrics, then the 19 silver shekels mentioned above, 52 other coins, as well as eighteen Latin and four Greek papyri.[468]

---

[460] Malka Hershkovitz and Shua Amorai-Stark, "The Gems from Masada," in *Masada VIII: the Yigael Yadin excavations 1963–1965, Final Reports* (ed. Joseph Aviram et al.; Jerusalem: Israel Exploration Society; The Hebrew University of Jerusalem, 2007), 219.
[461] Guy D. Stiebl and Jodi Magness, "Military Equipment from Masada," in *Masada VIII: the Yigael Yadin excavations 1963–1965; Final Reports* (ed. Joseph Aviram et al.; Jerusalem: Israel Exploration Society; The Hebrew University of Jerusalem, 2007), 8.
[462] Stiebl and Magness, "Military Equipment," 10.
[463] Stiebl and Magness, "Military Equipment," 11.
[464] Stiebl and Magness, "Military Equipment," 12.
[465] Daily meetings were held to discuss the finds and possible interpretations of each locus during the excavations. These were always recorded on audio tapes.
[466] Ehud Netzer, *Masada III: The Yigael Yadin Excavations 1963–1965; Final Reports, The Buildings, Stratigraphy and Architecture* (Jerusalem: Israel Exploration Society; The Hebrew University of Jerusalem, 1991), 417.
[467] Netzer, *Masada III*, 418.
[468] Netzer, *Masada III*, 418.

Also found in Locus 1039 were fifteen parchment fragments written in Hebrew. These fragments included part of a Ben-Sira scroll[469] and a fragment of שרות עולת השבת ("Songs of Sabbath Sacrifice"), a document associated with Qumran and the Essenes in modern scholarship.[470] There were also fragments from Genesis, Deuteronomy, Leviticus, and Psalms.[471] The audio discussions relating to the contexts in which these fragments were found are the ones that were lost.[472]

As digging continued in Locus 1039, it turned out that the layer with the densest concentration of objects was about 40 cm deep. Beneath this, a new layer was exposed, containing a few hundred ballistas and rolling stones, which must have fallen in from a room or a rooftop above when the roof of Locus 1039 collapsed.[473]

While it is clear that Locus 1039 was occupied during the period of the rebellion, it is not clear to what use it was put. It may have been some sort of a workroom or cook room because of the basin, silo, and oven. Perhaps this was one of many kitchens for the groups of the rebels on Masada. It should be noted that there are difficulties in associating Locus 1039 with Locus 1042, as there are two other chambers in between them which have the same sort of domestic installations in them. The only noteworthy difference is the number and variety of materials, especially written texts, found in Locus 1039.

Although numerous documents were found in Locus 1039, many of them seem to have fallen in from the floor above when it collapsed. If we assume that the biblical and extra-biblical scrolls fell into this room from above, then it would appear that they had been or were being kept elsewhere. Much has been made of this room because of what was found in it (and it is publicised and published specifically as "The Casemate of the Scrolls"), but it seems rather unlikely that it was ever used as an archive.

Adding to these difficulties is the loss of the discussions about the finds as well as their specific contexts. This is important because the material lost relates to which of the items fell into Locus 1039 from above and which may have been gathered there from elsewhere. If Locus 1039 was not an archive, then why were such a variety of scrolls and Latin military papyri found there? Locus 1039 contained the great majority of Hebrew scrolls found on Masada. However, Greek and Latin papyri were also found here.[474] At the very least, it would appear that

---

[469] Yigael Yadin, *The Ben Sira Scroll from Masada* (Jerusalem: Israel Exploration Society; The Shrine of the Book, 1965).
[470] Carol Newsom and Yigael Yadin, "The Masada Fragments of the Qumran Songs of the Sabbath Sacrifice," *IEJ* 34.2/3 (1984): 77–88.
[471] Shemaryahu Talmon, "Hebrew Written Fragments from Masada," *DSD* 3.2 (1996): 168.
[472] Netzer, *Masada III*, 417.
[473] Netzer, *Masada III*, 419.
[474] Cotton and Geiger, *Masada II*, 19.

the collection of papyri and scrolls was placed there (or in the room above) deliberately at some point, probably in order to either prepare them for removal or for destruction, or perhaps even just as part of an inventory of items found for those who might divide the spoils between them.

We cannot assume that the random collection of written materials found in Casemate 1039 implies that it was used by the rebels as an archive. The archive or administrative centre is much more likely to have been the Water Gate, as discussed above, the place where people most likely entered onto the Masada acropolis. Much of the material found in Locus 1039 is unrelated to any religious purpose, being letters to and from Roman legionaries, receipts, bills of sale, and so on, suggesting that much of this motley collection of documents postdates the rebellion period and the end of the siege. That this particular casemate is designated in the mythology of Masada as bearing upon the identification of Locus 1042 as a synagogue is difficult to understand outside the nationalistic fervour of the time of the excavations.

The presence of fragments of שרות עולת השבת ("Songs of Sabbath Sacrifice") could perhaps suggest the existence of a first-century Jewish liturgy which *might*, in turn, imply that there was a fixed location wherein this liturgy was enacted.[475] This document may well have been brought to Masada from elsewhere in order to ensure its survival. If the connection with Jerusalem and Qumran was as simple as people fleeing to Masada after the destruction of those places, taking with them the moveable paraphernalia of their lives and religious beliefs, and parts of their libraries, then this is probably sufficient to explain the presence of such a wide assortment of objects, written, and otherwise. The evidence, such as it is, does not lend itself to a more concrete conclusion as to the existence of a synagogue at Locus 1042 or the existence of an archive at Locus 1039.

THE EXCAVATION REPORTS

LOCUS 1042 (EXCAVATORS' PHASE 1)

According to the excavators, the first phase of Locus 1042 belongs to the Herodian period, when it was constructed as part of Herod the Great's building programme on Masada (Herodian construction on Masada began between 37–31 BCE). According to the excavators, the Herodian building is basically—but not exactly—rectangular in shape, and measures 10.5 m x 12 m. It comprised a main chamber (10.5 m x 8.0 m) and an antechamber adjoining it on the east (10.5 m x 3.6 m). The entrance (1.35 m) to the building was in the middle of its eastern

---

[475] I am grateful to Dr. Benjamin Wold of Trinity College Dublin for advice about the Essenes, Qumran, and first-century Jewish liturgy.

wall.[476] In the main chamber were five columns, in a U-shaped configuration (see fig. 27 below).[477] The entrance to the building is on the east.

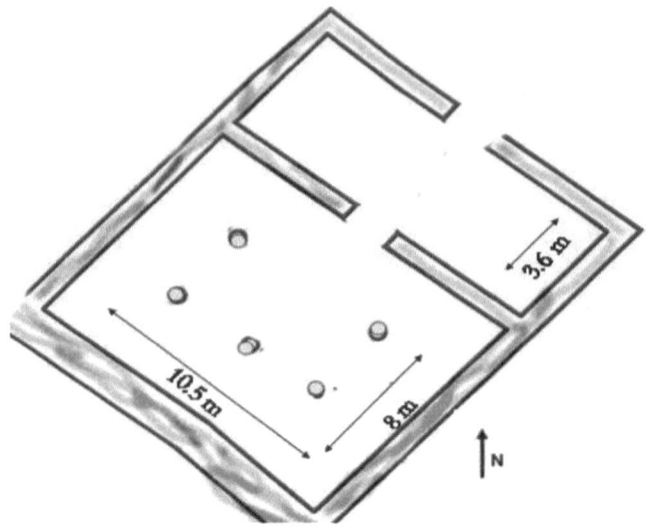

Figure 27 – Locus 1042 (excavators' phase 1)

In Locus 1042, all five columns stood on square (70 x 70 cm) bases, none of which are visible now. The floor of the building was white lime plaster laid on a thick gravel fill which levelled the ground above the bedrock.[478] There were no traces of white lime plaster on the inner walls either above or below the later floor. The inner facings of the walls were covered with earth plaster, patches of which have survived. The outer facing was coated with white lime plaster, large sections of which have been preserved, particularly on the northern wall. No evidence was found of installations or other details related to the original building.[479]

There is not very much to add to the excavators' description of the first phase of Locus 1042. No evidence of installations or other details related to the original building were found during the excavations, and it is therefore not possible to do other than speculate as to how it may have been used. In context, Locus 1042 stands just 25 m from Herod's Northern Palace, and just 50 m to its north is the Water Gate leading to the cisterns in the cliff face 80 m below (see figure 26 above). Locus 1042 was close enough to the Northern Palace to have been used

---

[476] Netzer, *Masada III*, 402–4.
[477] Netzer, *Masada III*, 404.
[478] Netzer, *Masada III*, 405.
[479] Netzer, *Masada III*, 405. As we shall see below, it seems that the earth-plastered walls relate to a later phase of Locus 1042.

by some sort of support staff for some official function which was necessary to the occupants of the palace and/or garrison. At this original Herodian stage in its life, Locus 1042 did not have benches and could have been used for virtually any purpose. It is notable that its inner walls were coated with a rough earth plaster, and not a hard white lime plaster. At the very least, given that the original phase of Locus 1042 had a white lime plastered floor, it might be useful to assume that it also originally had white plastered or painted walls, but it is impossible to say if this was the case. Nevertheless, it would be difficult to imagine why the builders of Locus 1042 would put a hard white lime plaster floor into a building with rough earth plastered walls. It may be that this brown earth plaster belongs to the post-Herodian period, and that it is related to the second and/or third phases of Locus 1042 (see below).

LOCUS 1042/1043 (EXCAVATORS' PHASE 2/3)

Major structural changes were made in the second/third phase of the building's existence, and the excavators attribute these changes to the "Zealots" (see fig. 28 below).[480]

Once the building had undergone these major structural changes, benches were built in tiers along all sides of the merged chamber. Four tiers were located along most of the available wall space—the northern wall, the eastern wall (with the exception of the central section between the two pilasters), the southern wall, and the shortened western wall (up to Locus 1043). Only one tier was installed along the wall between Locus 1043 and the main chamber, facing the entrance. The average width of the benches was 45 cm, their average height 35 cm. They were built of fieldstones, sandstone, and fragments of capitals and other reused architectural elements. Like the walls of the hall, the benches were covered with earth plaster, much of which survived *in situ*.[481] Trial sections in the tiers of benches revealed how they were constructed. For some reason, the first to be built was not the lowest tier but the two upper ones. These two upper benches were erected on the *original* Herodian white lime plaster floor of the hall.[482]

---

[480] Netzer, *Masada III*, 406; Marilyn Joyce Segal Chiat, *Handbook of Synagogue Architecture* (BJS 29; Chico, CA: Scholars Press, 1982), 249–51.
[481] Netzer, *Masada III*, 406.
[482] Netzer, *Masada III*, 407. The reason this is important will become clear in my analysis of the construction phases of Locus 1042/1043 below.

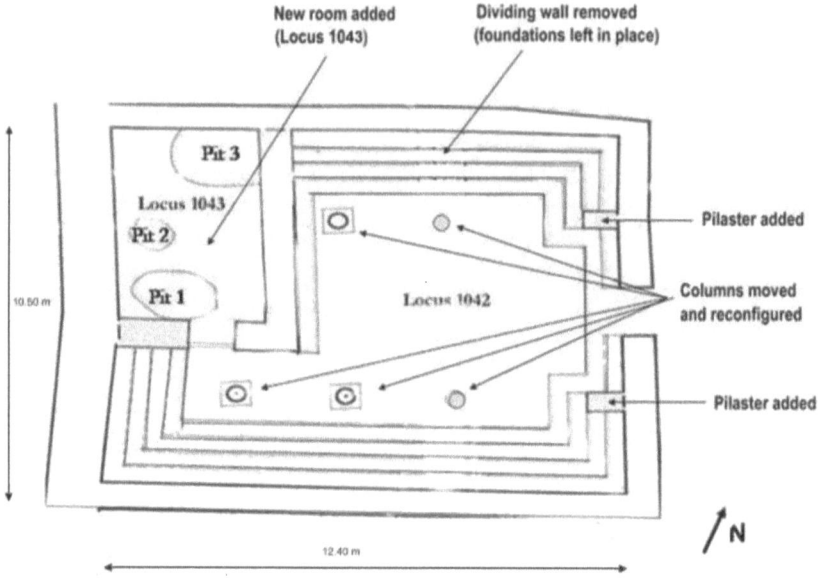

Figure 28 – Locus 1042 (excavators' phases 2/3)

The lowest bench was added later, above the plaster floor laid by the rebels. A similar technique was employed along the eastern wall, except that there the two upper tiers were built first and the lower ones added later. The excavators had two possible explanations for this: technical considerations or a change of plan while work was in progress.[483]

In the rebellion period, the floor of Locus 1042 was a grey ash lime plaster laid on a bedding of small stones intermixed with sherds.[484] Excavations revealed that this floor sat about 20 cm above the original Herodian floor. Below the new floor was a layer of soil which had been levelled and covered with gravel and stones. Also exposed in the excavations were the foundations of the wall that originally separated the inner and outer chambers. While the wall itself had been dismantled down to the bedrock, its foundations were left intact to a height of 30 cm to support the new columns. Seventeen coins were found here.[485]

Twenty Herodian period lamps were uncovered in Locus 1042, most of which were found in the northwestern corner.[486] On the southwestern floor were fragments of glass vessels and the above-mentioned ostracon inscribed with מעשר

---

[483] Netzer, *Masada III*, 407.
[484] Netzer, *Masada III*, 407.
[485] Netzer, *Masada III*, 409.
[486] Yadin, "Excavation of Masada," 78.

כהן.[487] This ostracon was found just outside the threshold of Locus 1043. Also in the southeastern corner of Locus 1042 were visible traces of a fire.[488]

The floor of the new room, Locus 1043, was beaten earth, and it was not plastered over when the new floor was laid in Locus 1042. This beaten earth floor was found covered with debris, including the remains of an oven and evidence of a fire. The oven led Yadin to suggest that this room served as a dwelling for the person responsible for the maintenance of the building, and he said that this person was a priest.[489]

Among the burnt items found scattered on the floor were fragments of clay chalices, portions of a bronze bowl, and a large quartz hand-bowl. There were also some coins, cloth fragments, and a strip of sacking twisted and dipped in asphalt (possibly a torch), all overlying a layer of animal dung some 10 cm thick (and as much as 20 cm or more in some places).[490] At some point, when the dung layer was already in place, three pits were dug in the floor of Locus 1043: one in the middle, near the western wall, another in the southern section of the room, by the doorway, and one running beneath the wall that divided Locii 1042 and 1043.

THE THREE PITS IN LOCUS 1043

The first pit found was roughly circular, about 80 cm in diameter and about 70 cm deep, and contained fragments of the book of Deuteronomy as well as 15 coins dating to the first century CE (but not the rebellion).[491] The second pit discovered was roughly oval, about 2.0 m long, 1.4 m wide and also about 70 cm deep. The second pit was later filled by a layer which included, as well as gravel, pottery sherds, dung, and small fragments of the book of Ezekiel. A further fill was then deposited, up to a height of some 30 cm, in layers consisting of ashes and dung. The third pit contained the same mix of gravel, pottery sherds, dung, and four Latin *tituli picti* (two of which related to consignments of wine for Herod).[492]

According to the excavators, in terms of the identification of the usage of this building in this phase as a synagogue, one should "envisage the Zealots' efforts to find the most suitable location for assembling in prayer and/or reading the Torah," where the only alternatives would have been either on the lower terrace of the Northern Palace or on the upper terrace, but that these rooms were situated in a section of Masada that may have been out of bounds for most of the Zealot

---

[487] Yadin and Naveh, *Masada* I, 32.
[487] Netzer, *Masada III*, 410.
[488] Yadin, "Excavation of Masada," 78.
[489] Yadin, "Excavation of Masada," 78–79.
[490] Netzer, *Masada III*, 409.
[491] Netzer, *Masada III*, 410.
[492] Netzer, *Masada III*, 410.

community. Locus 1042 provided enough space, according to the excavators, for at least 250 persons, if some were seated on the floor.[493]

MY ANALYSIS OF THE EXCAVATION REPORTS AND BUILDING PHASES

The second/third phase of Locus 1042/1043, as set out in the final excavation reports above, is confusing and needs to be unpacked. This is because, contrary to the excavation reports, there appear to be four to five discrete construction phases, not two to three.

The first phase of Locus 1042 (see fig. 27 above) seems straightforward, and I am in agreement with the analysis outlined under Phase One above. However, my interpretation of the second and subsequent phases differs substantially from that of the excavators. Locus 1042 was used as a stable at some point (something the excavators themselves suggest, but only in relation to the original Herodian phase 1 of the structure).[494]

Locus 1042 is large enough to have contained wooden stalls and/or tethering areas for perhaps ten or fifteen mules, donkeys or horses, with the outer chamber being used for tack, equipment, feed, etc. (it measured 10.5 x 12.4 m). At any rate, and in relation to its use as a stable, Locus 1042 was close to a number of buildings which might have need of such facilities. For instance, it is just 50 m south of the Water Gate, 60 m from the Western Palace, and 25 m from the Northern Palace (see fig. 26 above). It is possible that this was a place used to stable pack animals which were used to carry water up to the acropolis. During the rebellion period, it would have been necessary to have a place to keep horses needed for raiding neighbouring areas, such as En Gedi, as mentioned in Josephus (*B.J.* 4.402–405).

LOCUS 1042 / MY PHASE 2A

Whether its use as a stable extended into the rebel period is impossible to say, but at some point during the period of the rebellion, Locus 1042 was converted for use as an assembly space. The construction of the benches using architectural fragments from elsewhere suggests that other areas of the palace had gone out of use by the time they were put in place, and the fill in the pits in which the scroll fragments had been found contained dung. The construction of the benches, in particular, is quite interesting. The lowest bench was not added until *after* the rebel period floor was laid (discussed in detail below). In my Phase 2a (see fig. 29 below), the inner and outer chambers were merged into one large room by removing the partition wall and rearranging the columns to support a new roof

---

[493] Netzer, *Masada III*, 412.
[494] Netzer, *Masada III*, 412.

over the entire structure.[495] As stated in the excavation reports, only three of the original column bases remained in place when this structural change was made, the other two (the northwestern and middle columns in the western row) were dismantled and moved (their foundations remained in place), and a sixth column was added.

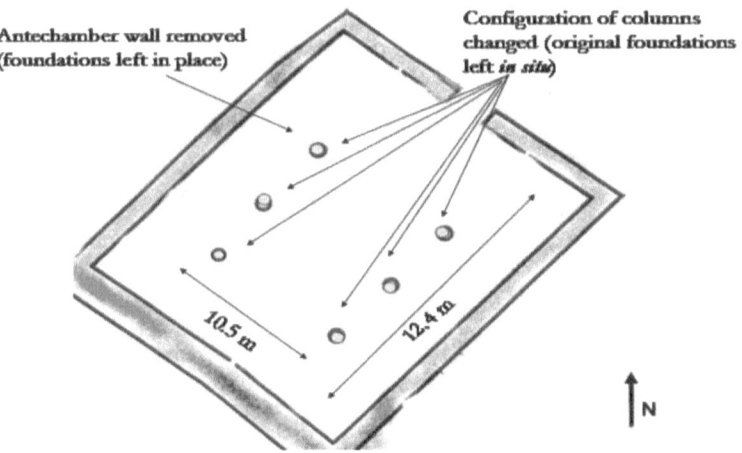

Figure 29 – Locus 1042 (My phase 2a)

It is quite possible that these changes were made to make the stable (if that is what it was) more capacious. Given that its walls were coated in a rough brown earth plaster, it would appear to make sense that the earth plaster on the walls dates to this phase, and not to the earlier Herodian phase; otherwise, it is difficult to imagine why a structure with an expensive, hard white lime plaster floor could be plastered with rough brown earth plaster. This also, in turn, suggests that in its earlier phases (when it was white-plastered) it was not a stable.

LOCUS 1042 / MY PHASE 2B

In my Phase 2b of Locus 1042, two rows of benches were added above the original white plaster Herodian period floor (see fig. 30 below).[496] The top bench in this phase was 135 cm high and 45 cm wide. The second bench was 100 cm high and 45 cm wide. *The height of these benches is the clearest possible indication that they were not originally intended as seating, but as places for holding water troughs, hay, straw, feedbags, and other equipment for use with the animals housed in the building. It is important, for the purposes of the seating argument,*

---

[495] Netzer, *Masada III*, 404.
[496] Netzer, *Masada III*, 407.

to keep in mind the fact that the two benches of this phase rested on the original Herodian floor. The reason for this will be clear in relation to my phase 3.

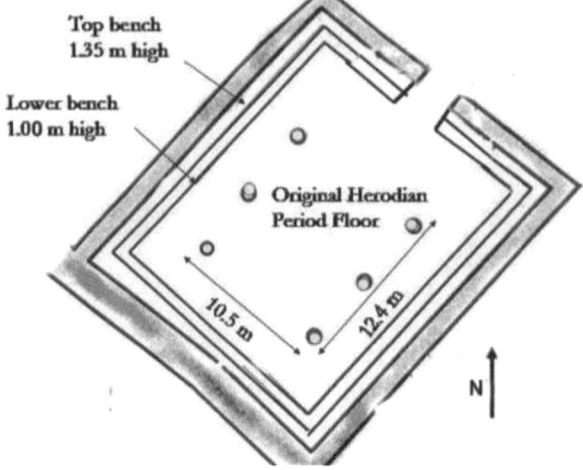

Figure 30 – Locus 1042 (my phase 2b)

The argument in relation to the benches (or, perhaps more correctly, the *shelves*) not being used for seating is made on the basis that the first two rows of benches which are constructed over the original Herodian period floor are too high to be used as seating. The height of the *then*-bottom row (100 cm) would make it difficult to step onto to get to the bench above it, but this height is ideal for shelves holding water, feed troughs, and tack for animals standing in stalls. Furthermore, these two tiers of shelves were plastered with a simple brown earth plaster rather than a more stable white or grey hydraulic lime plaster, as were the internal walls of Locus 1042, and it must therefore be the case that the brown earth plastered internal walls of Locus 1042 probably belong to this phase.

LOCUS 1042 / MY PHASE 3

Only in my phase 3 of Locus 1042, is the lowest (third) tier of benching added (see fig. 31 below). In the rebellion period, a new floor made of grey lime plaster was laid approximately 20 cm above the original Herodian period floor. The third (and lowest) bench was added only after the new floor was laid, and rests on it. It was at this point that the two pilasters at the entrance were also added. It becomes clear *only* at this point that Locus 1042 had been converted from probable use as a stable to use as an assembly space.[497]

---

[497] Netzer, *Masada III*, 407.

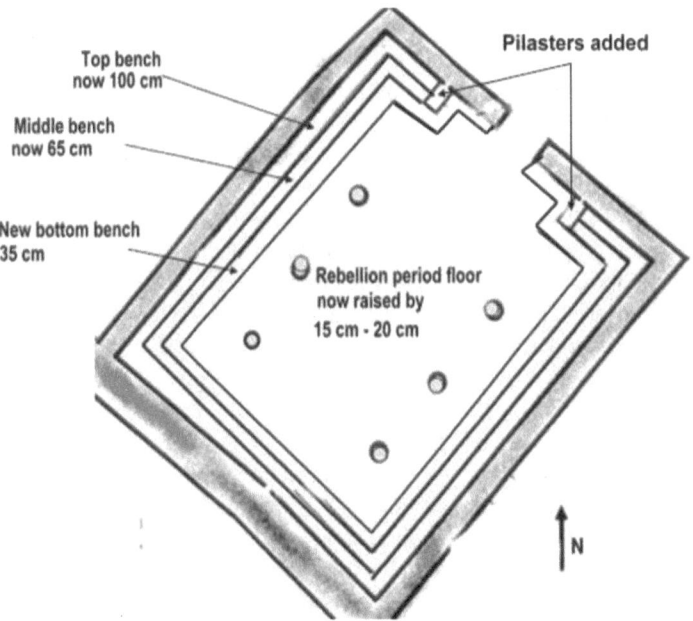

Figure 31 – Locus 1042 (my phase 3)

There is no way of knowing whether the merging of the two original chambers and the construction of the "benches" was contemporary, immediately consecutive, or separated by an unknown period of time, but we can say for sure that the bottom row of benches and the two pilasters went in only *after* the new floor was laid. This is certain, because the excavations revealed that the first two rows of benches sat on the original Herodian floor, and the bottom row of benches sat on the rebellion period floor, and, the pilasters sat on the same level as the bottom row of benches.[498] The addition of the lowest row of benching and the new floor meant that the two upper benches were now easily accessible for people stepping from one row to the next.[499] The bottom row was now 35 cm high, the middle row was 65 cm high and the top row 100 cm high, making it possible to step up onto them.

Another major difference between the excavators' understanding of this phase and mine is that the way in which the benches were constructed makes it evident that there are only three rows of benches along the north and south walls of Locus 1042, not four. Somewhere between Yadin's excavations, the subsequent conservation work (including the replastering of the benches), and the writing-up

---

[498] Netzer, *Masada III*, 407.
[499] Netzer, *Masada III*, 407.

of the final excavation reports, some information seems to have been lost. The loss of this information (pertaining to the removal of the entire rebel period floor) appears to have happened at the point at which conservation and plastering was carried out and the rebel period floor level was mistaken for a bottom bench. Because this lowest tier is not a bench, there is also no single bench along the western wall.[500]

The proof for this is a simple physical observation, one which can be made from the photographic evidence, even without referring to the supporting information in the excavation reports. The composition of the rebel period floor—which the excavators removed in its entirety to search for more pits which they hoped would contain more scrolls/scroll fragments—can still be seen in the entranceway of Locus 1042 in the photograph at figure 32 below.[501] In the photograph, you can also see that the rebel period floor was level with what the excavators described as the bottom tier of benches.[502] After the excavations were completed, the conservators of the site plastered the benches with white plaster as part of the reconstruction of Locus 1042, which has added to the confusion. Lending still more support to this observation is the fact that you can clearly see tide marks on the columns showing where the rebellion period floor reached before the excavators removed it. These tide marks are visible on all of the columns in Locus 1042, although only one is in view in this photograph (there is another view of the columns at fig. 35 below). You can also see in the photograph above that the two pilasters are sitting on the bottom row of benches, which was laid above the rebel period floor. In the photograph, you can also clearly see where the rebellion period floor *would have been* had it not been removed during the excavation process. The excavation reports themselves refer to the removal of the rebel period floor in its entirety.[503]

---

[500] Netzer, *Masada III*, 406.
[501] Netzer, *Masada III*, 407.
[502] Yadin, *Masada: Herod's Fortress*, 187. Here Yadin describes the events around the discovery of the pits containing the scroll fragments, and how this "spurred" the excavators on to remove the *entire* rebel period floor level.
[503] Netzer, *Masada III*, 407.

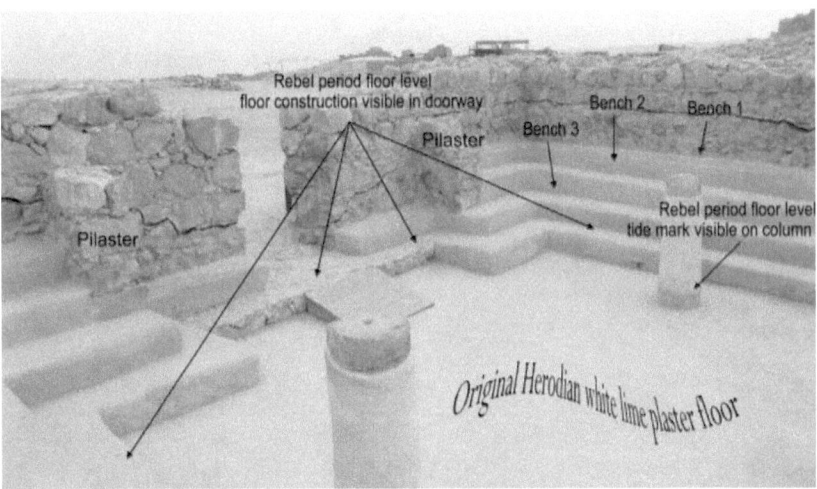

Figure 32 – Locus 1042 (floor level and benches)

The absence of the fourth row of benches along the western wall has implications for the seating, which I will discuss in detail below.

LOCUS 1042 (MY PHASE 4)

The final structural change to Locus 1042 was the addition of the smaller inner room (see fig. 33 below). This necessitated the removal of the benches along the western wall, which is why the benches as preserved today have such a peculiar configuration. Leading up to the construction of Locus 1043 (*before* Locus 1042 was used for assembly but *after* it was used as a stable) dung was brushed into the northwestern corner of the building and never removed. This corner of the building ended up being contained within the walls that created Locus 1043. The dung which had been brushed into the corner of the two merged chambers was left in place, and a layer of beaten earth was laid over it. The fact that the floor of Locus 1043 was never plastered, but rather had a covering of beaten earth, suggests that it was something of an *ad hoc* addition to the structure of Locus 1042, during the period of the rebellion, and was put in place *after* the first two rows of benches had been first constructed and then amended and, therefore, probably *after* the structure had begun to be used as a meeting space.

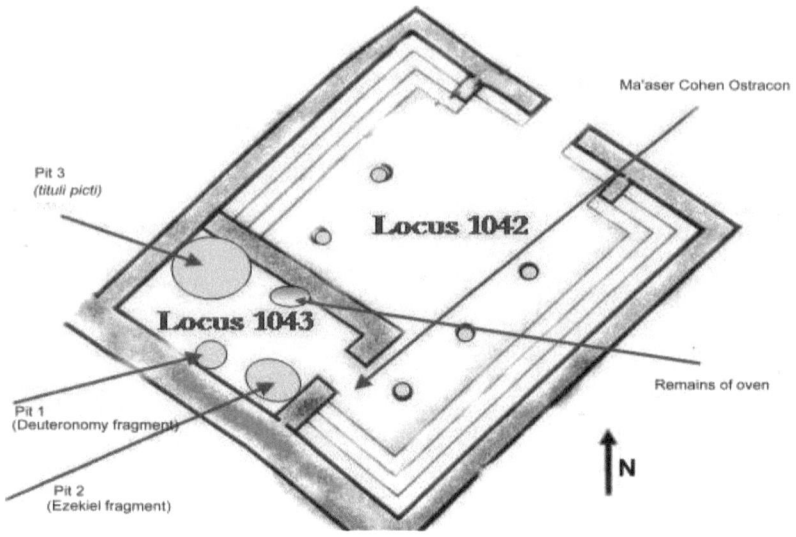

Figure 33 – Locus 1042/1043 (my phase 4)

Three pits were excavated in Locus 1043. They are numbered in figure 33 above in the order in which they were uncovered. But despite the excavators' interpretation (see above), there is nothing in the contents of the pits to differentiate their ages or their fill.

Pit 1 was found in the middle of the room, near the western wall. It was roughly circular, some 80 cm in diameter and about 70 cm deep. This pit was found to contain a small scroll fragment from the book of Deuteronomy. Pit 2 was roughly oval, some 1.4 m in diameter and about 70 cm deep. It contained a fragment of the book of Ezekiel. Pit 3, ran underneath the wall between Locus 1042 and Locus 1043, suggesting it predated the wall which, in turn, suggests that the other two pits also predated the wall, since they contained the same fill mix. In any event, contained within this pit were, besides gravel, potsherds, organic material (dung), four Latin *tituli picti* (two of which specified shipments of wine for Herod), and coins. A further fill was then deposited, up to a height of about 30 cm, in layers consisting of ashes and more dung.

It is worth repeating that all three pits contained the same fill mixture, comprising potsherds, burnt material, and dung—a clear indication that they were contemporary. Pit 3 also contained Latin *tituli picti* and coins, covered over with layers of burn material and more dung, but it was not identified as belonging to the *"genizah."*[504] The scroll fragments from Pits 1 and 2 were found near the sides

---

[504] Netzer, *Masada III*, 410.

and bottoms of the pits.[505] It was the discovery of these fragments of biblical text that resulted in Locus 1043 being identified as a *genizah*. However, there are considerable difficulties with this interpretation, in that the random nature of the items found in the pits in Locus 1043 is confused, and the pit fill from all three pits includes the dung that was found all over the floor of Locus 1043.[506] It is this which rules out a *genizah* identification, as it would seem to be impossible for anyone of a religious sensibility to deliberately dispose of sacred texts in a dung-filled pit. Moreover, unlike Locus 1042, there was never any separation between the pits and the dung because the floor of Locus 1043 was never plastered over. It is no longer possible to know why the items found in these three pits came to be buried there, but they would appear to be a random mix, rather than a deliberate method of putting textual fragments out of use.

Of course, it is also possible that the scroll fragments found in Pits 1 and 2 could have been disposed of during the frantic last hours or minutes of the siege, thereby explaining the carelessness of the deposit. They could also have been deposited during the inevitable looting by the Romans after the siege had ended. There is also another possibility, that the pit deposits were made during a later period, for instance, when Masada was occupied by Christian monks during the Byzantine period.[507]

Locus 1043 was not the only structure in which biblical scroll fragments and other items were found. Only two chambers away to the south, in Locus 1039 (the "Casemate of the Scrolls") there was a large collection of scroll fragments, in Hebrew, Aramaic, Greek, and Latin, as well as numerous other articles all apparently deliberately gathered together (see section on Locus 1039 above).

It is something of a leap of faith to assume that Locus 1042 was used by Zealots for the purposes of assembly and for reading Torah. Locus 1042 is a strategically important place. It is just two casemate rooms away from Tower 1038, which looks out over the Roman siege ramp (see fig. 34 below) and which was used for defensive purposes.

---

[505] Netzer, *Masada III*, 410.
[506] Netzer, *Masada III*, 409.
[507] Feldman, Louis H. "Masada: a critique of recent scholarship," in *Christianity, Judaism and Other Greco-Roman Cults, Studies for Morton Smith at Sixty* (ed. Jacob Neusner; Leiden: Brill, 1975), 3:224.

140   INVENTION OF THE FIRST-CENTURY SYNAGOGUE

Figure 34 – View of Loci 1038, 1039 and 1042 (looking west)

It makes far more sense to interpret Locus 1042 as a military field office designated for planning battle strategies, especially in light of the seating capacity available. Remains of a rebellion period oven were found in Locus 1043 (see fig. 33 above), and certainly it would make sense to have cooking facilities available for people using this Locus 1042 for strategic planning or other meetings.[508]

SEATING IN LOCUS 1042

Now, to the number of people Locus 1042 could contain: the excavators' estimate of 250 is highly suspect, even with people sitting or standing on the floor.[509] Unfortunately, during my many visits to Masada, I never thought to measure the building and now have a sadly unfulfilled sense that the excavators' measurements relate to the external dimensions of Locus 1042, not its internal dimensions. At most, 100 people could have sat in this building; 12–13 people on each row of benches and the rest standing or sitting on the floor. Even if I am wrong about the existence of a fourth tier of benches, only another twenty or so people could fit in. Either way, these people would have been very cramped indeed, and their presence would have rendered the space impossible to use for anything other than squashing people into it. There would be no logical reason to have a community assembly area located in such a confined space.

Moreover, if this was a synagogue for the general community, services would have had to have been conducted in shifts to accommodate everyone, adding

---

[508] See chapter on Jericho herein.
[509] Netzer, *Masada III*, 412.

another level of improbability to the argument for use of this space as a synagogue in a militarily and strategically significant area.

Even packed in like sardines, and including people standing on the floor, nothing like 250 people could have fitted into this space: there are only two walls of three rows of benches available (or four, if my explanation for the structure of the benches is rejected). Figure 35 (below) is a photograph taken in February 2009, showing six people sitting along the northern wall of Locus 1042, which is the wall with the most available seating space, and I am standing on the middle bench of the southern wall to take the photograph.[510]

Figure 35 – Locus 1042 (seating capacity)

While Locus 1042 could of course have been used as a synagogue or a place to read the Torah, or just a multi-purpose assembly area, there were plenty of locations far away from the siege engines and assorted offensive weaponry of the Romans which could have been used for this purpose. It is difficult to envisage a situation where the rebel commanders of Masada could allow such a strategically important space to be used by one group, and a group, moreover, which was made up of men, women, and children. It simply does not make sense to have Locus 1042 used for this purpose, when it would have been important to the rebels as an enclosed defence and strategic planning area.

The excavators have claimed that there were only two possible alternatives for the location of an assembly area: one on the lower terrace of the Northern Palace and one on the upper terrace, and that these "may well have been off

---

[510] You can also see in this photograph that the so-called single bench on the western wall is in fact the floor level of the rebel period chamber. Note also the tide marks on the columns, showing where the rebel period floor level reached. The floor you can now see in Locus 1042 is the *original* floor level from Phase 1 (the Herodian period building). See also fig. 40 in the Herodium chapter, a comparison of the seating there and at Masada.

bounds for most of the Zealot community."[511] This is demonstrably a straw man argument. There were any number of places that could have been used for religious or other assembly. The southern end of the acropolis was relatively open (see fig. 26), the casemate chambers there were occupied by refugees, rebels, and their families during the siege, and there was no immediate risk of attack by the Romans as it was inaccessible, there being no southern access to the Masada acropolis. There was a southern gate (see fig. 26 above), but it led only to a group of cisterns in the southeastern cliff, not to the bottom of the mountain, and it was not accessible from the ground.

If there was a synagogue on Masada, the southern end of the acropolis would be the likeliest and safest place for it to be. Moreover, many huts had been built on the southern end of the acropolis during the period of the rebellion to solve a housing problem. These huts were built of mud and stones and were concentrated around the Herodian structures on the southern end of the acropolis, adjacent to the walls. These were built during the final stages of the rebellion, when there appears to have been an influx of refugees. Most of the coins from Year 4 of the rebellion were found in these huts.[512] It would seem logical to construct an assembly hall here, where the refugees lived, not at the northern end of the acropolis where the rebels were based, and where *all* of the defensive action against the Romans took place.

LITERATURE REVIEW

HERSHEL SHANKS (1979)

According to Shanks, readers unfamiliar with the history of synagogues assumed that Yadin's discovery of a synagogue on Masada was the only evidence for a pre-70 CE synagogue, but, in fact, Yadin's discovery only marked "the first synagogue *remains* which predated the Roman destruction."[513] Shanks goes on to say that we even "have archaeological evidence for a synagogue in Israel which pre-dates the Masada synagogue, although no trace has been found of the synagogue building itself, and only the dedication inscription survives: this is the synagogue referred to in the Theodotos inscription.[514]

According to Shanks, in 66 CE a small group of Jewish "Zealots" occupied Masada and held it until 73 CE when it fell to the Romans. Describing Locus 1042, Shanks says that a small room was built in the corner of the synagogue, and that we do not know the purpose of the small room, but it could only be entered

---

[511] Netzer, *Masada III*, 412.
[512] Netzer, "Masada," 980.
[513] Herschel Shanks, *Judaism in Stone: The Archaeology of Ancient Synagogues* (New York: Harper & Row, 1979), 17.
[514] Shanks, *Judaism in Stone*, 17–18.

from the synagogue. Perhaps, he says, Torah scrolls and a wooden ark to house them were stored here. The portable ark would then be brought into the synagogue for service. Shanks says that "this was a common arrangement before a permanent structure for the Torah ark was built into the synagogue's prayer room."[515] He asks how we know this building was a synagogue, and answers that the evidence is provided in the two pits which the "Zealots" dug, in which biblical scrolls were found. This, he says, was the "Zealot" *genizah,* the traditional burial ground for worn out holy writings.[516] Shanks offers other reasons to support his argument: that the architecture is similar to some Galilaean synagogues; that an ostracon inscribed "priestly tithe" was found in Locus 1042; and that the building was clearly used as a public structure.[517]

Shanks began his discussion of Masada with reference to the Theodotos inscription and the synagogue to which it belonged, stating that it belongs to the pre-destruction period in Jerusalem. He noted that the synagogue itself had not been found. He does not mention, however, that there is debate about the dating of the Theodotos inscription, that it was found *entirely* out of context (see introduction), and that we do not know to what period it belonged. It is far too ambiguous a piece of evidence on which to hang an argument about pre-70 synagogues.

Shanks goes on to describe how Locus 1043 might have been used to house a wooden ark and Torah scrolls for use in the synagogue. Here, he has made an assumption about the use of Torah shrines and arks—the use of which are not, in any event, established until at least the third century CE—and projected the assumption backwards in time, with no evidence—archaeological or otherwise—to support the claim. Moreover, as I have shown above, the dating of the pit finds in Locus 1043 is by no means clear, and the deposits contain other material, such as *tituli picti* and potsherds, which would not be required to be disposed of in a *genizah.* If Locus 1043 really was a *genizah,* then surely a better method of disposing of sacred texts could be found than burying them in a crudely dug and unlined pit with rubble and rubbish?

Shanks's final argument, that the identification of Locus 1042 as a synagogue was made because the architecture is similar to other first-century, Galilaean synagogues, is entirely circular since all other supposed first-century synagogues (*all of them!*) are compared with Locus 1042 on Masada and are identified on the basis of their similarity with Masada. Compounding this problem, Locus 1042 on Masada is then compared to those other sites!

To this, Shanks adds the evidence of the ostracon inscribed "priestly tithe" and the fact that the building was used for assembly. The ostracon, as we have

---

[515] Shanks, *Judaism in Stone,* 23–25.
[516] Shanks, *Judaism in Stone,* 25.
[517] Shanks, *Judaism in Stone,* 26.

seen above, is interesting, and there is some evidence that the ostracon was in fact the shoulder of a jug in which something was contained which was probably kept for a tithe. Not that this means, of course, that a priest could not have lived in Locus 1043. A priest could have lived in Locus 1043, but we do not know this. And if a priest did live in Locus 1043, how can this possibly support a *genizah* identification? In a debris-strewn context, one small ostracon/potsherd does not an identification make.

As to the use of Locus 1042 as an assembly space: there is no question about this. In its last phase, whenever that was, Locus 1042 was clearly and unequivocally designed to be used as an assembly space. However, it is quite small and its location in terms of use by the general civilian population is problematic in that it is slap-bang in the middle of the most heavily besieged area of the acropolis of Masada; it sits beside Tower 1038 (see fig. 34), which was itself just above the Roman siege ramp. Is it likely that a place of religious assembly was located amongst the military activity of the rebels when there was ample and relatively peaceful space hundreds of metres away to the southern end of the acropolis?

GIDEON FOERSTER (1981)

Foerster concurs with the excavators, although his article was written some ten years before the volume of final archaeological reports dealing with Locus 1042. He says that the structure at Masada in its initial Herodian phase was divided into two elements: a vestibule and a hall. During the rebellion, he says, the partition between the two chambers was removed and a smaller room was built in the northern corner. Along the walls of this expanded hall, three rows of stone benches were constructed, built of ashlars taken from Herod's palace structures.[518] He goes on to say that while no fixed place was found for a Torah shrine at Masada, the smaller room (Locus 1043) might have functioned as such.[519]

Foerster also says that early synagogue plans might be compared with theatre-like structures, such as the *pronaoi* of the Greek temples at Arargatis, Artemis, and Tyche, in which benches are arranged in a horseshoe shape around the walls, and the general plan resembles a very small theatre or *Odeon*, which may be either covered or open. In these structures, the benches along two or three walls are also plastered. Foerster says that these halls served for the assembly of worshippers who were barred from entering the temples proper.[520] The most characteristic feature of the assembly halls at Masada and Herodium is their

---

[518] Gideon Foerster, "The Synagogues at Masada and Herodium," in *Ancient Synagogues Revealed* (ed. Lee I. Levine; Jerusalem: Israel Exploration Society, 1981), 24.
[519] Foerster, "The Synagogues at Masada and Herodium," 26.
[520] Foerster, "The Synagogues at Masada and Herodium," 28.

uniform orientation, the entrance is from the east, as in the Temple in Jerusalem, he says, and this uniformity cannot be regarded as coincidental, but must be seriously considered in any discussion of the function and date of these structures.[521]

Foerster has accepted Yadin's and Netzer's identification of Locus 1042 as a synagogue, and while he does suggest interesting architectural comparisons for the building in Greek architecture, he does not examine the reasons for the identification, or the difficulties and inconsistencies inherent in that identification, such as the fact that Locus 1042 is not actually orientated towards Jerusalem.[522] In mitigation of this, however, and as stated above, he wrote this article before the excavation reports had been published. Nevertheless, other than the Greek architectural comparisons, this is a straightforward recitation of Yadin's and Netzer's opinions.

SHAYE COHEN (1982)

Cohen does not deal with the identification of Locus 1042 as a synagogue, but does discuss Josephus's suicide narrative, which at least sheds some light on the nature of the people on Masada. He says that Josephus exaggerated and embellished events, and that it is safe to suppose that the Masada narrative is not "an unalloyed version of the truth."[523] Cohen argues convincingly that the speeches made by Eleazar on Masada were literary devices and that this being the case, the use of lots as described by Josephus must be fictitious too. As twelve ostraca (not ten) were found, they cannot *a priori* have been the lots described in Josephus, even if Josephus's account was a precise representation of what had transpired at the end of the siege on Masada.[524] He goes on to say that perhaps some Sicarii killed themselves at the end of the siege, but it is most unlikely that all of them did so. The very idea that all of the rebels on Masada killed themselves is derived from another instance of this motif used by Josephus in his account of the episode at Jotapata, where he and another commander survived the same sort of suicide pact and where he then surrendered himself to the Romans.[525] Cohen points out that, had the Romans massacred the Sicarii, Josephus would have had no reason to disguise this fact because, from the Roman point of view, they

---

[521] As already noted, the orientation of Locus 1042 is not towards the east. The excavators described the axis of Masada as facing north for convenience, but it actually faces somewhat to the northwest.
[522] Netzer, *Masada III*, 410.
[523] Shaye J. D. Cohen, "Masada: Literary Tradition, Archaeological Remains and the Credibility of Josephus," *JJS* 33.1–2 (1982): 393.
[524] Cohen, "Masada: Literary Tradition," 397. For details on the *twelve* lots found, see Yadin and Naveh, *Masada I*, 30–37.
[525] Cohen, "Masada: Literary Tradition," 397.

deserved to die since they had participated in the siege of the royal palace in Jerusalem in 66 CE, and had killed some Romans during that siege (*B.J.* 2.434–440). Moreover, from the Jewish point of view, the Sicarii deserved death, since they had raided and killed 700 women and children in the town of En Gedi (*B.J.* 4.402–405). Finally, from Josephus's point of view, the Sicarii were guilty of all sorts of crimes, not the least of which was the launching of the war against Rome (*B.J.* 7.253–262).[526]

Cohen's arguments are cogent and convincing, and while they do not help with the identification of Locus 1042 as a synagogue, they do go some way to explaining why a literal interpretation of Josephus's Masada narrative has served to skew the historical record, both in terms of the nature of the people occupying Masada and their likely behaviour. The confusing representation of the Sicarii on Masada as both heroic and despicable is particularly troubling, given the foregoing, but there does not seem to be a clear way to resolve this issue.

DAVID LADOUCEUR (1989)

Like Cohen, Ladouceur does not deal with the identification of Locus 1042, but he does reinforce Cohen's arguments (above), in terms of the mythology of the Masada narrative. He says that the archaeological excavations neither "serve nor discredit" the central suicide story, but that there might be a nugget of truth in the story and perhaps an unknown number of the defenders did commit suicide rather than be taken captive by the Romans. Like Cohen, he notes the fictivity of Eleazar's speeches, that they are part of an ancient and traditional historiographic rhetorical pattern and prove nothing. He concludes in the end that the suicide narrative at least is not entirely implausible.[527]

As Ladouceur's article covers much the same ground as Cohen's, there is little to disagree with in terms of Josephus's rendering of the Masada narrative. Like Cohen, he says that it is entirely possible that some of the rebels may have killed themselves rather than be taken captive by the Romans and that, in this respect, the narrative is not entirely implausible.[528] There is perhaps some issue to be taken with Ladouceur's comment that the suicide narrative "is not entirely implausible because some Sicarii probably did commit suicide." He seems to suggest that there was some truth to the Eleazar's speeches and to the casting of lots *because* there might have been some suicides. In other respects, Ladouceur's article, like Cohen's, is a useful survey of suicide motifs in the ancient world.

---

[526] Cohen, "Masada: Literary Tradition," 399–400.
[527] Ladouceur, "Josephus and Masada," 109.
[528] Ladouceur, "Josephus and Masada," 109.

PAUL VIRGIL MCCRACKEN FLESHER (1995)

Flesher says of Masada that its structure does not have any features that identify it as a synagogue. Even the architectural features that have been used to identify it as a synagogue—such as the benches and the columns—also appear in other buildings that are not identified as synagogues, not all of which are Jewish. He also says that the discipline of archaeology is dependent on the timely publication of excavation reports to allow scholars access to the information and that, in the case of Masada, these reports took almost three decades to appear, and thus most discussion of the subject has been on the basis of brief preliminary remarks, rather than on a complete presentation of the data.[529] Flesher describes the building that Yigael Yadin identified as a synagogue, and notes its construction during the Herodian period. He notes Yadin's claim that the rebels on Masada converted it into a synagogue by removing a wall, adding a floor, constructing a storage room, and adding four levels of stone benches around the inside walls. He acknowledges Yadin's reasons for the identification as being: that it was an assembly hall; that it was orientated towards Jerusalem; and that fragments of Deuteronomy and Ezekiel were found buried in the storage room.[530]

Flesher deals with Yadin's claim on the orientation by saying that it derives not from the rebels but from the original Herodian structure, and is therefore coincidental. However, since Locus 1042 is actually aligned on a northwest-southeast axis for convenience, the orientation argument is not in any event correct.[531] Flesher goes on to say that the original (Herodian) floor of the building was covered with a deep layer of animal dung, indicating that it had been a barn. The dung was not removed before the new floor was laid down. Finally, he argues that the buried scroll fragments do not prove that this was a synagogue on the basis that the literary and archaeological evidence from Qumran show that there was no synagogue there and, since Qumran's scrolls are nowhere associated with a synagogue, Masada's fragments cannot on their own indicate such a structure.[532] Flesher says that the identification of this structure as a synagogue is uncertain. Indeed, it could have been a place for the rebels to meet and plan strategy, a need common to most armies. Certainly, it is well situated for that purpose, overlooking the area where the Romans built their siege ramp.[533]

Flesher's discussion is the only truly critical one in the scholarship. While he has not dealt with the archaeological evidence closely (for example, he has not noticed the problem with the number of benches identified by the excavators, or the fact that the second ostracon ascribed to Locus 1042 came from Locus 1044),

---

[529] Flesher, "Palestinian Synagogues," 35.
[530] Flesher, "Palestinian Synagogues," 35–36.
[531] Flesher, "Palestinian Synagogues," 36.
[532] Flesher, "Palestinian Synagogues," 36.
[533] Flesher, "Palestinian Synagogues," 37.

he comes to the conclusion that Locus 1042 was used as a strategic centre for military planning, because of its location so close to the siege ramp and access to Masada from the valley below.[534] He clearly wrote this article on the basis of all the evidence available to him, and not on the basis of a pre-existing theory which he wished to shore up. He has looked for evidence to support the synagogue identification, but has not found it. In methodological terms, this is the ideal approach to take.

E. JAN WILSON (1996)

Wilson reiterates Yadin's description of Locus 1042, saying that it was identified on the basis of its orientation and the presence of the ostraca inscribed "priestly tithe" and another marked "Hezekiah."[535] She adds that although it had been modified by the "Zealots," it was quite likely to have been constructed as a synagogue by Herod.[536] Wilson goes on to say that if "any doubts remained that this structure represented a synagogue, those doubts were removed during the second season when Yadin's team discovered a *genizah*." Wilson describes the fragments of scrolls found and then asserts that since "these scrolls were buried there before the destruction of Masada by the Romans, they must be dated no later than AD 73."[537] Wilson argues that scholars "generally assume that the institution of the synagogue arose after the destruction of Jerusalem and the First Temple in 586 BC because of a need to find a substitute form of worship when temple worship was no longer possible." This is based on Ezek 11:16, where God states that although he has moved his people to distant places and scattered them in various lands, he will nevertheless be to them as a "small sanctuary."[538] Wilson also refers to Jer 39:8, which refers to the destruction of a structure called a *beth ha'am*, saying that if the *beth ha'am* represents a synagogue or even a forerunner to the synagogue, then the institution was in place before the destruction of the first temple."[539]

---

[534] I came to these same conclusions independently before I had read Flesher's account. His account provided both a deflation of ego—because he had come to these conclusions long before I even began to study the subject—and a sense of comfort and reassurance—because I was not the only person who thought this way about early synagogue identifications.

[535] In fact, the Hezekiah ostracon, as I have stated above, was found in Locus 1044, the storerooms north of Locus 1042. E. Jan Wilson, "The Masada Synagogue and Its Relationship to Jewish Worship during the Second Temple Period," *Brigham Young University Studies* 36.3 (1996): 269.

[536] Wilson, "The Masada Synagogue," 269.

[537] Wilson, "The Masada Synagogue," 270.

[538] The same passage that *t. Sukkah* 4.5 uses to interpret מעט מקדש (a small sanctuary) as *house of assembly* (בית הכנסת).

[539] Wilson, "The Masada Synagogue," 271.

Wilson states that one thing that may be very significant in relation to the Masada synagogue is the lack of a Torah shrine, adding that from the third century CE onward, it was always present in some form and that such a niche is lacking from all structures of the Second Temple period (Masada, Herodium, Gamla, and Delos).[540] The Masada, Gamla, and Herodium synagogues, according to Wilson, also lacked the *bema* that was characteristically present in later synagogues. Wilson then argues that this supports the assumption that synagogues of the Second Temple period were not just religious structures, but instead were communal structures where religious functions *also* took place on specific days.[541]

Although her article is entitled "The Masada Synagogue and Its Relationship to Jewish Worship during the Second Temple Period," Wilson has not actually discussed the material pertaining to Masada. It is difficult to understand the reasons for this because when this article was written in 1996, *Masada III*—relating to Locus 1042 (amongst other things)—had been published, so there was certainly material available which could have been discussed. Moreover, Wilson has taken Yadin's argument that Locus 1042 was a synagogue even during the Herodian period literally, even though Yadin himself only offered it as a possibility.[542] At the very least, it would have been possible for Wilson to discuss the items found in the pits in Locus 1043 in some detail had the excavation reports been consulted, since it is not clear whether in fact the pit fills do have a *terminus post quem* of 73 CE. As I have suggested above, this is not necessarily the case. Wilson argues that the *lack* of a Torah shrine in Locus 1042 shows that the "synagogues" at Masada, Gamla, and Herodium were early stages in the development of the synagogues of the third century CE because they *share the same lack* of Torah shrine!

So, in this article the only work specifically about Locus 1042 that Wilson consulted was Yigael Yadin's 1966 popular book. Otherwise, the works consulted in preparing this article were Azriel Eisenberg's 1974 work entitled *The Synagogue Though the Ages*, the referenced section of which refers only to the Ezekiel passage referenced in Wilson's work; Eric Meyers's 1994 article in the *Anchor Bible Dictionary* relating to the same Ezekiel passage; Leopold Loew's 1875 work in *Gesammelte Schriften* (unnamed in Wilson's article) on the same passage; Louis Finkelstein's 1975 work "The Origin of the Synagogue" in *The Synagogue: Studies in Origins, Archaeology and Architecture*; Lee Levine's 1987 article "The Second Temple Synagogue: The Formative Years" in *The Synagogue in Late Antiquity*—but not in relation to Masada, only in relation to the theories around the development of the early synagogue; Richard Horsley's 1995 work, *Galilee: History, Politics, People*; Rachel Hachlili's 1976 article, "The Niche and

---

[540] Wilson, "The Masada Synagogue," 272–73.
[541] Wilson, "The Masada Synagogue," 273.
[542] Yadin, *Masada: Herod's Fortress*, 185–87.

the Ark in Ancient Synagogues" (*BASOR*); and Solomon Zeitlin's 1975 article, "The Origin of the Synagogue" in *The Synagogue: Studies in Origins, Archaeology and Architecture*. Thus, despite its title, other than Yadin's 1966 book, Wilson's bibliography does not relate to the identification of Locus 1042 as a synagogue.

Wilson's article does not add anything to the scholarship on the subject of Locus 1042, and instead discusses tangential material relating to the development of early synagogues. While these materials are certainly not irrelevant to the subject of synagogue development, they are irrelevant to the subject of the identification of a synagogue on Masada.

DONALD BINDER (1999)

Binder, like Foerster and others, repeats Yadin's assertions about the identification and the interpretations contained in the later excavation reports. He says that because the renovated hall consists of rows of benches on four sides with columns intervening between the benches and the centre of the hall, and because scriptures were found deposited within the room adjoining the main hall, it seems highly likely that the building served as a synagogue for the rebels and that this identification has been established.[543]

In relation to Locus 1043, Binder says that while this space was "certainly" used as a *genizah,* it must also be noted that the presence of an oven suggests that a priest lived in this room, a point originally made by Yadin,[544] and that the ostracon bearing the words מעשר כהן found near this room supports this contention.[545] He finds further support for this hypothesis in other ostraca attesting to the presence of priests at Masada during the revolt.[546] He also notes that stoves and personal items were found in other casemate rooms, pointing to the conclusion that many of the rebels had used these areas as dwelling places.[547] Finally, he notes that the placement of "sleeping quarters" in the Masada "synagogue" parallels the arrangement of the synagogue of Theodotos, which also contained such rooms.[548]

Binder turns to the size of Locus 1042 and its seating capacity. He notes Netzer's estimate of 250.[549] He says that, since Josephus numbered the rebels at Masada at 967, including women and children, only a segment of the community could have met inside the structure at any one time. He adds that if the synagogue

---

[543] Binder, *Into the Temple Courts*, 177.
[544] Binder, *Into the Temple Courts*, 177.
[545] Binder, *Into the Temple Courts*, 177.
[546] Binder, *Into the Temple Courts*, 177.
[547] Binder, *Into the Temple Courts*, 177.
[548] Binder, *Into the Temple Courts*, 178.
[549] Binder, *Into the Temple Courts*, 178.

served as a Sabbath meeting place "as the literature indicates," perhaps this problem was solved by having different assembly times for different groups or by having the overflow crowds sit outside (or both).[550]

Binder asserts that the discovery of the Ezekiel scroll in the small room of the synagogue suggests that not only did services include the recitation of Torah, but also readings from the Prophets. He supports this contention by reference to Locus 1039, where a number of additional scrolls were found, all dating to the rebel occupation. He says that these scrolls were all in Hebrew, and included fragments of Genesis, Leviticus, Psalms, and the *Songs of the Sabbath Sacrifice*.[551] He makes a connection with Qumran here because the *Songs of Sabbath Sacrifice* were also found there, and he says that it is possible that it too was used within services held in the synagogue. He goes on to claim that this also applies to the other scrolls found elsewhere at Masada, including fragments of Sirach and Jubilees.[552] Binder has accepted the identification of Locus 1043 as a genizah on the basis that the ostracon inscribed with the words מעשר כהן belonged there and that this contention is supported by the existence of other ostraca on Masada relating to the presence of priests.

There are a number of problems with Binder's assertions. The first, and most obvious one, is the contention that Locus 1042 is a synagogue on the basis of its internal configuration. It is not sufficient to say that because a space is intended for assembly that it is a synagogue. This, especially in the case of Masada, has created a circular argument where other so-called first-century synagogues are compared to the structure at Masada and then the structure at Masada is compared to them. Moreover, as already stated, Locus 1042 is potentially one of the least likely places (in strategic terms), and certainly one of the least safe places on Masada, to locate a synagogue or even an assembly area for the community on Masada.

Binder then turns to the fragments of scrolls found in Locus 1043, which he says served to establish its identification as a *genizah*.[553] Again, as stated above, the pit finds are by no means proof of a *genizah*. The fills are a mixture of items, including Herodian *tituli picti*, potsherds, dung, and the Ezekiel and Deuteronomy scroll fragments. As stated above, while the excavators have claimed that the first two pits (with the scroll fragments) are contemporary and belong to the *genizah*, there is in reality nothing to separate them from the third pit which extends under the wall of Locus 1043 into Locus 1042 and which contains the same mix, including dung, *except* for scroll fragments.

---

[550] Binder, *Into the Temple Courts*, 178.
[551] Binder, *Into the Temple Courts*, 179.
[552] Binder, *Into the Temple Courts*, 179.
[553] Binder, *Into the Temple Courts*, 177.

Binder goes on to discuss the presence of the oven and the ostraca inscribed "priestly tithe." He suggests that a priest lived in this room and that the ostracon supports this. As I have said above and elsewhere, it is possible that a priest *did* live in Locus 1043, but it is highly unlikely given the location of Locus 1042 in the most heavily besieged area of the acropolis. Moreover, as stated above, the ostraca (or jar shoulder) could have come from elsewhere, since it was part of a debris layer.

Binder goes on to compare Locus 1043, the *genizah,* with the facilities available in the Jerusalem Theodotos synagogue (remains of which have never been found). As stated above, the Theodotos inscription has not been definitively dated, and it was found in rubble, entirely out of context. Moreover, even if the comparison were a valid one, one could hardly compare the "hostel" arrangements described in the Theodotos inscription with the small, rough-stamped earth and dung-floored chamber of Locus 1043.[554]

Binder notes, too, that stoves and personal items were found in other casemate rooms. This is of course correct. However, it does not lend any support to his genizah and/or hostel arrangement argument. Every single casemate room on Masada was occupied during the rebel period. Since there are other references on Masada to priestly tithes, and since there was an exodus from Jerusalem leading up to and after its fall, one might expect priests to be living in various places on Masada and elsewhere.

Next, following Netzer's estimate of the seating capacity of Locus 1042 at around 250 and Josephus's assertion that there were 960 rebels on Masada, Binder suggests a sort of staggered synagogue service with groups of worshippers moving in and out. As stated above, the capacity is not, in fact, so large. It also bears repeating that this area is not suitable for the placement of a synagogue or even an assembly space for the general population. It was heavily besieged, heavily defended, and the notion that hundreds of men, women, and children could have had access to this area and moved in and out of the defensive systems is incredible. How this could possibly have worked with the Roman siege ramp just 20 m away is impossible to imagine.

Binder then goes on to claim that the Ezekiel and Deuteronomy scroll fragments found in Locus 1043 indicate that services included a Torah recitation and readings from the prophets. He suggests that this claim is supported by reference to the scrolls found in Locus 1043 which, he says, "were *all* [my emphasis] in Hebrew, and included fragments of Genesis, Leviticus, Psalms, and the *Songs of the Sabbath Sacrifice.*"[555] There is no evidence for any of this; it is an extrapolation from an assumption—and it is a faulty assumption to begin with: Binder has either misunderstood the excavation reports, and/or has ignored the

---

[554] Discussed in the introduction chapter herein.
[555] Binder, *Into the Temple Courts*, 179.

other material found in Locus 1039. As listed above in the section on Locus 1039, these materials included biblical and extra-biblical texts, letters and lists in Greek, Latin, Aramaic, and Hebrew, including a papyrus scroll which contained parts of lines from Virgil's *Aeneid*, and many other items, such as a seal of Victory/Nike, a hoard of rebel period shekels, eighteen Latin and four Greek papyri, a multiplicity of militaria including a broken and burnt bone sword pommel, a scabbard mount and a dagger suspension loop, shield fragments, a belt-buckle tongue, ballista balls, arrows, arrowheads, and rolling stones.

Binder has taken Yadin's claims on face value and has embellished them. Moreover, he has misunderstood the information contained in the excavation reports in relation to Locus 1039 in order to support his claims.[556] In any case, and in general, Binder's claims rely on assumptions and suppositions which the evidence does not support.

AVRAHAM NEGEV AND SHIMON GIBSON (2001)

Writing more recently, Avraham and Gibson reiterated, in a very short passage, the opinions of the excavators. They were careful not to deal too closely with the issue of the synagogue identification, and instead merely reported that it had been made by the excavators. They said that Locus 1042 was built over two construction phases. In the original Herodian phase the building had two rows of columns, three in each row, supporting the roof, while the entrance was on the east.[557] During the period of the Jewish rebellion, a room was built into the northwestern corner. Benches were also built along the walls, and in this way two of the columns went out of use. They also note that the excavators believe that this structure was originally a synagogue in the Herodian period and that it was certainly used as a prayer house at the time of the Revolt.[558]

LEE I. LEVINE (2000)

Levine says that Masada is "undoubtedly" the most famous synagogue from the Second Temple period and that it served the revolutionaries on Masada for meeting purposes generally, as well as for religious services, i.e., it functioned as a synagogue.[559] Levine says that, in synagogues such as those at Gamla, Masada, and Herodium, the reading of scriptures would also have been carried out in the centre of the hall, since the benches and columns left no room for a platform at one end.[560] Levine notes that three synagogues from pre-70 Judæa, Masada,

---

[556] Much as he did in relation to the Delos material (see Delos chapter herein).
[557] This detail is incorrect; in the first phase it had only five columns, in a U-shaped pattern.
[558] Negev and Gibson, *Archaeological Encyclopedia of the Holy Land*, 324.
[559] Levine, *The Ancient Synagogue*, 59–60.
[560] Levine, *The Ancient Synagogue*, 86.

Gamla, and Herodium, had nearby cisterns, which could be *mikva'ot*. He goes on to say that there is no information for any other Judæan synagogues, and generalisations cannot be made about these three in relation to others, although the practice of performing ablutions before worship is well attested in the ancient world.[561]

Levine says that the placing of stone benches in synagogue buildings is not uniform, and that generally they were placed along two or three walls of the main assembly hall, although at 'En Gedi and 'Anim in Southern Judæa they were found on only one side and at Gamla, Masada, and Herodium they were found on four sides, and that only rarely were there no benches at all (such as at Sardis and Sepphoris).[562] He also says that, up to the third century CE, focus in synagogue halls was in the centre of the room and that halls such as those at Masada, Gamla, and Herodium seem to confirm this.[563]

Levine has been careful in what he has said about the synagogue identification at Masada in his 2000 work, *The Ancient Synagogue*, for he has not made any broad claims, except his apparent acceptance of the Yadin identification of the structure as a synagogue. However, on the other hand, he devoted only one paragraph to it.

LEVINE (2004)

By 2004, Levine was able to describe the "religiously motivated population" of Masada and the room adjacent to Locus 1042 which was "probably used to store Torah scrolls used in synagogue worship." He says that while there are no inscriptions or artistic evidence that point explicitly to the identification of any of those early structures (Masada, Herodium, Delos, or Gamla) as synagogues, it is reasonable to acknowledge the public nature of these buildings and consider the possibility that a (if not *the*) key role of a synagogue in the first century was its communal function, with the religious component being ancillary—as least as reflected in the building's architectural plan and physical appearance.[564]

Again, there can be no argument with that latter statement, because it opens the door of synagogue identification so wide that any building in a demonstrably Jewish context and capable of accommodating communal activity becomes a possible synagogue. In the context of Levine writing specifically about Masada, there is nothing new here as he has, *ipso facto*, accepted the identification on the grounds put forward by Yadin and the other excavators.

---

[561] Levine, *The Ancient Synagogue*, 310.
[562] Levine, *The Ancient Synagogue*, 313–14.
[563] Levine, *The Ancient Synagogue*, 354.
[564] Lee I. Levine, "The First-Century Synagogue: Critical Reassessments and Assessments of the Critical," in *Religion and Society in Roman Palestine. Old Questions, New Approaches* (ed. Douglas R. Edwards; New York: Routledge, 2004), 79.

STEPHEN K. CATTO (2007)

Catto's discussion of Masada is another recitation of Yadin's and the excavators' opinions. He is careful, however, not to refer to the occupants of the building as "Zealots," and instead uses the term "Sicarii."[565] He says of Locus 1043 that it seems likely that it was used to house the Torah when it was not in use.[566] He further says that the discovery of scroll fragments in pits in Locus 1043 makes it certain that this was a *genizah* and that, while the foregoing are individually poor arguments, cumulatively they add up to a stronger conclusion.[567]

There is nothing in Catto's text that in any way advances the scholarship on the subject identification. However, as noted above, he is careful not to make assumptions about who the rebels were, and unlike the excavators does not refer to them generally as Zealots.

RUNESSON, BINDER, AND OLSSON (2008)

This work contains a two-paragraph recitation of Yadin's and the excavators' arguments, and it is not particularly useful in relation to the plethora of material evidence available to us. It is notable, however, that in the bibliography for the section, the authors do not include any reference to Flesher's contrary and cogent opinions.[568]

CONCLUSIONS

Unfortunately, with Locus 1042, it is only possible to suggest a number of functional possibilities for the building's use without being able to link it with specific texts and even with the material found within it and nearby. While there is certainly material evidence at Masada that suggests the possibility of some sort of religious activity during the period of the rebellion, none of it relates to the identification of a synagogue, or to whether those materials belonged to the rebels on Masada or were brought there by refugees fleeing Jerusalem and elsewhere. Indeed, if there had been a synagogue on Masada (or even an assembly hall for the general population), Locus 1042 would have been a terrible choice because of its location among the defensive structures overlooking the Roman siege ramp (see figure 34 above) and would therefore have been a dangerous place for non-combatants to have had access to.

---

[565] Stephen K. Catto, *Reconstructing the First-Century Synagogue: A Critical Analysis of Current Research*, LNTS 363 (London: T&T Clark, 2007), 91.
[566] Catto, *Reconstructing*, 92.
[567] Catto, *Reconstructing*, 92.
[568] Anders Runesson, Donald D. Binder, and Birger Olsson, *The Ancient Synagogue from its Origins to 200 CE* (Leiden: Brill, 2008), 55–57.

The evidence uncovered in Locus 1042, such as the ostracon with מעשר כהן written on it, seems to point towards some elements of religious activity on Masada but, even so, this activity, whether simple observance and a continuance of temple-based practices, simply cannot be tied to Locus 1042 because of the jumble of materials found both there and elsewhere after the fall of Masada. According to Yigael Yadin, it was during the period of the war that Locus 1042 was used as an assembly place and as a synagogue.[569] According to Yadin, while the original function of Locus 1042 is not known, it was converted into a synagogue between 66 and 74 CE. In the same work, he also made a suggestion that Locus 1042 could have been used as a synagogue even during the Herodian period, and described Locus 1043 as a *genizah* where sacred documents were put out of use.[570] His argument for this was threefold: that it was unlikely that Herod would have denied a place of worship for the Jewish members of his family and for other Jews who were members of his court; that the architectural plan of Locus 1042 with its pillars and benches is very reminiscent of the plan of several early synagogues discovered elsewhere; and that there is a strong tradition in the siting of houses of worship which would also explain why the original building was oriented toward Jerusalem.[571]

As it turns out, this is an entirely circular argument. Locus 1042 was the first structure in the land of Israel to be identified as a first-century synagogue and is invariably used as the comparator for all subsequent identifications, as I have stated above. Locus 1042 is therefore, in effect, being compared to itself. Furthermore, the orientation of Locus 1042 is not towards the east; the excavators described the axis of Masada as facing north for convenience, it actually faces north-northwest.[572] Moreover, there is no mention in Josephus or elsewhere of a synagogue or multi-purpose assembly hall at Masada. Ultimately, only the rebels on Masada, and possibly the Romans, could have known whether Locus 1042 was used as a place of religious significance and a place of general assembly or, indeed, as a synagogue. While there are some archaeological and historical reasons to support the argument that this might have been the case, as demonstrated above, the excavators' interpretation of that material is far from being beyond dispute. The above analysis has highlighted difficulties with the number of phases, the nature of the use before adaptation into an assembly space, the dating of the adaptation, as well as the capacity for seating. Furthermore, I would suggest the historical context points to a location elsewhere on Masada, if a synagogue existed there at all.

---

[569] Netzer, *Masada III*, 402; Netzer, "Masada," 974.
[570] Yadin, *Masada: Herod's Fortress*, 185, 187.
[571] Netzer, *Masada III*, 411. In any event, Locus 1042 is not oriented towards Jerusalem. The north-south axis of Masada is not precise and is used for convenience only. Locus 1042 actually faces southeast.
[572] Netzer, *Masada III*, 410.

In sum, there is no evidence to support the claim that Locus 1042 was a synagogue or general assembly hall or, indeed, that there was *any* synagogue or general assembly hall on Masada during the period of the first Jewish rebellion or any other time.

5
HERODIUM

Figure 36 – Herodium (looking south from Bethlehem)

INTRODUCTION

Herodium is one of Herod the Great's mountain fortress sites in the Judaean desert, built during the years he was establishing his kingship in Israel and is a site at which a first-century synagogue CE was identified. The identification is generally accepted in the scholarship, but when we look at the archaeological and epigraphical evidence, many flaws are revealed. Herodium (consisting of an upper fortress and a lower palatial area) is located 12 km south of Jerusalem, just below the hills of Bethlehem (see fig. 36 above).

The archaeology of upper Herodium is such that destruction layers from both Jewish rebellions against Rome are mixed together.[573] Indeed, there is only one space in the immediate area of the building identified as a synagogue that could be specifically identified as belonging to the period of the first rebellion. This chapter addresses the basis on which the synagogue identification was made, using the excavation reports, as well as the epigraphical and source material relating thereto.

Virgilio Corbo, who excavated Herodium, uncovered a Roman *triclinium* in the upper fortress of Herodium, which he said may have been adapted for use as a synagogue. He attributed the structure as belonging to the period of the Jewish *Wars*, deliberately avoiding any specific chronological ascription. By the time the final excavation reports were published, however, Corbo had found sufficient archaeological evidence to be able to say that *if* the *triclinium* had been adapted for use as a synagogue, then that usage belonged to the period of the *second* rebellion. Other scholars have since then argued that the changes to the *triclinium* belonged to the period of the first Jewish rebellion, and it is this argument that is generally accepted in the scholarship.

There is a strange disconnect between the two arguments, primarily because those who have ascribed the changes to the *triclinium* as belonging to the period of the first Jewish rebellion have quite simply ignored Corbo's findings. There is a paucity of primary material, both textual and archaeological, relating to Herodium for the period of the first Jewish rebellion. Josephus, our only comprehensive source, deals with the construction of Herodium by Herod the Great and his funeral procession to that place, but Josephus barely mentions Herodium in the context of the first rebellion. This is something that is again ignored by scholars who chose to ascribe a synagogue identification to the earlier period.

JOSEPHUS'S HERODIUM NARRATIVE

Josephus tells us that Herodium was built on the spot where Herod, retreating from Jerusalem to Masada in flight from Antigonus and the massed Parthian armies in 40 BCE, achieved one of his most important victories over the Hasmonaeans and their allies. Herodium was built sometime between 24 BCE and 15 BCE (*A.J.* 14.359–360; *B.J.* 1.265), and consists of a lower palace with gardens and swimming pools, and an upper palace-fortress. This layout, according to Josephus, gave Lower Herodium the appearance of a town, and Upper Herodium the appearance of a castle stronghold (*A.J.* 15.323–325; 17.196–199; *B.J.* 1.419; 1.670–673; 3.55).

---

[573] First Jewish rebellion: 66–73 CE; second Jewish rebellion (the Bar Kokhba rebellion): 132–135 CE.

Josephus said that Herod furnished both the upper and lower parts lavishly and brought in an abundant water supply to an area which was generally arid. He says that the upper site was adorned with round towers and that there was a route to the summit via two hundred steps of pure white marble (*A.J.* 15.323–325; 16.13; 17.196–199; *B.J.* 1.419; 1.670–673; 3.55).

As well as building Lower and Upper Herodium, Herod also designed Herodium as the site of his mausoleum, and Josephus tells us of the lavish funeral procession culminating in his burial (*A.J.* 17.199; *B.J.* 1.670–673).[574] The account of the funeral procession is the last mention of Herodium by Josephus until he begins his account of the Jewish rebellion against Rome in the late 60s CE.

Josephus tells us that during the Jewish rebellion, the mountain fortresses of Herodium, Masada, and Machaerus were the last three rebel desert strongholds to hold out still against Roman forces. In 71 CE, Herodium became the first of these three to fall to the Tenth Legion *Fretensis*, then under the command of Legate Lucilius Bassus (*B.J.* 4.554–555).

Given the foregoing, we might expect that Josephus would have then spent some time describing what happened at Herodium during the first Jewish rebellion, but, in fact, he barely touches on the subject. The rebel occupation of Herodium does not seem to have posed much of a threat to the Romans, and Herodium was captured by them *en route* to Machaerus (*B.J.* 7.163). Josephus does not give us any detail relating to the fall of Herodium to the Romans. For Herodium during the first Jewish rebellion, there was to be no grand narrative relating heroic deeds by brave defenders, no motif of mass-suicide, no account of the final desperate hours before the fall, and no mention of survivors or deaths on either side.

THE ANCIENT SOURCES

Most references to Herodium prior to the second Jewish rebellion relate to its construction during the reign of Herod the Great, to its location, and to Herod's burial there. Material relating to the occupation of Herodium during the first Jewish rebellion is sparse and what we do know comes to us in its entirety from Josephus. Unlike his descriptions of the fortress at Masada (in the previous chapter), Josephus does not give any details of numbers, time-span, alterations, or even details of the siege and eventual taking of Herodium by the Romans.[575]

---

[574] In 2009, Ehud Netzer, Emeritus Professor of Archaeology at the Hebrew University of Jerusalem, discovered what he has identified as Herod's tomb on the southeastern side of the hill of Upper Herodium.

[575] See *B.J.* 1.265; 1.419; 1.670–673; 3.55; 4.554–555; 4.503–508; 4.509–513; 4.514–520; 7.163; *A.J.* 14.359–360; 15.323–325; 16.12–13; 17.196–199; Pliny the Elder, *Nat.* 5.15.

[...] When Cerealis had conquered them he went to Hebron, another very ancient city. I have told you already, that this city is situated in a mountainous country not far off Jerusalem; and when he had broken into the city by force what multitude and young men were left therein he slew and burnt down the city; so that as now all the places were taken, excepting Herodium and Masada, and Machaerus, which were in possession of the robbers, so Jerusalem was what the Romans at present aimed at. (Josephus, *B.J.* 4.554–55, Thackeray, LCL)

In the foregoing passage we are told only that the strongholds of Masada, Herodium, and Machaerus were in the hands of the rebels. The Roman strategy was to deal with the rebellious cities such as Hebron and Jerusalem before concerning themselves with ridding themselves of the rebels at Masada, Herodium, and Machaerus:

Meanwhile, Lucilius Bassus had been dispatched to Judæa as legate, and, taking over the command from Cerealis Vetilianus, had reduced the fortress of Herodium with its garrison to surrender. He next concentrated all the numerous scattered detachments of troops, including the tenth legion, having determined to march against Machaerus. This fortress it was absolutely necessary to eradicate, lest its strength should induce many to revolt; since the nature of the place was specially adapted to inspire its occupants with high hopes of security and to deter and alarm its assailants. [...] (Josephus, *B.J.* 7.163, Thackeray, LCL)

In this second passage, it would appear that Herodium did not pose any great military difficulty to the Romans. The implication may be that the scattered troops referred to by Josephus were not deemed necessary to besiege Herodium, and, perhaps, that only troops immediately available were sent. Josephus does not describe the capture of Herodium, but instead discusses the strategic importance of the mountain fortress of Machaerus. One might expect, if the rebels at Herodium had also posed a threat to the Romans, that Josephus would have included some detail as to its defensive systems and its occupiers, as he had done with Masada:

The Zealots, in consequence, alarmed at his designs and anxious to forestall one whose growing strength was to their injury, went out with their main body under arms; Simon met them and in the ensuing fight killed many of them and drove the remainder into the city. Misgivings about his forces, however, still deterred him from an assault on the walls; instead he resolved first to subdue Idumaea, and now marched with an army of twenty thousand men towards the frontiers of that country. The chieftains of Idumaea hastily mustered from the country their most efficient troops, numbering about twenty-five thousand, and leaving the mass of the population to protect their property against incursions of the *Sicarii* of Masada, met Simon at the frontier. There he fought them and, after a battle lasting all day, left the field neither victor nor vanquished; he then withdrew to

Nain and the Idumaeans disbanded to their homes. Not long after, however, Simon [bar Gioras] with a yet larger force again invaded their territory, and, encamping at a village called Tekoa, sent one of his comrades named Eleazar to the garrison at Herodion, which was not far off, to persuade them to hand over that fortress. The guards, ignorant of the subject of his visit, promptly admitted him, but at the first mention of the word "surrender" drew their swords and pursued him, until, finding escape impossible, he flung himself from the ramparts into the valley below and was killed on the spot. (Josephus, *B.J.* 4.514–520, Thackeray, LCL)

This passage at least gives us some information about the group of rebels in control of Herodium; still, we do not know whether they occupied Herodium during the entire period of the first rebellion. We do not know when they arrived there, whether they had to wrest control of it from the Romans through force or treachery (as at Masada, *B.J.* 2.408), or whether it was unoccupied and their taking of it was unopposed. We do not know what condition Herodium was in when it was occupied during the period of the first rebellion. Nor do we have any idea of the number of rebels there, or how they were organised. We know only that a faction of rebels who were opposed to Simon bar Gioras occupied and had control of Herodium, although we do not know for how long, or what people comprised that group. These three references represent the totality of material from Josephus relating to Herodium during the period of the first rebellion. They are clearly of no assistance in any discussion of a synagogue identification, nor are they of great assistance in identifying who exactly (or even approximately) occupied Herodium, and for how long.

CONSTRUCTION OF THE FORTRESS OF HERODIUM

Herod went to extraordinary lengths—even by his standards—to construct Upper Herodium, first creating an artificial hill on which to locate it, and then building the fortress on the hill, raising it well above the local landscape (see fig. 36 above). The circular upper palace-fortress is surrounded by a casemate wall with four towers protruding from it (see fig. 37 below).

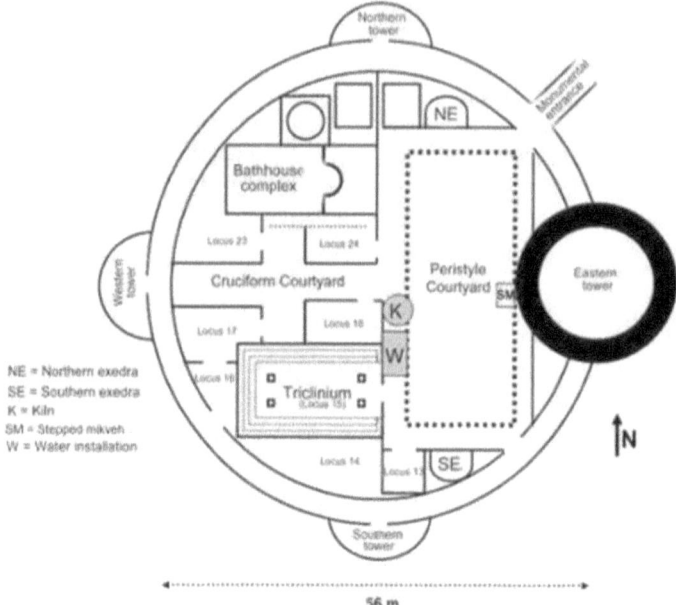

Figure 37 – Plan of the upper palace-fortress

The outer diameter of the casemate wall is 63 m and the inner diameter of the palace-fortress is 56 m. The casemate is made up of two parallel walls 3.4 m apart, forming a circular corridor around the footprint of Upper Herodium. When it was built, this structure extended some 25 m above the artificial hill and was possibly divided into as many as seven storeys, including two underground cellar/cistern levels. The upper storeys had ceilings and floors supported on wooden beams and were each encircled by the casemate corridor/rooms, which probably served for habitation, storerooms, and access.[576] Four towers protrude out from the casemate wall; three semicircular ones (on the south, west and north) and one circular one on the east (see fig. 37 above). The circular eastern tower is the only one of the towers to extend inside the fortress as well as out.[577] Access to the palace-fortress was from the northeast, via a stairway that Josephus described as having 200 stone steps of white marble (*B.J.* 1.420).[578] When the construction work was completed, earth and gravel was piled up around the walls of the upper palace-fortress,

---

[576] Netzer, *Architecture of Herod*, 183.
[577] Virgilio C. Corbo, "L'Herodion de Giabel Fureidis," *Liber Annuus* 117 (1967): 74.
[578] Netzer, *Architecture of Herod*, 187.

creating steep slopes and giving the hill its iconic conical volcanic shape (see fig. 36 above).[579]

Internally, the fortress is divided into two main sections. The structure with which this chapter is concerned—a converted *triclinium*—is located in the western section (see figs. 37 and 38 above). The western section contains the *triclinium*, various ancillary rooms, and a bathhouse complex. A cross-shaped courtyard separates the *triclinium* and ancillary rooms from the bathhouse complex just 30 m to the north of the triclinium. The eastern section of the palace-fortress is almost completely taken up by a large peristyle courtyard.[580]

History of the Excavations

Between 1962 and 1967, Virgilio Corbo conducted excavations at the site on behalf of the Studium Biblicum Franciscanum, during which time the main buildings on the summit were uncovered and mapped.[581] Between 1967 and 1970, Gideon Foerster of the Hebrew University of Jerusalem carried out preservation and restoration works for the National Parks Authority. During these works, a network of cisterns and a system of tunnels dug in the hill that dated to the time of the Bar-Kokhba revolt were uncovered.[582] In 1970, Ehud Netzer excavated sections of Lower Herodium.[583] Netzer is currently involved in the ongoing excavation of what he has identified as Herod's tomb, as well as in preservation works on Upper Herodium.[584]

The Identification of the Converted *Triclinium* as a Synagogue

In his preliminary report published in 1967, Virgilio Corbo, the excavator of Upper Herodium, identified the *triclinium* as a synagogue. He said that the *triclinium* was occupied and transformed during the period of the Jewish *wars* ("le guerre giudache") and that it was the construction of benches around its walls that identified it as a synagogue.[585] Outside the northeastern wall of the *triclinium* he

---

[579] Netzer, *Architecture of Herod*, 188.
[580] Ehud Netzer, "Herodium," *NEAEHL*, Vol. 2 (ed. Ephraim Stern; Jerusalem: The Israel Exploration Society; Carta, 1993), 619.
[581] Corbo, "L'Herodion de Giabel Fureidis," 103.
[582] Netzer, "Herodium," 618.
[583] Netzer, "Herodium," 618.
[584] Announced on website *News@HebrewU*, http://www.hunews.huji.ac.il/articles.asp?cat=6&artID=935 (accessed 2 September 2008) [No longer extant, see https://web.archive.org/web/20090628050801/http://www.hunews.huji.ac.il/articles.asp?cat=6&artID=935 —Eds]
[585] Corbo, "L'Herodion de Giabel Fureidis," 103.

found a 3-pool water installation which he identified as a *mikveh,* as well as a large kiln (see fig. 38 below).[586]

In the final excavation reports published in 1989, Corbo went further than in his preliminary reports, and categorised the converted *triclinium* as belonging to the period of the second Jewish rebellion (132–135 CE).[587] Corbo's identification of the synagogue as belonging to the second rebellion period has given subsequent scholars something of a headache and, indeed, nearly all of those who have written about the *triclinium*/synagogue have simply ignored Corbo's reports and followed the line taken by Netzer, Foerster, and others, saying that the use of the *triclinium* as a synagogue dates to the period of the first rebellion. However, as Corbo found, and as is discussed below, there is little or no evidence to substantiate a first Jewish rebellion period identification.

THE EXCAVATION REPORTS

Corbo's identification of the converted *triclinium* as a synagogue is based on the fact that the room has benches around three walls and, presumably, because it was occupied by Jews during the period of both rebellions.[588] It is worth noting here that Corbo made his identification in 1967, and Yigael Yadin had identified Locus 1042 on Masada as a synagogue (see previous chapter) in 1965.[589]

THE CONVERTED *TRICLINIUM*

Corbo described the Herodian-period *triclinium* as a large rectangular room measuring 15.15 x 10.60 m, with an entrance overlooking the peristyle courtyard to the east. There were a number of rooms around the *triclinium,* but only two of these were connected with it when it was excavated (Loci 14 and 18—see fig. 38 below). Corbo said that these two loci were not related to its usage as a synagogue, since the northern and southern access doorways from the *triclinium* to those rooms had been bricked-up when the *triclinium* was converted. There were two windows on the eastern façade that had also been bricked up when the *triclinium* was converted.[590]

The area of the *triclinium* was the single largest space excavated in Upper Herodium. During the Herodian phase, according to Corbo, it had a wooden roof supported by four or possibly six columns, although only one column base was

---

[586] Virgilio C. Corbo, *Herodion: Gli Edifici della Reggia-Fortezza,* Vol. 1 (Jerusalem: Franciscan Printing Press, 1989): 74–75.
[587] Corbo, *Herodion,* 1:74–75.
[588] Corbo, *Herodion,* 1:102.
[589] Previous chapter; Netzer, "Masada," 974.
[590] Corbo, *Herodion,* 1:101.

found *in situ* (see fig. 38 below).[591] The conversion of the *triclinium* into a synagogue, according to Corbo, involved the construction of benches around the walls and the blocking off of the northern and southern doors and the two windows on the eastern façade. The entrance on the eastern façade was also made narrower at this time.[592] Three benches/steps were added in the *triclinium*, and these were built of stone blocks taken from the walls of the *triclinium* and some reused architectural pieces from elsewhere on Upper Herodium.

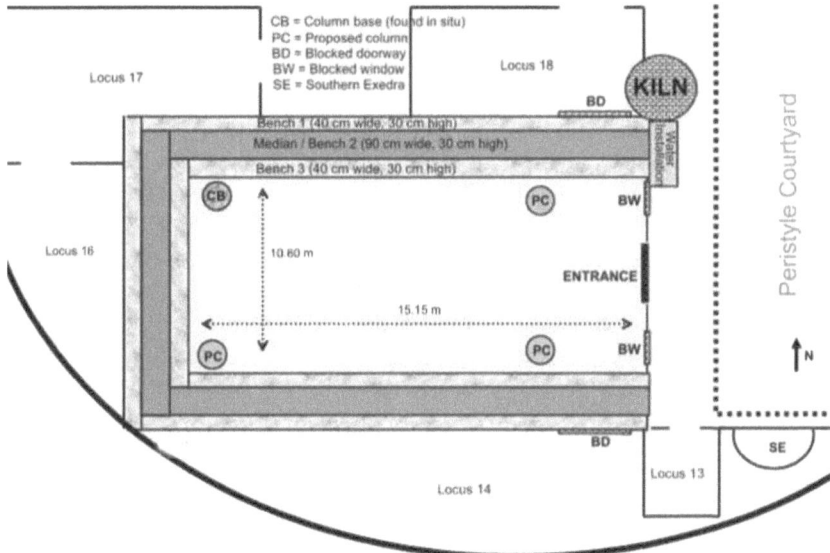

Figure 38 – Plan of the *triclinium*

The top bench is 40 cm wide and 30 cm high, the middle bench (or median) is 90 cm wide and 30 cm high, and the bottom bench is 40 cm wide and 30 high. The benches/steps run from the jamb of the blocked door on the north wall, around the western wall and almost to the jamb of the blocked door on the southern wall (see fig.38 above). Corbo could not determine whether the steps/benches broke off at the northern and southern doors intentionally, or whether this was due to subsequent destruction.[593] Corbo said that pieces of capitals built into the benches around the north, south and western walls may have come from the columns that originally supported the roof, and that the structural changes, such as the blocking

---

[591] Corbo, *Herodion*, 1:101.
[592] Corbo, *Herodion*, 1:102.
[593] Corbo, *Herodion*, 1:103.

up of the windows and doors and the construction of the benches, signalled the change of usage from *triclinium* to synagogue.[594]

By the northeastern façade of the *triclinium,* Corbo uncovered what he described as a three-pooled *mikveh*.[595] Abutting the northern edge of this installation is a large kiln (see figs. 37 and 38 above).[596] Nowhere in the excavation reports does Corbo address the reasons a *mikveh* and a kiln might be associated together in this way.

By the time he published the final excavation reports (the first volume was published in 1989), Corbo had come to the conclusion that the structural changes in the *triclinium,* which he said transformed it into a synagogue, had to be attributed to the period of the second Jewish rebellion.[597] The basis on which Corbo came to this conclusion was very simply that that the material evidence pointed to the period of the second rebellion and that very little evidence existed to point to an earlier period. In fact, the *only* evidence—other than coins—that could be safely attributed to the period of the first revolt were some wooden plates found in context with some first rebellion period coins. The wooden plates and coins were found in Locus 17, which had no connection with the *triclinium* itself. Its access was via the cruciform courtyard (see fig. 38 above).[598]

According to Corbo, the Herodian period floor of Locus 17 had been completely destroyed and was about one metre lower than the floor of the first rebel period. On the rebel period floor, sixteen coins were found (nine of year 2 of the rebellion, one of year 3, and six which were too worn to date).[599] The wooden plates were also found in this context.[600] Also found were a Corinthian capital, a section of hypocaust from the bathhouse, and a large ballista.[601]

Locus 18 borders the *triclinium* and the cruciform courtyard (see fig. 38 above). Originally, there was a connection between Locus 18 and the *triclinium*. The original doorway between the north wall of the *triclinium* and Locus 18 mirrors the doorway between the south wall of the triclinium and Locus 14.

---

[594] Corbo, *Herodion*, 1:102.
[595] The water installation was completely buried beneath the sand in the years after the Corbo excavations. From 1999 through to my most recent visit to the site in February 2009, only the kiln remained visible above ground. However, since then conservation work being undertaken by the Hebrew University of Jerusalem has uncovered the water installation again.
[596] Corbo, *Herodion*, 1:75.
[597] Corbo, *Herodion*, 1:75.
[598] Corbo, *Herodion*, 1:107.
[599] Augusto Spijkerman, *Herodion III: Catologo delle Monete* (Jerusalem: Franciscan Printing Press, 1972), 21.
[600] Corbo, *Herodion*, 1:107.
[601] Corbo, *Herodion*, 1:107.

However, both of these doors were blocked up during the conversion of the *triclinium*.[602]

Locus 13 is the room to the south of the peristyle courtyard, in front of the southern tower. It measures 4.21 x 4.10 m and to its east is the southern exedra (see fig. 37 above). Its entrance was via the peristyle courtyard. It was occupied during the period of the second rebellion and, when it was excavated, was buried beneath a debris layer almost 2 metres deep. Amongst the debris of this layer was one coin from the second rebellion (which was too worn to be dated).[603] In the area between Locus 13 and the wall of the *triclinium*, a hoard of 770 second rebellion period coins and some scattered coins of the same period were excavated.[604] The importance of the level around this area was derived, according to Corbo, from the fact that it dated to the period of the second rebellion and the deep destruction layer indicated the intensity of the rebel defence of Herodium against the Romans in 135 CE.[605]

Corbo's identification of a synagogue in Upper Herodium in 1967 seems to have been influenced by Yigael Yadin's identification of what he claimed was a synagogue at Masada only two years earlier. The building Yadin identified had benches around its walls. Indeed, Corbo mentioned Yigael Yadin's synagogue identification (which was widely publicised and which has subsequently achieved iconic status).[606]

Without reference to the Yadin synagogue identification, all there is at Herodium to identify the structure as a synagogue is a converted *triclinium* with stepped benches around three of the walls, two blocked up doors, two blocked up windows, and a nearby *mikveh* (not the one identified by Corbo, but another one, belonging to the period of the second rebellion, on the other side of the peristyle courtyard, beside the eastern tower). Nor was any material found inside or near the *triclinium* which might indicate its use.

Corbo's identification of a synagogue has been widely accepted by scholars, although those who have written about it have ascribed it to the period of the first Jewish rebellion, even though no material was found in the *triclinium* or even in any of the rooms which had previously been connected to it (Loci 14 and 18). The only locus in which material was discovered in a context which could be clearly identified as belonging to the first Jewish rebellion was Locus 17, which was **not** connected to the *triclinium* (see figs. 37 and 38 above) in the period when it had been converted.

---

[602] Corbo, *Herodion*, 1:109.
[603] Spijkerman, *Herodion III*, 17–21.
[604] Spijkerman, *Herodion III*, 23–83.
[605] Corbo, *Herodion*, 1:76.
[606] Corbo, *Herodion*, 1:75.

170   INVENTION OF THE FIRST-CENTURY SYNAGOGUE

Since most of the material discovered in this area (and elsewhere in Upper Herodium) belongs to the period of the second rebellion, Corbo concluded that the amendments to the *triclinium* were contemporary with that period. Of course, it is possible that the benches were put in place earlier, but there is no evidence to support this. And even if the benches had been put in during the period of the first or second rebellion, there is nothing to link this with usage of the building as a synagogue.

THE WATER INSTALLATION/*MIKVEH* AND KILN

Abutting the *triclinium* is what Corbo described as a *mikveh*. This structure itself is located beside a large second rebellion period kiln (see fig. 38 above). The water installation is a three-pool system,[607] so that if it were a *mikveh*, one might have had to enter one pool, exit it, enter the next, exit that and then enter and exit the final pool, a curious arrangement which is unlikely to be connected to any sort of organised religious ritual relating to purification rites.

Josephus is silent on the subject of *mikva'ot*, although he does mention purification procedures elsewhere and in different periods (*A.J.* 12.145; 18.116–119; *B.J.* 4.205; *Vita* 11–12). The starting point for all information we have about *mikva'ot* comes from the tractates *mikva'ot* of the Mishnah and the Tosefta.[608] The purpose of the *mikveh* was to ritually cleanse the flesh, and it may also have been used before eating, before reading the Torah, or praying. Ritual bathing could be conducted in the comfort of a person's home, but there were also public *mikva'ot*. The *mikveh* was not used for bathing, which instead was done in alternative water installations located within the household, or in public bathhouses.[609] Indeed, people appear to have washed themselves (or parts of their bodies, notably the feet and hands) before entering them (*m. Miqw.* 9:2).[610]

In the Mishnah, at least six grades of *mikva'ot* are listed: (1) ponds; (2) ponds during the rainy season; (3) immersion pools containing more than forty *se'ahs*[611] of water; (4) wells with natural groundwater; (5) salty water from the sea and hot springs; and (6) natural flowing *living* waters from springs and in rivers (*m. Miqw.* 1:1–8).[612] Stepped and plastered water installations fell in the middle of the grades of *mikva'ot*, and we are told that "More excellent is a pool of water containing

---

[607] Although this is not fully visible because sand from the desert blows into it and fills it up.
[608] Shimon Gibson, "The Pool of Bethesda in Jerusalem and Jewish Purification Practices of the Second Temple Period," *Proche-Orient Chrétien* 55.3–4 (2005): 274.
[609] Gibson, "Pool of Bethesda," 280.
[610] Gibson, "Pool of Bethesda," 276.
[611] Somewhat less than one cubic litre of water.
[612] Gibson, "Pool of Bethesda," 274; *The Mishnah*, trans. Herbert Danby (Oxford: Oxford University Press, 1933; repr. 1985).

forty *se'ahs*; for in them men may immerse themselves and immerse other things [i.e., vessels]" (*m. Miqw.* 1:7).[613]

A *mikveh* must also be watertight because leakage invalidated it. Its depth was to be 120 cm so that a person may be completely immersed, even if they had to bend their knees to achieve this.[614] Indeed, "if the water of an immersion pool was too shallow it may be dammed [to one side] even with bundles of sticks or reeds, that the level of water may be raised, and so he may go down and immerse himself" (*m. Miqw.* 7:7).[615] *Mikva'ot* were required to be sunken into the ground, either through construction or by cutting into the rock. Into these sunken cisterns natural water from a spring or from surface rainwater would flow.[616]

It is not known when the first stepped and plastered *mikveh* appeared, but it is thought to have been in the late Hasmonaean period, toward the end of the second century BCE or early in the first century BCE. A large number of *mikva'ot* are known from the Herodian period and up to the destruction of Jerusalem in 70 CE in both public and private contexts.[617] Because *mikva'ot* could be found in many contexts, both public and private, it is not known whether there is a particular association between synagogues and *mikva'ot*. Indeed, even the relationship of synagogue and *mikveh* is not certain, and it appears to be an occasional association only. A synagogue did not need to have a *mikveh* attached to it, and a *mikveh* did not need to be attached to a synagogue to qualify as a *mikveh*.

In the case of the water installation outside the converted *triclinium* in the upper fortress of Herodium, the size of the adjoining kiln (with a diameter of 2 m) suggests it could have been used on an industrial scale, and it would seem logical that the three pools, rather than being a mikveh, relate directly to the kiln and were used for the purpose of processing clay and firing pottery, or for some other manufacturing process.

No tests have ever been conducted on residues in either the water installation or the kiln that could have indicated the purposes for which they were used.[618] Other than this *sort* of explanation, the association of a kiln and a water installation just does not make sense. The radiating heat from the kiln would cause the water in the *mikveh* to evaporate, making it difficult to maintain the volume required for ritual purification purposes, and perhaps even making it uncomfortable to use. Most important, however, is that there is no reason to have

---

[613] Gibson, "Pool of Bethesda," 275.
[614] David Kotlar and Judith Baskin, "Mikveh," *Encyclopaedia Judaica* (2nd ed.; Detroit: Thomson, 2007), 225.
[615] Gibson, "Pool of Bethesda," 277.
[616] Gibson, "Pool of Bethesda," 277.
[617] Gibson, "Pool of Bethesda," 279.
[618] Corbo, *Herodion*, 1:75.

a three-pooled structure for purification, when all that is required is ritual immersion—not facilities for a sequence of ablutions.

Moreover, there *is* what appears to be a simple *mikveh* on the other side of the peristyle courtyard, just 25 m away, and it is a simple stepped pool into which a person could step, immerse, and exit quickly and easily (see figure 39 below). If the converted *triclinium were* a synagogue, and if it *was* established that synagogues were found in association with *mikva'ot,* then the stepped *mikveh* on the far side of the peristyle courtyard would be the one related to the *triclinium*.

Figure 39 – Location of *mikveh, triclinium,* kiln and water installation

The *mikveh* shown on the bottom left of figure 39 (above) is a second rebellion period structure, constructed out of the same sorts of material used to convert the *triclinium*.[619] This *mikveh* is large enough for a person to stand in and to be immersed in water to chest level. This, while not being conclusive evidence, lends some weight to Corbo's identification of the structural changes in the *triclinium* as belonging to the second rebellion period.[620] The stepped pool outside the converted *triclinium* is part of a three-pool installation and the stepped section

---

[619] Corbo, *Herodion*, 1:76.
[620] Corbo, *Herodion*, 1:76.

HERODIUM 173

(bottom right of fig. 39) is barely deep enough to reach to the knees of an adult, rendering it useless as a *mikveh* for ritual immersion.

During the period of the second rebellion, the occupants of the fortress made minor structural changes to most of the buildings to suit their needs. Evidence of their work was found in the area of the peristyle courtyard on the east and in the bathhouse and the *triclinium* on the west. Ovens for domestic use were also found, as well as the aforementioned large kiln and associated water installation. All of these installations contained material from the second rebellion period only.[621]

THE COINS FROM THE UPPER FORTRESS

Over the four seasons of excavations on Herodium between 1962 and 1967, a total of 873 coins were found. The coins and where they were found during the four seasons of Corbo's excavations are as follows:

Table 1 – The coins from the period of the first rebellion

Catalogue No	Quantity	Date	Location
33–55[622]	23	FR (13 x year 2; 10 year 3)	Room XXXIII
58[623]	1	FR (1 x year 2)	Garden / Peristyle Area
70–71[624]	2	FR (2 x undated)	Garden / Peristyle Area
76[625]	1	FR (1 x year 2)	Garden Area VIII
77	1	FR (1 x year 2)	Garden Area VIII
79–80[626]	2	FR (2 x year 2)	Garden / Peristyle Area
81[627]	1	FR (1 x year 3)	Garden Area VIII
85–98[628]	14	FR; (7 x year 2; 1 x year 3; 6 x unclear)	Room XVII
99–100[629]	2	(2) FR year 2	XVII
TOTAL	**47**		

---

[621] Corbo, *Herodion*, 1:76.
[622] Spijkerman, *Herodion III*, 18.
[623] Spijkerman, *Herodion III*, 19.
[624] Spijkerman, *Herodion III*, 19.
[625] Spijkerman, *Herodion III*, 20.
[626] Spijkerman, *Herodion III*, 21.
[627] Spijkerman, *Herodion III*, 20.
[628] Spijkerman, *Herodion III*, 21.
[629] Spijkerman, *Herodion III*, 21.

Table 2 – The coins from the period of the second rebellion

Catalogue	Number of Coins	Date	Location
Hoard[630]	770	SR	Southern Exedra
59	1	SR; year 1	Garden / Peristyle Area
60	1	SR; unclear	Garden / Peristyle Area
61	1	SR; undated	Garden / Peristyle Area
62	1	SR; year 2	Garden / Peristyle Area
63	1	SR; undated	Garden / Peristyle Area
64	1	SR; undated	Garden / Peristyle Area
65	1	SR; undated	Garden / Peristyle Area
66	1	SR; undated	Garden / Peristyle Area
67	1	SR; undated	Garden / Peristyle Area
69	1	SR; unclear	Garden / Peristyle Area
73	1	SR; year 2	Garden / Peristyle Area
74	1	SR; undated	Eastern Tower, bottom of cistern
75	1	SR; undated	Eastern Tower, bottom of cistern
82	1	SR; undated	Room XX, apse of church
84	1	SR; undated	Apse of church
102	1	SR; undated	Room XIII
TOTAL	**786**		

Table 3 – The coins from miscellaneous periods

Catalogue No.	Number of Coins	Date	Location
1	1	7th century CE	XXVIII (Tepidarium)
2	1	5th–6th century CE	XXX (Frigidarium)
3	1	6th century CE	XXX (Frigidarium)
4	1	6th century CE	XXXI (monastery)
5–20	16	5th century CE	XXIX (monastery)
21	1	5th century CE	XXVIII (monastery)
22–23	2	4th century CE	XXVIII (monastery)
24	1	2nd century CE	XXXII (coin of Caesarea)
25	1	1st century BCE	External wall (Herod the Great)
26	1	1st century BCE	External wall (Herod the Great)
27	1	2nd–1st century BCE	?? Possibly external wall
28	1	6th century CE	XXXII
29	1	1st century CE	XXXIV (Nero)

---

[630] Spijkerman, *Herodion III*, 23–83.

30	1	1st century BCE	XXXIV (Herod the Great)
31	1	??	XXXIV (Imitation Jannaeus)
32	1	2nd century BCE	? very small coin
32a	1	?? unique	XXXIII Large heavy coin
56	1	??	XXXIII Completely Fragmented
57	1	2nd century CE	XXXIII
68	1	Umayyad	Eastern tower
72	1	4th century BCE	Garden / Peristyle Area
78	1	1st century BCE	Garden / Peristyle Area
83	1	1st century CE	XXXVIII (Coin of Pilate)
101	1	1st century CE	XX (Coin of Ethnarch Archelaus)
Total	**40**		

As can be seen from table 2 above, the majority of these coins belonged to the period of the Bar Kokhba revolt. Of these, 770 were found in a single hoard buried in the space between Locus 13 and the *triclinium* (see fig. 37 above). A further sixteen coins were found in rooms elsewhere in the fortress, giving a total of 786 second rebellion period coins. Another forty coins of miscellaneous dates (belonging neither to the first nor second rebellions) were found. These included coins from the second century BCE though the seventh century CE.[631] Only 47 coins relating to the period of the first revolt were found, and these were found scattered in various rooms around the fortress. Of these forty-seven coins, twenty-seven were from year two of the rebellion, twelve from year three, two were undated, and six were too faded and/or damaged and/or worn to be read.[632]

The coins can tell us a little about the period of the first rebellion. They tell us that Herodium may have been occupied from at least the second year of the rebellion (67–68 CE) and that this occupation may have lasted until at least the third year (68–69 CE). Of course, none of this is certain. It is possible that the first rebel period coins may have been in the hands of the rebels during the second rebellion. Coins of bronze, silver, and gold retained the value of the metal they were made of and did not go out of use, unless they were melted down to make something else.

---

[631] Spijkerman, *Herodion III*, 17–21.
[632] Spijkerman, *Herodion III*, 17–21.

176   INVENTION OF THE FIRST-CENTURY SYNAGOGUE

THE INSCRIPTIONS AND OSTRACA

There was little written material found at Herodium, certainly nothing that would indicate the system of organisation of the occupants during the first rebellion period. In fact, most of the written material found on Herodium comprised graffiti scratched on the plaster of the bathhouse walls, various ostraca, and on writing on jars.[633] The ostraca and jar inscriptions were written in Greek, Aramaic, and Hebrew, and, according to the excavation reports, belong to the main periods of settlement; that is, to the Herodian and/or to the first and second Jewish rebellions. On the basis of archaeological remains and finds, Corbo said it was impossible to differentiate between inscriptions from the time of Herod and from the two revolts.[634]

Some of the material could be safely attributed to the second century CE. An *abecedary* was found in the kiln adjacent to the triclinium, containing two complete Hebrew alphabets on one side and an incomplete alphabet (up to the letter ס) on the other. At nearby Wadi Murabba'at, nine very similar *abecedaries* dating to the second century CE were found.[635] The presence of an *abecedary* does suggest that some sort of teaching or scribal activity was taking place here during the second century, which is interesting, and one could certainly imagine there being a school or *bet midrash* of some sort on the site during the second century, especially given the extent and length of the occupation in the period of the Bar Kokhba rebellion.[636]

Even so, the ostraca provide strangely mixed evidence. A small ostracon, for example, was found in the large kiln abutting the *triclinium*. In the excavation reports of 1972, Emmanuelle Testa translated the text of this ostracon דגון סבי ספח גדול as "Dagon my ancestor is among the nobility."[637] The verb ספח means "to grow, or to swell, or to add to," or possibly "to spontaneously regrow." *Dagon* is the name of a Philistine deity, and since the kiln and the water installation are associated together, it is difficult to understand how this might relate to a religious Jewish context.

Another ostracon was found in the adjacent water installation on which was inscribed two words in Aramaic lettering. These two words are תן גלא, which Testa tentatively translated as "instructs the exiles" or, possibly, "repeat again the exile."[638] The word גלא can also be translated as a "heap" (i.e., of stones or bones), "to be uncovered," or to "go into exile." This text could therefore be translated as

---

[633] There were only around 100 ostraca found in all at Herodium.
[634] Emmanuele Testa, *Herodion IV. I Graffiti e gli Ostraka* (Jerusalem: Franciscan Printing Press, 1972), 93.
[635] Testa, *Herodion IV*, 77–78.
[636] Testa, *Herodion IV*, 107.
[637] Testa, *Herodion IV*, 80.
[638] Testa, *Herodion IV*, 81.

"give [a] heap [of something]," or "give [into] exile." It is impossible to know now to what this refers and it may be that the text of the ostracon is incomplete.

Another inscription, written on the belly of a large jar, was found in the water installation. This inscription comprised two words in Aramaic script. The words are ירסא רבא, which Testa suggested could translate as "poison the high power."[639] The term ירסא רבא is not found in biblical texts. It is, however, cited in Jastrow's dictionary of the Mishnah, suggesting a later date.[640] Testa's translation of these words as "poison the high power" is an interesting possibility, but is it a likely one? ריס is found in Jastrow as a masculine noun, meaning "a drop" or "poison," and Testa has coupled it in this form with רבא and translated it as "poison the high power." However, Testa clearly thought the first word was a verb rather than a noun, and the second word a noun (and an accusative object). Jastrow says that the word ירסא appears in the same form in the Targum to Psalms 58:5 and is identical to *eres*, "poison." Therefore "great poison" could be the meaning. This text might have been attached to goods or merchandise that was poisonous. Ultimately, however, the meaning remains elusive.[641]

None of the ostraca from Herodium speak to the existence of, or the necessity for, a synagogue during the period of either the first or second rebellions, although the *abecedary* certainly suggests the existence of some sort of scribal or teaching activity on the site. And, unlike at Masada (where the ostraca numbered almost a thousand and attested to the existence of an administrative system of some complexity), there were only a hundred or so ostraca found on Herodium. Against this, however, the *abecedary* suggests that there was some form of organised administration going on at Herodium during the second century revolt, and, perhaps, that this was taking place in the assembly space into which the *triclinium* had been converted.

LITERATURE REVIEW

The scholarship on the subject of Herodium follows the same pattern as the scholarship on Delos, Jericho, and Masada. That is, an archaeologist (usually the excavator) declares that the building is a synagogue, and thereafter practically every scholar repeats the claim, sometimes with variations and often with embellishments.

It is noteworthy that, as with Masada, the excavators, including Corbo, have referred throughout their reports to the rebels on Herodium as "Zealots," although Josephus never identifies any of the occupants of Herodium specifically as

---

[639] Testa, *Herodion IV*, 82.
[640] Marcus Jastrow, *A Dictionary of the Targumim, the Talmud Babli and Yerushalmi, and the Midrashic Literature* (New York: The Judaica Press, 1996).
[641] In an email discussion with Prof. Catherine Hezser, Chair of Jewish Studies at SOAS.

Zealots. Describing the rebel occupants of Herodium (and elsewhere) as Zealots clearly sets up a scenario where there *could* be reason to establish a synagogue, even if there is no other evidence to support that identification. If the rebels are identified as brigands, *Sicarii*, mercenaries, political rebels, and so forth, then the identification of religious buildings becomes far more problematic.

GIDEON FOERSTER (1981)

Foerster performed conservation work at Upper Herodium after the Corbo excavations had ceased. He describes the physical layout of the *triclinium*, attributing the post-Herodian structural changes as belonging to the period of the first Jewish rebellion, particularly the benches, which were built of architectural fragments taken from other areas of Herod's palace.[642] He goes on to compare the Herodium *triclinium* with the building identified as a synagogue on Masada, saying that their layout is "essentially identical." He attributes this similarity to "Zealot construction" on the site. He says that in neither Masada nor Herodium has a fixed Torah shrine been found, although at Masada a side room may have functioned as a repository, since scroll fragments were discovered there. He goes on to say that at Herodium, one of the smaller rooms flanking the hall may have served this purpose.[643] He also goes on to note that in the cases of both Herodium and Masada there is a nearby *mikveh*, and that at Herodium the *mikveh* actually abutted the eastern wall of the synagogue.[644]

Foerster argues that the two structures identified as synagogues on Masada and Herodium are almost identical in dimensions: Masada 12 x 15 m; Herodium 10.5 x 15 m, and that they were undoubtedly constructed along with the other structures at these sites, although significant modifications were made in both of them during the First Revolt against Rome, when these buildings fell into the hands of the insurgents.[645] Foerster does not explain his reasons for rejecting Corbo's dating, other than saying that the *triclinium*'s structural changes "most likely" occurred in the period of the first rebellion, on the basis of a comparison with the structure at Masada which has also been identified as a belonging to the first rebellion period synagogue and that the two structures are "essentially identical: oblong halls lined with benches and with supporting columns in the space of the hall proper."[646]

However, the identification of a synagogue at Masada is debatable (as argued in the previous chapter herein) and arguments for it are themselves based only on comparisons with—in essence—itself and a structure at Gamla also identified as

---

[642] Foerster, "Synagogues at Masada and Herodium," 24.
[643] Foerster, "Synagogues at Masada and Herodium," 26.
[644] Foerster, "Synagogues at Masada and Herodium," 26.
[645] Foerster, "Synagogues at Masada and Herodium," 24.
[646] Foerster, "Synagogues at Masada and Herodium," 24.

a first-century synagogue. This does not appear to be sufficient evidence to make such an identification at Herodium. There is no question that the structures at Masada and Gamla do share some features: the benches, the rectangular shape of the room, but that is as far as the similarities go. The *triclinium* at Herodium is in fact easily twice the size of Locus 1042 on Masada, although this does not bear on its identification. I neglected to take measurements when visiting the sites in 1999, 2004, 2005, 2006, and 2009, but the photographs I took *do* show the size difference between the two structures.

Figure 40 – Comparison of Locus 1042 on Masada and the Herodium *triclinium*

Foerster accepted the details of Corbo's excavation reports in relation to the triclinium on Herodium, but has attributed them to the period of the first rebellion on the basis of a superficial similarity with the building identified as a synagogue at Masada. His short article, published in *Ancient Synagogues Revealed* in 1981, is the point at which the identification of the *triclinium* as a synagogue dating to the first rebellion became well established and the point from which most other scholarship has followed.

Joseph Patrich (1992)

In a review of Corbo's final excavation reports, Patrich says that "the synagogue" is better dated to the period of the first Jewish rebellion because of its resemblance to the structures at Masada and Gamla. He says that the majority of coins scattered about the site date from the First Jewish War. Then he says that of the coins found on the site, 47 relate to the period of the first rebellion, and only 16 coins to the period of the second rebellion "[…] if we disregard a hoard of approximately 1,000 bronze coins from this period found in the southern exedra."[647] Patrich says that it is hard to understand why Corbo insisted on attributing most of the installations and alterations in the Herodian palace-fortress to the Second Revolt. He says that there is no plan in the final reports illustrating the state of the construction during the period of the first rebellion and that only in room 17 could Corbo define a stratigraphic distinction between the remains from the two revolts.[648] He goes on to say that his conclusions are further supported because the Zealots at Masada went through significant efforts to build a synagogue and several *mikva'ot*. Thus, he claims, because a similar group inhabited Herodium during the period of the first Jewish rebellion, it seems likely that their activities would have followed the same pattern. Moreover, since the fortress was in the possession of the rebels from about 66 to 71 CE, they certainly had ample time to make renovations to the *triclinium*.[649]

Patrich disregards the lack of evidence relating to the period of the first rebellion, and he sets out an unsupported conclusion based on a comparison and some assumptions. First, we do *not* know that Zealots occupied Herodium. Second, the reason there is no plan in Corbo's final excavation reports showing the construction phase relating to the period of the first rebellion, is that *there were no built structures that could be so identified*. Corbo was quite clear on this point.[650]

The fact that 47 coins of the period of the first rebellion were found scattered around the site (but not in the triclinium itself) must be weighed against the discovery of the hoard of 770 coins of the period of the second rebellion being found (they were found between Locus 13 and the *triclinium*, not in the southern

---

[647] Joseph Patrich, "Corbo's Excavations at Herodium: a Review Article," *IEJ* 42.3–4 (1992): 243.

[648] Patrich, "Corbo's Excavations at Herodium," 243.

[649] Patrich, "Corbo's Excavations at Herodium," 243.

[650] Corbo, *Herodion*, 1:69–70: "In our excavations, given the huge build up of the second Roman destruction, it is difficult to distinguish what belonged to the first destruction of the Herodian fortress. We could only safely differentiate wooden plates which were found associated with coins of the first revolt. Coins of the first revolt were also found between the peristyle and the north exedra, in the peristyle, and in the tower" (my translation from the Italian).

HERODIUM   181

exedra as Patrich states).⁶⁵¹ Another sixteen second rebellion period coins were found in various rooms. Patrich has simply disregarded this evidence and has treated the first rebellion period coins as though they could *only* have been in use during the first rebellion. All in all, Patrich's contentions are not supported by the evidence.

EHUD NETZER (1993)

Netzer reiterates Foerster's position, describing the architectural layout of the palace-fortress. He says that many archaeological traces of settlement were found from both the first and second revolts, and that settlement is also known from the literary sources. He says that the rebels' building activities were generally limited to the addition of walls in dry construction and the reuse of stones, but that more basic changes—of a religious and cultic nature—were made in the *triclinium*, where rows of stone benches were added along three of the walls. Netzer says that this structure was apparently used as a synagogue by the rebels who had taken refuge here and that a *mikveh* "appears to have been added when the building became a synagogue."⁶⁵²

Netzer's contention that many archaeological traces of settlement changes were found relating to the period of the first rebellion is not supported by the excavation reports or any of the material evidence found on the site. Netzer links the water installation to the structural changes in the *triclinium* which, since they most likely belong to the period of the second rebellion, does not support his argument. While Netzer has written extensively on the subject of Herod's building programme, he does not add anything new to the identification argument, merely repeating Foerster's contention that the structural changes in the triclinium belong to the period of the first rebellion.

PAUL FLESHER (1995)

Flesher takes a more cautious approach, and deals with the issue of the identification in general, saying of Masada, Herodium, and Gamla that their Jewish character is evident only from their locations, which are within areas identified with Jews, and that the architectural features that have been used to identify them as synagogues—the benches around the walls and the columns—appear also in structures not identified as synagogues, and only some of which are Jewish.⁶⁵³ Flesher says that there is no way to identify what the *triclinium* was used for in the rebel period and that Herodium was the location of a rebel army

---

⁶⁵¹ Spijkerman, *Herodion III*, 23–83.
⁶⁵² Netzer, "Herodium," 620.
⁶⁵³ Flesher, "Palestinian Synagogues," 37.

who, like the rebels at Masada, needed a place to plan military strategy.[654] Flesher goes on to say that there is also a chronological problem with the dating "of the synagogue" at Herodium. He notes that the main proponent of this argument was Gideon Foerster, who supervised the restoration of the site after the primary excavations had been completed and who argued that the synagogue dates to rebels who used the site as a fortress during the first Jewish rebellion, but that Corbo—the site's excavator—states (in the final report) that the synagogue belongs to the Bar Kokhba rebellion. Flesher concludes that the structure at Herodium provides "no sure evidence of a synagogue in the first century; if it is a synagogue, it most likely stems from the early second century."[655]

DONALD BINDER (1999)

Binder repeats Foerster's assertions in some detail and acknowledges that the synagogue identification was made on the basis of similarities with the structures on Masada and Gamla, and that Foerster and Netzer defended this proposal, which has since been adopted by many other archaeologists.[656] Binder reiterates Foerster's work, adding that the structure was "hewn out of the western side of the Herodian peristyle court by the rebels."[657] While Binder acknowledges Corbo's attribution of the structure changes to the period of the second rebellion, he says that "nowhere in his report does Corbo defend his new position with arguments from archaeology."[658] In fact, Corbo based his conclusion on the material found in each archaeological context. Moreover, Binder can suggest no archaeological reason for Foerster's and Netzer's time line other than the superficial similarities between the structures at Masada, Herodium, and Gamla.

LEE I. LEVINE (2005)

Levine takes a minimalist's cautious position, merely pointing out the architectural layout of the *triclinium*. He does not undertake any analysis of the excavation reports or add any new information or analysis.[659]

STEPHEN CATTO (2007)

Catto reiterates the same argument as Foerster, Netzer, Binder, and others, referring to the rebel occupants as "Zealots." He also attributes the structural

---

[654] Flesher, "Palestinian Synagogues," 37.
[655] Flesher, "Palestinian Synagogues," 37–38.
[656] Binder, *Into the Temple Courts*, 184.
[657] Binder, *Into the Temple Courts*, 183.
[658] Binder, *Into the Temple Courts*, 184.
[659] Levine, *Ancient Synagogue*², 60.

changes to the period of the first rebellion. He say that Herodium offers little in the way of allowing a comfortable assertion that this room is a synagogue,[660] but also that it is capable of seating around 200 people, so it was clearly used for communal purposes. The *mikveh* next to the building suggests that it was used for some ritual purpose, and the benches are "very similar to the ones found in other places which have been more confidently identified as synagogue buildings."[661] Catto's entire argument is based on Foerster's, Netzer's, and Binder's, and he does not add anything new, nor does he attempt to analyse the excavation reports for himself.

Conclusions

Jewish rebels took control of Herodium some time after the beginning of the first rebellion against Rome.[662] It was eventually recaptured by the Romans before the fall of Masada and Machaerus. The site was then abandoned until the Bar Kokhba rebellion, when a group of rebels used it as an administrative and military base. In 135 CE, the Romans once more conquered Herodium and the site was again abandoned.

Given that the foregoing is all we know about Herodium from the period of its construction to the first rebellion, the identification of a synagogue there is perplexing, and there is no evidence to support it. Even the debate about the dating of the structure is potentially irrelevant, as to whatever period the triclinium related, there is still no evidence that it functioned as a synagogue, although, clearly, it *could* have been used as a synagogue, and may have been used for scribal and teaching activity during the Bar Kokhba period.

Discussions about the architectural reconfiguration of the *triclinium* are irrelevant because beyond being a rectangular room with benches, there was nothing found in or near it to indicate it was used for religious purposes.

While material relating to the period of the first rebellion is lacking, there is specific reference to the period of the second rebellion found in Dio Cassius and in documents found at Wadi Murabba'at near Qumran. The Wadi Murabba'at documents say that Simeon Bar Kokhba had a command post at Herodium.[663] Corbo cites two documents found at Wadi Murabba'at, both of which refer to land leases made "in Year Two of the liberation of Israel [...] by the authority of Simon bar Kokhba, Prince of Israel, who lives at Herodium."[664]

---

[660] Catto, *Reconstructing the First-Century Synagogue*, 93.
[661] Catto, *Reconstructing the First-Century Synagogue*, 93.
[662] Actually, there is nothing in the sources or the archaeological record to indicate whether they wrest it from Roman control or whether it lay abandoned before they occupied it.
[663] Netzer, "Herodium," 618.
[664] Corbo, *Herodion*, 1:70.

The documents found at Wadi Murabbaʿat suggest that there was a settled community at Herodium during the period of the second rebellion, and that that community required administration. There is nothing, however, to suggest that this was the case for the occupation of Herodium during the period of the first rebellion. This may be because of the extent of the destruction of the site after the second rebellion, but there is unfortunately no way to know if this is the case.

While Corbo initially struggled with the process of attributing structural changes in the buildings of the palace-fortress to either the first and/or second rebellion periods, by the time he wrote his final report he was convinced that most of the changes belonged to the period of the second rebellion. This seems somewhat safe on the basis that there is a large second rebellion period kiln and related water installation adjacent to the *triclinium*. We can perhaps surmise that whatever processes the kiln was used to facilitate, they required water either before or afterwards. The kiln is very large (2 m in diameter), and it would seem logical to suggest that it was used for some industrial and/or military purpose, rather than for simple cooking or bread-making.

Corbo identified the *triclinium* as a synagogue on the basis of its similarity to a structure at Masada, but attributed it and its structural changes (the addition of benches, the blocking up of the northern and southern doors and the two windows) to the period of the second rebellion, on the basis that these changes were contemporary with the kiln and water installation.[665]

In general, it is likely that the changes to the *triclinium* were made at the same time as the development of the kiln and the associated water installation (which Corbo identified as a *mikveh*). The *mikveh* identification is problematic on the basis that the installation Corbo describes is a 3-pool complex in which one would first have to enter into a small pool, exit that pool, enter and exit a larger pool, and then enter and exit a third pool, all in a chamber directly connected to the large kiln. It seems improbable that a *mikveh* would be constructed in this manner, when it would be so easy to excavate a single pool with steps in the same space. And, as already stated, there is a stepped *mikveh* just 20 m away, across the peristyle courtyard, beside the eastern tower, which dates to the period of the second rebellion. It is constructed in the same manner as the benches in the *triclinium*, using reused blocks of stone and architectural fragments (see figure 39 above).

Another possible use for the *triclinium* would be if it had been converted for administrative use. The benches in the *triclinium* would have created a perfect space for a command and/or administrative centre and for a public meeting place to discuss issues in general with the population of Herodium. Thus, while the structure at Herodium seems to be an assembly space, there is nothing to indicate that it was used for religious purposes. Since we know from the Wadi Murabbaʿat documents that the site was used as a command post by Simon bar Kokhba, the

---

[665] Corbo, *Herodion*, 1:75.

leader of the second rebellion, the assembly hall, the single largest space in the upper fortress, would be most reasonably attached to that time period because the rebels would have needed a place to assemble for military and strategic planning purposes.[666] It also appears, because of the discovery of the *abecedary* in the kiln, that some sort of administrative/scribal/teaching function was going on in this place during the period of the second revolt.

Taking all of this into consideration and, in particular, the placement of a kiln and associated water installation beside the *triclinium*, the identification of this site as a synagogue is vexing and is difficult to explain because of the lack of supporting evidence. At best, if the *triclinium* were used as a synagogue, it was probably during the period of the second rebellion on the basis of the finds associated with that period.

---

[666] Flesher, "Palestinian Synagogues," 37.

6
GAMLA

Figure 41 – Gamla (looking west across to Galilee)

INTRODUCTION

During excavations at Gamla in the Golan in 1976, the archaeologist Shmarya Gutmann uncovered a large building. Because of its internal layout, with benches encircling the walls and three entrances, Gutman said that it was a public building, designed for the assembly of large numbers of people for some common activity.[667] The building is purpose-built and is part of a large complex of rooms,

---

[667] Shmarya Gutmann, *Gamla, A City in Rebellion* (Tel Aviv: Misrad ha-Bitahon, 1994), 108 [Hebrew].

188   INVENTION OF THE FIRST-CENTURY SYNAGOGUE

some of which have not yet been excavated. In the second season of excavations, when an adjoining *mikveh*/cistern was uncovered, Gutmann identified the public building as a first-century synagogue.

The ancient city of Gamla is located in the southern part of the Golan, in what is now the Yehudiyah Nature Reserve, through which two rivers flow, the Nahal Gamla in the north and the Nahal Dalyot in the south. Gamla sits on the southern side of a ridge between these two rivers and is surrounded by deep gorges. There is a shallow depression on the eastern side of the Gamla ridge that creates a degree of separation between ancient Gamla and the rest of the ridge. The top of the ridge is narrow and pointed, with a steep slope in the north. In figure 41 above, you can see Gamla on the southern side of the ridge above Nahal Dalyot, as well as the shallow depression mentioned above.

The city of Gamla occupies around 141,639 m^2 (c. 35 acres) and is built entirely on the southern slope of the ridge, which is slightly less steep than the northern one. The buildings of Gamla are constructed of local black basalt, built on terraces cut into the soft chalky ground. Surveys conducted on the northern slope during the Gutmann excavations did not reveal any archaeological remains.[668]

The public building excavated by Gutmann and identified as a synagogue is situated on the main road into Gamla, and everyone who entered Gamla by this road would have passed it. The gap between the public building and the building complex immediately to its south was another formal entryway into the city. The large public building Gutmann discovered would have been very visible in the landscape, and it is by far the largest single space excavated in Gamla.[669]

The area of Gamla has been occupied since at least the early Bronze Age. There are about 200 dolmens in the area of the Yehudiyah Nature Reserve.[670] While the extent of the Bronze Age settlement at Gamla has not been established, it was apparently as large as the Second Temple period settlement.[671] There was Hasmonaean (and earlier) occupation in the western section of the city of Gamla which, for some unknown reason, fell into disuse in around 10 CE. Subsequently, the entire city moved a few steps to the right.[672]

---

[668] Zvi Yavor, "The Architecture and Stratigraphy of the Eastern and Western Quarters," in *Gamla II: The Shmarya Gutmann Excavations, 1976–1989: The Architecture* (ed. Danny Syon and Zvi Yavor; Jerusalem: Israel Antiquities Authority, 2010). [The author cited the prepublished version of this report, but the citation data has been updated –Eds.].

[669] Yavor, "Architecture and Stratigraphy."

[670] Structures built of unworked basalt stones, arranged one on top of another to form rectangles or trapezoids, with one or two short sides open. These usually served as graves.

[671] Danny Syon and Zvi Yavor, "Gamla 1997–2000," *Atiqot* (2005): 46.

[672] David Goren, "The Architecture and Stratigraphy of the Hasmonean Quarter (Areas D and B) and Area B77," in *Gamla II: The Shmarya Gutmann Excavations, 1976–1989: The Architecture* (ed. Danny Syon and Zvi Yavor; Jerusalem: Israel Antiquities Authority, 2010).

Josephus's Gamla Narrative

The fortification of Gamla by Josephus and Vespasian's ultimately successful siege are related to us by Josephus (*B.J.* 4.1–83) and very briefly by Suetonius (*Tit.* 4.3).[673] Josephus relates the lead-up to the siege, including Gamla's initial loyalty to Rome (under Agrippa II), its eventual rebellion, the fortification of the city, Agrippa II's part in besieging it, and the later Roman attack leading to its catastrophic destruction and abandonment on or around 10 November 67 CE (*B.J.* 5.58–61).[674]

Josephus, according to his account, was appointed a commander of Galilee during the rebellion (*B.J.* 2.566–568), and, in 66 CE, as part of his commission, he fortified Gamla and other cities (*B.J.* 2.574; 4.2–10). However, by the time Gamla was besieged by the Romans, Josephus had already become a prisoner of Vespasian, having surrendered after the fall of Jotapata in July of 67 CE (*B.J.* 3.340–407). In his account of the siege and fall of Gamla, Josephus gives detailed descriptions of the local topography and the layout of the city (*B.J.* 4.1–83), and from his narrative it is clear that he had firsthand knowledge of the city and its fortifications.[675]

Josephus says that even after the fall of Jotapata, the inhabitants of Gamla were confident in the security of their city, relying on the hostile terrain on which their city stood for protection (*B.J.* 4.4–10). This, of course, proved no real obstacle to the Romans when they made their final assault on the city. According to Josephus, after the razing of Jotapata by the Romans, and Josephus's surrender to Titus and Vespasian (*B.J.* 3.392), Gamla came under a ferocious attack (*B.J.* 3.393–408).

Agrippa II, against whom Gamla had initially rebelled, had besieged the city for seven months, with no success. Roman reinforcements were sent for, and Vespasian arrived at Gamla at the head of units from three Roman legions. A month later, the Romans breached the wall and entered Gamla, but were beaten back by the rebels. A few days later Roman soldiers managed to creep unnoticed to the bottom of a watchtower along the city walls. They removed five stones from its base (it did not have foundations), and the whole construction collapsed,

---

[The author cited the prepublished version of this report, but the citation data has been updated –Eds.]. Also in conversation with Motti Aviam of the University of Rochester during a visit with him to Gamla in 2005.

[673] Suetonius mentions Vespasian's triumph at Rome after his successes against the Jews in Judæa (Suetonius, *Vesp.* 8.3).

[674] Danny Syon, "Gamla. City of Refuge," in *The First Jewish Revolt: Archaeology, History, and Ideology* (ed. Andrea M. Berlin and J. Andrew Overman; London: Routledge, 2002), 134.

[675] Syon, "Gamla: City of Refuge," 135.

causing panic among the defenders. A few days later, on 10 November 67 CE, Gamla fell to the Romans (*B.J.* 4.83).

Josephus says that on the last days of the siege, thousands of the inhabitants of Gamla were slaughtered, while others chose to jump to their deaths from the top of the cliff rather than be captured by the Romans. According to Josephus, the only survivors of the siege were two women (*B.J.* 4.1–81).[676] After the razing of the city by the Romans, Gamla was abandoned. This gives us the rare comfort of the destruction of a site with an exact *terminus ad quem* and, consequently, a safe identification of the catastrophe as pertaining only to a specific event.[677]

GEOGRAPHICAL CONTEXT

The main approach road to Gamla runs along the length of the ridge to the eastern part of the city (you can see part of the road in fig. 41 above), up to the city walls which had been fortified by Josephus (*B.J.* 2.572–576). The fortified city wall is as much as 6 metres thick in places, has several square towers situated along its length, and has a circular tower at the crest of the hill. In the low-lying southern part of the wall, two square towers guarded a narrow gateway into the city.[678]

THE BREACH IN THE FORTIFICATIONS

Along the most vulnerable areas of the fortification wall, houses were put out of use and filled with stones and rubble to add strength to the wall. This is the case with the city wall at the point where the wide breach was discovered just above the building with which this chapter is concerned (see fig. 42 below). Scattered inside and around the breach were dozens of ballista stones and arrowheads. A siege hook was found still attached to the wall at the breach.[679] Vast amounts of weapons and ammunition were uncovered at Gamla, mostly along the city wall, and their distribution shows that most of the fighting took place within a section about 50 m wide on the eastern side of the city along the wall.[680]

---

[676] This is echoed in Josephus's Masada narrative, but the ridge of Gamla is not really conducive to mass suicide as, although it is steep, nowhere is it sheer enough to drop to your death.

[677] Unlike Herodium, for instance, where usage continued to the second century and beyond and the destruction layers from the first and second Jewish rebellions were muddled together beyond the point of accurate distinction.

[678] Syon, "Gamla: A City of Refuge," 137.

[679] Syon, "Gamla: A City of Refuge," 145.

[680] Syon, "Gamla: A City of Refuge," 145.

Figure 42 – The breach in the fortifications

Units from three Roman legions under the command of Vespasian took part in the siege of Gamla (*Fifth Macedonica*, *Tenth Fretensis*, and *Fifteenth Apollinaris*). This overwhelming weight of numbers is reflected in the enormous quantity of arrowheads, ballista balls, and catapult bolts found at Gamla.[681]

The eastern end of Gamla was bombarded with ballista balls and bolts fired from catapults located further back along the ridge. The national park authorities have placed two replica Roman catapults, one for firing ballistas and one for firing bolts, on the site across the ridge where it is thought the catapults and other siege weapons were located (see figure 43 below).[682]

IDENTIFICATION OF THE SYNAGOGUE

In 1976, the archaeologist Shmarya Gutmann began fourteen seasons of excavations at Gamla (1976–1989).[683] In the first season of digging, inside the walls of Gamla, in the building complex immediately behind the breached wall, a large public building was uncovered. According to Gutmann, who had been involved with the excavations at Masada, the layout of the building was somewhat

---

[681] Syon, "Gamla: A City of Refuge," 141.

[682] The effects of catapult bombardment were cruel. At Jotapata, where Josephus was present during the final days of the siege, he had this to say: "One of the men standing on the wall beside Josephus had his head carried away by a stone, and his skull was shot, as from a sling, to a distance of three furlongs; a woman with child was struck on the belly just as she was leaving her house at daybreak, and the babe in her womb was flung half a furlong away." (*B.J.* 3.245–247)

[683] Excavations and conservation work restarted in 1997, see Syon and Yavor, "Gamla 1997–2000," 37.

similar to the building identified as a synagogue there (in that it had benches around its walls).[684]

Figure 43 – Replica catapult (looking west to the breached wall)

Figure 44 – The public building (looking southwest)

Although Gutmann was not initially certain how to interpret the building he excavated at Gamla, by the second season, when the adjacent stepped mikveh/cistern was uncovered, he became confident enough to make his identification.[685] According to Gutmann, the internal configuration of the public

---
[684] Syon, "Gamla: City of Refuge," 136.
[685] In conversation variously with Motti Aviam, Danny Syon, and Shimon Gibson.

building—with benches around the walls, ancillary rooms, and a *mikveh* just outside the western entrance of the building—was such that it could safely be described as a *bet knesset* (a house of assembly).[686] Another indication for Gutmann that this was a public building—specifically an assembly hall and, indeed, even a synagogue—was the presence of three entrances: a main entrance in the centre of the western wall (visible in the photograph above), a second smaller entrance along the western wall leading to a raised ambulatory area, and a third entrance: a doorway and staircase in the southeastern section of the southern wall leading up from the street below. Gutmann thought the separate entrances might also have had significance in relation to the function that this building fulfilled, perhaps even in terms of separation of people for reasons of gender, seniority, etc., as well as serving to facilitate traffic in and out of the building.[687] Gutmann's excavations revealed a large building whose internal measurements were 20 x 16 m with an east-north-east/west-south-west longitudinal axis (for convenience, the excavators treated it as an east-west axis and I have followed suit).[688] The building was constructed on a wide terrace on the ridge, carved out of the soft chalk bedrock in the north and supported by a massive retaining wall in the south.[689] It is built entirely of the local black basalt. It is part of a larger complex, consisting of a main hall, ancillary rooms on the east and west, a large plastered and stepped-*mikveh* just outside the eastern ancillary rooms, and an unexcavated section north of the main hall (see fig. 45 below).[690]

---

[686] Gutmann, *Gamla: A City in Rebellion*, 106. This section of Gutmann's book was kindly translated for me by Dr. Orit Peleg of the Institute of Archaeology at the Hebrew University of Jerusalem.
[687] Gutmann, *Gamla: A City in Rebellion*, 106.
[688] Gutmann, *Gamla: A City in Rebellion*, 99. This section of Gutmann's book was kindly translated for me by Orit Peleg of the Institute of Archaeology at the Hebrew University of Jerusalem.
[689] Gutmann, *Gamla: A City in Rebellion*, 99.
[690] The [modern] roof of the *mikveh* can be seen the centre background of the photograph (fig. 45 above) just past the western rooms (marked A and B) of the complex.

194   INVENTION OF THE FIRST-CENTURY SYNAGOGUE

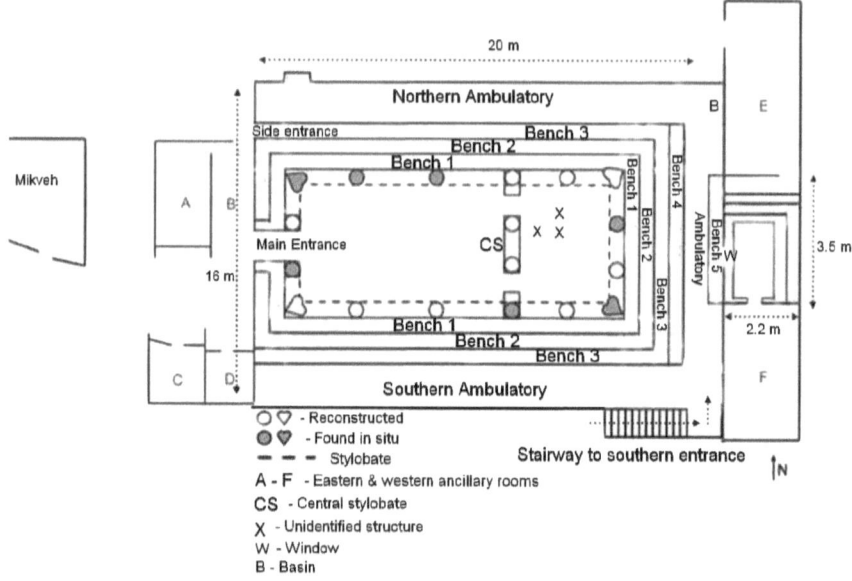

Figure 45 – The public building (floor plan)

THE EXCAVATION REPORTS

The orientation of the main hall was wholly dictated by the topography of the ridge on which the complex is built.[691] The southern wall of the public building is also the retaining wall of this terrace and did not survive above the level of the remaining surface of the hall.[692]

The hall of the public building consists of a central space surrounded by rows of steps/benches leading to a raised ambulatory that runs around all the walls.[693] At the bottom of the benches is a stylobate on which the supporting columns stood. While only bits and pieces of the columns survived, most of the stylobate on which they stood remains intact. Two heart-shaped column bases survived *in situ* in the southeastern and northeastern corners of the stylobate. Some column drums were found scattered on the floor, but the majority of drums, capitals, and

---

[691] Zvi Yavor, "The Architecture and Stratigraphy of the Eastern and Western Quarters," in *Gamla II: The Shmarya Gutmann Excavations 1976–1989: The Architecture* (ed. Danny Syon and Zvi Yavor; IAA Reports 44; Jerusalem: Israel Antiquities Authority, 2010), 41–42. [The author cited the prepublished version; the editors thank Danny Syon for aid in updating the citation to the subsequently published version –Eds.].
[692] Gutmann, *Gamla: A City in Rebellion*, 100.
[693] Visible in the photograph at fig. 3 above.

bases are missing; many rolled down the slope, possibly during the destruction. The few capitals that remain are Doric order, but there is one Ionic capital.[694]

There is a short stylobate in the centre of the floor towards the eastern end of the hall (see figs. 44 and 45 above). This carried two columns and divided the hall into two parts in a ratio of 2:3. The columns on this stylobate aligned exactly with the central columns of the north and south stylobates. Because of its layout and the columns which stood on it, it is unlikely to have been the base of a podium for reading the torah scrolls, as was suggested by one of the excavators.[695] However, there is a structure just behind the central stylobate, which might relate to this purpose, and which is not fully explained in the forthcoming *Gamla II* publication.[696] An alternative and tentative explanation for this structure is offered in the section below labelled "Food for thought."

The position of the central stylobate, along with the destruction in the hall, led the excavators to query whether the entire hall might originally have been paved over. To answer this question, a series of test pits were dug under the floor, including under sections of the stylobate. This revealed that beneath the floor surface there is a tightly packed layer (some 15 cm thick) of stone chips. The stone chips seem to have originated from the construction process. This layer in turn lies on a layer of small to medium sized fieldstones.[697] Beneath the stones making up the stylobate strip surrounding the perimeter of the hall was a layer of rough field stones arranged to form a foundation. The paving as it appears now (around the bottom of the benches and the central short stylobate) would therefore appear to be practically the full extent of the original paving and was meant to serve partly as a walkway and partly as a stylobate. This in turn means that the central space of the assembly room was unpaved when in use.[698]

On the northern ambulatory near the eastern wall, a circular plastered hand-basin was discovered, sitting on a foundation of earth and stones (see fig. 45 above). This basin was fed with water from one of two large cisterns discovered about 30 m east of the hall. The channel that fed this basin continues west beyond the basin, along the length of the northern wall of the hall, and empties into the mikveh outside the western ancillary rooms. The foundation on which the basin sat was partly destroyed during the siege, during which time it was unlikely to have been used, because the channel supplying it (and the *mikveh*/cistern)

---

[694] Yavor, "Architecture and Stratigraphy," 43.
[695] Yavor, "Architecture and Stratigraphy," 47; Zvi Uri Ma'oz, "The Synagogue of Gamla and the Typology of Second-Temple Synagogues," in *Ancient Synagogues Revealed*, ed. Lee I. Levine (Jerusalem: Israel Exploration Society, 1982), 38.
[696] [Matassa refers to the pre-published version; Gamla has subsequently been fully published. –Eds.]
[697] Yavor, "Architecture and Stratigraphy," 47.
[698] Yavor, "Architecture and Stratigraphy," 52.

originates from a cistern outside the city wall, in an area controlled by the Romans.[699]

The main entrance to the building is in the centre of the western wall and is 1.5 m wide, constructed of dressed ashlars including a threshold made of three stones, with two hinge sockets and a bolt hole. The construction and width of the doorframe suggests that it was the formal entrance to the space within. Near the entrance a fragment of a lintel with an engraved rosette was found (see fig. 49 below).[700]

There is a second entrance, 85 cm wide, also in the western wall, 3.20 m north of the main entrance. This entrance led to the northwestern corner of the ambulatory and its threshold is appropriately higher.[701] The rosette lintel fragment mentioned above belonged to this entrance.[702]

There is a third entrance, again around 85 cm wide, via a staircase leading from the street beneath the south side of the building onto the eastern end of the southern ambulatory (see fig. 47 below).

Along both the north and south walls of the assembly hall there are three rows of benches rising to the ambulatory.[703] Along the western wall there are two rows of benches, which continue into the entrance corridor.[704] Along the eastern wall there are four rows of benches. There is a fifth bench against the eastern wall.[705] The benches around the walls are 30 cm high, 40 cm wide and built of basalt ashlars.[706] At the foot of the benches and encircling the room is the stylobate on which the supporting columns sat.[707]

When excavated, there were signs of fire damage on the northern ambulatory, apparently as a consequence of cooking. Gutmann thought that this may have been the remains from the last days of the siege, when residents used the building as a shelter.[708] Further evidence of conditions during the siege came in the form of the

---

[699] Yavor, "Architecture and Stratigraphy," 54.
[700] Yavor, "Architecture and Stratigraphy," 42.
[701] Yavor, "Architecture and Stratigraphy," 42.
[702] Orit Peleg-Barkat, "Architectural Decoration," in *Gamla II: The Shmarya Gutmann Excavations, 1976–1989: The Architecture* (ed. Danny Syon and Zvi Yavor; Jerusalem: Israel Antiquities Authority, 2010) [The author cited the prepublished version –Eds.].
[703] The benches are not all intact, but there is sufficient survival to infer the remainder of their layout.
[704] Gutmann, *Gamla: A City in Rebellion*, 106.
[705] Gutmann, *Gamla: A City in Rebellion*, 107.
[706] The entire structure and most of the monumental city of Gamla is built of local basalt.
[707] Gutmann, *Gamla: A City in Rebellion*, 100.
[708] This is an inexplicable and peculiar choice for a shelter, since this building abuts the fortification wall and is within a few metres of the breached wall. It was under heavy bombardment (as is evidenced by the quantity of ballista balls, arrowheads, and catapult bolts found in the destruction layer). 350 ballista balls were found in the hall and its immediate

remains of cooking hearths on the northern ambulatory, which indicated that the space had been used to house refugees. Fragments of two knife-pared lamps were found in this area, as well as an intact juglet, a complete cooking pot, and large quantities of broken household pottery.[709] Many ballista balls and arrowheads were also found here, and it would appear that the wooden roof of the hall collapsed at some point during the bombardment.[710]

Several column drums were found in the main hall. The corner columns were heart-shaped (see fig. 44 above). Gutmann also found various capitals, mostly Doric, but also an Ionic one, and a fragment of a Doric column base decorated with a meander pattern. Several column drums were found standing on the stylobate, and along the northern and southern sides of the hall stood four columns, while two more stood on the west and east. Most of the column drums have disappeared, some down the slope. Several corbel stones that supported the roof beams were retrieved from the debris layer in the hall.[711] In the western corner of the northern wall, close to the smaller entrance to the hall, there is a large cupboard, which was preserved to the height of the wall. Gutmann suggested that this space may have been used to store Torah scrolls.[712]

Figure 46 – The northern wall (cupboard)

---

vicinity, more than at the breach in the fortification wall! See Syon, "Gamla: City of Refuge," 141.
[709] Yavor, "Architecture and Stratigraphy," 54.
[710] Gutmann, *Gamla: A City in Rebellion*, 100.
[711] Gutmann, *Gamla: A City in Rebellion*, 103.
[712] Gutmann, *Gamla: A City in Rebellion*, 100.

The cupboard should be imagined as being lined with wood and as having shelves. As can be seen from figure 46 above, it is located just inside the building on the left of the smaller western doorway (light is streaming through the smaller doorway in this photograph, although you cannot see the doorway itself from the angle the photograph was taken). While Gutmann thought this cupboard could have been used as a place to store Torah scrolls, this does not seem very likely, for a number of reasons. The cupboard is located on the northern ambulatory, close to the side entrance, and there would be far too much movement in front of it and too much access to it by anyone in the vicinity.

Gutmann was unable to determine the date of the founding of the building as a whole and relied mainly on coin finds in the building and nearby.[713] He argued that it may have been established as early as the reign of Alexander Jannaeus and was probably renovated towards the end of the first century BCE, during Herod the Great's lifetime.[714]

The finds (other than the knife-pared Herodian lamp found buried underneath the floor, suggesting a Herodian foundation) were found scattered all over the hall, along with the large quantities of ballista balls and other ammunition, which illustrated the heavy bombardment this section of Gamla faced. Only thirty-five arrowheads were found in the hall itself, but archers were not usually deployed in constricted spaces. Most of the arrowheads found were from the eastern ambulatory and were probably shot after the roof had collapsed.[715] Many nails were found, including a large cluster in the northeastern corner. These may have come from furniture and from ceiling rafters that collapsed. Spots of black soot were identified on the floor and ambulatories, also probably from the rafters.[716]

THE ANCILLARY ROOM

In the third season of digging, a small ancillary room behind the eastern wall of the assembly hall was uncovered (see figure 47 below). This room measures 3.5 x 2.2 m and is only a third of the width of the main hall. The entry to this room is via a porch or vestibule to its south and there is another room to its north. When excavated, it was found completely filled with stones and rubble and had apparently been used to buttress the fortification wall on its eastern side. Along two walls there are rows of benches; three along the northern wall and two along the eastern. There is an ambulatory along the northern wall, along which the water channel that feeds the mikveh at the western end of the complex and the water basin in the main hall runs, and these elements are contemporary with the building

---

[713] As at 2000, over 6,000 coins had been found; see Syon and Yavor, "Gamla 1997–2000," 61.
[714] Gutmann, *Gamla: A City in Rebellion*, 109.
[715] Yavor, "Architecture and Stratigraphy," 54.
[716] Yavor, "Architecture and Stratigraphy," 54.

complex and therefore also purpose-built. In the western wall there is a window, opening onto the main hall. The short fifth bench in the main assembly space (mentioned above) is located directly beneath this window. According to the excavators, this room could seat around twenty-five people.[717]

Figure 47 – The ancillary room

This configuration of this room with benches and a connection to the main hall was evidently for some related function, and it suggested, to Gutmann, a place for study. Gutmann thought the most obvious parallel was the *bet midrash* of rabbinic literature. This room is certainly unique in the architecture and archaeology of this period (so far), and it is perhaps best seen as a prototype for something specific to its design which is, alas, unknown.[718]

In any event, because of the benches and because it looks out onto the main hall, Gutmann interpreted the small room as a study room or *bet midrash*, which, he said, strengthened the case for a pre-70 CE synagogue functioning as a centre for cultural and religious activity.[719] Gutman said that the Gamla assembly hall would have been used for conducting secular assemblies, meetings, and celebrations, and not just for praying.[720] There is certainly no doubt that this ancillary room is in some way related to the functioning of the main hall, and that it, also, was purpose-built (it is contemporary with the rest of the building complex).

---

[717] Yavor, "Architecture and Stratigraphy," 56. It seems unlikely that so many people (even small and slender people) could sit together in this space. [According to Danny Syon, the excavators fit twenty people into the room, and their published estimate is for the full extent of the original room –Eds.]

[718] Yavor, "Architecture and Stratigraphy," 57. [which agrees with Gutmann –Eds.]

[719] Gutmann, *Gamla: A City in Rebellion*, 109.

[720] Gutmann, *Gamla: A City in Rebellion*, 109. This argument is highly speculative.

The *Mikveh*/Cistern

A stepped *mikveh*/cistern associated with the building is located just 4.5 m west of the assembly hall, just outside the western ancillary rooms (its modern roof is visible in fig. 44 above). The *mikveh*/cistern is constructed of field stones and partly dressed stones, cemented together and covered with several layers of heavy plaster. The inner dimensions of the *mikveh* are 4.5 x 4 m.[721] Four complete steps and some partly destroyed steps into the structure were found. The steps were also covered with several layers of thick plaster.[722]

Figure 48 – The *mikveh*/cistern

The channel that feeds this water installation comes directly along the northern wall of the assembly hall, feeding the hand-basin along its way, through the eastern ancillary room, before emptying into it.[723] While the link between early synagogues and *mikva'ot* has not been established in the scholarship, there is no question that the assembly hall here and this water installation are contemporary and part of the same complex.

Architectural Decoration

Some of the decorative architectural pieces in this public building, as well as its internal configuration, link it in form to late Roman/Byzantine synagogues.[724]

---

[721] Yavor, "Architecture and Stratigraphy," 58.
[722] Yavor, "Architecture and Stratigraphy," 58.
[723] Yavor, "Architecture and Stratigraphy," 53.
[724] Peleg-Barkat, "Architectural Decoration."

Specifically, two door lintels were found at Gamla, the first of which was found outside the secondary entrance along the western wall of the assembly hall complex. This lintel is decorated with a low-relief encircled rosette.[725]

Figure 49 – The rosette lintel from the second western door[726]
© Danny Syon/ Gamla Excavations. Used by permission

The six-petalled rosette is by far the most common type of rosette motif in Jewish art of the period and later, perhaps because it is so easily executed (by drawing a circle and using a compass to draw semi-circles which intersect at the centre of the primary circle).[727] A second lintel, also decorated with a low-relief encircled rosette was found in the lower city near another large public building (the basilica).[728] The second lintel was unbroken and was inscribed with a six-petalled rosette engraved into a raised circle between two simple engraved palm trees.[729] The palm trees on either side of the rosette have eleven branches each, arranged symmetrically.[730] The second lintel appears to have been carved by a

---

[725] Syon and Yavor, "Gamla 1997–2000," 16–23; Peleg-Barkat, "Architectural Decoration."
[726] I am very grateful to Danny Syon of the Israel Antiquities Authority for letting me use this photograph of the lintel in this dissertation. The photograph is from the original 1976 excavations of Gamla. I was unable to take a photograph of the lintel because—during conservation works undertaken in 1989—it was accidentally bricked into a wall and is no longer visible. [© Danny Syon/ Gamla Excavations. The editors are grateful for permission to republish this photograph].
[727] Peleg-Barkat, "Architectural Decoration."
[728] Syon and Yavor, "Gamla 1997–2000," 16–23; Peleg-Barkat, "Architectural Decoration."
[729] The basilica is a public building, but it contains no open spaces sufficient for general assembly, and it is therefore ruled out as being another possible synagogue.
[730] Syon and Yavor, "Gamla 1997–2000," 16–23; Peleg-Barkat, "Architectural Decoration."

more experienced artisan as, rather than having a simple incised circle around the rosette, the circle is carved in very low relief (although the palms trees and the rosette are incised).[731]

Figure 50 – The rosette lintel from the basilica[732]
Photo by O. Peleg-Barkat. Used by permission

Although this type of decorated lintel became common in the Late Roman and Byzantine periods, the only other contemporary first-century examples come from En-Gedi, where lintels and doorposts were decorated with a rosette, an amphora, and grape clusters.[733] The rosette also appears on the Late Roman/Byzantine period synagogues at En Neshut (on a column pedestal); an encircled rosette also appears on a capital decorated with an eagle relief at Umm-el Kanatir; and a modified encircled (it is slanted) rosette appears on a lintel fragment from the synagogue at Kokhav Hayarden.[734]

In general, the decorative elements in the assembly hall tend to attest to the prosperity of the inhabitants of Gamla before the outbreak of the rebellion and to their familiarity with current fashions—albeit the execution of those elements was

---

[731] Peleg-Barkat, "Architectural Decoration."

[732] I am very grateful to Orit Peleg for letting me use a photograph of the basilica rosette lintel from her personal collection for use in this book [Photo by O. Peleg-Barkat. The editors are grateful for permission to use the image –Eds.]

[733] Peleg-Barkat, "Architectural Decoration"; B. Mazar and I. Dunayevsky, "En-Gedi, Third Season of Excavations: Preliminary Report," *IEJ* 14.3 (1964): 128.

[734] Levine, *Ancient Synagogues Revealed*, 106, 108, 95–97.

a simple, and sometimes inaccurate, rendering of the decorative patterns, and reflect local workmanship.[735]

In the hall, there were originally at least sixteen columns, each comprised of several drums. Only fourteen of the column drums were found; most of the architectural elements had tumbled or been rolled down the steep southern slope.[736] Each of the corner columns in the hall is heart-shaped. Typically, heart-shaped columns were used at the junctions of colonnades of peristyle courtyards or reception halls, for example in the banqueting hall of Herod's northern palace at Masada.[737] Each of the four heart-shaped capitals at Gamla differs slightly from the others.[738] All but one of the columns found in the assembly hall were carved in a simplified Doric style (one column was Ionic) and rather than standing directly on the ground as in the classical Doric order, they stood on a stylobate.[739] The single Ionic capital in the main hall was found broken in two. Its faulty decoration suggests it was carved by an unskilled artisan, or one who was not wholly familiar with the design being executed, as both the volutes of the capital spiral clockwise, whereas the left volute should spiral anti-clockwise and the right clockwise (see fig. 51 below, the capital on the left).[740]

Figure 51 – The badly carved capitals

One of the Doric capitals from the synagogue is decorated with what is usually described as an incorrectly executed Greek meander pattern (see fig. 51

---

[735] Peleg-Barkat, "Architectural Decoration."
[736] Gutmann, *Gamla: A City in Rebellion*, 103.
[737] Gideon Foerster with Naomi Porat, *Masada V: The Yigael Yadin Excavations 1963–1965: Final Reports, Art and Architecture* (Jerusalem: Israel Exploration Society, 1995), fig. 33.
[738] Peleg-Barkat, "Architectural Decoration."
[739] Peleg-Barkat, "Architectural Decoration."
[740] Peleg-Barkat, "Architectural Decoration."

above, the capital on the right).[741] This description is not correct; it is instead a crude rendering of another fairly common motif in Jewish art of the period: the swastika (or double meander). Exactly the same pattern is seen in synagogues of the Late Roman/Byzantine period at Ma'oz Hayim on a mosaic floor, on the doorway of the synagogue at Kokhav-Hayarden, and on a doorpost at Dabbura.[742] It is also seen in a sixth century CE building at Bet She'an (fig. 52 below).[743]

Figure 52 – The swastika/double meander pattern at Bet She'an

Of course, whether the capital is decorated with a badly executed single meander pattern or a correctly executed swastika (double meander) pattern does not make any difference to the identification of the public building at Gamla, but it does correct an error that is repeated in the scholarship in relation to its decoration.[744] In either event, these are unquestionably patterns that occur in later Jewish art and architecture.

The public building at Gamla is a clear example of something that was built for the function it served; the question is whether it is safe to say it functioned as a synagogue. The structure has elements one would expect (and indeed hope) to find in an early synagogue: seating, and perhaps even an adjacent study area. It stands in close proximity to a stepped *mikveh* or cistern just a few metres outside the western entrance, as well as a hand basin within the hall itself, both of which were fed by a single water channel whose route through the building is contemporary with its construction. There is no ambiguity about the construction or configuration of the hall, and the archaeology is well documented and reported

---

[741] Peleg-Barkat, "Architectural Decoration."

[742] Levine, ed., *Ancient Synagogues Revealed*, 87, 95, 109.

[743] Author's photograph of meander pattern in bathhouse at Bet She'an, 2005. The swastika is another form of meander pattern, but the design of the capital at Gamla is always compared to the Greek meander, which is altogether different in composition. The classical Greek meander consists of continuous squared-off "S" shapes, with no central "cross," thus:

[744] See also Goodenough, *Jewish Symbols*, 46–47, on the use of the Swastika in Jewish art.

(although not yet fully published).[745] Moreover, the hall was constructed in one single phase, and was not adapted or changed afterwards.[746] In addition, there is an absolute *terminus ad quem* for the city as a whole, not that this is relevant to a synagogue identification.

There can be no doubt that the assembly hall was used for public business. Perhaps it was even used as a trading floor, for the sale of the olive oil and flour (produced on an industrial scale in the city's numerous oil presses and flour mills centred in the western and lower part of the city).[747] One could easily imagine trading going on in what must have been a busy and bustling city, with clerks taking details, producing receipts and storing other documentation in the back room of the assembly hall. The town council most likely also met there and the space was probably also used as a law court. The seating in the hall is well-designed and ample and could probably accommodate well over 300 people when required.

Access to the hall and circulation around it was well-planned from the three entrances and from the ancillary rooms. Proceeding from the western side of the city, one would pass the mikveh/cistern on the left. Coming from the upper ridge, access could probably be had via the ancillary room marked "E" in figure 45 above, and from the lower city access could be had via the southern entrance. All of this shows that the assembly hall was a central element in the life of Gamla, and, since the complex was purpose built, we must assume that the centrality and particular configuration was meaningful.

The quantity and quality of datable material found in this structure (other than relating directly to the siege) was very scant. The latest datable material under the floor was the nozzle of a knife-pared lamp, found during test probes into the floor

---

[745] I am very grateful to Danny Syon of the Israel Antiquities Authority in Akko for so generously giving me access to the relevant chapters from the forthcoming publication of the Gamla excavation reports, as well as for taking the time to meet with me in 2006 at his offices in Akko to discuss the excavation of Gamla and the archaeologists involved in those excavations. During our conversation, I said to Danny that the floor plan, with its 3:2 division by the extra stylobate, looked a little like that of a tripartite Greek temple, and he replied that its layout was one of the reasons Gutmann was not initially convinced that it was a synagogue, and only changed his mind in the second season when the adjoining *mikveh*/cistern was excavated. Then in the third digging season, the discovery of the ancillary room with benches behind the eastern wall added weight to argument for that identification. Certainly, it is to be hoped that if further excavations take place to uncover the rooms to the north of the complex some of the mystery will be alleviated. [The excavations are now fully published, and the footnotes have been updated accordingly –Eds.]

[746] Yavor, "Architecture and Stratigraphy," 61.

[747] Such as room 1703 (a complete flour mill); shop row 5018 (a row of shops entirely dedicated to flour production); buildings 5000, 5010, and 5011 (a large oil press in a large complex—130 m^2—for the production of olive oil); building 5005 (a large room for the storage of oil). See Yavor, "The Architecture and Stratigraphy."

in 1983, as well as a rim of a stew-pot found in test probes in 1997, whose first appearance is dated to the early first century CE. Gutmann suggested a possible founding date under Alexander Jannaeus, which simply does not accord with the fact that a Herodian lamp of a type manufactured only in the late first century BCE and early first century CE was found in the floor fill (especially since the floor fill is contemporary with the construction of the building) and the building is itself a single-phase development.[748] The style of the building also accords with the style of many of the buildings in the western section of the city as well as the "basilica-style" building of the lower city, all of which are safely dated to the first century CE, on architectural, archaeological, and evidential grounds.[749] For these reasons, even if we accept Gutmann's identification of the assembly hall, we must reject his dating of it to the late Hasmonaean period.

FOOD FOR THOUGHT (A PROTOTYPE AEDICULA?)

An element of the internal structural configuration which is perplexing is the central stylobate. It is not clear what function this could have served, and the excavators do not offer any suggestions. Ma'oz suggested that it could possibly be the base of a *bema*, but this was rejected by the excavators on the basis that the layout of the extra stylobate and its relationship to the other stylobates was too symmetrical to allow for this.[750] It is also possible that the central stylobate was there to separate the larger section of the main space from sight and hearing of activity in the ancillary room (or vice versa). Perhaps it was used to separate people—men from women, or even senior members of the community from juniors—though it is not clear how this could have worked in practice, since circulation along the benches and ambulatories was not affected by the stylobate. There is no parallel for this extra stylobate in any later synagogue so far known.

However, there is another structure immediately behind the central stylobate that is most interesting. In an email, Danny Syon of the Israel Antiquities Authority confirmed to me that the excavators consider this structure to be possibly part of the structural underpinning of the building. And, as mentioned above (in the section labelled the "Layout of the Public Building"), this structure is discussed in only one short sentence in the excavation reports, as follows:

---

[748] Dan Barag and Malka Hershkovitz, "Lamps," in *Masada IV: the Yigael Yadin Excavations 1963–65: Final Reports: Lamps, Textiles, Basketry, Cordage and Related Artifacts, Wood Remains, Ballista Balls* (ed. Joseph Aviram et al.; Jerusalem: Israel Exploration Society; Hebrew University of Jerusalem, 1995), 45; Yavor, "Architecture and Stratigraphy," 54, 61. I am grateful to Orit Peleg-Barkat for pointing this out as it had not occurred to me.

[749] Syon and Yavor, "Gamla 1997–2000," 52–59. A second encircled rosette lintel was found by the basilica-style building in the lower part of the city. This lintel has an incised rosette beside an incised palm tree. See image above; Peleg-Barkat, "Architectural Decoration."

[750] Ma'oz, "Synagogue of Gamla," 38; Yavor, "Architecture and Stratigraphy," 47.

At some points, deep and continuous foundation walls were found, constructed of roughly dressed stones. These gave support to the colonnades and in the southern half also supported the podium and relieved part of the load from the south retaining wall. *The top of one of these walls is flush with the floor* [my emphasis].[751]

Figure 53 – The unidentified structure behind the central stylobate

The excavators' explanation (above) is somewhat unsatisfying. The structures are not located so as to support the stylobate or the benches along the eastern wall, and it is not clear how they could be load-bearing for the southern retaining wall. If these were foundation walls, as is suggested, then their height is problematic. The square structure seen in the photograph above is the same height as the central stylobate, not the floor—which suggests it may not have been a sub-surface element. If it was part of the foundations, one might expect it to run centrally along the spine of the main hall. It is also aligned with a stylobate flagstone (this can be seen in the photograph above), suggesting it is part of the stylobate structure; indeed, not only that it was part of the stylobate structure, but that it was part of the original purpose-built public building, and not a later addition.

---

[751] [This text comes from the unpublished report that Matassa had used, but it is not in the published version, as the excavators now believe that the structure is "an improvised hearth constructed by the refugees in the synagogue hall." Communication to the editors by Danny Syon –Eds.]

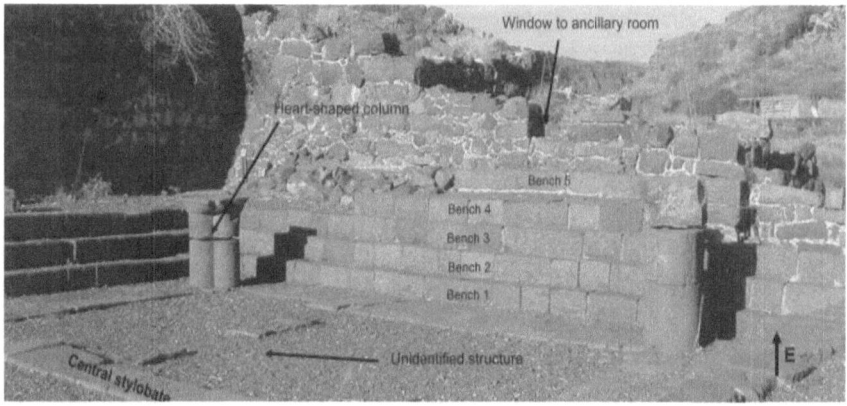

Figure 54 – Another view of the unidentified structure (looking northeast)

The fact that the structures are located off-centre is puzzling. If they are supporting the structural integrity of the space behind the central stylobate, then this should imply that there was paving covering this area which was shored up by these piles—but the excavators have correctly shown that the paving, as it survives, is near enough complete. If these were foundations, without paving on top, then they would not need to extend up to the surface. A foundation above the bedrock but beneath the floor would be sufficient and stable. The sub-surface foundations in other areas of the hall are constructed of variously sized field stones, roughly fitted together.[752]

The square structure behind the stylobate is also odd in that it is constructed of cut basalt, not field stones like other elements of the foundations. Moreover, the stones are regular in size and have been shaped, although they are by no means as well dressed as the stylobate paving slabs. Still, they *could* be foundations. They could be shoring up the nearby structures, though it is not clear how this might work. There may have been some warping of the floor area in the intervening two thousand years since this building's destruction, resulting in these structures breaking the surface.

However, and while hesitant to make the claim, it is not beyond the realm of possibility that this structure is integral to the hall as a whole and that, perhaps, the central stylobate was closed off on one side by either a wall or a column, giving the area to the northern side (behind the central stylobate) the look of a sort of *prototype* aedicula (see figure 55 below).[753] In this context, the aedicula would

---

[752] Yavor, "Architecture and Stratigraphy," 52.

[753] In this context, we could imagine the aedicula as a raised and covered area.

be a squared-off and covered structure, perhaps with the central stylobate as its front, and the east-west short wall partially closing it off behind.

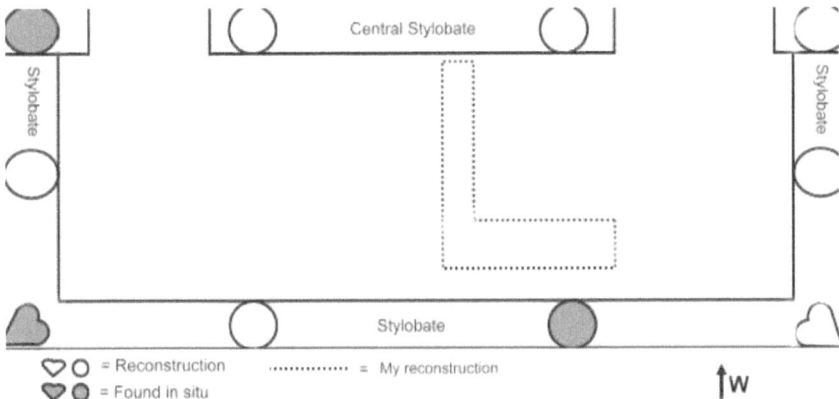

Figure 55 – A prototype aedicula?

If this was such a prototype structure, then we could have in the Gamla assembly hall a squared-off section, behind which something could have been kept, or done, or a platform (such as a *bema*) on which someone could have stood. Certainly, we see in late Roman/Byzantine synagogues single aediculae which are off-centre.[754] And, according to Hachlili, "nearly every excavated synagogue yields fragments, traces of a site, or the actual site of the Torah shrine as early as the second century CE."[755]

If synagogues from the second century CE are yielding this sort of structural evidence (and later synagogues are outside the remit of this monograph), then I think it likely that the origins of those structures are somewhat earlier. And if they are earlier, then perhaps Gamla is the first excavated site in which we see their physical manifestation.

This reconstruction is pure speculation, however, and, whether this odd structure is an integral part of the Gamla assembly hall, or part of its structural underpinning as the excavators say, it remains problematic, because it leaves the 2:3 division of the hall and the benches behind the stylobate unexplained, which is in itself odd in a building designed for public assembly.

---

[754] Rachel Hachlili, "Torah Shrine and Ark in Ancient Synagogues: A Re-Evaluation," *ZDPV* 116.2 (2000): 147.
[755] Hachlili, "Torah Shrine," 147.

Conclusions

While there were no documents found within the building which might support a synagogue identification, or which might refer to a synagogue, and no references in Josephus or Suetonius to a synagogue, the combination of the architectural elements leave no doubt that this building was designed for public assembly and was most likely a multi-purpose building, used for council meetings, as a trade floor, as a law court, etc. Since it is located in a flourishing Jewish city, it has to be likely that one of the uses to which it was put was as a place to read the Torah and to study. It is well laid out for this purpose. The ancillary benched room with its window into the main hall, which Gutmann thought might be a study room, is also persuasive in this regard. Moreover, this is the only building of the five case studies herein to have had any recognisable decorative architectural features that *could* be Jewish in character; in particular, the rosette motif on the door lintel (which becomes a common motif in later Jewish art and architecture) lends some support to this identification. The meander pattern capital (be it a single meander or a swastika/double meander), is another motif which, as I have shown, occurs in later synagogues and other Jewish buildings (although both the rosette and meander also occur in non-Jewish buildings).

Consequently, the public building at Gamla is likely to have been, *among other things*, a synagogue—in the very broadest sense of the word—in that it could have been used for reading the law and studying the Torah in this Jewish town. In some ways, it is difficult to argue that it could not have been a synagogue, because of how it is designed, where it is, and access to it. If it was a synagogue, it is probably the earliest one so far excavated in the land of Israel, since it must date to at least the late Herodian period.

7
CONCLUSIONS

This monograph was intended to examine the identification of so-called early synagogues on the basis of the available archaeological, epigraphic, and literary evidence. A close examination of the first case study of this book, Delos, quickly revealed a pattern of dubious connections and identifications which simply could not be relied upon. Exploring that issue revealed that the identification problem extended to the other four case studies, and the evidential trail for each site was followed with no presumptions of where it might lead.

In the case of Delos, the first case study in this book, the difficulty with the identification of a synagogue was not immediately apparent. An extended visit to the site allowed for a proper analysis of the material, and it was possible to put together a cohesive account of the contrast between the scholarship and the physical reality of the site, and to piece together the body of evidence that both supports the claims made in this study and shows that those claims are objective and fully reasoned. From assumptions relying on the tangential source material in Maccabees and Josephus, to the interpretations of six inscriptions found within and without the building, to the claims made about specific features in the building, such as a *mikveh* (with no room for human ingress) and a Torah shrine (into which it would be difficult to fit an adult hand), examination of the putative synagogue on Delos led to the realisation that there was no relationship between the physical structure, its furniture and fittings, and its identification as a synagogue. Indeed, on Delos, there were other buildings, such as Sarapeion A in the theatre district, which could have functioned as a synagogue if the basis on which the building identified as a synagogue on Delos were correct, and, thus, the certainty of the identification of the synagogue on Delos crumbled.

The second case study in this monograph, Hasmonaean/Herodian Jericho, was identified as a synagogue only in 1998 (although the site was excavated some years earlier), and so it was possible to discuss it with a number of the people involved with its excavation, including Ehud Netzer of the Institute of Archaeology at the Hebrew University of Jerusalem, who made the synagogue identification. While the identification of this particular site is not unanimously accepted in the scholarship, it is commonly referred to as a *possible* synagogue

212   INVENTION OF THE FIRST-CENTURY SYNAGOGUE

and thus, consequently, *possibly* the earliest synagogue in the land of Israel. At Jericho, with the benefit of the process developed with the Delos site, it was possible to make some quite specific *dis*identifications of the various architectural and archaeological elements its excavator had interpreted as belonging to a synagogue.

While there is no textual, epigraphic, or other material relating to the existence of a synagogue on this site, it was relatively easy to correct much of the information surrounding the site's context, architecture, and archaeology. This process involved, among other things, a close and detailed analysis of the water systems feeding the entire site, which, in turn, allowed for the re-identification of the structure the excavator claimed was a Torah niche, but which was actually a sluice-gate on the main Na'aran aqueduct.[756] Moreover, the excavator had described benches around the main assembly space (actually a simple peristyle courtyard) for which there is simply no physical evidence.[757] As was made clear in the Jericho case study herein, the matter of the benches and the Torah niche, as well as other evidence presented in terms of the identification of a synagogue in the final excavation reports, is seriously flawed and is, again, unsafe to use as a comparison to support a synagogue identification on any other site.

The third case study, the most complex and enigmatic of the sites, is the one on Masada. There is a veritable mountain of epigraphical and archaeological evidence relating to Masada, and Josephus was generous enough to give a long and detailed account of events on Masada during the first Jewish rebellion, as well as some fairly accurate descriptions of the physical layout and architecture of the palatial site as a whole. There were many hundreds of biblical and extra-biblical scrolls and scroll fragments found on Masada, as well as coins, ostraca, ceramics, and textiles. And, as is shown in the case study, there is much tangential material in the case of Masada which has been used to make and/or support the case for a synagogue identification and to construct the Masada synagogue myth, which is in no way borne out by the archaeological, epigraphical, or source material.

Despite the vast quantity of material relating to Masada, the material pertaining to the identification of a synagogue is minute. The identification was made on the basis of the benches around the walls and two scroll fragments found in pits in the connected ancillary room. As is clear from the case study, the mixture of material found in the pits in the so-called *genizah,* as well as the construction of the main area of the structure identified as a synagogue and its location in the overall context of first rebellion period Masada, is insufficient to support a synagogue identification.

Arguments about the so-called *genizah* are themselves quite telling: that sacred documents could be intentionally interred in a dung-filled room, that

---

[756] Netzer, *Hasmonaean and Herodian Palaces at Jericho*, 2:168.
[757] Netzer, *Hasmonaean and Herodian Palaces at Jericho*, 2:165–66.

someone could live in the same space and use a domestic oven in it seem quite extraordinary. Add to this the fact that the putative synagogue is located in the area of the Masada acropolis that was most under attack during the siege and is beside the Roman siege ramp, and the peculiarity of the accepted position of mainstream scholarship on the Masada synagogue identification becomes truly baffling.

The fourth case study in this monograph, the identification of the *triclinium* in the upper fortress of Herodium as a synagogue, presented an entirely new set of problems. The first was that its destruction at the end of both the first *and* second Jewish rebellions is such that it is not certain which parts of which destruction belong to what period. This difficulty was fully rehearsed by the site's excavator, Virgilio Corbo, in his series of excavation reports. Corbo argued that if the structure were a synagogue, then, because of the material found in and close by it, it belonged to the period of the second rebellion in the second century CE.[758]

Some specifics can be added to this: the structure adjacent to the *triclinium* identified as a *mikveh* is associated with an industrial-size kiln,[759] an ostracon found in the kiln relates to the Philistine deity *Dagon*,[760] an *abecedary* found in the kiln is datable to the second century;[761] moreover, there was nothing in or around the *triclinium* to suggest a first-century date or usage, there is no connection between the *triclinium* and the rooms surrounding it (they were blocked off during its final phase), the vast majority of coins found throughout the entire upper fortress site belong to the period of the second revolt (including coins minted by the Bar Kokhba rebels), and none of the graffiti or ostraca from the site can be identified as belonging to the first century. Corbo's argument for a later date was subsequently rejected by Foerster, Netzer, and others. However, as is illustrated in the case study, it is clear that their rejection of Corbo's argument is fraught with difficulties and inconsistencies and is not based on any physical evidence. Moreover, as with the Jericho identification, there is no textual, epigraphic, or other material relating to a synagogue on the site, whereas there is sufficient textual, epigraphic, and archaeological material relating to the later date to suggest that Corbo's analysis is, on balance, probably correct. In any event, even without resolution of the chronological issues, there is no evidence to suggest that the *triclinium* was used as a synagogue in any of its phases.

And then we come to the fifth case study, Gamla, where the building identified as a synagogue is a purpose-built assembly space, central both to the town and to entry into the town. In this site, and *only* in this site, are there a few architectural, archaeological, and decorative features that might be linked in

---

[758] Corbo, "L'Herodion de Giabel Fureidis," *LA* 117 (1967): 103.
[759] Corbo, *Herodion*, 1:75.
[760] Testa, *Herodion IV*, 80.
[761] Testa, *Herodion IV*, 77–78.

character to later Galilaean synagogues. The evidence is sparse and very open to debate, but it may nonetheless point to a link between first-century and later Galilaean synagogues. There is, as with the other sites, no textual or epigraphic material relating to the presence of a synagogue at Gamla in the first century or earlier. As with Masada, Josephus gives a full account of events leading to the rebellion of the city against Agrippa II and the Romans, to its being besieged and, finally, to its destruction by the Romans, after which it was abandoned forever. There is, again, no reference anywhere in the historical texts or in epigraphy to the existence of a synagogue at Gamla.

Thus the evidence that may point to a synagogue identification at Gamla is purely contextual. Specifically, there is a decorated door lintel with a low-relief rosette carved into it, and an ancillary room connected with the main assembly space (the main space and the adjacent room both have benches around their walls, though benches, in and of themselves, cannot indicate synagogue usage).

Of all the physical elements in the assembly hall at Gamla, the most exciting is the unidentified structural feature, just off-centre of the north-east axis of the main assembly space, which might represent the base of an aedicula. Of course, the conclusions in the case of Gamla are tentative and open to interpretation. The authors of the excavation reports have suggested in an email that the unidentified subsurface structure referred to above may be pilings to support the building complex as a whole, or even the remains of an earlier structure. As outlined in the Gamla chapter, aediculae were typically constructed close to existing columns, near walls, and their most common feature is a base consisting of a platform of stones.[762] Moreover, aediculae in later synagogues are found in the same position as the unidentified structure in the Gamla assembly hall. In the case of Gamla, this structure may have been a simple raised platform on which a person could have stood to read, or it may have been covered by a canopy. In later synagogues, such an aedicula would have had a façade of columns and a lintel, and would have been built against or close to an existing wall, possibly the Jerusalem-facing wall, and access to it would have been from the front or with steps leading up to it from the side.[763] This is consistent with the position of the unidentified structure at Gamla.

However, even with limited archaeological evidence in this case, and only relying on the decorated door lintel and other decorative carved elements linking it to later Galilaean synagogues, as well as its location on the main road into the city, it may be that the Herodian-period assembly hall complex at Gamla functioned, amongst other things, as a synagogue.

The methodological approach taken in this monograph has had the benefits of allowing the illustration of many of the lacunae between modern theory and the *actual* material record. And, because each case was approached from the same

---

[762] Hachlili, "Torah Shrine and Ark," 147–48.
[763] Hachlili, "Torah Shrine and Ark," 147.

CONCLUSIONS 215

point (local history, ancient texts, epigraphy, and archaeology), it has been possible to highlight specific errors in relation to each of the sites. This method has not been used before (in this context), but it should be used as a component of synagogue identification, as it makes inconsistencies, errors, misidentifications, and archaeological red herrings more easily identifiable. In the search for an accurate historical record, it may be just as important to define what is not supported by the evidence and based on mere conjecture as it is to record what is or could be correct.

To establish a truly reliable identification system, it is vital to deal with the gap between theory and the material record. Attempts to match theory and material evidence by assuming and presuming links has already produced results (in the cases of Delos, Jericho, Herodium, Masada, and perhaps Gamla) that are untenable and should never have been used to shore up what remains an unproven theory of development in relation to other sites. For example, while the undated and decontextualised Theodotos inscription is important and fills in some of the gaps for the function of the early synagogue, it does not support the identification of, say, a particular first-century synagogue at Masada, nor any other location. Nor is it possible then to use the structure at Masada, in conjunction with the Theodotos inscription, to make a case for all first-century synagogues being laid out with ancillary buildings and a water supply.[764]

There is, unfortunately, little material to suggest a clear identification method, and the gap between modern theory and the material record remains the central problem in the field of synagogue studies, especially in relation to pre-70 CE structures. While it is neither possible nor desirable to disprove synagogue identifications, it is fair to say that there has to be *some* evidence present, be it textual, epigraphical, architectural, or archaeological, before a positive identification can be made and before a synagogue so identified should be accepted into the body of scholarship on the subject and used as a basis on which to identify other structures.

If we view the synagogue as the successor to the Jerusalem temple, and as the vehicle that enabled Judaism to survive the destruction of the temple, we must acknowledge that there remains the problem of identifying how that institution came into being. This issue is difficult, and possibly impossible to resolve, because there is no source that describes the process of development or the physical structures that are referred to in the New Testament, and there is as yet no clear way to reconcile the distance between the first century CE and the safely established and identified synagogues of the late Roman/Byzantine period.

There is little evidence in the sources to help us to make specific identifications. Even though it is widely accepted that the *proseuchai* of Hellenistic and Roman Egypt evolved into the institution we know as the

---

[764] Flesher, "Palestinian Synagogues," 33, n. 21.

synagogue, there is nothing in the material record to support this claim. By the time we see the emergence of the synagogue in the late first-century CE texts of the New Testament, the use of the word *proseuchē* has once again come to refer to prayer and praying, not place (as it is used in the Delos inscription). And while there are numerous references to Jesus and his disciples preaching in synagogues in Israel and the diaspora, there is still not a single physical structure that can be identified as a synagogue before the late Roman/Byzantine period.

There can be little doubt that the synagogue began to take on its more sacral functions after the destruction of the Jerusalem temple in 70 CE, and that this happened far from Jerusalem. There can be little doubt that it was in this period, also, that the physical structure of the synagogue began to take shape (leading to the more canonical structures we see from the late Roman/Byzantine period). However, since we cannot yet ascertain precisely how and where this happened, we must take care to make it clear that speculation is not presented as fact, so that, as more data emerges to fill in the gaps in the historical and archaeological record, what we come to is an accurate representation of an ancient reality rather than a mythological one.

While there must be, of necessity, a certain nebulous quality to making specific synagogue identifications when there is no supporting physical or textual signal, what has emerged through this research project is evidence of a series of identifications having been made—in the main—without sound archaeological, architectural, or historiographic bases. As has been made clear from the case studies presented in this monograph, the processes by which early synagogues have been identified up to this point are seriously flawed and serially inconsistent. There has to be a better way of making identifications, even in the absence of corroborating material, and it is far better to leave the way open for future scholarship to make identifications by posing questions than by forcing unsubstantiated conclusions which can only serve to skew the historical and chronological record.

BIBLIOGRAPHY

Adan-Bayewitz, David, and Mordechai Aviam. "Jotapata, Josephus, and the Siege of 67: Preliminary Report on the 1992–1994 Seasons." *JRA* 10 (1997): 131–65.

Alderink, Larry J., and Luther H. Martin. "Prayer in Greco-Roman Religions." Pages 123–27 in *Prayer from Alexander to Constantine: A Critical Anthology*. Edited by Mark Kiley et al. London: Routledge, 1997.

Ameling, Walter, ed. *Inscriptiones Judaicae Orientis. Band II. Kleinasien*. TSAJ 99. Tübingen: Mohr Siebeck, 2004.

Amiran, David H. K., E. Arieh, and T. Turcotte. "Earthquakes in Israel and Adjacent Areas: Macroseismic Observations since 100 BCE." *IEJ* 44 (1994): 260–305.

Amit, David. "Architectural Plans of Synagogues in the Southern Judæan Hills and the 'Halakah.'" Pages 129–56 in *ASHAD*.

Amit, David, Joseph Patrich, and Yizhar Hirshfeld, eds. *The Aqueducts of Israel*. Journal of Roman Archaeology Supplementary Series 46. Portsmouth, RI: Journal of Roman Archaeology, 2002.

Applebaum, Shimon. "The Legal Status of the Jewish Communities in the Diaspora; The Organization of the Jewish Communities in the Diaspora." Pages 420–503 in *The Jewish People in the First Century*. Vol. 1. Edited by Shmuel Safrai and Menahem Stern. Assen: Van Gorcum, 1974.

Athanassiadi, Polymnia, and Michael Frede, eds. *Pagan Monotheism in Late Antiquity*. Oxford: Oxford University Press, 1999.

Atkinson, Kenneth, and Jodi Magness. "Josephus's Essenes and the Qumran Community." *JBL* 129.2 (2010): 317–42.

Ault, Bradley A., and Lisa C. Nevett, eds. *Ancient Greek Houses and Households*. Philadelphia: University of Pennsylvania Press, 2005.

Avery-Peck, Alan J., and Jacob Neusner, eds. *Judaism in Late Antiquity*. Leiden: Brill, 2001.

Aviam, Mordecai. "Yodefat/Jotapata. The Archaeology of the First Battle." Pages 121–33 in *The First Jewish Revolt: Archaeology, History and Ideology*. Edited by Andrea M. Berlin and J. A. Overman. London: Routledge, 2002.

———. *Jews, Pagans and Christians in the Galilee: 25 Years of Archaeological Excavations and Surveys*. Land of Galilee 1. Rochester, NY: University of Rochester Press, 2004.

Avigad, Nahman. "The 'Galilean' Synagogue and its Predecessors." Pages 42–44 in *Ancient Synagogues Revealed*. Edited by Lee I. Levine. Jerusalem: Israel Exploration Society, 1982.

———. *Discovering Jerusalem*. Jerusalem, 1980. Repr., Nashville, TN: Nelson, 1983.

———. *The Herodian Quarter in Jerusalem: Wohl Archaeological Museum*. Jerusalem: Keter House, 1991.

Aviram, Joseph, Gideon Foerster, and Ehud Netzer, eds. *Masada IV, Final Reports, Textiles, Basketry, Cordage and Related Artifacts; Wood Remains; Ballista Balls; Addendum: Human Skeletal Remains*. Jerusalem: Israel Exploration Society; Hebrew University of Jerusalem, 1994.

———. *Masada VI, Final Reports. Hebrew Fragments from Masada by Shemaryahu Talmon; The Ben Sira Scroll from Masada by Yigael Yadin*. Jerusalem: Israel Exploration Society; the Hebrew University of Jerusalem, 1999.

Aviram, Joseph, Gideon Foerster, Ehud Netzer, and Guy D. Stiebl, eds. *Masada VIII, the Yigael Yadin Excavations 1963–1965, Final Reports*. Jerusalem: Israel Exploration Society; the Hebrew University of Jerusalem, 2007.

Avi-Yonah, Michael. "Synagogue Architecture in the Classical Period." Pages 157–90 in *Jewish Art*. Edited by Cecil Roth. Tel-Aviv: Massadah-P.E.C. Press; New York: McGraw Hill, 1961.

———. *Hellenism and the East*. Ann Arbor, MI: for the Institute of Languages, Literature and the Arts, the Hebrew University, Jerusalem by University Microfilms International, 1978.

———. *Art in Ancient Palestine*. Jerusalem: Magnes, 1981.

Avni, Gideon, and Zvi Greenhut, and Tamar Shadmi. *The Akeldama Tombs: Three Burial Caves in the Kidron Valley, Jerusalem*. IAA Reports 1. Jerusalem: Israel Antiquities Authority, 1996.

Barag, Dan, and Malka Hershkovitz. "Lamps." Pages 7–147 in *Masada IV: the Yigael Yadin Excavations 1963–65: Final Reports: Lamps, Textiles, Basketry, Cordage and Related Artifacts, Wood Remains, Ballista Balls*. Edited by Joseph Aviram et al. Jerusalem: Israel Exploration Society; the Hebrew University of Jerusalem, 1995.

Bar-Kokhva, Bezalel. "Gamla in Gaulanitis." *ZDPV* 92 (1976): 54–71.

Bar-Nathan, Rachel. *Hasmonaean and Herodian Palaces at Jericho. Final Reports of the 1973–1987 Excavations*. Volume 2. Jerusalem: Israel Exploration Society; Institute of Archaeology, the Hebrew University of Jerusalem, 2002.

———. *Masada VII, The Pottery of Masada, Final Reports*. Jerusalem: Israel Exploration Society; the Hebrew University of Jerusalem, 2006.

Barclay, John M. G. *Jews in the Mediterranean Diaspora: From Alexander to Trajan (323 BCE to 117 CE)*. Edinburgh: T&T Clark, 1996.

Barkai, Ran. "Midsummer Sunset at Neolithic Jericho." *Time and Mind* 1.3 (2008): 273–83.

Bartlett, John R. *Jericho*. Cities of the Biblical World. Guildford: Lutterworth, 1982.

———. *Jews in the Hellenistic World*. Cambridge: Cambridge University Press, 1995.

———. *1 Maccabees*. Sheffield: Sheffield Academic Press, 1998.

———. *Jews in the Hellenistic and Roman Cities*. London: Routledge, 2002.

Baslez, M. F. "Déliens et étrangers domiciliés à Délos (166–155)." *REG* 89 (1976): 343–60.

Bauckham, Richard, ed. *The Book of Acts in its Palestinian Setting*. Grand Rapids: Eerdmans, 1995.

———. *Gospel Women: Studies of the Named Women in the Gospels*. Grand Rapids: Eerdmans, 2002.

———. *Jesus and the Eyewitnesses: The Gospels as Eyewitness Testimony*. Grand Rapids: Eerdmans, 2006.

———. *The Jewish World Around the New Testament*. Tübingen: Mohr Siebeck, 2008.

Benoit, Pierre, J. T. Milik, and Roland de Vaux, eds. *Les Grottes de Murabba'at*. DJD 2. Oxford: Clarendon, 1961.

Ben-Yehuda, Nachman. *The Masada Myth*. Madison, WI: The University of Wisconsin Press, 1995.

———. *Sacrificing Truth: Archaeology and the Myth of Masada*. New York: Humanity Books, 2002.

Berlin, Andrea. *Gamla I: The Hellenistic and Roman Pottery*. IAA Reports 29. Jerusalem: Israel Antiquities Authority, 2006.

Bickerman, Elias J. *The Jews in the Greek Age*. Cambridge, MA: Harvard University Press, 1988.

Binder, Donald D. *Into the Temple Courts: The Place of the Synagogues in the Second Temple Period*. SBLDS 169. Atlanta: Society of Biblical Literature, 1999.

Bingen, Jean. "L'asylie pour une synagogue." Pages 11–16 in *Studia Paulo Naster oblata II: Orientalia Antiqua*. Edited by J. Quaegebeur. OLA 23. Leuven: Peeters, 1982.

Blau, Soren. "An Analysis of Human Skeletal Remains from Two Middle Bronze Age Tombs from Jericho." *PEQ* 138.1 (2006): 13–26.

Bliss, Frederick Jones, and Robert Alexander Stewart MacAlister. *Excavations in Palestine during the Years 1898–1900*. London: Committee of the Palestine Exploration Fund, 1902.

Bloedhorn, Hanswulf. "The Capitals of the Synagogue of Capernaum—Their Chronological and Stylistic Classification with Regard to the Development of Capitals in the Decapolis and in Palestine." Pages 49–54 in *Ancient Synagogues in Israel: Third-Seventh Century CE: Proceedings of Symposium, University of Haifa, May 1987*. Edited by Rachel Hachlili. BAR International Series 499. Oxford: BAR, 1989.

Boardman, John, Jasper Griffin, and Oswyn Murray. *Greece and the Hellenistic World*. Oxford: Oxford University Press, 1988.

Bohak, Gideon. "Ethnic Continuity in the Jewish Diaspora in Antiquity." Pages 175–92 in *Jews in the Hellenistic and Roman Cities*. Edited by John R. Bartlett. London: Routledge, 2002.

Bonz, Marianne. "The Jewish Community of Ancient Sardis: Deconstruction and Reconstruction." Pages 106–22 in *Evolution of the Synagogue: Problems and Progress*. Edited by Howard Clark Kee and Lynn H. Cohick. Harrisburg, PA: Trinity Press Intl, 1999.

Botti, Giuseppe. "Le inscrizioni cristiane di Alessandria d'Egitto." *Bessarione* 7 (1900): 270–81.

———. "Les inscriptions de Schédia." *BSKG* 10 (1901): 611–17.

Bottini, Giovanni Claudio, Leah Di Segni, and Lesław Daniel Chrupcala, eds. *One Land—Many Cultures*. Jerusalem: Franciscan Printing Press, 2003.

Bowersock, Glen Warren, Peter Brown, and Oleg Grabar, eds. *Late Antiquity: A Guide to the Postclassical World*. Cambridge, MA: The Bellknap Press of Harvard University Press, 1999.

———. *Interpreting Late Antiquity: Essays on the Postclassical World*. Cambridge, MA: The Bellknap Press of Harvard University Press, 2001.

Bowman, John, ed. *Samaritan Documents Relating to Their History, Religion and Life*. Pittsburgh Original Texts and Translations Series 2. Pittsburgh, PA: The Pickwick Press, 1977.

Boyarin, Jonathan, and Daniel Boyarin. *Powers of Diaspora: Two Essays on the Relevance of Jewish Culture*. Minneapolis, MN: University of Minnesota Press, 2002.

Boyaval, B. "Quelques remarques sur les épithètes funéraires grecques d'Égypte." *ZPE* 23 (1976): 225–30.

Bromiley, Geoffrey W., Everett F. Harrison, Roland K. Harrison, William Sanford LaSor, Lawrence T. Geraty, and Edgar W. Smith Jr., eds. *The International Standard Bible Encyclopedia*. Volume 2. Grand Rapids: Eerdmans, 1982.

Brooten, Bernadette J. *Women Leaders in the Ancient Synagogue*. BJS 36. Chico, CA: Scholars, 1982.

Broshi, Magen. "Date Beer and Date Wine in Antiquity." *PEQ* 139.1 (2007): 55–59.

Brown, Francis, Samuel R. Driver, and Charles A. Briggs. *Hebrew and English Lexicon*. Peabody, MA: Hendrickson, 2001.

Bruneau, Philippe. *Recherches sur les Cultes de Délos à l'Époque Hellénistique et à l'Époque Impériale*. Paris: De Boccard, 1970.

———. "Les Israélites de Délos et la juiverie délienne." *BCH* 106 (1982): 465–504.

Bruneau, Philippe and Jean Ducat. *Guide de Délos*. 3rd Ed. Paris: De Boccard, 1983.

Brunet, Michèle. "Contribution à l'histoire rurale de Délos aux époques Classique et hellénistique."*BCH* 114.2 (1990): 669–82.

Burtchaell, James T. *From Synagogue to Church: Public Services and Offices in the Earliest Christian Communities.* Cambridge: Cambridge University Press, 1992.

Cahill, Nicholas. *Household and City Organization at Olynthus.* New Haven: Yale University Press, 2002.

Calderini, A. *Dizionario dei nomi geografici e topografici dell'Egitto greco-romano.* Vol. 1. Cairo: Società reale di geografia d'Egitto, 1935.

Cartwright, C. R. "The Bronze Age Wooden Tomb Furniture from Jericho: the Microscopical Reconstruction of a Distinctive Carpentry Tradition." *PEQ* 137. 2 (2005): 99–138.

Catto, Stephen K. *Reconstructing the First-Century Synagogue: A Critical Analysis of Current Research.* LNTS 363. London: T&T Clark, 2007.

Chancey, Mark A. "City Coins and Roman Power in Palestine: from Pompey to the Great Revolt." Pages 103–12 in *Religion and Society in Roman Palestine. Old Questions, New Approaches.* Edited by Douglas R. Edwards. London: Routledge, 2004.

———. *The Myth of a Gentile Galilee: The Population of Galilee and New Testament Studies.* Cambridge: Cambridge University Press, 2002.

———. *Graeco-Roman Culture and the Galilee of Jesus.* Cambridge: Cambridge University Press, 2005.

Charlesworth, James H. *Jesus and Archaeology.* Grand Rapids: Eerdmans, 2006.

———, ed. *The Old Testament Pseudepigrapha.* 2 vols. Peabody, MA: Hendrickson, 2009.

Chen, D. "The Design of the Ancient Synagogues in Judea: Masada and Herodium." *BASOR* 239 (1980): 37–40.

Chiat, Marilyn J. S. *Handbook of Synagogue Architecture.* BJS 29. Chico, CA: Scholars, 1982.

Claussen, Carsten. "Meeting, Community, Synagogue—Different Frameworks of Ancient Jewish Congregations in the Diaspora." Pages 144–67 in *The Ancient Synagogue from its Origins until 200 CE.* Edited by Birger Olsson and Magnus Zetterholm. ConBNT 39. Stockholm: Almqvist & Wiksell Intl, 2003.

Clutton-Brock, Juliet. "The Mammalian Remains from the Jericho Tell." *Proceedings of the Prehistoric Society* 45 (1979): 135–57.

Coggins, Richard J. *Samaritans and Jews: The Origins of Samaritanism Reconsidered.* Oxford: Blackwell, 1975.

Cohen, Naomi G. "Jewish Names as Cultural Indicators in Antiquity." *JSJ* 7 (1976): 97–128.

———. "The Names of the Translators in the Letter of Aristeas." *JSJ* 15 (1984): 32–64.

Cohen, Shaye J. D. *Josephus in Galilee and Rome: His Vita and Development as a Historian.* Leiden: Brill, 1979.

———. "Masada: Literary Tradition, Archaeological Remains and Credibility of Josephus." *JJS* 33.1–2 (1982): 385–405.

———. "The Significance of Yavneh: Pharisees, Rabbis and the End of Sectarianism." *HUCA* 55 (1984): 27–53.

———. *The Beginnings of Jewishness: Boundaries, Varieties, Uncertainties*. Berkeley, CA: University of California Press, 1999.

———. "Were Pharisees and Rabbis the Leaders of Communal Prayer and Torah Study in Antiquity? The Evidence of the New Testament, Josephus, and the Early Church Fathers." Pages 89–105 in *Evolution of the Synagogue. Problems and Progress*. Edited by Howard C. Kee and Lynn H. Cohick. Harrisburg, PA: Trinity Press Intl, 1999.

Cohen, Shaye J. D., and J. J. Schwartz, eds. *Studies in Josephus and the Varieties of Ancient Judaism: Louis H. Feldman Jubilee Volume*. Leiden: Brill, 2007.

Cohen, Shaye. "The Judaean Legal Tradition and the *Halakhah* of the Mishnah." Pages 121–43 in *The Cambridge Companion to the Talmud and Rabbinic Literature*. Edited by C. E. Fonrobert and M. S. Jaffee. Cambridge: Cambridge University Press, 2007.

Cohon, Beryl David. *Men at the Crossroads, Between Jerusalem and Rome, Synagogue and Church. The Lives, Times, and Doctrines of the Founders of Talmudic Judaism and New Testament Christianity*. London: Thomas Yoseloff, 1970.

Collins, John J. *Between Athens and Jerusalem: Jewish Identity in the Hellenistic Diaspora*. 2nd ed. The Biblical Resource Series. Grand Rapids: Eerdmans, 2000.

Collins, John J., and Gregory E. Sterling, eds. *Hellenism in the Land of Israel*. Notre Dame, IN: University of Notre Dame Press, 2001.

Conder, Claude R., and Horatio H. Kitchener. *Survey of Western Palestine*. Vol 3: *Memoirs (Judæa)*. London: Committee of the Palestine Exploration Fund, 1883.

Cook, Arthur B. *Zeus: A Study in Ancient Religion*. Volume 2.2. Cambridge: Cambridge University Press, 1926.

Corbo, Virgilio C. "The Excavation at Herodium." *Qadmoniot* 4 (1968): 132–36.

———. "Gébel Fureidis (Hérodium)." *RB* 75 (1968): 424–28.

———. "L'Herodion de Giabel Fureidis." *LA* 113 (1962–1963): 219–77.

———. "L'Herodion de Giabel Fureidis." *LA* 117 (1967): 65–121.

———. *Herodion: Gli Edifici della Reggia-Fortrezza*. Vol. 1. Jerusalem: Franciscan Printing Press, 1989.

Cotton, Hannah M., and Joseph Geiger (with J. David Thomas). *Masada II: The Latin and Greek Documents, Final Reports*. Jerusalem: Israel Exploration Society; the Hebrew University of Jerusalem, 1989.

Crown, Alan D. "New Light on the Interrelationships of Samaritan Chronicles from Some Manuscripts in the John Rylands Library." *BJRL* 54 (1971/2): 282–313; and *BJRL* 55 (1972/3): 86–111.

———. *The Samaritans*. Tübingen: Mohr Siebeck, 1989.

Crudden, Michael. "Hymn 3 to Apollo." Pages 23–42 in *The Homeric Hymns*. Edited by Michael Crudden. OWC. Oxford: Oxford University Press, 2001.

Danby, Herbert D. D., trans. *The Mishnah: Translated from the Hebrew with Introduction and Brief Explanatory Notes.* Oxford: Oxford University Press, 1933; repr. 1985.

Dar, Shimon and Johanan Mintzker. "The Synagogue of Hurvat Sumaqa." Pages 17–20 in *Ancient Synagogues in Israel: Third-Seventh Century CE: Proceedings of symposium, University of Haifa, May 1987*. Edited by Rachel Hachlili. BAR International Series 499. Oxford: B.A.R., 1989.

Davies, Graham I. *Ancient Hebrew Inscriptions*. Cambridge: Cambridge University Press, 1991.

Davies, Philip R. and Richard T. White, eds. *A Tribute to Geza Vermes: Essays on Jewish and Christian Literature and History.* Sheffield: JSOT Press, 1990.

Deines, Roland and Karl-Wilhelm Niebuhr, eds. *Philo und das Neue Testament: Wechselseitige Wahrnehmungen. 1. Internationales Symposium zum Corpus Judaeo-Hellenisticum, 1.–4. Mai 2003, Eisenach, Jena*. Tübingen: Mohr Siebeck, 2004.

Deissmann, Adolf. *Light from the Ancient East.* London: Hodder & Stoughton, 1927.

Déonna, Waldemar. *Exploration Archéologique de Délos. 18 (Planches)*. Par Écoles Françaises d'Athènes. Paris: de Boccard, [1938].

———. *Le Mobilier délien, Délos*. Pl. CXII. Paris: de Boccard, 1938.

———. *La Vie Privée des Déliens*. Paris: de Boccard, 1948.

Develin, Robert. *Athenian Officials 684–321 B.C.* Cambridge: Cambridge University Press, 1989.

De Vries, LaMoine F. *Cities of the Biblical World*. Peabody, MA: Hendrickson, 1997.

Dillon, John. "The Essenes in Greek sources: some reflections." Pages 117–28 in *Jews in the Hellenistic and Roman Cities*. Edited by John R. Bartlett. London: Routledge, 2002.

Dothan, Moshe. *Hammath Tiberias: Early Synagogues and the Hellenistic and Roman Remains.* Jerusalem: Israel Exploration Society, 1983.

Dudman, Helga and Elisheva Ballhorn. *Tiberias*. Jerusalem: Carta, 1988.

Durrbach, Félix. *Inscriptions de Délos. Comptes des Hiéropes (Nos. 290–371)*. Librairie Ancienne. Paris: Honoré Champion, 1926.

———. *Inscriptions de Délos. Comptes des Hiéropes (Nos. 372–498). Lois ou Réglements, Contrats d'Entreprises et Devis (Nos. 499–509)*. Librairie Ancienne. Paris: Honoré Champion, 1929.

Durrbach, Félix, and P. Roussel, *Inscriptions de Délos. Actes des Fonctionnaires Athéniens Préposés à l'Administration des Sanctuaires Après 166 AV. J.-C. (Nos. 1400–1479). Fragments des Actes Divers (Nos. 1480–1496)*. Librairie Ancienne. Paris: Honoré Champion, 1935.

Dvorjetski, Estee. "The Synagogue-Church at Gerasa in Jordan. A Contribution to the Study of Ancient Synagogues." *ZDPV* 121 (2005):140–67.

Dyck, Jonathan. "Philo, Alexandria and Empire: the Politics of Allegorical Interpretation." Pages 149–174 in *Jews in the Hellenistic and Roman Cities*. Edited by John R. Bartlett. London: Routledge, 2002.

Edwards, Douglas R. "Constructing the World of Roman Palestine: An Introduction." Pages 1–6 in *Religion and Society in Roman Palestine. Old Questions, New Approaches*. Edited by Douglas R. Edwards. New York: Routledge, 2004.

———. *Religion and Power: Pagans, Jews and Christians in the Greek East*. Oxford: Oxford University Press, 1996.

Ego, Beate, Armin Lange, and Peter Pilhofer, eds. *Gemeinde ohne Tempel: zur Substituierung und Transformation des Jerusalemer Tempels und seines Kults im alten Testament, antiken Judentum und frühen Christentum*. WUNT 118. Tübingen: Mohr Siebeck, 1999.

Eilers, Claude. "The Date of Augustus' Edict on the Jews (Jos. *AJ* 16.162–165) and the Career of C. Marcius Censorinus." *Phoenix* 58.1–2 (2004): 86–95.

Eisenman, Robert. *Maccabees, Zadokites, Christians and Qumran*. Leiden: Brill, 1983.

Eitan, Avraham. "Rare sword of the Israelite period found at Vered Jericho." *IMJ* 12 (1994): 61–62.

Elbogen, Ismar. *Jewish Liturgy: A Comprehensive History*. Philadelphia: The Jewish Publication Society, 1993.

Eliav, Yaron Z. "The Roman Bath as a Jewish Institution: Another Look at the Encounter Between Judaism and the Greco-Roman Culture." *JSJ* 31.4 (2000): 416–54.

Ellis, Simon P. *Roman Housing*. London: Duckworth, 2002.

Elsner, Jaś and Ian Rutherford. *Pilgrimage in the Graeco-Roman and Early Christian Antiquity*. Oxford: Oxford University Press, 2005.

Eschel, Hanan. "Josephus' View on Judaism without the Temple in Light of the Discoveries at Masada and Murabba'at." Pages 229–38 in *Gemeinde ohne Tempel/Community without Temple: Zur Substituierung und Transformation des Jerusalemer Tempels und seines Kults im Alten Testament, antiken Judentum und frühen Christentum*. WUNT 118. Edited by Beate Ego, Armin Lange, and Peter Pilhofer. Tübingen: Mohr Siebeck, 1999.

———. "Roman Coins from the 'Cave of the Sandal' West of Jericho." *INJ* 13 [1994–1999] (1999): 70–77.

Evans, Craig A., and H. Daniel Zacharias, eds. *Jewish and Christian Scripture as Artifact and Canon*. Edinburgh: T&T Clark, 2009.

[unattributed]. *Excavations and Surveys in Israel 1982*. Vol 1. Jerusalem: Israel Department of Antiquities and Museums, 1984. English Edition of *Hadashot Arkheologiyot*, Archaeological Newsletter of the Israel Department of Antiquities and Museums, Numbers 78–81, Jerusalem, 1982.

[unattributed]. *Excavations and Surveys in Israel 1983*. Volume 2. English Edition of *Hadashot Arkheologiyot*, Archaeological Newsletter of the Israel Department of Antiquities and Museums, Numbers 82–83, Jerusalem 1983.

[unattributed]. *Excavations and Surveys in Israel 1984*. Volume 3. English Edition of *Hadashot Arkheologiyot*, Archaeological Newsletter of the Israel Department of Antiquities and Museums, Numbers 84–85, Jerusalem 1984.

Feldman, Louis H. "Masada: A Critique of Recent Scholarship." Pages 218–48 in *Christianity, Judaism and Other Greco-Roman Cults, Studies for Morton Smith at Sixty*. Edited by Jacob Neusner. Vol 3. Leiden: Brill, 1975.

———. *Josephus and Modern Scholarship (1937–1980)*. Berlin: de Gruyter, 1984.

———. *Jew and Gentile in the Ancient World*. Princeton, NJ: Princeton University Press, 1993.

———. "Diaspora Synagogues: New Light from Inscriptions and Papyri." Pages 48–66 in *Sacred Realm: The Emergence of the Synagogue in the Ancient World*. Edited by Steven Fine. Oxford: Oxford University Press, 1996.

———. *Studies in Hellenistic Judaism*. Leiden: Brill, 1996.

Feldman, Louis H., and G. Hata, *Josephus, Judaism and Christianity*. Detroit: Wayne State University Press, 1989.

Ferguson, John. *Among The Gods: An Archaeological Exploration of Ancient Greek Religion*. London: Routledge, 1989.

Fiensy, David A. "The Hellenistic Synagogal Prayers: One Hundred Years of Discussion." *JSP* 5 (1989): 17–27.

———. *The Social History of Palestine in the Herodian Period, Studies in the Bible and Early Christianity*. Vol. 20. Lewiston, NY: The Edwin Mellen Press, 1991.

Figueras, Pau. *Decorated Jewish Ossuaries*. Leiden: Brill, 1983.

Fine, Steven, ed. *Sacred Realm. The Emergence of the Synagogue in the Ancient World*. New York: Oxford University Press, 1996.

———. "From Meeting House to Sacred Realm." Pages 21–47 in *Sacred Realm: The Emergence of the Synagogue in the Ancient World*. Edited by Steven Fine. Oxford: Oxford University Press, 1996.

———. *This Holy Place: On the Sanctity of Synagogues During the Greco-Roman Period*. Christianity and Judaism in Antiquity Series. Notre Dame: University of Notre Dame Press, 1997.

———. *Jews, Christians, and Polytheists in the Ancient Synagogue: Cultural Interaction during the Greco-Roman Period*. London: Routledge, 1999.

———. "Synagogues in the Land of Israel." Pages 455–64 in *Near Eastern Archaeology: A Reader*. Edited by Suzanne Richard. Winona Lake, IN: Eisenbrauns, 2003.

Fischel, Henry A. *Rabbinic Literature and Greco-Roman Philosophy: A Study of Epicurea and Rhetorica in Early Midrashic Writings*. Leiden: Brill, 1973.

Fishbane, Michael. *Biblical Myth and Rabbinic Mythmaking.* Oxford: Oxford University Press, 2003.

Fittschen, Klaus and Gideon Foerster, eds. *Judaea and the Greco-Roman World in the Time of Herod in the Light of Archaeological Evidence: Acts of a Symposium Organized by the Institute of Archaeology, the Hebrew University of Jerusalem and the Archaeological Institute, Georg-August-Universität Göttingen at Jerusalem November 3–4, 1988.* Göttingen: Vandenhoeck & Ruprecht, 1996.

Fitzpatrick-McKinley, Anne. "Synagogue communities in the Graeco-Roman cities." Pages 55–87 in *Jews in the Hellenistic and Roman Cities.* Edited by John R. Bartlett. London: Routledge, 2002.

Flesher, Paul V. M., "Palestinian Synagogues Before 70 CE: A Review of the Evidence." Pages 27–39 in *ASHAD.* Leiden: Brill, 1995.

———. "Prolegomenon to a Theory of Early Synagogue Development." Pages 121–15 in *Judaism in Late Antiquity.* Vol. 4. Edited by Alan J. Avery-Peck and Jacob Neusner. Leiden: Brill, 2001.

Foerster, Gideon. "The Synagogues at Masada and Herodion." *Journal of Jewish Art* 3–4 (1977): 6–11.

———. "The Synagogues at Masada and Herodium." Pages 24–29 in *Ancient Synagogues Revealed.* Edited by Lee I. Levine. Jerusalem: Israel Exploration Society, 1981.

———. "Dating Synagogues with a 'Basilical' Plan and an Apse." Pages 87–94 in *ASHAD.* Leiden: Brill, 1995.

———. "Sarcophagus Production in Jerusalem from the Beginning of the Common Era up to 70 CE." Pages 295–310 in *Akten des Symposiums "125 Jahre Sarkophag-Corpus," Marburg 4–7 Oktober 1995.* Edited by Guntram Koch. Mainz: von Zabern, 1998.

Foerster, Gideon (with Naomi Porat). *Masada V: The Yigael Yadin Excavations 1963–1965: Final Reports, Art and Architecture.* Jerusalem: Israel Exploration Society, 1995.

Fonrobert, Charlotte E., and Martin S. Jaffee, eds. *The Cambridge Companion to the Talmud and Rabbinic Literature.* Cambridge: Cambridge University Press, 2007.

Forbes, Richard J. *Studies in Ancient Technology.* 2nd ed. Vol 1. Leiden: Brill, 1964.

———. *Studies in Ancient Technology.* 2nd Ed. Vol 2. Leiden: Brill, 1965.

Fraade, Steven D. "The Early Rabbinic Sage." Pages 417–36 in *The Sage in Israel and the Ancient Near East.* Edited by John G. Gammie and Leo G. Perdue. Winona Lake, IN: Eisenbrauns, 1990.

Fraade, Steven D., A. Shemesh, and R. A. Clements, eds. *Rabbinic Perspectives: Rabbinic Literature and the Dead Sea Scrolls: Proceedings of the Eighth International Symposium of the Orion Center for the Study of the Dead Sea Scrolls and Associated Literature, 7–9 January, 2003.* Leiden: Brill, 2007.

Frankel, Rafael. *Wine and Oil Production in Antiquity in Israel and Other Mediterranean Countries*. Sheffield: Sheffield Academic Press, 1999.

Fraser, Peter M., and Elaine Matthews, eds. *A Lexicon of Greek Personal Names, Volume 1: The Aegean Islands, Cyprus, Cyrenaica*. Oxford: Clarendon, 1987.

Frey, Jörg B. *Corpus inscriptionum judaicarum*. Vols. 1 and 2. Rome: Pontificio Istituto di Archeologia Cristiana, 1936–1952.

Frey, Jörg B., Daniel R. Schwartz, and Stephanie Gripentrog, eds. *Jewish Identity in the Greco-Roman World*. Leiden: Brill, 2007.

Freyne, Seán. *Galilee, Jesus and the Gospels: Literary Approaches and Historical Investigations*. Dublin: Gill & Macmillan, 1988.

———. *The Geography, Politics and Economics of Galilee and the Quest for the Historical Jesus*. Leiden: Brill, 1994.

———. *Galilee: From Alexander the Great to Hadrian, 323 BCE. to 135 CE: A Study of Second Temple Judaism*. Edinburgh: T&T Clark, 1998.

———. "Behind the Names: Galilaeans, Samaritans, *Ioudaioi*." Pages 39–56 in *Galilee through the Centuries*. Edited by Eric M. Meyers. Winona Lake, IN: Eisenbrauns, 1999.

———. *Galilee and Gospel: Collected Essays*. WUNT 125. Tübingen: Mohr Siebeck, 2000.

Fritz, Volkmar. *The City in Ancient Israel*. Sheffield: Sheffield Academic Press, 1995.

Furneaux, Rupert. *The Roman Siege of Jerusalem*. London: Hart-Davis MacGibbon, 1973.

Garbrecht, Günter, and Yehuda Peleg. "The Water Supply of the Desert Fortresses in the Jordan Valley." *BA* 57.3 (1994): 161–70.

Galil, Gershon, and Moshe Weinfeld, eds. *Studies in Historical Geography and Biblical Historiography*. Brill: Leiden, 2000.

Gammie, John G., and Leo G. Perdue, eds. *The Sage in Israel and the Ancient Near East*. Winona Lake, IN: Eisenbrauns, 1990.

Garstang, John. *Joshua, Judges: The Foundations of Bible History*. London: Constable, 1931.

Garstang, John, and John B. E. Garstang. *The Story of Jericho*. London: Hodder & Stoughton, 1940.

Gibson, Shimon. *The Cave of John the Baptist*. New York: Doubleday, 2004.

———. "The Pool of Bethesda in Jerusalem and Jewish Purification Practices of the Second Temple Period." *Proche-Orient Chrétien* 55.3–4 (2005): 270–93.

———. *The Final Days of Jesus: The Archaeological Evidence*. New York: HarperOne, 2009.

Gibson, Shimon, and David M. Jacobson. *Below the Temple Mount in Jerusalem: a Sourcebook on the Cisterns, Subterranean Chambers and Conduits of the Ḥaram al-Sharīf.* BAR International Series 637. Oxford: Archaeopress, 1996.

Goldstein, Jonathan A. *1 Maccabees.* AB. Garden City, NJ: Doubleday, 1976.

Goodenough, Erwin. *Jewish Symbols in the Greco-Roman Period.* Princeton, NJ: Princeton University Press, 1988.

Goodman, Martin. "The First Jewish Revolt: Social Conflict and the Problems of Debt." *JJS* 33.1–2 (1982): 417–27.

———. *State and Society in Roman Galilee, AD 132–212.* Totowa, NJ: Rowman & Allanheld, 1983.

———. *The Ruling Class of Judaea: The Origins of the Jewish Revolt against Rome AD 66–70.* Cambridge: Cambridge University Press, 1987.

———. "Kosher Olive Oil in Antiquity." Pages 227–45 in *A Tribute to Geza Vermes: Essays on Jewish and Christian Literature and History.* JSOTSup 100. Edited by Philip R. Davies and Richard T. White. Sheffield: Sheffield Academic Press, 1990.

Goren, David. "The Architecture and Stratigraphy of the Hasmonean Quarter (Areas D and B) and Area B77." Pages 113–52 in *Gamla II: The Shmarya Gutmann Excavations, 1976–1989: The Architecture.* Edited by Danny Syon and Zvi Yavor. Jerusalem: Israel Antiquities Authority, 2010.

Goren, Yuval, A. Nigel Goring-Morris, and Irena Segal. "The Technology of Skull Modelling in the Pre-Pottery Neolithic B (PPNB): Regional Variability, the Relation of Technology and Iconography, and Their Archaeological Implications." *JAS* 28.7 (2001): 671–90. doi: https://doi.org/10.1006/jasc.1999.0573.

Grabbe, Lester L. "Synagogues in Pre-70 Palestine: A Re-assessment." *JTS* 39 (1988): 401–10.

———. *Judaism from Cyrus to Hadrian.* London: SCM, 1992.

———. "Synagogues in Pre-70 Palestine: A Re-Assessment." Pages 17–26 in *Ancient Synagogues, Historical Analysis and Archaeological Discovery.* Vol. 1. Edited by Dan Urman and Paul V. M. Flesher. Leiden: Brill, 1995.

———. *An Introduction to First Century Judaism.* Edinburgh: T&T Clark, 1996.

Griffiths, J. Gwyn. "Egypt and the Rise of the Synagogue." *JTS* 38 (1987): 1–15.

Gruen, Erich S. *Heritage and Hellenism: The Reinvention of Jewish Tradition.* Berkeley, CA: University of California Press, 1998.

———. *Diaspora: Jews amidst Greeks and Romans.* Cambridge, MA: Harvard University Press, 2002.

Gutmann, Shmarya. "Gamla." Pages 459–63 in *NEAEHL.* Vol. 2. Edited by Ephraim Stern. Jerusalem: The Israel Exploration Society, 1993.

———. *Gamla: A City in Rebellion.* Tel Aviv: Misra ha-Bitahon, 1994 [Hebrew].

Gutmann, Shmarya, and Herschel Shanks. "Gamla—Masada of the North." *BAR* 5.1 (1979): 12–27.

Gutmann, Joseph, ed. *The Synagogue: Studies in Origins, Archaeology and Architecture.* New York: KTAV, 1975.

———, ed. *Ancient Synagogues: The State of Research.* Vol. 22. Chico, CA: Scholars, 1981.

———. "Synagogue Origins: Theories and Facts." Pages 1–6 in *Ancient Synagogues: The State of Research.* Edited by Joseph Gutmann. Chico, CA: Scholars, 1981.

———. "The Synagogue of Dura-Europos: A Critical Analysis." Pages 73–88 in *Evolution of the Synagogue: Problems and Progress.* Edited by Howard Clark Kee and Lynn H. Cohick. Harrisburg, PA: Trinity Press Intl, 1999.

Hachlili, Rachael. "The Niche and the Ark in Ancient Synagogues." *BASOR* 223 (1976): 43–53.

———. *Ancient Jewish Art and Archaeology in the Holy Land.* HdO 7.1.2.4. Leiden: Brill, 1988.

———. "The State of Ancient Synagogues Research." Pages 1–6 in *Ancient Synagogues in Israel: Third–Seventh century CE: Proceedings of Symposium, University of Haifa, May 1987.* BAR International Series 499. Edited by Rachel Hachlili. Oxford: BAR, 1989.

———. "Unidentical Symmetrical Composition in Synagogal Art." Pages 65–68 in *Ancient Synagogues in Israel: Third–Seventh Century CE: Proceedings of Symposium, University of Haifa, May 1987.* BAR International Series 499. Edited by Rachel Hachlili. Oxford: BAR, 1989.

———. "Late Antique Jewish Art from the Golan." Pages 183–212 in *The Roman and Byzantine Near East: Some Recent Archaeological Research.* Journal of Roman Archaeology, Supplemental Series 14. Edited by John H. Humphrey. Ann Arbor, MI: Journal of Roman Archaeology, 1995.

———. "The Origin of the Synagogue: A Reassessment." *JSJ* 28.1 (1997): 34–47.

———. "A Jericho Ossuary and a Jerusalem Workshop." *IEJ* 47.3–4 (1997): 238–47.

———. "Aspects of Similarity and Diversity in the Architecture and Art of Ancient Synagogues and Churches in the Land of Israel." *ZDPV* 113 (1997): 92–125.

———. "Torah Shrine and Ark in Ancient Synagogues: A Re-evaluation." *ZDPV* 116.2 (2000): 146–83.

———. "Names and Nicknames at Masada." Pages 93–108 in *These Are the Names: Studies in Jewish Onomastics.* Vol. 3. Edited by Aaron Demsky. Ramat-Gan: Bar-Ilan University Press, 2002.

Hachlili, Rachel and Ann Killebrew. "Jewish Funerary Customs during the Second Temple Period, in the Light of Excavations at the Jericho Necropolis." *PEQ* 115 (1983): 109–32.

Hamburger, Herman. "A Hoard of Syrian Tetradrachms from Tiberias." *Atiqot* (English Series) 2 (1959): 133–45.

Harland, Philip A. *Associations, Synagogues, and Congregations: Claiming a Place in Mediterranean Society.* Minneapolis, MN: Fortress, 2004.

———. "Familial Dimensions of Group Identity (II):1 'Mothers' and 'Fathers' in Associations and Synagogues of the Greek World." *JJS* 38 (2007): 57–79.

Hayes, John H, and Sara R. Mandell. *The Jewish People in Classical Antiquity from Alexander to Bar Kochba.* Louisville, KY: Westminster John Knox, 1998.

Hengel, Martin. "Die Synagogeninschrift von Stobi," *ZNW* 57 (1966): 145–83.

———. "Proseuche und Synagoge: Jüdische Gemeinde, Gotteshaus und Gottesdienst in der Diaspora und in Palästina." Pages 157–84 in *Tradition und Glaube: Das frühe Christentum in seiner Umwelt.* Eds. Gert Jeremias, Heinz-Wolfgang Kuhn, and Hartmut Stegemann. Göttingen: Vandenhoeck & Ruprecht, 1971.

———. *Judaism and Hellenism.* 2 Vol. London: SCM, 1974.

———. *Acts and the History of Earliest Christianity.* London: SCM Press, 1979.

———. *Jews, Greeks, and Barbarians: Aspects of the Hellenization of Judaism in the Pre-Christian Period.* First American edition. Philadelphia: Fortress, 1980.

———. *Judaism and Hellenism. Studies in their Encounter in Palestine during the Early Hellenistic Period.* 2 vols. in 1. London: SCM, 1981.

———. *The Zealots: Investigations into the Jewish Freedom Movement in the Period from Herod I until 70 A.D.* Edinburgh: T&T Clark, 1989.

———. *The "Hellenization" of Judea in the First Century after Christ.* London: SCM, 1989.

———. *The Four Gospels and the One Gospel of Jesus Christ.* London: SCM, 2000.

———. "Judaism and Hellenism Revisited." Pages 6–37 in *Hellenism in the Land of Israel.* Edited by John J. Collins and Gregory E. Sterling. Notre Dame, IN: University of Notre Dame Press, 2001.

Hepper, F. Nigel, and Joan E. Taylor. "Date Palms and Opobalsam in the Madaba Mosaic Map." *PEQ* 136 (2004): 35–44.

Hershkovitz, Malka, and Shua Amorai-Stark. "The Gems from Masada." Pages 217–32 in *Masada VIII: The Yigael Yadin Excavations 1963–1965, Final Reports.* Edited by Joseph Aviram et al. Jerusalem: Israel Exploration Society; the Hebrew University of Jerusalem, 2007.

Hezser, Catherine. *Form, Function, and Historical Significance of the Rabbinic Story in Yerushalmi Neziqin.* TSAJ 37. Tübingen: Mohr Siebeck, 1993.

———. *The Social Structure of the Rabbinic Movement in Roman Palestine.* Tübingen: Mohr Siebeck, 1997.

———. "The (In)Significance of Jerusalem in the Talmud Yerushalmi." Pages 11–49 in *The Talmud Yerushalmi and Graeco-Roman Culture*. Vol. 2. Edited by Catherine Hezser and Peter Schäfer. Tübingen: Mohr Siebeck, 2000.

———. "Interfaces Between Rabbinic Literature and Graeco-Roman Philosophy." Pages 161–87 in *The Talmud Yerushalmi and Graeco-Roman Culture*. Vol. 2. Edited by Catherine Hezser and Peter Schäfer. Tübingen: Mohr Siebeck, 2000.

———. *Jewish Literacy in Roman Palestine*. TSAJ 81. Tübingen: Mohr Siebeck, 2001.

———, ed. *Rabbinic Law in Its Roman and Near Eastern Context*. TSAJ 86. Tübingen: Mohr Siebeck, 2003.

———. "Slaves and Slavery in Rabbinic and Roman Law." Pages 133–78 in *Rabbinic Law in its Roman and Near Eastern Context*. Edited by Catherine Hezser. Tübingen: Mohr Siebeck, 2003.

———. "Literacy and the Use of Writing in Jewish and Roman Society of Late Antiquity." Pages 149–95 in *Jewish Culture and Society Under the Christian Roman Empire*. Edited by Richard Kalmin and Seth Schwartz. Leuven: Peeters, 2003.

———. "The Exposure and Sale of Infants in Rabbinic and Roman Law." Pages 3–28 in *Jewish Studies Between the Disciplines*. Edited by Klaus Herrmann, Margarete Schlüter and Giuseppe Veltri. Leiden: Brill, 2003.

———. "Slaves and Slavery in Rabbinic and Roman Law." Pages 133–76 in *Rabbinic Law in Its Roman and Near Eastern Context*. Edited by Catherine Hezser. Tübingen: Mohr Siebeck, 2003.

———. *Jewish Slavery in Antiquity*. Oxford: Oxford University Press, 2005.

———. "'The Slave of a Scholar is Like a Scholar': Stories About Rabbis and Their Slaves in the Babylonian Talmud." Pages 198–217 in *Creation and Composition: The Contribution of the Bavli Redactors*. Edited by Jeffrey L. Rubenstein. Tübingen: Mohr Siebeck, 2005.

———. "The Impact of Other Disciplines Upon Biblical Scholarship: Diaspora and Rabbinic Judaism." Pages 120–32 in *The Oxford Handbook of Biblical Studies*. Edited by John W. Rogerson and Judith M. Lieu. Oxford: Oxford University Press, 2006.

———. "From Study House to Marketplace: Rabbinic Guidelines for the Economy of Roman Palestine." *Antiquité Tardive* 14 (2006): 39–45.

———. "Roman Law and Rabbinic Legal Composition." Pages 144–63 in *The Cambridge Companion to the Talmud and Rabbinic Literature*. Edited by Charlotte Elisheva Fonrobert and Martin S. Jaffee. Cambridge: Cambridge University Press, 2007.

———. "Ben-Hur and Ancient Jewish Slavery." Pages 121–39 in *A Wandering Galilean: Essays in Honour of Sean Freyne*. SJSJ 132. Edited by Zuleika Rodgers, Margaret Daly-Denton, and Anne Fitzpatrick-McKinley. Leiden: Brill, 2009.

Hezser, Catherine, and Peter Schäfer, eds. *The Talmud Yerushalmi and Graeco-Roman Culture*. Vol. 2. TSAJ 93. Tübingen: Mohr Siebeck, 2000c.

Hirschfeld, Yizhar. *A Guide to Antiquity Sites in Tiberias*. Translated by Edward Levin and Inna Pommerantz. Jerusalem: Israel Antiquities Authority, 1992.

———. *The Palestinian Dwelling in the Roman-Byzantine Period*. Studium Biblicum Franciscanum, Collectio Minor 34. Jerusalem: Franciscan Printing Press; Israel Exploration Society, 1995.

———. "Architecture and Stratigraphy." Pages 235–370 in *Ramat Hanadiv Excavations*. Edited by Yizhar Hirschfeld. Jerusalem: Israel Exploration Society, 2000.

Hjelm, Ingrid. *The Samaritans and Early Judaism*. Copenhagen International Seminar 7; JSOTSup 303. Sheffield: Sheffield Academic Press, 2000.

Hodge, A. Trevor. *Roman Aqueducts and Water Supply*. 2nd ed. London: Duckworth, 2002.

Hobsbawm, Eric and Terence Ranger, eds. *The Invention of Tradition*. Cambridge: Cambridge University Press, 1992.

Holleaux, Maurice. *Mélanges Holleaux. Recueil de Mémoires Concernant l'Antiquité Grecque. Offert a Maurice Holleaux en souvenir de ses anneés de direction à l'École française d'Athènes (1904–1912)*. Paris: Auguste Picard, 1913.

Holum, Kenneth G., et al. *King Herod's Dream: Caesarea on the Sea*. New York: W. W. Norton, 1988.

Honigman, Sylvie. *The Septuagint and Homeric Scholarship in Alexandria. A Study in the Narrative of the Letter of Aristeas*. London: Routledge, 2003.

Horbury, William. *Hebrew Study from Ezra to Ben-Yehuda*. Edinburgh: T&T Clark, 1999.

Horbury, William, and David Noy. *Jewish Inscriptions of Graeco-Roman Egypt*. Cambridge: Cambridge University Press, 1992.

Horsley, Richard A. *Galilee*. Valley Forge, PA: Trinity Press Intl, 1995.

———. *Archaeology, History, and Society in Galilee: The Social Context of Jesus and the Rabbis*. Valley Forge, PA: Trinity Press Intl, 1996.

———. "Synagogues in Galilee and the Gospels." Pages 46–69 in *Evolution of the Synagogue: Problems and Progress*. Edited by Howard C. Kee and Lynn H. Cohick. Harrisburg, PA: Trinity Press Intl, 1999.

Horwitz, L. K., "A Study of Diachronic Change in Bone Mass of Sheep and Goats, Jericho (Tel-es Sultan)." *ArchaeoZoologia* 4.1 (1991): 29–38.

Hoss, Stefanie. *Baths and Bathing: The Culture of Bathing and the Baths and Thermae in Palestine from the Hasmonaeans to the Moslem Conquest*. BAR International Series 1346. Oxford: BAR, 2005.

Humphrey, John H., ed. *The Roman and Byzantine Near East: Some Recent Archaeological Research*. Journal of Roman Archaeology Supplementary Series 14. Ann Arbor, MI: Journal of Roman Archaeology, 1995.

———. *The Roman and Byzantine Near East*. Vol. 2. Journal of Roman Archaeology Supplementary Series 31. Portsmouth, RI: Journal of Roman Archaeology, 1999.

Hüttenmeister, Frowald Gil, and Gottfroed Reeg. *Die Antiken Synagogen in Israel*. 2 vols. Wiesbaden: Reichert, 1977.

Idelsohn, Abraham Z. *Jewish Liturgy and Its Development*. New York: Dover Publications, 1995.

Ilan, Tal. "New Jewish Inscriptions from Hierapolis and Questions of Jewish Diaspora Cemeteries." *SCI* 25 (2006): 71–86.

Ilan, Zvi. "The Synagogue and Bet Midrash of Meroth." Pages 21–42 in *Ancient Synagogues in Israel:Third–Seventh century CE. Proceedings of Symposium, University of Haifa, May 1987*. BAR International Series 499. Edited by Rachel Hachlili. Oxford: BAR, 1989.

Jastrow, Marcus. *A Dictionary of the Targumim, the Talmud Babli and Yerushalmi, and the Midrashic Literature*. New York: The Judaica Press, 1996.

Jeanrond, Werner G., and Andrew D. H. Mayes, eds. *Recognising the Margins: Developments in Biblical and Theological Studies. Essays in Honour of Seán Freyne*. Blackrock: Columba Press, 2006.

Jones, Christopher P. "Towards a Chronology of Josephus." *SCI* 21 (2002): 113–21.

Jones, Siân. *The Archaeology of Ethnicity: Constructing Identities in the Past and Present*. London: Routledge, 1997.

Jones, Siân and Sarah Pearce, eds. *Jewish Local Patriotism and Self-Identification in the Graeco-Roman Period*. JSPSup 31. Sheffield: Sheffield Academic Press, 2002.

Jossa, G. "Josephus' Action in Galilee during the Jewish War." Pages 265–78 in *Josephus and the History of the Graeco-Roman Period: Essays in Memory of Morton Smith*. Edited by Fausto Parente and Joseph Sievers. Leiden: Brill, 1994.

Kalms, Jürgen U., ed. *Internationales Josephus-Kolloquium, Åarhus 1999*. Münsteraner Judaistische Studien, 6. Münster: Lit Verlag, 2000.

Kamesar, Adam, ed. *The Cambridge Companion to Philo*. Cambridge: Cambridge University Press, 2009.

Kaplan, Julius. *The Redaction of the Babylonian Talmud*. New York: Bloch, 1933.

Kasher, Aryeh. "Three Jewish Communities of Lower Egypt in the Ptolemaic Period." *SCI* 2 (1975): 113–23.

———. "First Jewish military units in Ptolemaic Egypt." *JSJ* 9 (1978): 57–67.

———. *Jews, Idumaeans, and Ancient Arabs*. Tübingen: Mohr Siebeck, 1988.

———. *Jews and Hellenistic Cities in Eretz-Israel*. Tübingen: Mohr Siebeck, 1990.

———. "Synagogues as 'Houses of Prayer' and 'Holy Places' in the Jewish Communities of Hellenistic and Roman Egypt." Pages 205–20 in *Ancient Synagogues: Historical Analysis and Archaeological Discovery*. Vol 1. Edited by Dan Urman and Paul V. M. Flesher. New York: Brill, 1995.

Kasher, Aryeh, Aharon Oppenheimer, and Uriel Rappaport, eds. *Synagogues in Antiquity*. Jerusalem: Ben Zvi, 1987.

Kee, Howard C. "Defining the First-Century CE Synagogue: Problems and Progress." Pages 7–26 in *Evolution of the Synagogue: Problems and Progress*. Edited by Howard C. Kee and Lynn H. Cohick. Harrisburg, PA: Trinity Press Intl, 1999.

Kee, Howard C., and Lynn H. Cohick, eds. *Evolution of the Synagogue: Problems and Progress*. Harrisburg, PA: Trinity Press Intl, 1999.

Kenyon, Kathleen. *Digging Up Jericho*. London: Benn, 1957.

———. *Excavations at Jericho*. 5 vols. London: British School of Archaeology in Jerusalem, 1960–1983.

———. *The Bible and Recent Archaeology*. Atlanta: John Knox Press, 1987.

Kloner, Amos. "The Synagogues of Horvat Rimmon." Pages 43–48 in *Ancient Synagogues in Israel: Third–Seventh Century CE: Proceedings of Symposium, University of Haifa, May 1987*. BAR International Series 499. Edited by Rachel Hachlili. Oxford: BAR, 1989.

Kloppenborg, John S. *The Shape of Q: Signal Essays on the Sayings Gospel*. Minneapolis, MN: Augsburg Fortress, 1994.

———. *Excavating Q: The History and Setting of the Sayings Gospel*. Minneapolis, MN: Augsburg Fortress, 2000.

———. "The Theodotos Inscription and the Problem of First-Century Synagogue Buildings." Pages 236–82 in *Jesus and Archaeology*. Edited by James H. Charlesworth. Grand Rapids: Eerdmans, 2006.

Kloppenborg, John S., and Stephen G. Wilson, eds. *Voluntary Associations in the Graeco-Roman World*. London: Routledge, 1996.

Kohl, Heinrich, and Carl Watzinger. *Antike Synagogen in Galilaea*. Peilzig: Hinrichs, 1916.

Kokkinos, Nikos. *The Herodian Dynasty*. JSPSup 30. Sheffield: Sheffield Academic Press, 1998.

———. "Justus, Josephus, Agrippa II and his Coins." *SCI* 22 (2003): 163–80.

Kotlar, David, and Judith Baskin. "Mikveh." Pages 225–30 in *Encyclopaedia Judaica*. 2nd ed. Vol. 14. Detroit: Thomson, 2007.

Kraabel, Alf Thomas. "The Diaspora Synagogue: Archaeological and Epigraphic Evidence since Sukenik." *ANRW* II, 19.1 (1979): 477–510.

———. "New Evidence of the Samaritan Diaspora has been Found on Delos." *BA* (1984): 44–46.

Kraemer, Ross Shepherd. "Hellenistic Jewish Women: the Epigraphical Evidence." Pages 183–200 in *SBL 1986 Seminar Papers*. Atlanta: Society of Biblical Literature, 1986.

———. "Non-literary Evidence for Jewish Women in Rome and Egypt." Pages 75–101 in *Rescuing Creusa: New Methodological Approaches to Women in Antiquity*. Edited by Marilyn Skinner. Lubbock, TX: Texas Tech University Press, 1986.

———. "On the Meaning of the Term 'Jew' in Greco-Roman Inscriptions." *HTR* 82 (1989): 35–54.

Krauss, Samuel. *Synagogale Altertümer*. Berlin: Hildesheim, 1922.

Kushnir-Stein, A. "Another Look at Josephus' Evidence for the Date of Herod's Death." *SCI* 14 (1995): 73–86.

———. "The Coinage of Agrippa II." *SCI* 21 (2002): 123–31.

———. "Agrippa I in Josephus." *SCI* 22 (2003): 153–161.

Ladouceur, David J. "Josephus and Masada." Pages 95–113 in *Josephus, Judaism and Christianity*. Edited by Louis H. Feldman and Gōhei Hata. Detroit: Wayne State University Press, 1989.

Lass, Egon H. E. *The Seasons of Tulul*. [No location]: Xlibris, 2005.

LaVerdiere, E. A. "Masada—The Zealot Synagogue." *BT* 46 (1970): 3176–89.

Lawrence, Arnold Walter. *Greek Architecture*. Pelican History of Art. 5th ed., rev. by Richard Allen Tomlinson. New Haven: Yale University Press, 1996.

Leclercq, H. "Judaïsme." *DACL* 8.1 (1932): col. 1–254.

Lefèbvre, Gustave. "Inscriptions grecques d'Égypte." *BCH* 26 (1902): 440–66.

———. "Inscriptions gréco-juives." *ASAE* 24 (1924): 1–5.

Leiser, B. M. "The 'Mezuzah' Column in Hungary's Egyptological Collection." *JQR* 50 (1960): 365–70.

Levine, Lee I. *Caesarea Under Roman Rule*. Leiden: Brill, 1975.

———. "Ancient Synagogues: A Historical Introduction." Pages 1–10 in *Ancient Synagogues Revealed*. Edited by Lee I. Levine. Detroit: Wayne State University Press; Jerusalem: Israel Exploration Society, 1982.

———, ed. *Ancient Synagogues Revealed*. Detroit: Wayne State University Press; Jerusalem: Israel Exploration Society, 1982.

———. *The Rabbinic Class of Roman Palestine in Late Antiquity*. Jerusalem: Ben-Zvi, 1989.

———. "How Anti-Roman Was the Galilee?" Pages 95–102 in *The Galilee in Late Antiquity*. Edited by Lee I. Levine. New York: Jewish Theological Seminary; Harvard University Press, 1992.

———. "Synagogue Officials: The Evidence from Caesarea and Its Implications for Palestine and the Diaspora." Pages 392–400 in *Caesarea Maritima. A Retrospective After Two Millennia*. Edited by Avner Raban and Kenneth G. Holum. Leiden: Brill, 1996.

———. "The Nature and Origin of the Palestinian Synagogue Reconsidered." *JBL* 115.3 (1996b): 425–48.

———. "The Revolutionary Effects of Archaeology on the Study of Jewish History: The Case of the Ancient Synagogue." Pages 166–89 in *The Archaeology of Israel. Constructing the Past, Interpreting the Present*. JSOTSup 237. Edited by Neil Asher Silberman and David B. Small. Sheffield: Sheffield Academic Press, 1997.

———. *Judaism and Hellenism in Antiquity: Conflict or Confluence?* Seattle: University of Washington Press, 1998.

———. "The Development of Synagogue Liturgy in Late Antiquity." Pages 123–44 in *Galilee through the Centuries*. Edited by Eric M. Meyers. Winona Lake, IN: Eisenbrauns, 1999.

———. *The Ancient Synagogue: The First Thousand Years*. New Haven: Yale University Press, 2000.

———. *Jerusalem: Portrait of the City in the Second Temple Period*. Philadelphia: Jewish Publication Society, 2002.

———. "The First-Century Synagogue: Critical Reassessments and Assessments of the Critical." Pages 70–102 in *Religion and Society in Roman Palestine. Old Questions, New Approaches*. Edited by Douglas R. Edwards. New York: Routledge, 2004.

———. *The Ancient Synagogue: The First Thousand Years*. 2nd Ed. New Haven: Yale University Press, 2005.

Levy, Thomas Evan, ed. *The Archaeology of Society in the Holy Land*. London: Leicester University Press, 1998.

Lewis, David M. "The Jewish Inscriptions of Egypt." Pages 138–66 in *Corpus Papyrorum Iudaicarum*. Vol. 3. Edited by V.A. Tcherikover, A. Fuks, and M. Stern. Jerusalem: Magness Press, 1964.

Liddell, Henry G., and Robert Scott. *A Greek-English Lexicon, Ninth Edition with a Revised Supplement*. Rev. by Henry S. Jones. Oxford: Oxford University Press, 1996.

Lieu, Judith, John A. North, and Tessa Rajak, eds. *The Jews Among Pagans and Christians in the Roman Empire*. London: Routledge, 1992.

Lifschitz, Baruch. *Donateurs et fondateurs dans les synagogues juives: Répertoire des dédicaces grecques relatives à la construction et à la réfection des synagogues*. Cahiers de la *RB* 7. Paris: Gabalda, 1967.

Lim, Timothy H., Larry W. Hurtado, and A. Graeme Auld, eds. *The Dead Sea Scrolls in Their Historical Context*. Edinburgh: T&T Clark, 2000.

Lyons, William J., Jonathan G. Campbell, and Lloyd K. Pietersen, eds. *New Directions in Qumran Studies*. London: T&T Clark, 2005

Magen, Yitzhak. "Mt. Gerizim—A Temple City." *Qadmoniot* 33.2 (120) (2000): 74–118 [Hebrew].

———. "Tombs Decorated in Jerusalem Style in Samaria and the Hebron Hills." *Qadmoniot* 123 (2002): 28–37.

———. "Mt. Gerizim during the Roman and Byzantine Periods."*Qadmoniot* 33.2 (120) (2000): 133–43 [Hebrew].

Magen, Yitzhak, L. Tsafania and H. Misgav, "The Hebrew and Aramaic Inscriptions from Mt. Gerizim." *Qadmoniot* 33.2 (120) (2000): 125–32.

Magen, Yitzak, Haggai Misgav, and Levana Tsafania. *Mount Gerizim Excavations I: The Aramaic, Hebrew and Samaritan Inscriptions.* JSP 2. Jerusalem: Israel Antiquitites Authority, 2004.

Magen, Yitzhak, et al. *The Land of Benjamin*. JSP 3. Jerusalem: Civil Administration of Judea and Samaria; Israel Antiquities Authority, 2004.

Magness, Jodi. *The Archaeology of Qumran and the Dead Sea Scrolls*. Grand Rapids: Eerdmans, 2002.

———. "[On] Rachel Bar-Nathan, Hasmonean and Herodian Palaces at Jericho: Final Reports of the 1973–1987 Excavations, Volume III: The Pottery." *Dead Sea Discoveries* 10.3 (2003): 420–28.

———."The Golan: Hellenistic Period to the Middle Ages." in *NEAEHL* (1993). Vol. 2: 234–46.

———. "The Judæan Synagogues—As a Reflection of Alexandrine Architecture." Pages 192–201 in *Alessandria e il Mondo Ellenistico-Romano, Atti del II Congresso Internazionale Italo-Egiziano*. Edited by Nicola Bonacasa et al. Rome: L'Erma di Bretschneider, 1995.

———. "The Synagogue at Capernaum: a Radical Solution." Pages 137–48 in *The Roman and Byzantine Near East, Volume II.* Journal of Roman Archaeology Supplementary Series 31. Edited by John H. Humphrey. Portsmouth, RI, 1999.

———. "Golan Synagogues." Pages 465–72 in *Near Eastern Archaeology: A Reader*. Edited by Suzanne Richard. Winona Lake, IN: Eisenbrauns, 2005.

Ma'oz, Zvi Uri. "The Synagogue of Gamla and the Typology of Second-Temple Synagogues." Pages 35–41 in *Ancient Synagogues Revealed*. Edited by Lee I. Levine. Jerusalem: Israel Exploration Society, 1982.

———. "The Synagogue in the Second Temple Period." *EI* 23 (1992): 331–34 (English summary: 157–58).

———. "The Judaean Synagogues—As a Reflection of Alexandrian Architecture." Pages 192–201 in *Alessandria e il Mondo Ellenistico-Romano, Atti del II Congresso Internazionale Italo-Egiziano*. Eds. Nicola Bonacasa et al. Rome: L'Erma di Bretschneider, 1995.

Marcadé, Jean. *Au Musée de Délos: Étude Sur la Sculpture Hellénistique en Ronde Bosse Découverte Dans l'Île*. Paris: de Boccard, 1969.

Marchetti, N. "Preliminary Report on the First Season of Excavations of the Italian-Palestinian Expedition at Tell es-Sultan/Jericho, April-May 1997." *PEQ* 130.2 (1998): 121–44.

Martin, Matthew J. "Interpreting the Theodotos Inscription: Some Reflections on a First Century Jerusalem Synagogue Inscription and E.P. Sanders' 'Common Judaism.'" *ANES* 39 (2002): 160–81.

Matassa, Lidia D. "Unravelling the Myth of the Synagogue on Delos." *BAIAS* 25 (2007): 81–116.

———. "Magdala." Page 335 in *Encyclopaedia Judaica*. 2nd ed. Vol 13. Detroit: Thomson, 2007.

———. "The Samaritans in the Second Temple Period." Pages 720–22 in *Encyclopaedia Judaica*. 2nd ed. Vol 17. Detroit: Thomson, 2007.

———. "Delos." Pages 544–45 in *Encyclopaedia Judaica*. 2nd ed. Vol. 5. Detroit: Thomson, 2007.

———. "Elephantine." Pages 311–14 in *Encyclopaedia Judaica*. 2nd ed. Vol. 6. Detroit: Thomson, 2007.

———. "Problems with the Identification of a Synagogue in the Hasmonaean Estate at Jericho." Pages 95–132 in *Text, Theology, and Trowel: Recent Research into the Hebrew Bible*. Edited by Lidia D. Matassa and Jason M. Silverman. Eugene, OR: Pickwick, 2011.

Mayer, Leo A., and Adolf Reifenberg. "A Jewish Titulus from Egypt." *ASAE* 33 (1933): 81–82.

Mazar, Benjamin, and Immanuel Dunayevsky. "En-Gedi, Third Season of Excavations: Preliminary Report." *IEJ* 14.3 (1964): 121–30.

Mazar, Eilat. *The Complete Guide to the Temple Mount Excavations*. Jerusalem: Shoham Academic Research, 2002.

Mazur, Belle D. *Studies on Jewry in Greece* Athens: Printing Office "Hestia," 1935.

Martínez, Florentino G., and Donald W. Parry. *A Bibliography of the Finds in the Desert of Judah 1970–95*. Leiden: Brill, 1996.

McGing, Brian. "Population and Proselytism: How Many Jews Were There in the Ancient World?" Pages 88–106 in *Jews in the Hellenistic and Roman Cities*. Edited by John R. Bartlett. London: Routledge, 2002.

McKay, Heather A. *Sabbath and Synagogue: The Question of Sabbath Worship in Ancient Judaism*. Leiden: Brill, 1995.

McLaren, James S. *Turbulent Times? Josephus and Scholarship on Judaea in the First Century CE*. JSPSup 29. Sheffield: Sheffield Academic Press, 1998.

———. "The Coinage of the First Year as a Point of Reference for the Jewish Revolt (66–70 CE)." *SCI* 22 (2003): 135–52.

McLean, B. Hudson. "The Place of Cult in Voluntary Associations and Christian Churches on Delos." Pages 186–225 in *Voluntary Associations in the Graeco-Roman World*. Edited by John S. Kloppenborg and Stephen G. Wilson. London: Routledge, 1996.

Meeks, Wayne A. *In Search of the Early Christians: Selected Essays*. New Haven: Yale University Press, 2002.

Mendels, Doron. *Identity, Religion, and Historiography*. JSPSup 24. Sheffield: Sheffield Academic Press, 1998.

Meshorer, Ya'akov. *The City Coins of Eretz-Israel and the Decapolis in the Roman Period*. Translated by Ina Pomerantz. Jerusalem: The Israel Museum, 1985.

———. "The Coins of Masada." Pages 71–132 in *Masada I: The Yigael Yadin Excavations 1963–1965. Final Reports*. Jerusalem: Israel Exploration Society; The Hebrew University of Jerusalem, 1989.

Metzger, Bruce M., and Michael D. Coogan, eds. *The Oxford Companion to the Bible*. Oxford: Oxford University Press, 1993.

Meyers, Carol, Toni Craven, and Ross Shephard Kraemer, eds. *Women in Scripture: A Dictionary of Named and Unnamed Women in the Hebrew Bible, the Apocryphal / Deuterocanonical Books and New Testament*. New York: Houghton Mifflin, 2000.

Meyers, Eric M. "Aspects of Everyday Life in Roman Palestine with Special Reference to Private Domiciles and Ritual Baths." Pages 193–220 in *Jews in the Hellenistic and Roman Cities*. Edited by John R. Bartlett. London: Routledge, 2002.

Meyers, Eric M., James F. Strange, Carol L. Meyers, Dennis E. Groh, Martin Goodman, Patricia Smith, and Joseph Zias. *Excavations at Ancient Meiron, Upper Galilee, Israel 1971–2, 1974–5, 1977*. Meiron Excavation Project Volume 3. Cambridge, MA: The American Schools of Oriental Research, 1981.

Meyers, Eric M., and James F. Strange. *Archaeology, the Rabbis, and Early Christianity*. Nashville, TN: Abingdon, 1981.

Meyers, Eric M., and Steven Fine. "Ancient Synagogues: An Archaeological Introduction." Pages 3–20 in *Sacred Realm: The Emergence of the Synagogue in the Ancient World*. Edited by Steven Fine. Oxford: Oxford University Press, 1996.

Middlemass, Jill. *The Troubles of Templeless Judah*. OTM. Oxford: Oxford University Press, 2005.

Miller, Robert J., ed. *The Complete Gospels: Annotated Scholar's Version*. 3rd ed. San Franscico: Harper San Francisco, 1994.

Miller, Stuart S. "Stepped Pools, Stone Vessels, and Other Identity Markers of 'Complex Common Judaism.'" *JJS* 41 (2010): 214–43.

Milson, David W. "The Stratum IB Building at Hammat Tiberias: Synagogue or Church?" *PEQ* 136 (2004): 45–56.

Mitchell, Stephen. *Anatolia: Land, Men, and Gods in Asia Minor. Vol 2: The Rise of the Church*. Oxford: Clarendon Press, 1993.

———. "The Cult of Theos Hypsistos between Pagans, Jews and Christians." Pages 81–148 in *Pagan Monotheism in Late Antiquity*. Edited by Polymnia Athanassiadi and Michael Frede. Oxford: Clarendon, 1999.

Mélèze-Modrzejewski, Joseph. *The Jews of Egypt: From Rameses II to Emperor Hadrian.* Edinburgh: T&T Clark, 1995.

Mosser, Carl. "Torah Instruction, Discussion, and Prophecy in First-Century Synagogues." Pages 523–51 in *Christian Origins and Hellenistic Judaism: Literary and Social Contexts for the New Testament.* Edited by Stanley E. Porter and Andrew Pitts. Leiden: Brill, 2012. doi: 10.1163/9789004236394_020.

Murphy, Frederick J. *An Introduction to Jesus and the Gospels.* Nashville, TN: Abingdon, 2005.

Mußner, Franz. *Jesus von Nazareth im Umfeld Israels und der Urkirche.* WUNT 111. Tübingen: Mohr Siebeck, 1999.

Naveh, Joseph. "Did Ancient Samaritan Inscriptions Belong to Synagogues?" Pages 61–64 in *Ancient Synagogues in Israel: Third–Seventh Century CE: Proceedings of Symposium, University of Haifa, May 1987.* BAR International Series 499. Edited by Rachel Hachlili. Oxford: BAR, 1989.

Negev, Avraham, and Shimon Gibson, eds. *Archaeological Encyclopedia of the Holy Land.* Rev. ed. New York: Continuum, 2001.

Netzer, Ehud. "The Hasmonaean and Herodian Winter Palaces at Jericho." *IEJ* 25 (1975): 89–100.

———. *Greater Herodium.* Qedem 13. Jerusalem: Institute of Archaeology, the Hebrew University of Jerusalem, 1981.

———. "Did the Spring-House at Magdala Serve as a Synagogue?" Pages 165–72 in *Synagogues in Antiquity.* Edited by Aryeh Kasher, Aharon Oppenheimer, and Uriel Rappaport. Jerusalem: Ben Zvi, 1987 [Hebrew].

———. "Architecture in Palaestina Prior to and During the Days of Herod the Great." Pages 37–50 in *Akten Des XIII Internationalen Kongresses für Klassische Archäologie.* Edited by Edmund Buchner. Mainz: von Zabern, 1988.

———. "Jericho." Pages 723–40 in *ABD.* Vol. 3. New York: Doubleday, 1990.

———. "The Last Days and Hours at Masada." *BAR* 17 (1991): 20–32.

———. *Masada III: The Yigael Yadin Excavations 1963–1965. Final Reports, the Buildings, Stratigraphy and Architecture.* Jerusalem: Israel Exploration Society; the Hebrew University of Jerusalem, 1991.

———. "Herodium." Pages 618–26 in *NEAEHL.* Vol 2. Jerusalem: The Israel Exploration Society; Carta, 1993.

———. "Masada." Pages 973–85 in *NEAEHL,* Vol 2. Jerusalem: The Israel Exploration Society; Carta, 1993.

———. *Hasmonaean and Herodian Palaces at Jericho. Final Reports of the 1973–1987 Excavations.* Vol. 1. Jerusalem: Israel Exploration Society; Institute of Archaeology, The Hebrew University of Jerusalem, 2001.

———. *Hasmonaean and Herodian Palaces at Jericho. Final Reports of the 1973–1987 Excavations*. Vol. 2. Jerusalem: Israel Exploration Society; Institute of Archaeology, The Hebrew University of Jerusalem, 2004.

———. "The Rebels' Archives at Masada." *IEJ* 54.2 (2004): 218–29.

———. *The Architecture of Herod, the Great Builder*. Tübingen: Mohr Siebeck, 2006a.

———. "A Synagogue in Jericho from the Hasmonaean Period." Unpublished Hebrew article. Translated by Orit Peleg. 2006.

Netzer, Ehud, and Günter Garbrecht. "Water Channels and a Royal Estate of the Late Hellenistic Period in Jericho's Western Plains." Pages 366–79 in *The Aqueducts of Israel*. Journal of Roman Archaeology, Supplementary Series 46. Edited by David Amit, Joseph Patrich, and Yizhar Hirshfeld. Portsmouth, RI: 2002.

Netzer, Ehud (with Ya'akov Kalman and Rachel Laureys). "A Synagogue from the Hasmonean Period Recently Exposed in the Western Plain of Jericho." *IEJ* 49.3–4 (1999): 203–21.

Neusner, Jacob, ed. *Christianity, Judaism and Other Greco-Roman Cults: Studies for Morton Smith at Sixty*. 4 vols. Leiden: Brill, 1975.

———. "The Formation of Rabbinic Judaism: Yavneh (Jamnia) from AD 70 to 100." Pages 3–42 in *Aufstieg der römischen Welt: Principat*, vol. 19: *Religion*. Edited by W. Haase. Berlin: de Gruyter, 1979.

———. *The Mishnah: A New Translation*. New Haven, CT: Yale University Press, 1988.

———. *The Mishnah: An Introduction*. Northvale, NJ: Jason Aronson, 1989.

———. *Rabbinic Judaism: The Documentary History of Its Formative Age (70–600 CE)*. Bethesda, MD: CDL Press, 1994.

———. *The Four Stages of Rabbinic Judaism*. London: Routledge, 1999.

———. *Judaism When Christianity Began*. Louisville, KY: Westminster John Knox, 2002.

———. *The Talmud. What It Is and What It Says*. Lanham, MD: Rowman & Littlefield, 2006.

Nevett, Lisa C. *House and Society in the Ancient Greek World*. Cambridge: Cambridge University Press, 1999.

Newman, Hillel. *Proximity to Power and Jewish Sectarian Groups of the Ancient Period*. Leiden: Brill, 2006.

Newsom, Carol, and Yigael Yadin. "The Masada Fragments of the Qumran Songs of the Sabbath Sacrifice." *IEJ* 34.2/3 (1984): 77–88

Newsome, James D. *Greeks, Romans, Jews: Currents of Culture and Belief in the New Testament World*. Philadelphia: Trinity Press Intl, 1992.

Nielsen, Inge. "Issues of Current Interest: Synagogue (*synagogé*) and Prayerhouse (*proseuché*): The Relationship between Jewish Religious Architecture in Palestine and the Diaspora." *Hephaistos* 23 (2005): 63–111.

Nodet, Etienne. *A Search for the Origins of Judaism: From Joshua to the Mishnah*. JSOTSup 248. Sheffield: Sheffield Academic Press, 1997.

Noy, David. "A Jewish Place of Prayer in Roman Egypt." *JTS* 43.1 (1992): 118–22.

———. *Jewish Inscriptions of Western Europe*. Volume 1. Italy (excluding the City of Rome), Spain, and Gaul. Cambridge: Cambridge University Press, 1993.

Noy, David, Alexander Panayotov, and Hans-Wulf Bloedhorn, eds. *Inscriptiones Judaicae Orientis. Volume I. Eastern Europe*. TSAJ 101. Tübingen: Mohr Siebeck, 2004.

Noy, David, and Hans-Wulf Bloedhorn, eds. *Inscriptiones Judaicae Orientis. Volume III. Syria and Cyprus*. TSAJ 102. Tübingen: Mohr Siebeck, 2004.

Nutton, Vivian. *Ancient Medicine*. London: Routledge, 2004.

Ó Ferghail, F. "The Jews in the Hellenistic Cities of Acts." Pages 39–54 in *Jews in the Hellenistic and Roman Cities*. Edited by John R. Bartlett. London: Routledge, 2002.

Oleson, John Peter. *Greek and Roman Mechanical Water-Lifting Devices: The History of a Technology*. Phoenix Supplement 16. Toronto: University of Toronto Press, 1984.

Olsson, Birgir, Dieter Mitternacht, and Olof Brandt, eds. *The Synagogue of Ancient Ostia and the Jews of Rome: Interdisciplinary Studies*. Stockholm: Åströms, 2001.

Olsson, Birgir, and Magnus Zetterholm, eds. *The Ancient Synagogue from Its Origins Until 200 CE.: Papers Presented at an International Conference at Lund University October 14–17*. ConBNT 39. Stockholm: Almqvist & Wiskell Intl, 2003.

Oppenheimer, A., "The Separation of the First Tithes During the Second Temple Period." Pages 70–83 in *Benjamin de Vries Memorial Volume*. Edited by Ezra Zion Melamed. Jerusalem: Tel Aviv University Research Authority, 1968.

Otzen, Benedikt. *Judaism in Antiquity: Political Development and Religious Currents from Alexander to Hadrian*. Biblical Seminar 7. Sheffield: Sheffield Academic Press, 1990.

Overman, J. Andrew. "Jews, Slaves and Synagogues in the Black Sea: The Bosporan Manumission Inscriptions and Their Significance for Diaspora Judaism." Pages 141–57 in *Evolution of the Synagogue: Problems and Progress*. Edited by Howard C. Kee and Lynn H. Cohick. Harrisburg, PA: Trinity Press Intl, 1999.

Overman, J. Andrew, and Robert S. MacLennan, eds. *Diaspora Jews and Judaism: Essays in Honor of, and in Dialogue with, A. Thomas Kraabel*. South Florida Studies in the History of Judaism 41. Atlanta: Scholars Press, 1992.

Parente, Fausto, and Joseph Sievers, eds. *Josephus and the History of the Greco-Roman Period: Essays in Honor of Morton Smith*. Leiden: Brill, 1994.

Pastor, Jack. *Land and Economy in Ancient Palestine*. London: Routledge, 1997.

Patrich, Joseph. "Corbo's Excavations at Herodium: a Review Article." *IEJ* 42.3/4 (1992): 241–45.

Pearlman, Moshe. *Digging up the Bible*. London: Weidenfeld & Nicolson, 1980.

———. *The Zealots of Masada: Story of a Dig.* London: Hamish Hamilton, 1967.

Peleg-Barkat, Orit. "Architectural Decoration." Pages 159–74 in *Gamla II: The Shmarya Gutmann Excavations, 1976–1989: The Architecture.* Edited by Danny Syon and Zvi Yavor. Jerusalem: Israel Antiquities Authority, 2010.

———. "Roman Intaglio Gemstones from Aelia Capitolina." *PEQ* 135 (2003): 54–69.

Peleg, Yifat. "Gender and Ossuaries: Ideology and Meaning." *BASOR* 325 (2002): 65–73.

Plassart, André. *Exploration Archéologique de Délos 11: Les sanctuaires et les cultes du Mont Cynthe.* Par Ecoles Françaises d'Athènes. Paris: De Boccard, 1928.

———. "La Synagogue juive de Délos." Pages 201–15 in *Mélanges Holleaux, recueil de memoirs concernant l'antiquité grecque.* Paris: Picard, 1913.

———. "La synagogue juive de Délos." *RB* 23 (1914): 523–34.

———. *Inscriptions de Délos. Périodes de l'Amphictyonie Ionienne et de l'Amphictyonie Attico-Délienne, Dédicaces et Textes Divers. Ecrits dans les Alphabets Cycladiques (Nos. 1–35). Dédicaces, Bornes, Règlements, d'Alphabet Ionien Classique (Nos. 36–70). Décrets Déliens. Ordonnance Lacédemonienne. Décrets Athéniens (Nos. 71–88).* Librairie Ancienne Honoré Champion. Paris: Champion, 1915.

Pleket, H. W., R. S. Stroud, and J. H. M. Strubbe, eds. *Supplementum Epigraphicum Graecum.* Vol. 43. Amsterdam: J.C. Gieben, 1996.

Porat, Roi, Hanan Eshel, and Amos Frumkin. "Finds from the Bar Kokhba Revolt from Two Caves at En Gedi." *PEQ* 139 (2007): 35–54.

Porath, Yosef. "Hydraulic Plaster in Aqueducts as a Chronological Indicator." Pages 25–36 in *The Aqueducts of Israel.* Edited by David Amit, Joseph Patrich, and Yizhar Hirshfeld. Journal of Roman Archaeology Supplementary Series 46. Portsmouth, RI: Journal of Roman Archaeology, 2002.

Porten, Bezalel. *Archives from Elephantine: The Life of an Ancient Jewish Military Colony.* Berkeley, CA: University of California Press, 1968.

Poirier, John C. "Purity Beyond the Temple in the Second Temple Era." *JBL* 122.2 (2003): 247–65.

Price, Simon. "The History of the Hellenistic Period." Pages 364–89 in *Greece and the Hellenistic World.* Oxford History of the Classical World. Edited by John Boardman, Jasper Griffin, and Oswyn Murray. Oxford: Oxford University Press, 1988.

Price, Martin. "A Hoard of Tetradrachms from Jericho." *INJ* 11 [1990–91] (1993): 24–25.

Pucci Ben Zeev, Miriam. "Caesar and Jewish Law." *RB* 102 (1995): 28–37.

———. "Who Wrote a Letter concerning Delian Jews?" *RB* 103 (1996): 237–43.

———. *Jewish Rights in the Roman World: The Greek and Roman Documents Quoted by Josephus Flavius.* TSAJ 74. Tübingen: Mohr Siebeck, 1998.

Pummer, Reinhard. *The Samaritans.* Leiden: Brill, 1987.

———. "How to Tell a Samaritan Synagogue from a Jewish Synagogue." *BAR* 24 (1998): 24–35.

———. *The Samaritans in Flavius Josephus*. Tübingen: Mohr Siebeck, 2009.

Purdum, Stan. *He Walked in Galilee: The Days of Jesus' Ministry*. Nashville, TN: Abingdon, 2005.

Purvis, James D. *The Samaritan Pentateuch and the Origin of the Samaritan Sect*. Cambridge, MA: Harvard University Press, 1968.

Raban, Avner, and Kenneth G. Holum, eds. *Caesarea Maritima: A Retrospective After Two Millennia*. Leiden: Bill, 1996.

Rahmani, L. Y. "Stone Synagogue Chairs: Their Identification, Use and Significance." *IEJ* 40.2/3 (1990): 192–214.

———. *A Catalogue of Jewish Ossuaries: In the Collection of the State of Israel*. Jerusalem: Israel Antiquities Authority: Israel Museum, 1994.

Rast, Walter E. *Through the Ages in Palestinian Archaeology*. Philadelphia: Trinity Press Intl, 1992.

Rajak, Tessa. "Josephus and the 'Archaeology' of the Jews." *JJS* 33.1/2 (1982): 465–77.

———. "Was There a Roman Charter for the Jews?" *JRS* 74 (1984): 107–23.

———. "The Synagogue Within the Greco-Roman City." Pages 161–73 in *Jews, Christians, and Polytheists in the Ancient Synagogue. Cultural interaction during the Greco-Roman Period*. Edited by Steven Fine. London: Routledge, 1999.

———. *The Jewish Dialogue With Greece and Rome*. Leiden: Brill, 2001.

———. "Synagogue and Community in the Graeco-Roman Diaspora." Pages 22–38 in *Jews in the Hellenistic and Roman Cities*. Edited by John R. Bartlett. London: Routledge, 2002.

Rajak, Tessa, and David Noy. "Archisynagogoi: Office, Title, and Social Status in the Greco-Jewish Synagogue." *JRS* 83 (1993): 75–93.

Ramazzotti, M. "Appunti sulla semiotica delle relazioni stratigrafiche di Gerico neolitica." *Vicino Oriente* 12 (2000): 89–115.

Rappaport, Uriel. "John of Gischala: From Galilee to Jerusalem." *JJS* 33.1–2 (1982): 479–93.

———. "Where Was Josephus' Lying—in His Life or in the War?" Pages 279–89 in *Josephus and the History of the Graeco-Roman Period. Essays in Memory of Morton Smith*. Edited by Fausto Parente and Joseph Sievers. Leiden: Brill, 1994.

Rapuano, Yehudah. "The Hasmonaean Period 'Synagogue' at Jericho and the 'Council Chamber' at Qumran." *IEJ* 51.1 (2001): 48–56.

Regev, Eyal. "The Individual Meaning of Jewish Ossuaries: A Socio-Anthropological Perspective on Burial Practice." *PEQ* 133 (2001): 39–49.

Reich, Ronny. "The Hot Bath-House (Balneum), the Miqweh, and the Jewish Community in the Second Temple Period." *JJS* 39 (1988): 102–7.

———. "Baking and Cooking at Masada." *ZDPV* 119.2 (2003): 140–58.

———. "Spindle Whorls and Spinning at Masada." Pages 171–194 in *Masada VIII: The Yigael Yadin Excavations 1963–1965, Final Reports*. Edited by Joseph Aviram, Gideon Foerster, Ehud Netzer, and Guy D. Stiebel. Jerusalem: Israel Exploration Society; The Hebrew University of Jerusalem, 2007.

———. "Stone Mugs from Masada." Pages 195–209 in *Masada VIII: The Yigael Yadin Excavations 1963–1965, Final Reports*. Edited by Joseph Aviram, Gideon Foerster, Ehud Netzer, and Guy D. Stiebel. Jerusalem: Israel Exploration Society; The Hebrew University of Jerusalem, 2007.

———. "Stone Scale-Weights from Masada." Pages 210–16 in *Masada VIII: The Yigael Yadin Excavations 1963–1965, Final Reports*. Edited by Joseph Aviram, Gideon Foerster, Ehud Netzer, and Guy D. Stiebel. Jerusalem: Israel Exploration Society; The Hebrew University of Jerusalem, 2007.

Reif, Stefan C. "The Early History of Jewish Worship." Pages 109–36 in *The Making of Jewish and Christian Worship*. Edited by Paul F. Bradshaw. Notre Dame, IN: University of Notre Dame Press, 1991.

Reisner, Reiner. "Synagogues in Jerusalem." Pages 179–209 in *The Book of Acts in its Palestinian Setting*. Edited by Richard Bauckham. Grand Rapids: Eerdmans, 1995.

Renfrew, Colin. *The Archaeology of Cult: The Sanctuary at Phylakopi*. Supplementary Volume 18. Athens: British School of Archaeology at Athens; London: Thames & Hudson, 1985.

Rhoads, D. M. *Israel In Revolution 6–74 CE. A Political History Based on the Writings of Josephus*. Philadelphia: Fortress, 1976.

Richardson, Peter. "Early Synagogues as *Collegia* in the Diaspora and Palestine." Pages 90–109 in *Voluntary Associations in the Graeco-Roman World*. Edited by John S. Kloppenborg and Stephen G. Wilson. London: Routledge, 1996.

———. "Augustan-Era Synagogues in Rome." Pages 17–29 in *Judaism and Christianity in First Century Rome*. Edited by K. P. Donfried and Peter Richardson. Grand Rapids: Eerdmans, 1998.

Ridgway, Bunilde Sismondo. *Prayers in Stone: Greek Architectural Sculpture ca. 600–100 B.C.E*. The Sather Classical Lectures 1996. Berkeley, CA: University of California Press, 1999.

Rokeah, David. *Jews, Pagans and Christians in Conflict*. Jerusalem: The Magnes Press; Leiden: Brill, 1982.

Roller, Duane W. *The Building Program of Herod the Great*. Berkeley, CA: University of California Press, 1998.

Roth, Jonathan P. "The Length of the Siege of Masada." *SCI* 14 (1995): 87–110.

Roth-Gerson, Lea. *Greek Inscriptions from the Synagogues in Eretz-Israel*. Jerusalem: Ben Zvi Institute, 1987.

Rousseau, John J., and Rami Arav. *Jesus and His World: An Archaeological and Cultural Dictionary*. Minneapolis: Fortress, 1995.

Roussel, Pierre. *Délos, Colonie Athénienne*. Bibliothèque des Écoles Françaises d'Athènes et de Rome 111. Paris: de Boccard, 1916.

Roussel, Pierre, and Marcel Launey. *Inscriptions de Délos : Decrets Postérieurs à 166 av. J.-C. (Nos. 1497–1524). Dédicaces Postérieures à 166 av. J.-C. (Nos. 1525–2219)*. Librairie Ancienne. Paris: Honoré Champion, 1937a.

———. *Inscriptions de Délos : Dédicaces Postérieures à 166 av. J.-C. (Nos. 2220–2528). Textes Divers, Listes et Catalogues, Fragments Divers Postérieurs à 166 av. J.-C. (Nos. 2529–2879)*. Librairie Ancienne. Paris: Honoré Champion, 1937b.

Runesson, Anders. "The Oldest Synagogue Building in the Diaspora: A Response to L. M. White." *HTR* 92 (1999): 409–33.

———. *The Origins of the Synagogue: A Socio-Historical Study*. ConBNT 37. Uppsala: Almqvist & Wiksell, 2001.

Runesson, Anders, Donald D. Binder, and Birgir Olsson. *The Ancient Synagogue from Its Origins to 200 CE*. Leiden: Brill, 2008.

Runia, David T. *Philo in Early Christian Literature: A Survey*. Assen: Van Gorcum; Minneapolis: Fortress, 1993.

Rutgers, Leonard Victor, ed. *What Athens Has To Do With Jerusalem*. Leuven: Peeters, 2002.

Safrai, Shmuel. "Gathering in the Synagogues on Festivals, Sabbaths and Weekdays." Pages 7–12 in *Ancient Synagogues in Israel: Third–Seventh Century CE: Proceedings of Symposium, University of Haifa, May 1987*. BAR International Series 499. Edited by Rachel Hachlili. Oxford: BAR, 1989.

———. "Dukhan, Aron and Teva: How Was the Ancient Synagogue Furnished?" Pages 69–84 in *Ancient Synagogues in Israel: Third–Seventh Century CE: Proceedings of Symposium, University of Haifa, May 1987*. BAR International Series 499. Edited by Rachel Hachlili. Oxford: BAR, 1989.

———. *The Economy of Roman Palestine*. London: Routledge, 1994.

Saldarini, Anthony J. *Pharisees, Scribes, and Sadducees in Palestinian Society*. Edinburgh: T&T Clark, 1988.

Sanders, E. P. *Jesus and Judaism*. Philadelphia: Fortress, 1985.

———. *Judaism: Practice and Belief 63 BCE–66 CE*. London: SCM, 1998.

Schäfer, Peter, ed. *The Talmud Yerushalmi and Graeco-Roman Culture*. Tübingen: Mohr Siebeck, 1998.

Schiffman, Lawrence H. *From Text to Tradition: A History of Second Temple & Rabbinic Judaism*. Hoboken, NJ: KTAV, 1991.

———. *Texts and Traditions: A Source Reader for the Study of Second Temple and Rabbinic Judaism*. Hoboken, NJ: KTAV, 1998.

Schürer, Emil. *Die Gemeindeverfassung der Juden in Rom in der Kaiserzeit*. Leipzig: Hinrichs, 1879.

———. "Eine neue jüdische-griechische Inschrift." *TLZ* 28 (1903): 156.

———. *The History of the Jewish People in the Age of Jesus Christ (175 BC–AD 135)*. Translated and revised by Geza Vermes et al. 3 vols. Edinburgh: T&T Clark, 1973–87.

Schwabe, M. "On the Interpretation of a Jewish Inscription from Alexandria." *BEHJ* 1 (1946): 101–3.

Schwartz, Seth. *Josephus and Judaean Politics*. Leiden: Brill, 1990.

———. *Imperialism and Jewish Society 200 B.C.E. to 640 C.E.* Princeton, NJ: Princeton University Press, 2001.

Schweitzer, A. *The Quest of the Historical Jesus*. New York: Macmillan 1968.

Seager, Andrew R. "The Recent Historiography of Ancient Synagogue Architecture." Pages 85–92 in *Ancient Synagogues in Israel: Third–Seventh Century CE: Proceedings of Symposium, University of Haifa, May 1987*. BAR International Series 499. Edited by Rachel Hachlili. Oxford: BAR, 1989.

Seland, Torrey. *Establishment Violence in Philo and Luke: a Study of Non-conformity to the Torah and Jewish Vigilante Reactions*. Leiden: Brill 1995.

Sellin, Ernst, and Carl Watzinger. *Jericho, Die Eigebnisse del Ausgrabungen*. Leipzig, 1913. Repr. Osnabrück: Zeller, 1973.

Schwarzer, Holger and Sarah Japp. "Synagoge, Banketthaus oder Wohngebäude?: Überlegungen zu einem neu entdeckten Baukomplex in Jericho/Israel." *Antike Welt* 33.3 (2002): 277–88.

Shahar, Yuval. *Josephus Geographicus*. TSAJ 98. Tübingen: Mohr Siebeck, 2004.

Shanks, Hershel. *Judaism in Stone: The Archaeology of Ancient Synagogues*. New York: Harper & Row, 1979.

———. "Is It or Isn't It—A Synagogue? Archaeologists Disagree Over Buildings at Jericho and Migdal." *BAR* 27.6 (2001): 51–57.

Shatzman, I. "The Integration of Judaea into the Roman Empire." *SCI* 18 (1999): 49–84.

Silberman, Neil Asher, and David B. Small, eds. *The Archaeology of Israel: Constructing the Past, Interpreting the Present*. JSOTSup 237. Sheffield: Sheffield Academic Press, 1997.

Smith, Morton. "Zealots and Sicarii: Their Origins and Relation." *HTR* 64 (1971): 1–19.

Souza, Philip de. *Piracy in the Graeco-Roman World*. Cambridge: Cambridge University Press, 1999.

Sperber, Daniel. *Roman Palestine 200–400: Money and Prices*. 2nd ed. Ramat-Gan: Bar-Ilan University Press, 1991.

———. *The City in Roman Palestine*. Oxford: Oxford University Press, 1998.

Spijkerman, Augusto. *Herodion III. Catologo delle Monete*. Jerusalem: Franciscan Printing Press, 1972.

Stacey, David. "Was There a Synagogue in Hasmonaean Jericho?" in *The Bible and Interpretation*. No pages. Cited 2000. Online: http://www.bibleinterp.com/articles/Hasmonean_Jericho.shtml

Steinsaltz, Adin. *The Essential Talmud*. Northvale, NJ: Jason Aronson, 1992.

Sterling, Gregory E. "Explaining Defeat: Polybius and Josephus on the Wars with Rome." Pages 135–51 in *Internationales Josephus-Kolloquium, Åarhus 1999*. Edited by Jürgen Kalms. Münsteraner Judaistische Studien 6. Münster: Lit Verlag, 2000.

Stern, Ephraim. *Material Culture of the Land of the Bible in the Persian Period 538–332 B.C.* Warminster: Aris & Phillips; Jerusalem: Israel Exploration Society, 1982.

———. *The New Encyclopedia of Archaeological Excavations in the Holy Land*. Vol. 2–3. Jerusalem: The Israel Exploration Society; Carta, 1993.

Stern, Ephraim, and Yizhak Magen. "The First Phase of the Samaritan Temple on Mt. Gerizim—New Archaeological Evidence." *Qadmoniot* 33.2 (120) (2000): 119–24.

Stern, Menahem. "Zealots." Pages 135–53 in *Encyclopaedia Judaica Year Book*. Jerusalem: Encyclopaedia Judaica; New York: Macmillan, 1973.

Stiebl, Guy D., and Jodi Magness. "Military Equipment from Masada." Pages 1–94 in *Masada VIII: The Yigael Yadin Excavations 1963–1965, Final Reports*. Edited by Joseph Aviram et al. Jerusalem: Israel Exploration Society; the Hebrew University of Jerusalem, 2007.

Stone, Michael E., ed. *Jewish Writings of the Second Temple Period. Apocrypha, Pseudepigrapha, Qumran Sectarian Writings, Philo, Josephus*. Assen: Van Gorcum; Philadelphia: Fortress, 1984.

Strange, James F. "The Art and Archaeology of Ancient Judaism." Pages 64–114 in *Judaism in Late Antiquity, I: The Literary and Archaeological Sources*. Edited by Jacob Neusner. Leiden: Brill, 1995.

———. "Ancient Texts, Archaeology as Text, and the Problem of the First Century Synagogue." Pages 27–45 in *Evolution of the Synagogue: Problems and Progress*. Edited by Howard Clark Kee and Lynn H. Cohick. Harrisburg, PA: Trinity Press Intl, 1999.

———. "The Synagogue as Metaphor." Pages 93–120 in *Judaism in Late Antiquity*. Edited by Alan J. Avery-Peck, Jacob Neusner, and Bruce D. Chilton. Leiden: Brill, 2001.

Sukenik, Eleazar L. *The Ancient Synagogue of Bet Alpha: An Account of the Excavations Undertaken on Behalf of the Hebrew University of Jerusalem*. Jerusalem: The University Press, 1932 [Hebrew].

———. *Ancient Synagogues in Palestine and Greece*. Schweich Lectures of the British Academy. London: Oxford University Press, 1934.

———. "The Present State of Ancient Synagogue Studies." *Bulletin of the Lewis M. Rabinowitz Fund* 1 (1949): 8–23.

Syon, Danny. "Gamla: Portrait of a Rebellion." *BAR* 18.1 (1992): 21–37.

———. "The Coins from Gamla—An Interim Report." *INJ* 12 (1992–1993) (1994): 34–55.

———. "Gamla: City of Refuge." Pages 134–54 in *The First Jewish Revolt: Archaeology, History, and Ideology*. Edited by Andrea M. Berlin and J. Andrew Overman. London: Routledge, 2002.

———. "The Coins." Pages 109–223 in *Gamla III: The Shmarya Gutmann Excavations 1976–1989. Finds and Studies*. Part I. Edited by Danny Syon. Jerusalem: Israel Antiquities Authority, 2014.

Syon, Danny and Zvi Yavor. "Gamla 1997–2000." ʻ*Atikot* 50 (2005): 37–71.

———. eds. *Gamla II: The Shmarya Gutmann Excavations, 1976–1989: The Architecture*. Jerusalem: Israel Antiquities Authority, 2010.

Talmon, Shemaryahu. "Hebrew Written Fragments from Masada."*DSS* 3.2 (1996): 168–77.

———. "A Masada Fragment of Samaritan Origin." *IEJ* 47 (1997): 220–32.

Tcherikover, Victor A., Alexander Fuks, and Menahem Stern, eds. *Corpus Papyrorum judaicarum*. 3 vol. Cambridge, MA: Harvard University Press, 1957–1964.

Tcherikover, Victor A. *Hellenistic Civilization and the Jews*. New York: Atheneum, 1979.

Testa, Emmanuele. *Herodion IV. I Graffiti e Gli Ostraka*. Jerusalem: Franciscan Printing Press, 1972.

Theissen, Gerd, and Dagmar Winter. *The Quest for the Plausible Jesus: The Question of Criteria*. Louisville, KY: Westminster John Knox, 2002.

Tomasino, Anthony J. *Judaism Before Jesus*. Downers Grove, IL: InterVarsity, 2003.

Trümper, Monika. "The Oldest Original Synagogue Building in the Diaspora: The Delos Synagogue Reconsidered." *Hesperia* 73.4 (2004): 513–98.

Tsafrir, Yoram. *Ancient Churches Revealed*. Jerusalem: Israel Exploration Society, 1993.

———. "On the Source of the Architectural Design of the Ancient Synagogues in the Galilee: A New Appraisal." Pages 70–86 in *Ancient Synagogues, Historical Analysis and Archaeological Discovery*. Vol 1. Edited by Dan Urman and Paul V. M. Flesher. Leiden: Brill, 1995.

———. "The Synagogues at Capernaum and Meroth and the Dating of the Galilaean Synagogue." Pages 151–61 in *The Roman and Byzantine Near East*. Journal of Roman Archaeology Supplementary Series 14. Edited by John H. Humphrey. Ann Arbour, MI: Journal of Roman Archaeology, 1995.

Tsafrir, Yoram, L. Di Segni, and Judith Green. *Tabula Imperii Romani Iudaea-Palaestina: Eretz Israel in the Hellenistic, Roman, and Byzantine Periods.* Jerusalem: The Israel Academy of Sciences and Humanities, 1994.

Ullmann, Lisa, and Jonathan J. Price. "Drama and History in Josephus' *Bellum Judaicum.*" *SCI* 21 (2002): 97–112.

Urman, Dan, and Paul V.M. Flesher, eds. *Ancient Synagogues: Historical Analysis and Archaeological Discovery.* 2 vols. Leiden: Brill, 1995.

Vallois, René. *L'Architecture Hellénique à Délos, Jusqu'à l'Éviction des Déliens (166 av. J.-C.).* Première Partie: Les Monuments. Paris: de Boccard, 1944.

———. *Les Constructions Antiques de Délos (Documents).* Paris: de Boccard, 1953.

———. *L'Architecture Hellénique et Hellénistique à Délos, Jusqu'à l'Éviction des Déliens (166 av. J.-C.), Deuxième Partie (A): Grammaire Historique de l'Architecture Délienne.* Paris: de Boccard, 1966.

———. *L'Architecture Hellénique et Hellénistique à Délos, Jusqu'à l'Éviction des Déliens (166 av. J.-C.), Deuxième Partie (B): Grammaire Historique de l'Architecture Délienne.* Paris: de Boccard, 1978.

Van der Horst, Pieter William. *Ancient Jewish Epitaphs: An Introductory Survey of a Millennium of Jewish Funerary Epigraphy (300 BCE–700 CE).* Kampen: Kok Pharos, 1991.

Vermes, Geza. *The Religion of Jesus the Jew.* London: SCM, 1993.

Vermes, Geza, and Martin D. Goodman, eds. *The Essenes: According to Classical Sources.* Sheffield: JSOT Press, 1989.

Vincent, Louis-Hugues. "Un Hypogée Juif." *RB* 8 (1899): 414–18.

Walser, Georg. *The Greek of the Ancient Synagogue: An Investigation on the Greek of the Septuagint, Pseudepigrapha and the New Testament.* Stockholm: Almquist & Wiksell Intl, 2001.

Watzinger, Carl. "Zur Chronologie der Schichten von Jericho." *ZDMG* 80 (1926): 131–36.

Weinfeld, M. *Normative and Sectarian Judaism in the Second Temple Period.* London: T&T Clark Intl, 2005.

White, L. Michael. "The Delos Synagogue Revisited: Recent Fieldwork in the Graeco-Roman Diaspora." *HTR* 80.2 (1987): 133–60.

———. *Building God's House in the Roman World: Architectural Adaptation Among Pagans, Jews, and Christians.* Baltimore, MD: Johns Hopkins University Press, 1990.

———. "Reading the Ostia Synagogue: A Reply to A. Runesson." *HTR* 92 (1999): 435–64.

Wilson, Charles William. *Picturesque Palestine, Sinai and Egypt.* Vol. 1. London: J.S. Virtue and Co. [*possibly* 1892; the book is undated].

Wilson, E. Jan. "The Masada Synagogue and Its Relationship to Jewish Worship during the Second Temple Period." *Brigham Young University Studies* 36.3 (1996): 269–276.

Winter, Bruce W. *Philo and Paul Among the Sophists.* Cambridge: Cambridge University Press, 1997.

Wonder, Claude Regnier, and Horatio H. Kitchener. *The Survey of Western Palestine III: Judæa*. London: Committee of the Palestine Exploration Fund, 1883.

Yadin, Yigael. "The Excavation of Masada—1963/4; Preliminary Report." *IEJ* 15 (1965): 1–120.

———. *The Ben Sira Scroll from Masada*. Jerusalem: Israel Exploration Society; the Shrine of the Book, 1965.

———. *Masada: Herod's Fortress and the Zealots' Last Stand*. Translated by Moshe Pearlman. London: Weidenfeld & Nicholson, 1966. Repr. Paperback, London: Phoenix, 1997.

———. "Masada and the Limes." *IEJ* 17 (1967): 43–45.

———. "Masada." *EJ 11* (1971): 1078–91.

Yadin, Yigael, and Joseph Naveh. *Masada I: The Yigael Yadin Excavations 1963–1965, Final Reports*: *The Aramaic and Hebrew Ostraca and Jar Inscriptions*. Jerusalem: Israel Exploration Society; Hebrew University of Jerusalem, 1989.

Yavor, Zvi. "The Architecture and Stratigraphy of the Eastern and Western Quarters." Pages 13–112 in *Gamla II: The Shmarya Gutmann Excavations, 1976–1989: The Architecture*. IAA Reports 44. Edited by Danny Syon and Zvi Yavor. Jerusalem: Israel Antiquities Authority, 2010.

Yeivin, Z. "Khirbet Susiya, the *bema*, and Synagogue Ornamentation." Pages 92–100 in *Ancient Synagogues in Israel: Third–Seventh Century CE: Proceedings of Symposium, University of Haifa, May 1987*. BAR International Series 499. Edited by Rachel Hachlili. Oxford: BAR, 1989.

Yellin, J. "The Flowerpots from Herod's Winter Garden at Jericho." *IEJ* 39.1/2 (1989): 85–90.

Zangenberg, Jürgen, Harold W. Attridge, and Dale B. Martin, eds. *Religion, Ethnicity and Identity in Ancient Galilee.* Tübingen: Mohr Siebeck, 2007.

Zeitlin, Solomon. "Masada and the Sicarii." *JQR* New Series 55.4 (1965): 299–317.

———. "The Sicarii and Masada." *JQR* New Series 57.4 (1967): 251–70.

———. "An Historical Study of the first Canonization of the Hebrew Liturgy." Pages 15–61 in *Studies in the Early History of Judaism*. Edited by Solomon Zeitlin. New York: KTAV, 1973.

———. "The Origin of the Synagogue: A Study in the Development of Jewish Institutions." Pages 14–26 in *The Synagogue: Studies in Origins, Archaeology and Architecture*. Edited by Joseph Gutmann. New York: KTAV, 1975.

Zerubavel, Yael. *Recovered Roots: Collective Memory and the Making of Israeli National Tradition*. Chicago: The University of Chicago Press, 1995.

Zias, J. E. "Three Trephinated Skulls from Jericho." *BASOR* 246 (1982): 55–58.

Zias, J., L. Segal, and L. Carmi. "The Human Skeletal Remains from the Northern Cave at Masada—A Second Look." Pages 366–67 in *Masada IV*. Edited by Joseph Aviram, Gideon Foerster, and Ehud Netzer. Jerusalem: Israel Exploration Society; Hebrew University of Jerusalem, 1995.

Zissu, Boaz, and Amir Ganor. "Horvat 'Ethri—A Jewish Village from the Second Temple Period and the Bar Kokhba Revolt in the Judaean Foothills." *JJS* 60.1 (2009): 90–136. doi:10.18647/2876/JJS-2009.

ANCIENT AUTHORS

Cassius Dio. *Roman History*. Translated by Earnest Cary. LCL. London: William Heinemann, 1925.

Josephus, *Vita*. Translated by Henry St. J. Thackeray. LCL. London: William Heinemann, 1926.

Josephus, *Jewish Antiquities*. 11 vol. Translated by Henry St. J. Thackeray, Louis H. Feldman, Allen Wikgren, and Ralph Marcus. LCL. Cambridge, MA: Harvard University Press, 1930–1981.

Josephus, *Against Apion*. Translated by Henry St. J. Thackeray. LCL. London: William Heinemann, 1926.

Josephus. *Jewish War*. 3 vols. Translated by Henry St. J. Thackeray. LCL. London: William Heinemann, 1927–1928.

Juvenal. *Satires*. Translated by Susanna Morton Braund. LCL. Cambridge, MA: Harvard University Press, 2004.

Philo of Alexandria. 12 vol. Translated by Francis H. Colson, George H. Whitaker, Ralph Marcus. LCL. Cambridge, MA: Harvard University Press, 1939–1978.

Pliny the Elder. *Natural History*. Translated by Harris Rackham. LCL. Cambridge, MA: Harvard University Press, 1969.

Strabo. *The Geography of Strabo*. Translated by Horace L. Jones. LCL. London: William Heinemann, 1930.

Suetonius. *The Lives of the Caesars*. Translated by John C. Rolfe. LCL. Cambridge, MA: Harvard University Press, 1979.

Tacitus, *The Histories*. Translated by Clifford H. Moore. LCL. Cambridge, MA: Harvard University Press, 1931.

BIBLES

Attridge, H. W., ed. *The Harper Collins Study Bible, New Revised Standard Version*. New York: Harper One, 2006.

BIBLIOGRAPHY

Berlin, Adele, and Marc Z. Brettler, eds. *The Jewish Study Bible*. Jewish Publication Society, Tanakh Translation. Oxford University Press, 2006.

Kohlenberger, John R., ed. *The NIV Interlinear Hebrew-English Old Testament*. Grand Rapids: Zondervan, 1987.

Kohlenberger, John R., ed. *The NIV Triglot Old Testament*. Grand Rapids: Zondervan, 1981.

Ancient Sources Index

Hebrew Bible/Old Testament
Exodus
16:3	7 n. 15
16:22	7 n. 14
38:25	7 n. 14

Leviticus
4:13–4	7 n. 15
4:15	7 n. 14
4:21	7 n. 15
8:3–5	7 nn. 14–15
9:2	7 n. 14
9:5	7 n. 14
10:6	7 n. 14
10:17	7 n. 14
16:33	7 n. 15
24:14	7 n. 14
24:16	7 n. 14

Numbers
1:16	7 nn. 14–15
1:18	7 nn. 14–15
3:7	7 n. 14
4:34	7 n. 14
6:19	7 n. 14
8:9	7 nn. 14–15
10:2–3	7 nn. 14–15
13:26	7 n. 14
14:1–2	7 n. 14
14:1–10	7 n. 14
14:35–36	7 n. 14
15:15	7 n. 15
15:24	7 n. 14
15:33	7 n. 14
15:35–36	7 n. 14
16:3	457 n. 14
16:5	457 n. 14
16:9	457 n. 14
16:19	457 n. 14
16:21–22	457 n. 14
16:24	457 n. 14
16:26	457 n. 14
16:33	7 n. 15
17:7	7 n. 14
17:10–11	7 n. 14
17:12	7 n. 15
19:20	7 n. 15
20:1	7 n. 14
20:8	7 n. 14
20:11	7 n. 14
20:22	7 n. 14
20:27	7 n. 14
20:29	7 n. 14
20:2	7 n. 15
20:6	7 n. 15
20:10	7 n. 15
22:4	7 n. 15
25:7	7 n. 14
25:10ff	117 n. 242
26:9–10	7 n. 14
27:2–3	7 n. 14
27:14	7 n. 14
27:16	7 n. 14
27:19	7 n. 14
27:21–22	7 n. 14
31:13	7 n. 14
31:26–27	7 n. 14
31:43	7 n. 14
32:2	7 n. 14
35:12	7 n. 14

35:24–25	7 n. 14	29:31–32	7 n. 15
		30:2	7 n. 15
Deuteronomy		30:4	7 n. 15
4:10	7 n. 15	30:23	7 n. 15
9:10	7 n. 15	30:25	7 n. 15
10:4	7 n. 15		
18:6	7 n. 15	Proverbs	
31:12	7 n. 15	9:14	7 n. 14
Joshua		Ezra	
9:15	7 n. 14	2:34	81
9:18–19	7 n. 14	2:64	7 n. 15
9:21	7 n. 14	10:1	7 n. 15
18:1	7 n. 15	10:12	7 n. 15
20:6	7 n. 14	10:14	7 n. 15
20:9	7 n. 14		
22:12	7 nn. 14–15	Nehemiah	
22:30	7 nn. 14–15	5:13	7 n. 15
		7:66	7 n. 15
Judges		8:2	7 n. 15
20:1	7 n. 14	8:17	7 n. 15
21:8	7 n. 15		
21:10	7 n. 14	Esther	
21:13	7 n. 14	9:15	7 n. 15
21:16	7 n. 14		
		Job	
2 Samuel		15:34	7 n. 14
20:14	7 n. 15		
		Jeremiah	
1 Kings		6:18	7 n. 14
8:2	7 n. 15	39:8	148
12:20	7 n. 14		
		Ezekiel	
1 Chronicles		11:16	25, 148
13:4	7 n. 15	37	121
29:1	7 n. 15		
29:10	7 n. 15	**New Testament**	
29:20	7 n. 15	Matthew	
		4:17	16 n. 58
2 Chronicles		10:7	16 n. 58
1:3	7 n. 15	10:27	16 n. 58
5:3	7 n. 15	11:1	16 n. 58
20:14	7 n. 15	12:9	16 n. 58
23:3	7 n. 15	13:54	16 n. 58
28:14	7 n. 15	21:13	15
29:28	7 n. 15	28:19	16 n. 58

Ancient Sources Index

Mark		Acts	
1:4	16 n. 58	1:1	16 n. 58
1:21–23	16 n. 58	4:18	16 n. 58
1:29	16 n. 58	5:15–21	16 n. 58
1:38	16 n. 58	5:28	16 n. 58
3:1	16 n. 58	5:42	16 n. 58
3:14	16 n. 58	6:9	16 n. 58, 26, 33
4:1	16 n. 58	10:42	16 n. 58
5:22	16 n. 58	12:5	15
5:35	16 n. 58	13:14	16 n. 58
5:36	16 n. 58	13:15	16 n. 58
5:38	16 n. 58	13:42	16 n. 58
6:2	16 n. 58	14:1	16 n. 58
6:34	16 n. 58	14:15	16 n. 58
8:31	16 n. 58	15:2	16 n. 58
11:17	15	16:6	16 n. 58
16:15	16 n. 58	16:10	16 n. 58
		16:13	15
Luke		16:21	16 n. 58
4:16	16 n. 58	17:3	16 n. 58
4:18	16 n. 58	17:10	16 n. 58
4:19	16 n. 58	17:17	16 n. 58
4:20	16 n. 58	18:4	16 n. 58
4:28	16 n. 58	18:7–8	16 n. 58
4:33	16 n. 58	18:17	16 n. 58
4:38	16 n. 58	18:19	16 n. 58
4:43	16 n. 58	18:26	16 n. 58
6:6	16 n. 58	19:8	16 n. 58
7:5	16 n. 58	22:19	16 n. 58
8:41	16 n. 58	26:11	16 n. 58
8:49	16 n. 58		
9:2	16 n. 58	Romans	
9:60	16 n. 58	1:15	16 n. 58
11:1	16 n. 58	10:15	16 n. 58
12:12	16 n. 58	10:18	16 n. 58
13:14	16 n. 58	15:20	16 n. 58
19:46	15		
		1 Corinthians	
John		1:17	16 n. 58, 23
6:59	16 n. 58	9:14	16 n. 58
7:35	16 n. 58	9:16	16 n. 58
9:22	16 n. 58	9:18	16 n. 58
9:34	16 n. 58	15:11	16 n. 58
12:42	16 n. 58		
14:26	16 n. 58	2 Corinthians	
18:20	16 n. 58	2:12	16 n. 58

4:5	16 n. 58	15:15–23	42–43
4:17	16 n. 58		
10:16	16 n. 58	4 Maccabees	
11:14	16 n. 58	18:12	117 n. 242
14:19	16 n. 58		
		Greco-Roman Literature	
Galatians		Josephus, *A.J.*	
1:8–9	16 n. 58	1.10	17
2:2	16 n. 58	12.145	170
5:11	16 n. 58	14.54	85
		14.213–216	44, 52, 55, 70, 77
		14.258	13 n. 44, 14 n. 48
Ephesians		14.282	111 n. 398
3:18	16 n. 58	14.296	111
		14.359–360	161 n. 575
Philippians		15.96	85
1:15–16	16 n. 58	15.323–325	160–161
		16.12–13	161 n. 575
Colossians		16.13	161
1:28	16 n. 58	17.196–199	160–161
		18.116–119	170
1 Timothy		19.300–305	17
1:3	16 n. 58		
3:2	16 n. 58	Josephus, *B.J.*	
6:3	16 n. 58	1.170	82
		1.237–238	111
2 Timothy		1.265	161 n. 575
2:2	16 n. 58	1.267–285	111
2:4	16 n. 58	1.419	160–161
4:2	16 n. 58	1.670–673	160–161
		2.285	17 n. 62
Hebrews		2.289	17
5:12	16 n. 58	2.408	111, 163
8:11	16 n. 58	2.425	111 n. 400
		2.434–440	146
1 John		2.444	116
2:27	16 n. 58	2.566–568	189
		2.572–576	190
Revelations		2.574	189
2:9	16 n. 58	3.55	160–161
2:20	16 n. 58	3.245–247	191 n. 682
3:9	16 n. 58	3.340–407	189
14:6	16 n. 58	3.392	189
		3.393–408	189
Apocrypha		4.1–83	189, 190
1 Maccabees		4.2–10	189
9:50	82		

4.83	190	152	25
4.235	50	156–158	25
4.398–405	115	165	25
4.402	170	191	25
4.402–405	117, 132, 146	311	25
4.467–470	85, 98	346	25
4.503–508	161 n. 575	371	25
4.509–513	161 n. 575	Philo, *Flaccus*	
4.514–520	161 n. 575, 163	41	25
4.554–555	161–162	45	25
5.58–61	189	47–49	25
5.249	50	53	25
6.92	50	122	25
6.148	50		
6.380	50	Philo, *Good Person*	
7.44	17 n. 64	81–83	25
7.74	17		
7.163	161–162	Philo, *Hypothetica*	
7.252ff	117	7.13	12
7.253–262	146		
7.268–270	116	Philo, *Posterity*	
7.282	113	67	25
7.285–300	111		
7.305–309	113	Philo, *Special Laws*	
7.389–401	112	2.62	12
7.405–406	112		
		Pliny the Elder, *Natural History*	
Josephus, *Contra Apionem*		5.15	161 n. 575
2.10	13 n. 44	5.15.70	84
		5.17.29–31	122
Josephus, *Vita*			
11–12	170	Strabo, *Geography*	
277–295	13 nn. 44–47	16.2.40	82
295	26 n. 110	16.2.41	82–84
280	13 n. 45	16.2.44	122
293–294	13 n. 45		
		Suetonius, *Titus*	
Juvenal, *Satires*		4.3	189
3	2		
		Suetonius, *Vespasian*	
Philo, *Embassy to Gaius*		8.3	189 n. 673
132	25		
134	25	Tacitus, *Histories*	
137	25	5.12–14	115 n. 413
138–139	25		
149	25		

Virgil, *Aeneid*
4.9   124

Rabbinic Literature
Meg.
3:1, 738   27

m. Miqw.
1:1–8   170
1:7   171
7:7   171
9:2   170

b. Sanh.
82b   117 n. 242

t. Sukkah
4:5   8, 25, 148 n. 538

Modern Authors Index

Amit, David 97 n. 352, 98 nn. 357–58
Amorai–Stark, Shua 125 n. 460
Atkinson, Kenneth 114 n. 412
Attridge, Harold W. 4 n. 4, 15 n. 50
Ault, Bradley A. 87 n. 309, 95 n. 347
Aviam, Motti 189 n. 672, 192 n. 685
Aviram, Joseph 125 nn. 460–61, 206 n. 748
Avi–Yonah, Michael 20, 34
Avshalom–Gorni, Dina 1 n. 1
Barag, Dan 206 n. 748
Bartlett, John R. 43 n. 174–75
Baskin, Judith 171 n. 614
Bauckham, Richard 6 n. 9
Benoit, Pierre 122 nn. 450–51
Ben–Ami, Doron 19 n. 71
Ben–Yehuda, Nachman 115 n. 414
Berlin, Andrea M. 189 n. 674
Binder, Donald D. 29–30, 60, 64 n. 238, 65–66, 70–71, 74, 150–53, 155, 182–83
Bromiley, G.W. 82 n. 295
Bruneau, Philippe 40, 52 nn. 207–8, 53 nn. 209–13, 54, 59 n. 230, 60, 63, 64 n. 237, 65–66, 69–72, 74
Brunet Michelè 40 n. 168, 67 n. 245
Boardman, John 61 n. 234, 93 n. 335, 94 n. 341, 96 n. 349
Botti, Giuseppe 12 n. 42
Burtchaell, James Tunstead 24
Cahill, Nicholas 87 n. 309, 95 n. 344, 347
Catto, Stephen K. 155, 182–83

Chansey, Mark A. 14 n. 49
Claussen, Carsten 33
Cohen, Moshe 121
Cohen, Shaye J. D. 112 n. 402, 114 n. 412, 145–46
Cohick, Lynn H. 9 n. 26, 30 n. 132
Conder, C. R. 97 n. 353
Corbo, Virgilio C. 5, 160, 164 n. 577, 165–70, 172, 173 n. 621, 176–80, 182–84, 213
Cotton, Hannah M. 110 n. 397, 126 n. 474
Craven, Toni 6 n. 9
Crudden, Michael 38 n. 159
Danby, Herbert 170 n. 612
de Souza, Philip 39 nn. 160–61, 164–65
de Vaux, Roland 122 nn. 450–51
Déonna, Waldemar 47, 50, 51 n. 206, 59, 64, 67 n. 247
De Vries, LaMoine F. 6 n.9
Ducat, Jean 40, 59 n. 230
Dunayevsky, Munia–Immanuel 120 n. 442
Edwards, Douglas R. 154 n. 564
Ego, Beate 124 n. 459
Elbogen, Ismar 24
Eisenberg, Azriel 149
Eshel, Hanan 124 n. 459
Feldman, Louis H. 28, 112 n. 402, 114 n. 412, 119 n. 434, 139 n. 507
Fine, Steven 4 n. 6, 21 n. 77, 27 nn. 116–19, 28, 29 n. 125, 30 n. 131
Finkelstein, Louis 149

Flesher, Paul V. M.   4 n. 4, 18 n. 65, 19 n. 72, 26, 35 n. 157, 147–48, 155, 181–82, 185 n. 666, 215 n. 764
Foerster, Gideon   144–45, 165–66, 178, 181–83, 203 n. 737, 213
Forbes, Richard J.   94 n. 339
Fraade, Steven D.   8 nn. 18–19
Fraser, P. M.   48 n. 185
Frey, Jörg   14 n. 49
Freyne, Seán   14 n. 49
Gammie, John   8 n. 18
Ganor, Amir   1 n. 1
Garbrecht, Günter   82 n. 294, 97 nn. 352–55, 98 n. 356
Geiger, Joseph   110 n. 397, 126 n. 474
Gibson, Shimon   111 n. 399, 153, 170 nn. 608–10 and 612, 171 nn. 613 and 615–18, 192 n. 685
Grabbe, Lester L.   24–25, 31
Griffin, Jasper   61 n. 234, 93 n. 335, 94 n. 341, 96 n. 349
Griffiths, J. Gwyn   10 n. 38
Gripentrog, Stephanie   14 n. 49
Goldstein, Jonathan A.   43 n. 174
Goodenough, Erwin   20, 34, 204 n. 744
Goren, David   188 n. 672
Gutmann, Joseph   7 n. 16, 21 nn. 78–79, 22–23
Gutmann, Shmarya   5, 187–88, 191–93, 194 n. 692, 196–99, 203 n. 736, 206, 210
Hachlili, Rachel   4 n. 7, 7 n. 13, 29, 149, 209, 214 nn. 762–63
Hata, Gōhei   112 n. 402
Hengel, Martin   4 n. 4, 7 n. 13, 9–10, 14 n. 49, 22, 31, 114 n. 412, 116–18
Hershkoitvitz, Malka   125 n. 460, 206 n. 748
Hezser, Catherine   4 n. 4, 177 n. 641
Hirschfeld, Yizhar   87 n. 309, 89 n. 321, 90 n. 322, 92 n. 333, 95 n. 347, 97 n. 352, 98 nn. 357–58

Hodge, A. Trevor   100 nn. 372–74
Honigman, Sylvie   14 n. 49
Horbury, William   11, 12 n. 42, 16 n. 57
Horsley, Richard A.   29, 149
Hüttenmeister, Frowald Gil   4 n. 4
Japp, Sarah   105
Jastrow, Marcus   177
Jeanrond, W. G.   14 n. 49
Jones, H. L.   82 n. 296
Kalman, Ya'akov   102 n. 379, 104 n. 382, 106 nn. 392–93
Kasher, Aryeh   4 n. 4, 5 n. 8, 25, 31, 12 n. 42
Kee, Howard Clark   9 n. 26, 30
Kenyon, Kathleen   81
Kitchener, Horatio Herbert   97 n. 353
Kloppenborg, John S.   8 nn. 21–22, 14 n. 49, 17 n. 59, 18–19
Kohl, Heinrich   20
Kotlar, David   171 n. 614
Kraabel, Alf Thomas   26, 31, 70
Kraemer, Ross Shepherd   6 n. 9, 12 n. 42
Krauss, Samuel   7 n. 13
Ladouceur, David J.   112 n. 402, 114 n. 412, 146
Lange, Armin   124 n. 459
Lass, Egon H. E.   83 n. 297
Launey, Marcel   46 n. 179, 48 nn. 184 and 186–92, 49 nn. 194–96 and 198–99, 51 nn. 202 and 204
Laureys, Rachel   102 n. 379, 104 n. 382, nn. 392–93
Leclerq, H.   12 n. 42
Lefèbrvre, Gustave   12 n. 42
Levine, Lee I.   4 nn. 5 and 7, 6 n. 9, 8, 9 nn. 23–24, 21 nn. 76 and 80, 27, 30–31, 34 n. 156, 38, 71–72, 105–6, 149, 153–54, 182, 195 n. 695, 202 n. 734, 204 n. 742
Lewis, David M.   12 n. 42
Lidell, Henry George   11 n. 40, 16 n. 56

Modern Authors Index

Loew, Leopold 149
Loffreda, Stanslao 5
Magen, Yitzhak 2 n. 1
Magness, Jodi 114 n. 412, 125 nn. 461–64
Ma'Oz, Zvi Uri 195 n. 695, 206 n. 750
Marcus, Ralph 43 n. 176, 44 n. 177
Martin, Dale B. 4 n. 4
Matassa, Lidia D. 6 n. 9
Matthews, Elaine 48 n. 185
Mayer, L. A. 12 n. 42
Mayes, A. D. H. 14 n. 49
Mazur, Belle D. 55–56, 60, 62, 68–70, 74
McKay, Heather A. 25, 26 n. 108
McLean, B. Hudson 39 nn. 163 and 166, 40 n. 167, 70
Menzel, Ehud 120 n. 442
Meyers, Carol 6 n. 9
Meyers, Eric M. 14 n. 49, 27, 28 n. 120, 89 nn. 319–20, 91 nn. 330–31, 95 n. 347, 149
Milik, J.T. 122 nn. 450–51
Mitchell, Stephen 56 n. 221–24
Mosser, C. 12 n. 43
Murphy, Frederick J. 15 n. 49
Murray, Oswyn 61 n. 234, 93 n. 335, 94 n. 341, 96 n. 349
Najar, Arfan 1 n. 1
Naveh, Joseph 114 n. 412, 124 nn. 457–58, 131 n. 487
Negev, Avraham 111 n. 399, 153
Netzer, Ehud 5 n. 8, 79, 82 n. 295, 87 nn. 306–8, 88, 89 nn. 315–18, 90 nn. 323–24, 91, 92 n. 332, 93, 94 nn. 340 and 342–43, 95 nn. 345–46 and 348, 96–97, 98 nn. 356 and 360, 99 nn. 363–68, 101 nn. 375–77, 102 n. 379, 103–6, 107 n. 394, 112 nn. 404–5, 113, 114 n. 412, 123 nn. 453–55, 125 nn. 466–68, 126 nn. 472–73, 128 nn. 476–79, 129 nn. 480–82, 130 nn. 483–85, 131 nn. 487 and 490– 92, 132 nn. 493–94, 133 nn. 495– 96, 134 n. 497, 135 nn. 498–99, 136 nn. 500–501 and 503, 138 n. 504, 139 nn. 505–6, 140 n. 509, 142 nn. 511–12, 145, 150, 152, 156 nn. 569 and 571–72, 161 n. 574, 164 nn. 576 and 578, 165–66, 181–83, 211, 212 nn. 756–57, 213
Neusner, Jacob 8 n. 18, 119 n. 434, 139 n. 507
Nevett, Lisa C. 87 n. 309, 94 n. 338, 95 n. 347, 114 n. 412
Newsome, Carol 126 n. 470
Newsome, James D. 23, 24 n. 95
Nielsen, Inge 33–34, 105
Noy, David 11, 12 n. 42, 16 n. 57
Olsson, Birger 33 n. 148, 155
Oppenheimer, Aharon 5 n. 8
Overman, J. Andrew 70 nn. 257–58, 189 n. 674
Parente, Fausto 114 n. 412
Patrich, Joseph 97 n. 352, 98 nn. 357–58, 180–81
Pearlman, Moshe 114 nn. 411–12
Peleg–Barkat, Orit 193 nn. 686–88, 196 n. 702, 200 nn. 724, 201 nn. 725 and 727 and 730, 202, 203 nn. 735 and 738–40, 204 n. 741, 206 nn. 748–49
Peleg, Yehuda 82 n. 294
Perdue, Leo G.John 8 n. 18
Pilhofer, Peter 124 n. 459
Plassart, André 40–42, 45–51, 54–58, 60 n. 232, 62–63, 66–70, 72, 74–76
Pommerantz, Inna 80 nn. 286–87,
Porat, Naomi 203 n. 737
Porath, Yosef 98 nn. 357 and 359
Price, Jonathan J. 114 n. 412
Price, Simon 61 n. 234
Purdum, Stan 15 n. 49
Rackham, H. 84 n. 305
Rapuano, Yehudah 104
Rappaport, Uriel 5 n. 8, 114 n. 412
Reeg, Gottfried 4 n. 4

Reich, Ronny   26–27, 112 n. 403
Reifenberg, A.   12 n. 42
Renfrew, Colin   76
Richardson, Peter   17 n. 59, 27, 33, 70
Robert, S. MacLennan   70 nn. 257–58
Roth–Gerson, Lea   4 n. 4
Roussel, Pierre   46 n. 179, 48 nn. 184 and 186–92, 49 nn. 194–96 and 198–99, 51 nn. 202 and 204
Runesson, Anders   7 n. 13, 24 n. 101, 26 n. 113, 29 nn. 126–127, 30 n. 132, 31–33, 76, 155
Safrai, Z.   25
Sanders, E. P.   30
Schürer, Emil   8, 9 n. 25
Schwabe, M.   12 n. 42
Schwarzer, Holger   105
Schwartz, Daniel R.   14 n. 49, 114 n. 412
Schwartz, Seth   114 n. 412
Scott, Robert   11 n. 40, 16 n. 56
Segal Chiat, Marilyn Joyce   129 n. 480
Sellin, Ernest   81
Shanks, Hershel   103–4, 142–44
Silberman, Neil Asher   31 n. 137
Slievers, Joseph   114 n. 412
Small, David B.   31 n. 137
Smith, Morton   114 n. 412
Spijkerman, Augusto   186 n. 599, 189 nn. 603–4, 173 nn. 622–29, 174 n. 630, 175 nn. 631–32, 181 n. 651
Stacey, David   107 n. 395
Stern, Ephraim   81 nn. 290–92, 82 n. 295, 98 n. 361, 165 n. 580
Stern, Menahem   114 n. 412, 115–16, 118
Stiebl, Guy D.   125 nn. 461–64
Strange, James F.   9 n. 26
Sukenik, Eleazar L.   20, 21, 68, 70, 74, 113
Syon, Danny   4 n. 5, 188 nn. 668 and 671–72, 189 nn. 674–75, 190 nn. 678–80, 191 nn. 681 and 683, 192 nn. 684–85, 194 n. 691, 196

nn. 702 and 708, 198 n. 713, 199 n. 717, 201 nn. 725–26 and 728 and 730, 205 n. 745, 206
Talmon, Shemaryahu   126 n. 471
Testa, Emmanuelle   176–77, 213 nn. 760–61
Tomasion, Anthony J.   15 n. 49
Trümper, Monica   60, 72–76
Ullman, Lisa   114 n. 412
Urman, Dan   4 n.4
Walser, Georg   15 n. 49
Warren, Charles   81, 113
Watzinger, Carl   20, 81
White, L. Michael   54 nn. 215–16, 60, 69, 74
Wilson, E. Jan   148–50
Wilson, Stephen G.   8 nn. 21–22, 17 n. 59
Wold, Benjamin   127 n. 475
Yadin, Yigael   21 n. 81, 109–10, 113–14, 118–21, 124 nn. 456–58, 126 nn. 469–70, 130 n. 486, 131, 136 n. 502, 145, 147–50, 155, 156, 166, 169
Yavor, Zvi   4 n. 5, 188 nn. 668–69 and 671–72, 191 n. 683, 194 n. 691, 195 nn. 694–98, 196 nn. 699–702, 197 n. 709, 198 nn. 713 and 715–16, 199 nn. 717–18, 200 nn. 721–23, 201 nn. 725 and 728 and 730, 205 nn. 746–47, 206 nn. 748–750, 208 n. 752
Zangenber, Jürgen   4 n.4
Zeitlin, Solomon   22, 114–15 n. 412, 149
Zetterholm, Magnus   33 n. 148
Zissu, Boaz   1 n. 1

www.ingramcontent.com/pod-product-compliance
Lightning Source LLC
Chambersburg PA
CBHW030436300426
44112CB00009B/1026